P9-BYO-508

BIRDS
OF
AMERICA

BIRDS
OF
AMERICA

Frank Shaw

DRAGON'S WORLD

Dragon's World Ltd
Limpsfield
Surrey RH8 0DY
Great Britain

First published by Dragon's World 1990

© 1990 Dragon's World Ltd
© 1990 Text Frank Shaw
© 1990 Illustrations Dragon's World Ltd

Illustrations by Norman Arlott, Trevor Boyer, Malcolm Ellis, Robert
Morton, Maurice Pledger, Christopher Rose & David Thelwell of
Bernard Thornton Artists, London.

No part of this book may be reproduced in any form or by any electronic
or mechanical means, including information storage and retrieval
systems, without permission in writing from Dragon's World Ltd except
by a reviewer who may quote brief passages in a review.

All rights reserved.

BRITISH LIBRARY CATALOGUING IN PUBLICATION DATA

Shaw, Frank
    Birds of America
    1. North America. Birds
    I. Title
    598.297

ISBN 1−85028−082−7

EDITOR: Michael Downey
ART DIRECTOR: Dave Allen
EDITORIAL DIRECTOR: Pippa Rubinstein

Typeset by Bookworm Typesetting, Manchester, England
Printed in Singapore

CONTENTS

FOREWORD

From the earliest times birds have delighted and inspired us. In ancient Egypt certain gods were portrayed as birds: the god of the moon was as an ibis, the god of light a falcon – both were viewed as bearers of wisdom. It has been said that the Greek alphabet was partly inspired by the formation of flying cranes, and an ancient Persian legend states that men were once ruled by chickens. In ancient China certain species of birds were appointed as imperial officials, while in ancient Rome three of the most high-ranking officials were bird diviners responsible for predicting the future of the state by studying the flight, flocking habits, and even the entrails of birds.

The most famous of mythical birds is the Egyptian Phoenix. Legend has it that the Phoenix was the size of an eagle and had a lifespan of five hundred years. When burnt on the altar of the temple of Heliopolis it was miraculously reborn from its own ashes. This legend was still popular right up to the sixteenth century as an allegory for the resurrection of Christ.

The era of exploration and accurate mapping of the Earth's surface from 1400 to the 1700s ushered in the period of natural history exploration. This created an explosion of information about hitherto unknown species of birds from new territories. The first attempts at cataloguing the diversity of birds were made, and with these efforts came the first serious attempts to paint or draw birds as they appeared. Looking at much of this early artwork today we are struck by the stylized and romantic way in which much of it is presented. This style coincides with many of the notions held at the time about how birds lived and our perception of ourselves in relation to the natural world. This romanticized approach has gradually given way to a more naturalistic style which reflects more accurately the intricate subtlety of a bird's appearance and behaviour. This appearance is composed of a beauty of form and infinate diversity of color which can easily elude the eye of even the most careful observer.

In most cultures, birds (or any other creatures) are no longer considered in such mystical terms as was prevalent in ancient civilizations. Now, aside from the joy they provide to those who delight in their appearance and behaviour, they also provide us with an accurate indication of the state of the environment, a litmus test on pollution levels. An environment which once sustained birdlife, but does no more, is not a healthy one.

The artwork depicting North American birds in this volume is outstanding, among the best produced in recent years. For this reason The American Birding Association is very proud to sponsor the publication of this new work. The ABA exists to help those interested in bird distribution and identification to enjoy their avocation by learning more about where birds live and what they look like. We are confident this book will contribute to that goal.

Allan R. Keith
President
American Birding Association, Inc.

INTRODUCTION

Over 800 different species of birds have been found in North America at one time or another. Some may just nip across borders to breed or winter, albeit regularly in some areas; while still more are no more than vagrants that have occurred only once or twice, perhaps even a few times each year. To the avid birder these "rarities" have a magnetic attraction.

Every year, mostly in spring, the dedicated hard men and women of the birding fraternity set out for a remote Alaskan outpost across from Siberia. Here, new and rare birds for North America are drifted offshore to throw themselves before the binoculars of those prepared for primitive accommodations and miserable weather. Most of us, however, get our enjoyment from watching the birds in our back yard, the local park, a nearby marsh, or among the woods of summer.

This book is about North American birds - not necessarily birds that send listers into a state of frenetic twitching. Over 680 birds are treated here in the sort of detail that every bird-watcher needs. Each bird is described under standard headings picking out the salient points of its identification, distribution, migrations, habitat, and breeding routines. In addition, a comment is made that adds to the overall picture of the bird concerned. Although information is offered in a brief and concise, almost annotated, form, this is, then, considerably more than a "field guide". The illustrations show the adult male (in almost every case) in summer plumage. Together the text and illustrations form the basis for an understanding of the birds of North America, making this book a handy source of reference that can be consulted over and over again.

All of the birds fall naturally into groups such as vireos, flycatchers, and ducks. Each group, or amalgam of groups, is introduced by an essay that provides a summary of its main characteristics and, where relevant, picks out species of particular interest. These are inevitably somewhat discursive, but are aimed to enable anyone to understand a little more about the birds concerned in a form easy to assimilate.

The order in which the birds are listed is that in most common usage. Called the systematic or scientific order, it treats similar and, therefore, closely related birds consecutively in a way that no other order can do. Thus, if the book were arranged alphabetically, the first bird would be Anhinga, the second Ani, and the third Auklet — three totally unrelated birds from three unrelated families. Another, often proposed, order is based on habitats. By this method we would have, say, all marshland birds grouped together. Thus the Swamp Sparrow would be placed next to the Spoonbill - two birds that I doubt anyone could confuse.

However, the actual scientific order used in this book seeks to arrange the birds in the order in which they evolved. Thus it starts with the most primitive (earliest to evolve) and ends with the most advanced (latest to evolve). Inevitably, this is a matter of opinion and ornithologists that specialize in this aspect of birds are as liable as anyone to change their minds. Frankly, this makes little difference to us, the ordinary birders, just so long as similar birds are placed adjacently in order to facilitate comparisons. It takes a little while to get used to the order, but once it is realized that big birds are placed at the front and little birds at the rear, that birds of prey come before shorebirds, that the terns precede the auks, then it is easy to find your way around this and the vast majority of other bird books, no matter where in the world they are published.

North America has a rich and varied bird population with a wide variety of families represented. Other areas, notably South America, may have more species, but they do not have the diversity of North America. Canada and the U.S.A. are, for example, well blessed with breeding and migrating wildfowl, most of which are unknown farther south. The shorebirds, too, may be long-distance migrants, but many venture no farther south than Texas or California. Such regular toing and froing creates a sense of excitement that is unknown in the tropics. Migrating birds often get lost and an east coast bird may turn up in the west, and vice versa. Some birds occur in huge numbers on a seasonal basis and watching a huge flock of Snow Geese descend on some midwest refuge, for example, creates a quite unique thrill that some have called a "privilege." Surrounded by such riches, it is not surprising that so many people find birds completely absorbing. It is easy in North America to make the move from casual watcher to bird nut. Beware!

Watching birds is an easy thing to do — open your eyes and there they are. If you cannot see them well enough, or at close enough range, buy a pair of binoculars and get closer. Unless you are very lucky, it will not take long before you have seen most of the birds you can reasonably expect in your garden or the local park. At this point you have to start traveling to see new birds, or settle down to study the behavior of some common species nearby. Most of us make the choice and start traveling, but some become so engrossed by how birds behave that they study a single species year after year. During the Second World War several birders found themselves in prisoner-of-war camps where travel restrictions were, to say the least, rigorously enforced. So, instead of heading off to the nearest marsh or estuary, they started watching the birds around the camp. The result was several monographs on individual species in the post-war bird book boom.

Mostly, though, bird-watchers head away from home in their pursuit of yet more birds. The local reservoir or garbage dump will offer birds that are seldom, if ever, seen in the back yard. A nearby marsh may provide more, and for those who live near a coast, estuaries and shorelines are frequently alive with birds. So far, a couple of books and a pair of binoculars are the only costs involved. Now there is a sudden need for a telescope, then a tripod, then interchangable eye-pieces of different magnifications, then a better pair of binoculars, and the all-weather clothing that winter shorelines demand. Be careful — the next step is a four-wheel drive vehicle and an airline charge card.

It would be strange if somewhere along the way you did not get involved in conservation. Though America and Canada have only been settled for a few hundred years, there have been some extraordinary changes made to the landscapes. Forests have been felled and cleared, plains have been fenced, prairies have been plowed, rivers dammed, marshes drained, and large tracts of land converted to glass and concrete, lawn and flower bed. Along the way some birds have suffered while others have benefited.

Birds have also attracted hunters, and there are probably more sporting guns in North America today than there were a hundred years back, when hunting for the pot was an economic necessity. At first, a bird's culinary qualities were the main criterion in hunting; later, sporting qualities became more important. Sadly, the ignorant gun also took its toll on the birds of prey, scarce birds and, toward the end of the nineteenth century, the birds that boasted boldly-colored feathers and elaborate plumes. The ravages of these plume hunters was merciless and it was only a change in fashion that stopped the extermination of several species. Inevitably, some birds did not make it; the Passenger Pigeon and Carolina Parakeet are extinct, and the Eskimo Curlew all but so. The problem for the pigeon and curlew was that they occurred in such vast numbers that no one could conceive that they could ever be completely wiped out. In many ways, this is the very heart of the conservation problem on a worldwide scale today. When the birds around seem so abundant, it is difficult to understand the concern of those who tell you that they are the only ones left in the world. In the twentieth century we have seen the disappearance of the Ivory-billed Woodpecker and the wild California Condor, and the virtual disappearance of the Whooping Crane. Yet these are not birds that have been hunted to extinction, even if hunting did seriously reduce their numbers. Today the main problem is loss of habitat, and conservation is a much more complex business than the previous protection.

Like all good things, conservation costs money, but it also requires effort. If you want to get involved, contact your local Audubon Society or Nature Conservancy, join and contribute, but also offer your help, your skills, and your labor. All sorts of different projects need help, from the International Crane Foundation to save-the-local-wood campaigns. You don't have to be a millionaire to contribute, or a Charles Atlas to plant a tree. In fact, you can help for next to nothing by setting up a bird-feeding station in your own back yard.

Birds are particularly prone to hard weather, and when snow covers the ground many different species are unable to get at their natural food. A supply of nuts and kitchen scraps may make the difference between life and death. It is, of course, a good idea to start regular daily feeding before winter gains a grip but, whatever you do, don't feed the birds, until they get to know where you are, and then abandon them while you take off on your annual skiing holiday. During the short days of winter birds need to feed throughout the hours of daylight. If they waste time hanging around for you to feed them while you are hundreds of miles away sipping a bourbon and water or breaking a leg, they will be more at risk than if you hadn't fed them at all. Incidentally, a double feeding program with a co-operative next-door neighbor solves the problem completely. Unless, that is, you go on holiday together.

No man is an island, and no book the result of the efforts of a single individual. Thus my thanks go to all of the artists who have devoted their skills to making this book a much prettier affair and a more useful tool than it would otherwise have been. Thanks also to the typists and editors who between them have made sense of my scribbling. And to the publishers who have pulled all of us together in a truly team effort. Thank you all.

Frank Shaw

LOONS & GREBES

THESE are a group of relatively primitive birds whose origins can be traced back to the Upper Cretaceous period of prehistory. Indeed, the modern loons bear a strong resemblance to the huge, fish-eating and toothed *Hesperornis regalis* that was over 6ft/2m long. Today's loons are under half that size. All the four species of loons in the world breed in North America. They are well adapted to an aquatic lifestyle, spending their summers on lakes and their winters among coastal waters. The plumage is thick, insulating, and waterproof, while the large webbed feet are set well back on the body to act as highly efficient paddles. In fact, the feet are so well positioned for swimming that the birds are almost incapable of standing. When forced to dry land for nesting, they propel themselves over the ground on their breasts. Yet in their rightful element they are complete masters. These birds are great divers – indeed, they are called so in Europe – and are quite capable of diving to 200ft/60m and remaining submerged for several minutes. Most dives, however, last less than a minute. Loons are fine underwater fishermen and in this they bear a strong resemblance to the more numerous grebes.

There are 23 species of grebes in the world, of which seven breed in North America. Like the loons, they are expert swimmers and divers, though their feet are equipped with broad lobes rather than being fully webbed. They, too, are capable of lengthy dives, though none are capable of reaching the extreme depths of the larger birds. If anything, grebes are even more aquatic and several species never ever set foot (or web) on dry land. Instead they build a floating nest of vegetation anchored to an overhang, or to emergent growth. This floating structure has two major advantages: at times of flood the nest simply rises with the water level, while the decaying mass of vegetation rots like compost to create a warming heat that helps to incubate the eggs.

Many grebes have distinctive summer plumages which can be spectacularly colorful. These are an integral part of their courtship rituals, which are among the most elaborate of all birds. Early studies of bird behavior showed that grebe courtship was highly ritualized, consisting of a range of quite distinct movements, all of which are essential to successful breeding. One of the most spectacular is that of the Western Grebe, where members of the pair come together, then rise up and run side by side over the water. It is interesting that these birds, while showing the most bizarre behavior, are among the less colorful members of the family. Other less colorful grebes are highly vocal, and several sing quite definite duets.

Grebes are widespread in North America and can be seen in many parts according to season. Loons, on the other hand, are northern breeding birds that are most often seen along coasts in their dull winter plumage. While two species are regular along the Atlantic, four can be seen along the Pacific coast in winter.

Freshwater lakes and ponds attract many birds including Pied-billed, Horned, and Eared Grebes alongside a Common Loon. A pair of Western Grebes dance in the background while a flock of whistling swans flies over.

RED-THROATED LOON

Gavia stellata   21–23in/53–58cm

IDENTIFICATION Smallest of the loons. In summer, has gray head with rusty throat and striped nape and hind neck. At this season, is only loon that lacks checkerboard back. In winter is grayer above than other loons. Thin bill always held uptilted.

VOICE Wailing and cackling in summer.

HABITAT Breeds on small lakes moving to sea or larger lakes to feed; winters along coasts.

RANGE Breeds coastal and tundra Canada and Alaska.

MOVEMENTS Moves southward to winter on east and west coasts and along southern shores of Great Lakes.

BREEDING Small lakes and pools either near the coast or near a larger lake with plentiful food; May-June.

NEST AND EGGS A variable lining of vegetation in a hollow near the water's edge; the 2 eggs are olive brown, speckled brown or black.

INCUBATION Lasts for 24 to 29 days and is shared by both sexes.

COMMENT The short take-off abilities of this loon enable it to occupy smaller waters than its larger relatives.

PACIFIC LOON

Gavia pacifica   23–27in/58–68cm

IDENTIFICATION In summer, distinguished by gray crown, black throat, chequered back and boldly striped neck. In winter is the darkest of all the loons, with dark crown extending to below the eye. At this time most likely to be

confused with the Common Loon, but white patch on rear flank can be helpful.

VOICE Loud wailings in summer.

HABITAT Large lakes in summer; coasts in winter.

RANGE Breeds throughout Alaska, eastward through Canadian Arctic, south of tree line.

MOVEMENTS Winters west coast of Canada and US.

BREEDING Freshwater lakes of some size; May-June.

NEST AND EGGS A variable mass of vegetation close to the water's edge often built up as water rises to create an 'island'; the 2 eggs are olive brown, spotted black.

INCUBATION Lasts 29 days and is shared by male and female.

COMMENT East coast records may refer to Arctic Loon of Europe and northern Asia.

COMMON LOON

Gavia immer   27–32in/68–81cm

IDENTIFICATION A large, duck-like bird that dives easily. In summer, black head and boldly checkered back separate from all divers except Yellow-billed Loon which has pale ivory bill. In winter, back is barred gray and large, pointed, black bill is held horizontally. White extends above eye.

VOICE Wild, wailing cries in summer.

HABITAT Lakes in summer; coasts in winter.

RANGE Breeds throughout Canada to US borders.
MOVEMENTS Winters west and east coasts of Canada and US, including Gulf coast.
BREEDING Freshwater lakes; May-June.
NEST AND EGGS A mass of vegetation usually near the shoreline or an island; the 2 eggs are olive with brown spots.
INCUBATION Lasts for 29 days and is shared by both members of the pair.
COMMENT Usually a single pair occupies a lake, but larger waters may be shared by two or more pairs.

YELLOW-BILLED LOON

Gavia adamsii   33−39in/84−99cm

IDENTIFICATION Very similar to Common Loon, but separated at all times by large, pale bill with sharply, upwards-angled lower mandible. This creates impression of uptilted bill. Plumage pattern closely resembles Common Loon in both summer and winter.
VOICE Wailing cries in summer.
HABITAT Tundra lakes in summer; coasts in winter.
RANGE Breeds in western Canadian Arctic.

MOVEMENTS Migrates through Alaska to winter on west coast of Canada. Rare southward.
BREEDING Freshwater lakes among tundra; June-July.
NEST AND EGGS Placed close to the shoreline of an island and consists of a heap of vegetation; the 2 eggs are brownish olive, spotted brown.
INCUBATION Lasts 27 to 29 days and is shared by both members of the pair.
COMMENT The northern replacement of the Common Loon; the ranges do not overlap though there are rare cases of hybridization.

LEAST GREBE

Tachybaptus dominicus   8−10in/20−25cm

IDENTIFICATION Tiny grebe with dusky gray head, neck and upperparts in summer, but barred buffy on flanks. Bold yellow eye and tiny dark bill are best field marks. In winter, upperparts are less dusky and throat is white.
VOICE Distinctive clanging note.
HABITAT Overgrown ponds.
RANGE Breeds southern Texas; but distinctly local.
MOVEMENTS Resident.
BREEDING Pools and ponds with vegetation as well as slow stretches of streams; March-September.
NEST AND EGGS A mass of vegetation floating among emergent growth; the 2 to 7 eggs are white.
INCUBATION Lasts 21 days and is shared between the sexes.
COMMENT This grebe only just penetrates into North America.

PIED-BILLED GREBE

Podilymbus podiceps   12−15in/30−38cm

IDENTIFICATION A thick-set, chunky grebe with large conical bill. Upperparts brown, with boldly barred brown and buff flanks and square-cut, white rear end. In summer, there is a bold black patch on the throat and the heavy, pale bill has a vertical black bar near the tip. In winter, throat and bill are both whitish. Pale eye-ring at all times.
VOICE Various yelping calls.
HABITAT Shallow ponds with vegetation in summer; plus larger waters in winter.
RANGE Breeds throughout US and southern Canada.

VOICE Various squealing notes.

HABITAT Marshy lakes and ponds in summer; coastal in winter.

RANGE Breeds over most of western Canada, except extreme north.

MOVEMENTS Migrates across northern US to winter on Atlantic coasts, along Central Flyway to Gulf Coast and along Pacific coast as far as California.

BREEDING Shallow lakes, marshes and bays overgrown with vegetation; May-June.

NEST AND EGGS A floating mass of aquatic vegetation anchored to emergent plants; the 3 to 10 eggs are white.

INCUBATION Lasts 20 to 25 days and is shared between the pair.

COMMENT The large number of eggs is probably the result of two females laying in the same nest, though these are not normally colonial birds.

MOVEMENTS Leaves northern and central parts of range in winter.

BREEDING Shallow freshwater ponds, lakes and bays; April-May.

NEST AND EGGS A mass of aquatic plant material assembled to form a floating nest attached to emergent vegetation; the 5 to 7 eggs are white, washed blue or green.

INCUBATION Lasts 21 to 24 days and is shared between members of the pair.

COMMENT A non-colonial grebe that leaves the northern parts of its range only when ice begins to form, but which returns at the start of the spring melt.

RED-NECKED GREBE

Podiceps grisegena   15½–18in/40–46cm

HORNED GREBE

Podiceps auritus   12–14in/31–36cm

IDENTIFICATION A colorful grebe in summer with black head and golden "horns" extending as a crest. Foreneck and underparts are rust red. In winter, dark above and white below with distinctive capped appearance and white foreneck. Bill thickish and pointed. *See* Eared Grebe.

IDENTIFICATION Medium-sized grebe. In summer, black cap, silvery "face" and rust-red neck are distinctive. In winter, a black cap, whitish "face" and dusky foreneck are best identification features. Size and substantial bill should separate from smaller grebes at all times.

VOICE Wailing and loud *keck-keck* when breeding.

HABITAT Lakes with plentiful emergent vegetation; mainly coastal in winter.

RANGE Breeds from Alaska to the Great Lakes in Canada and to the US border country.

MOVEMENTS Some birds migrate across the eastern US to winter along the Atlantic coasts; others winter along Pacific coasts as far south as California.

BREEDING Freshwater lakes and marshes; May-June.

NEST AND EGGS A mass of aquatic vegetation placed among damp marshland plants; the 3 to 7 eggs are white.
INCUBATION Lasts 23 days and is shared by both members of the pair.
COMMENT Often a colonial breeder, this can be a noisy bird wherever numbers are found.

EARED GREBE

Podiceps nigricollis   11–13in/28–33cm

IDENTIFICATION Only a trifle smaller than Horned Grebe. In summer, head and neck black, with a gold fan on sides of "face". Breast black, underparts and flanks rusty. In winter, is dark above and white below. Cap darkish with paler hind crown, foreneck dusky – not white as Horned Grebe. Bill, thin and uptilted at all times.
VOICE Quiet *poo-cep* plus various raucous notes.
HABITAT Marshes and ponds in summer; winters on coasts and large lakes.
RANGE Breeds in prairie zone of western Canada southward over much of western US.
MOVEMENTS Winters along Pacific Coast, but many move southward into Mexico sometimes along Gulf coast states.
BREEDING Marsh bays of freshwater lakes; May-June.
NEST AND EGGS A mass of plant debris floats among dense emergent vegetation; the 1 to 6 eggs are white.
INCUBATION Lasts 20 to 22 days and is shared between the pair.
COMMENT A highly colonial grebe that nests close together, sometimes with other species, including gulls, in some parts of its range.

WESTERN GREBE

Aechmophorus occidentalis   22–29in/56–74cm

IDENTIFICATION Largest of grebes, with exceptionally long neck and bill. Upperparts dark gray, extending up hind neck to form a black cap that is curiously "bumped" at rear. White "face" and foreneck prominent at a distance. In flight, shows white bar across wing. Elaborate dancing display. In the closely related Clark's Grebe, the black cap does not extend below the eye and the bill is more yellow-orange.
VOICE *Kr-r-rick*, especially in summer.
HABITAT Lakes in summer; coasts in winter.
RANGE Breeds on lakes of the west as far as the prairie lakes.
MOVEMENTS Winters along west coast of British Columbia and the US as far as Mexico.
BREEDING Freshwater lakes with emergent vegetation; May-June.
NEST AND EGGS The nest is a mass of floating vegetation anchored to growing plants; the 3 or 4 eggs are white.
INCUBATION Lasts for 23 days and is shared by the pair.
COMMENT This is a colonial grebe that is gregarious at all seasons. It seems particularly prone to human disturbance in summer.

CLARK'S GREBE

Aechmophorus clarkii   c22in/56cm

IDENTIFICATION Very similar to Western Grebe and only recently recognized as a separate species. The black cap does not extend below the eye, and the bill is more yellow-orange.
VOICE Similar to Western Grebe.
HABITAT Lakes in summer; coastal in winter.
RANGE Overlaps with Western Grebe, though Clark's Grebe dominates in eastern and northern part of range.

ALBATROSSES, SHEARWATERS, FULMARS & STORM-PETRELS

THIS is a diverse group that includes most of the world's ocean-going seabirds, from the huge albatrosses to the dainty storm-petrels. They are divided into three main groups.

The albatrosses are the very epitome of ocean-going, or pelagic, birds. The huge Wandering Albatross is the world's longest-winged bird and takes a remarkable two years to rear its young. It is thus not surprising that it is among the longest lived of all birds. Two species of albatross regularly visit the west coast of North America. The Black-footed Albatross is common in summer, while the Laysan Albatross is decidedly rare at sea, off the Pacific coast.

Shearwaters are among the most superbly adapted of all seabirds. Their lives are spent combing the world's oceans, often hundreds or thousands of miles from land, coming to the shore only to breed. They fly on long, stiff wings, using the air currents created by rolling waves to keep them airborne and provide propulsion. Indeed, in a dead calm many just rest on the sea. Several of these birds make huge loop migrations from the southern hemisphere to reach our coasts and can truly be called "ocean wanderers". Inevitably, many are little known, being observed only from boats that follow the regular shipping lanes. Seeing such birds may involve lengthy watches from prominent headlands at the right time of the year, though there has been a boom in "pelagic" trips by boat in the past couple of decades. These pelagic trips now regularly produce records of birds that were formerly regarded as extremely rare in North American waters.

Perhaps the most abundant shearwater in North American waters is the Northern Fulmar, which breeds in the Canadian Arctic and Alaska and moves southward along both coasts. This bulky, stiff-winged bird is among the easiest to identify, as well as being among the most successful of the shearwaters. Though it lays only a single egg and does not breed until its seventh year of life, the Fulmar has increased and spread rapidly during the past hundred years. This population boom has been explained by the birds' ability to feed around modern trawlers on the waste thrown overboard.

There are many species of shearwaters in the world, but only two species breed in North America. The others are mainly migrants or wanderers from the southern oceans to either the east or west coast, though the Sooty Shearwater is commonly seen off both Pacific and Atlantic shores.

BLACK-FOOTED ALBATROSS

Diomedea nigripes   30–34in/76–86cm

IDENTIFICATION Only all-dark albatross found in North American waters, though beware immatures of other species. Slight pale area around base of bill and eye, and narrow white "horseshoe" on rump. Underwing shows distinctive series of bars, and undertail is white. Dark, not fleshy, bill separates from larger, immature albatrosses.
VOICE Silent at sea.
HABITAT Sea.
RANGE Pacific coast throughout year, most numerous in summer.
MOVEMENTS Migrant from breeding grounds off Hawaii.

LAYSAN ALBATROSS

Diomedea immutabilis   30–34in/76–86cm

IDENTIFICATION Dark wings and back contrast with white body. Tail black, underwing mostly white with distinct black pattern. Dark mark around eye.
VOICE Silent at sea.
HABITAT Sea.
RANGE Rare offshore visitor California and Alaska.
MOVEMENTS Migrant from breeding grounds off Hawaii.

BREEDING Cliff tops with wide grassy ledges; April-May.
NEST AND EGGS A simple hollow in grass or bare rock; the single egg is white.
INCUBATION Lasts 53 to 57 days and is shared between the sexes.
COMMENT The extraordinary boom in numbers enjoyed by this species is even more surprising in view of its inability to breed until seven years of age and then laying only a single egg each year.

NORTHERN FULMAR

Fulmarus glacialis   17–19½in/44–50cm

IDENTIFICATION A large, gull-like seabird that flies, shearwater-like, on stiff wings. Pale gray above, white below with a short, stubby yellow bill. At all times the thick neck is a good feature.
VOICE Harsh cackling at breeding sites.
HABITAT Breeds on remote northern cliffs, otherwise at sea, often well out of sight of land.
RANGE Breeds among Canadian archipelago as far south as Newfoundland and on islands of southern Alaska.
MOVEMENTS Winters in Pacific and northern Atlantic, may be abundant around fishing vessels.

BLACK-CAPPED PETREL

Pterodroma hasitata   15–17in/38–43cm

IDENTIFICATION Fast-flying, wing-fluttering "gadfly" petrel marked by angled wings, black cap often backed by white collar, and white "horseshoe-shaped" rump. Upperparts dark gray, underparts white. White underwing shows black leading edge.
VOICE Silent at sea.
HABITAT Sea.
RANGE Rare offshore from Florida to North Carolina.
MOVEMENTS Breeds Caribbean, wanders northward during the summer.

CORY'S SHEARWATER

Calonectris diomedea   17—19in/43—48cm

IDENTIFICATION Large, bulky shearwater, grayish-brown above, dirty white below. Shows no contrast between upperparts and underparts. Flies with slower wing-beats than other similar sized shearwaters.
VOICE Silent at sea.
HABITAT Sea.
RANGE Scarce off east coast in late summer and fall.
MOVEMENTS Transatlantic migrant from eastern Atlantic islands and Mediterranean.

PINK-FOOTED SHEARWATER

Puffinus creatopus   18—20in/46—51cm

IDENTIFICATION Uniform slate-gray upperparts with no distinguishing features. Underparts and underwing white, heavily mottled. Pink feet (and bill) useful only at close range.
VOICE Silent at sea.
HABITAT Sea.
RANGE Pacific coast migrant in summer.
MOVEMENTS Breeds offshore islands of Chile.

FLESH-FOOTED SHEARWATER

Puffinus carneipes   18—20in/46—51cm

IDENTIFICATION Uniformly sooty-colored shearwater, above and below; paler primaries. Pale bill and feet and lack of whitish underwing separate from more angular Sooty Shearwater.
VOICE Silent at sea.
HABITAT Sea.
RANGE Decidedly rare summer visitor to Pacific coast.
MOVEMENTS Migrant from breeding grounds off Australia and New Zealand.

GREATER SHEARWATER

Puffinus gravis   18—20in/46—51cm

IDENTIFICATION Brown above with narrow, white rump and bold, black cap. Underparts white, with smudged ventral patch. The distinctive black cap and white collar identifies.
VOICE Silent at sea.
HABITAT Sea.
RANGE Offshore along Atlantic coast in spring and summer.
MOVEMENTS Migrates from Tristan da Cunha to North Atlantic.

BULLER'S SHEARWATER

Puffinus bulleri   15—17in/38—43cm

IDENTIFICATION Gray above marked by black primaries extending across inner wing and lower back to form distinctive bar. Underparts white.
VOICE Silent at sea.
HABITAT Sea.
RANGE Scarce along Pacific coast in summer.
MOVEMENTS Loop migration in North Pacific from New Zealand breeding grounds.

SOOTY SHEARWATER

Puffinus griseus   15—17in/39—44cm

IDENTIFICATION A dusky, medium-sized shearwater. Upperparts are uniformly dusky brown; underparts similar, but with a distinctive pale center to the underwing. Though a typical shearwater, the long wings are held slightly more angled than other species and flight is more flapping.
VOICE Silent at sea.
HABITAT Oceans.
RANGE Breeds only in southern hemisphere. Fall visitor to east coast (common) and west coast (abundant).
MOVEMENTS Regular loop migration into both Pacific and Atlantic Oceans when not breeding.
BREEDING Southern hemisphere islands; December-February.

MANX SHEARWATER
Puffinus puffinus   12−15in/30−38cm

IDENTIFICATION A typical shearwater that careers over the sea showing alternately black upperparts and white underparts. Confusable only with Audubon's Shearwater, but is larger, longer-winged and less fluttering in flight.
VOICE Silent at sea.
HABITAT Oceans.
RANGE Regular offshore along northeastern coast.
MOVEMENTS Breeds in Europe and a few in Newfoundland. Mostly in North America in late summer and fall.
BREEDING Offshore islands in Atlantic; April-May.
NEST AND EGGS An unlined chamber at the end of a burrow; the single egg is white.
INCUBATION Lasts 52 to 54 days and is shared between the pair.
COMMENT North-eastern pelagic birders should keep an eye out for the dull brown Mediterranean races (probably separate species) of this bird in the fall. In North America the Manx Shearwater is only found breeding in a few colonies in Newfoundland.

NEST AND EGGS A bare rock crevice or burrow; the single egg is white.
INCUBATION Lasts about 56 days.
COMMENT West-coast birds come from New Zealand; east-coast birds from the area of Tierra del Fuego.

SHORT-TAILED SHEARWATER
Puffinus tenuirostris   13−14in/33−35cm

IDENTIFICATION Very similar to Sooty Shearwater, but smaller with more uniform underwing.
VOICE Silent at sea.
HABITAT Sea.
RANGE Scarce off western states in fall and sometimes winter.
MOVEMENTS Migrant from breeding grounds off Australia.

BLACK-VENTED SHEARWATER

Puffinus opisthomelas   13−15in/33−38cm

IDENTIFICATION Dark above, white below with sides of head and breast mottled dark and merging with underparts. Dark vent of little use in the field.
VOICE Silent at sea.
HABITAT Sea.
RANGE Regular off California from late summer into the fall.
MOVEMENTS Breeds off Baja California.

AUDUBON'S SHEARWATER

Puffinus l'herminieri   11−12in/28−30cm

IDENTIFICATION Small shearwater that is black above and white below; has black undertail coverts, but these are virtually impossible to see in the field. Shorter, more rounded wings than other shearwaters, with fluttering more murre-like, flight. Only confusable with rarer Manx Shearwater, but bill tiny in comparison.

VOICE Silent at sea.
HABITAT Oceans.
RANGE Regular visitor to Florida and east coast of US.
MOVEMENTS Disperses from breeding grounds in Bahamas.
BREEDING On rocky Caribbean islands.
NEST AND EGGS A bare crevice serves as a nest; the single egg is white.
INCUBATION Lasts 51 days and is shared between the pair.
COMMENT May well be a more frequent visitor to American eastern waters than appears from current reports.

WILSON'S STORM-PETREL

Oceanites oceanicus   6½−7in/17−18cm

IDENTIFICATION Small, black storm-petrel with white rump, rounded tail and long legs that extend or trail in flight. Gray in wing is similar to Leach's Storm-Petrel, but often follows ships and patters over the surface of the sea. Legs yellow if well seen. Swallow-like flight.

VOICE Silent at sea.
HABITAT Oceans.
RANGE Breeds only in southern oceans. Regular off east coast in fall and sometimes quite numerous off Grand Banks.
MOVEMENTS Performs huge loop migration in Atlantic.
BREEDING Remote islands in southern oceans; December-February.
NEST AND EGGS Rock crevices; the single egg is white.
INCUBATION Lasts 39 to 48 days and is shared by both sexes.
COMMENT Probably the world's most abundant bird.

FORK-TAILED STORM-PETREL

Oceanodroma furcata   8½in/21cm

IDENTIFICATION A long-tailed, all-gray storm-petrel with dark mark around eye and dark underwing coverts.
VOICE Silent at sea.
HABITAT Isolated islands.
RANGE Breeds from northern California northward to Aleutians.
MOVEMENTS Disperses in North Pacific.

LEACH'S STORM-PETREL

Oceanodroma leucorhoa   7½–8½in/19–22cm

IDENTIFICATION Small, black seabird with forked tail and bold white rump. In flight, shows gray coverts extending across the upper wing. In southern California white rump may be absent. Feet do not extend beyond tail, seldom follow ships. Flight consists of bat-like glides and wing flapping.
VOICE Various screeches and crooning at breeding colonies.
HABITAT Breeds on remote islands; winters at sea to the south.

RANGE Breeds along western coasts and in the north-east from Labrador to Maine.
BREEDING Remote offshore islands; May-June.
NEST AND EGGS A burrow or rock crevice serves as a nest; the single egg is white.
INCUBATION The egg is incubated for 41 or 42 days by both members of the pair.
COMMENT This is not an uncommon bird, though the isolation of its breeding colonies and its nocturnal and pelagic habits make it a difficult bird to see.

ASHY STORM-PETREL

Oceanodroma homochroa   8in/20cm

IDENTIFICATION All black, with a gray wash and paler gray underwing. Flight more direct than many other storm-petrels, but wing-beats still fast and fluttering.
VOICE Silent at sea.
HABITAT Offshore islands.
RANGE Breeds off California.
MOVEMENTS Except for winter, relatively common off California.

BAND-RUMPED STORM-PETREL

Oceanodroma castro   9in/23cm

IDENTIFICATION All-black storm-petrel with white, horseshoe-shape rump patch, that narrows below. Similar to Wilson's Storm-Petrel and Leach's Storm-Petrel, but flight more like shearwater with stiff-winged glides. Square-tailed.
VOICE Silent at sea.
HABITAT Sea.
RANGE Very rare off Atlantic and Gulf coasts.
MOVEMENTS Migrant from tropical islands such as Hawaii, Galapagos and Honshu in Japan.

BLACK STORM-PETREL

Oceanodroma melania   9in/23cm

IDENTIFICATION Large, all-black storm-petrel with deeply forked tail and long, slow wing-beats.
VOICE Silent at sea.
HABITAT Offshore islands.
RANGE Breeds Santa Barbara Island, California and off Baja peninsula.
MOVEMENTS Common off California coast from late summer through fall.

LEAST STORM-PETREL

Oceanodroma microsoma   6in/15cm

IDENTIFICATION Small, all-black storm-petrel with deep wing-beats in fast flight. Short, wedge-shaped tail creates unique shape.
VOICE Silent at sea.
HABITAT Sea.
RANGE Scarce visitor to southern California coast.
MOVEMENTS Migrant from Galapagos and Peruvian Islands in late summer and fall.

GANNETS, BOOBIES, PELICANS, CORMORANTS & DARTERS

THIS is a diverse grouping of bird families that consists of closely related waterbirds, many of which are essentially marine in habit. They are generally large, mostly gregarious and are generally of more southerly distribution.

The gannets and boobies are long-winged seabirds that use a rise and glide technique of flying relatively low and easily over the waves. When feeding they rise higher before plunging head-first into the water in search of fish. As they are essentially gregarious birds, feeding parties often perform quite dramatically as bird after bird dives spectacularly into the sea. The Northern Gannet breeds on islands and cliffs on the north-eastern coasts of North America and is a widespread visitor to the Atlantic seaboard outside the breeding season. The various species of boobies are of more tropical origins and are only occasional visitors to the southern United States.

There are only eight species of pelicans in the world, and two breed in North America. Typical of pelicans is the American White Pelican, a huge black and white bird with a mammoth bill and cavernous pouch. The pouch is used to catch rather than carry fish, despite the impression given by advertisements and cartoon pelicans. These are gregarious birds that often participate in co-operative fishing expeditions in which a half circle of birds drive a shoal of fish into the shallows. Despite their size, they are great fliers, being capable of "shearwatering" over the waves and soaring like a hawk over land. In contrast, the Brown Pelican is the world's only diving pelican. Gannet-like, it plunges into the sea from the air in the most spectacular fashion.

No less than six species of cormorants breed in North America out of a world total of 33 species. All are black birds that have the curious habit of hanging out their wings to dry. If a cormorant remains in the water too long, it becomes waterlogged and will drown. If this seems strange for what are essentially marine birds, it must be understood that all aquatic birds have made compromises to achieve a balance between efficiency in the water and safety in the air and on land. In the case of the cormorants, buoyancy has been sacrificed to underwater efficiency. The result is the need for an occasional dry out in the wind prior to total waterlogging. Perhaps the most evolved of all the cormorant-like birds is the Anhinga, or Snakebird as it is often called. This underwater hunter is unusual in actually spearing its prey with its sharp dagger-like bill before surfacing with an interesting problem. With a wriggling fish impaled on the end of its bill, the Anhinga tosses its prey in the air so that its open mouth can catch and consume the luckless fish.

WHITE-TAILED TROPICBIRD

Phaethon lepturus   29−31in/74−79cm

IDENTIFICATION Large, white seabird with bold, black marks in primaries and across the open wing. Extended central tail feathers are black and white. Bill yellow.
VOICE Silent at sea.
HABITAT Sea.
RANGE Rare straggler to Gulf and Atlantic coasts.
MOVEMENTS Migrant from Bermuda, Bahamas and Caribbean.

RED-BILLED TROPICBIRD

Phaethon aethereus   39−41in/99−104cm

IDENTIFICATION Large, red-billed, white seabird marked by barring above in all plumages and by black primaries. Extended tail feathers are white.
VOICE Silent at sea.
HABITAT Sea.
RANGE Rare offshore southern US coasts.
MOVEMENTS Some move northward at sea from Baja California and Caribbean islands.

MASKED BOOBY

Sula dactylatra   31−33in/79−84cm

IDENTIFICATION A black and white "gannet" with black extending from wing-tips along all flight feathers, black tail and black around base of bill. Bill and feet yellow.
VOICE Silent at sea.
HABITAT Sea.
RANGE Offshore in Gulf Coast.
MOVEMENTS Wanderer from Caribbean breeding grounds.

BLUE-FOOTED BOOBY

Sula nebouxii   31−33in/79−84cm

IDENTIFICATION Brown above, white below with buffy underwing stripe and heavily streaked head and neck. Gray bill, blue feet.
VOICE Silent at sea.
RANGE Scarce wanderer to southern California.
MOVEMENTS Breeds Baja peninsula.

BROWN BOOBY

Sula leucogaster   27½−31½in/70−80cm

IDENTIFICATION Closely related and similar to Northern Gannet in shape and behavior. Upperparts, head and neck brown, belly white. Underwing shows white centre. Bill, face and large feet, yellow. Basically a tropical species that just reaches North America.
VOICE Silent outside breeding season.
HABITAT Sea coasts, oceans.
RANGE Breeds in Mexico on Pacific coast and in Caribbean.
MOVEMENTS Wanders northward to coast of Gulf states and rarely to southern California and Salton Sea.
BREEDING Rocky coastal islands; March-May.
NEST AND EGGS A few pieces of vegetation and shells are drawn together to form the lip of a saucer on bare ground; the 2 eggs are pale blue.

INCUBATION Lasts 40 to 43 days and is shared by both members of the pair.

COMMENT Though easy enough to identify in adult plumage, immature birds should be treated with great care, especially where unexpected.

NORTHERN GANNET

Sula bassanus   34—38in/86—96cm

IDENTIFICATION Large black and white seabird that gathers at enormous colonies in favored localities. Large, cigar-shaped body with pointed head and tail. Long, stiffish wings with boldly black tips. Flies with series of flaps and long glides, dives from air into sea. Juveniles dark brown, becoming whiter over several years.

VOICE Grunts and cackles at colonies.

HABITAT Remote islands and stacks; winters at sea.

RANGE Breeds on islands off Newfoundland, Nova Scotia and in Gulf of St Lawrence.

MOVEMENTS Disperses over sea as far south as Florida and adjacent Gulf Coast in winter.

BREEDING Huge steep cliffs, isolated rocky stacks; April-June.

NEST AND EGGS Seaweed or grass, depending on location, formed into an untidy heap; the single egg is white.

INCUBATION Lasts 42 to 46 days and is shared between the sexes.

COMMENT A highly gregarious bird that depends on a territory that extends as far as it can reach with its bill.

AMERICAN WHITE PELICAN

Pelecanus erythrorhynchos   55—70in/140—178cm

IDENTIFICATION Unmistakable huge, white bird with large orange-pink bill and pouch. Adult is all white save for the bill; and black flight feathers that are particularly apparent in the air. Juvenile has brown crown and bill, but dirty-white body. Flies in formation on broad wings.

VOICE Usually silent.

HABITAT Marshes and lagoons.

RANGE Breeds in central west Canada southward through prairies.

MOVEMENTS Winters along coasts and inland in California and Gulf Coast.

BREEDING Coastal lagoons and lakes; March-May.

NEST AND EGGS A heap of earth and vegetation on an island, often among damp or marshy vegetation; the 2 or 3 eggs are white.

INCUBATION The eggs take 29 days to hatch and incubation is shared between the sexes.

COMMENT The huge, square-cut wings of this waterbird can be compared with those of other soaring birds, the hawks and eagles.

BROWN PELICAN

Pelecanus occidentalis   45—54in/114—137cm

IDENTIFICATION Unmistakable, being the only pelican that dives for its food. In summer, adult is silvery brown with large, dark-brown bill and pouch, creamy neck and chestnut hind neck and foreneck. In winter the chestnut is lost. Juvenile is brown and whitish, with dark upperparts. In flight, dark body contrasts with pale head. Usually gregarious.

VOICE Nestlings produce wide variety of calls; adults silent.

HABITAT Sea coasts and lagoons.

RANGE Breeds along both southern Pacific and Atlantic coasts and along Gulf coast.

MOVEMENTS Largely resident.

BREEDING Offshore islands; April-May.

NEST AND EGGS A huge heap of sticks placed in a bush or low tree, or on the bare ground; the 2 or 3 eggs are white.

INCUBATION Lasts some 28 days and is shared by male and female.

COMMENT The only one of the world's eight pelicans that dives for its food.

GREAT CORMORANT

Phalacrocorax carbo   35—39½in/89—100cm

IDENTIFICATION Largest of the cormorants. Dark bird that swims and dives well and often perches with its wings out to dry. Iridescent green and gold wash over mainly black plumage with, in summer adult, white chin and flank patches. Proportionally larger head and bill and thicker neck than similar species. Juvenile, pale on underparts and best identified by yellow base to bill and by structure.

VOICE Various grunts.

HABITAT Coastal, sometimes inland lakes.

RANGE Breeds on Atlantic coast of Canada.

MOVEMENTS Winters southward on Atlantic coast generally as far south as central Atlantic states.

BREEDING Coastal cliffs and stacks; April-May.

NEST AND EGGS An untidy pile of seaweed placed on an open ledge or among rocky debris at the foot of a cliff; the 3 or 4 eggs are pale blue.

INCUBATION Lasts 28 or 29 days and is shared by both members of the pair.

COMMENT These are colonial birds that often nest together with Double-crested Cormorants.

DOUBLE-CRESTED CORMORANT

Phalacrocorax auritus   30½−36in/77−91cm

IDENTIFICATION All-dark cormorant with golden sheen on wings like Great Cormorant. The most common and widespread member of the family. Orange "face" is almost the only distinguishing feature; the double crests are virtually impossible to see in the field. Juveniles are buffy below, brown above and show orange on face.
VOICE Grunts while breeding.
HABITAT Lakes, rivers and coastal waters.
RANGE Breeds throughout most of US and temperate Canada, though absent from hilly and mountain areas.
MOVEMENTS Winters along most coasts and inland along southern river systems.
BREEDING Coasts and estuaries, rivers and lakes; April-May.
NEST AND EGGS A large nest of sticks, seaweed and other materials placed on a cliff, island, or in a tree; the 2 to 7 eggs are green-blue.
INCUBATION Lasts 25 to 29 days and is shared between the pair.
COMMENT North America's only regular freshwater cormorant, often nests inland in colonies alongside gulls.

OLIVACEOUS CORMORANT

Phalacrocorax olivaceus   23½−25½in/60−65cm

IDENTIFICATION Small, dark cormorant with iridescent, olive plumage and orange-yellow throat patch bordered by white. Longish tail. Immature is brown above and buff below with orange-yellow throat. Smallest cormorant on the Atlantic coast.
VOICE Various grunting calls when breeding.
HABITAT Marshes, freshwaters and brackish lagoons.
RANGE Breeds along the coasts of Texas and Louisiana.
MOVEMENTS Moves southward along Gulf Coast to winter south of the Mexican border.
BREEDING Coastal marshes and freshwater lakes; March-April.
NEST AND EGGS A collection of twigs is lined with grasses and placed in a tree or on a rock; the 2 to 6 eggs are pale blue.
INCUBATION Undescribed.
COMMENT A colonial cormorant, confined to the Texas Gulf Coast, where it is relatively common.

BRANDT'S CORMORANT

Phalacrocorax penicillatus   33–35in/84–89cm

IDENTIFICATION Uniformly black cormorant marked by difficult-to-see blue throat patch bordered by a dull creamy patch that is a much better field mark. Shiny, iridescent plumage, lacks a crest.

VOICE Croaks and grunts while breeding.

HABITAT Coastal, breeds on offshore rocks.

RANGE Breeds from southern British Columbia to Mexico and confined to Pacific.

MOVEMENTS Local dispersal only.

BREEDING Rocky islands along coasts; April-May.

NEST AND EGGS A mass of seaweed together with other available materials placed on the ground; the 3 to 6 eggs are very pale blue.

INCUBATION Is shared between the pair.

COMMENT A highly gregarious cormorant at all times, even forming large flocks at feeding grounds.

VOICE Grunts at breeding colony.

HABITAT Coasts and offshore waters.

RANGE Breeds from Bering Straits to central California.

MOVEMENTS Local dispersal along Pacific coast.

BREEDING Prefers sheer cliffs along coasts and islands; May-June.

NEST AND EGGS A large collection of seaweed, grasses and other material is placed on a narrow ledge; the 3 to 7 eggs are pale blue.

INCUBATION Lasts 26 to 31 days and is performed by both members of the pair.

COMMENT Though very much a marine bird, it hardly merits the name Pelagic, which would indicate a life spent well out among the oceans. It is, in fact, a coastal bird.

PELAGIC CORMORANT

Phalacrocorax pelagicus   25–30in/64–76cm

IDENTIFICATION A small, all-black cormorant with thin bill and neck. A white flank patch develops during the breeding season and the "face" is red at all times. A double crest marks the crown, but is visible only at close range. Juvenile is brown with only structure to aid identification.

RED-FACED CORMORANT

Phalacrocorax urile   30–32in/76–81cm

IDENTIFICATION Medium-sized, all-dark cormorant marked by yellow bill, red face, and white flank patch in breeding adult. Beware smaller, dark-billed Pelagic Cormorant.

VOICE Growls and grunts on breeding grounds.

HABITAT Seas and islands.

RANGE Aleutian chain.

MOVEMENTS Resident.

ANHINGA

Anhinga anhinga   34–36in/86–91cm

IDENTIFICATION Like a large, slim cormorant. Adult male is greenish black with ragged upper neck and drooping silver plumes across the back and wings. The neck is extremely long, the head slim and the bill, long and dagger-like. The tail is long and broad. In soaring flight, the extending neck and tail form a "cross" in the sky. The female has buffy head and neck.

VOICE Various grunting calls.
HABITAT Freshwater marshes and overgrown swamps.
RANGE Breeds in southern states north to North Carolina.
MOVEMENTS Mostly coastal in winter.
BREEDING Marshes and shallow lakes with plentiful vegetation; March-April.
NEST AND EGGS A collection of sticks and leaves is placed in a tree or cypress; the 3 to 6 eggs are pale blue.
INCUBATION Is shared between the pair.
COMMENT The country name of 'snakebird' is a result of this species swimming with only neck and head above water.

MAGNIFICENT FRIGATEBIRD

Fregata magnificens   39–41in/99–104cm

IDENTIFICATION Large, all-black seabird with long, pointed and angled wings, and deeply forked tail. Flies easily on bowed wings. Orange-red throat sac.
VOICE Generally silent at sea.
HABITAT Seas and coasts.
RANGE Breeds on tropical islands and off Florida.
MOVEMENTS Wanderer to Gulf and Atlantic coasts, rarely to southern California.

HERONS, IBISES, SPOONBILLS & STORKS

THESE long-legged water birds are among the most obvious and attractive of all the world's birds. Even people with only a passing interest are impressed by their grace and beauty, by their stealth and wildness, and by their often colonial, tree-top nesting habits. In fact, if asked to show a layman the attraction of birds, most birders would head them off to a marsh where plenty of herons could be guaranteed. These birds are generally divided among three families. The Ardeidae consists of herons with some 64 species in the world, of which 12 breed in North America. There are 17 storks, all members of the Ciconiidae, only one of which, the American Wood Stork, breeds within North America. Finally, only four of the 33 species of Threskiornithidae, or ibises, are found in North America. Naturally the proportion of North American species varies from one family to another.

Herons are large birds, with species like the Great Blue Heron reaching almost 60in/150cm in height. They have long legs that enable them to wade in stream or marsh, and long necks that are extended when they strike at prey. Most have long, dagger-like bills, ideally suited to grabbing fish. The feet have a well-developed fourth toe which helps to spread their weight over soft mud, and the middle toe is equipped with a serrated claw that acts as a comb and is an essential aid to feather maintenance. Living in wet, muddy habitats, and feeding on slimy fish, keeping feathers clean is crucial to the herons. They also have unique patches of powder down feathers situated on the breast and rump. These grow continuously throughout the year and are broken down into a fine powder when rubbed. This is spread over the bird's body during preening and, having absorbed dirt, is then combed out by the middle claw. The toiletry is completed by oil taken from the bird's preen gland.

Herons fly with their necks tucked back in their shoulders, whereas storks fly with neck extended, so the two groups are quite distinct. The American Wood Stork, like other members of its family, is a highly gregarious and graceful bird but it is also something of a scavenger. Sadly, it is largely confined to the south-eastern U.S.A., though it ranges widely through Central and South America. It was doubtless the shape of its large, decurved bill that was responsible for its earlier misleading name of Wood Ibis.

MJPLEDGER

Ibises, of which there are four in North America, are similarly long-legged, long-billed water birds that fly with neck extended. Typically, they have decurved bills like a curlew, but several species have evolved a huge, spoon-shaped bill. The similarity between two of the three North American ibises, the Glossy Ibis, and White-faced Ibis, is so close that they are generally regarded as having a common ancestor. It seems highly likely that this was the Glossy Ibis of the Old World that colonized America in the past and evolved in isolation to become the White-faced Ibis. A more recent colonization then brought the Glossy Ibis to North American shores. These later arrivals are regarded as the same species as their relatives remaining across the Atlantic. In winter plumage these two species bear an even stronger resemblance to one another; while in immature plumages, they are identical.

Marshland is amongst the richest of all habitats, a place where large, long-legged waterbirds abound. While Sandhill Cranes fly in the distance a Reddish Egret raises its wings to balance its erratic hunting methods. The Great Blue Heron and American Bittern adopt a more stealthy technique while, in the foreground, an American Avocet and Semipalmated Sandpiper rest among the shallows.

AMERICAN BITTERN

Botaurus lentiginosus   23–34in/58–86cm

IDENTIFICATION Large, round-winged heron that skulks among reed beds and is usually seen briefly in flight. Whole plumage streaked in buffs and browns with a dark cap and broad dark moustachial streak. Bill is large and yellow, legs green. When caught in open, tries to merge with vegetation.
VOICE A booming *onk-a-sonk*.
HABITAT Marshes.
RANGE Breeds across southern Canada and much of US.
MOVEMENTS Leaves northern and central parts of range in winter.
BREEDING Well-vegetated marshes with cattails, bulrushes and other thickets.
NEST AND EGGS A platform of aquatic vegetation is built on wet ground among cover; the 3 to 7 eggs are brown buff.
INCUBATION Lasts about 28 days and is performed by the female.
COMMENT Attempting to liken the strange calls of this species to other sounds has created many local country names for this secretive bird.

LEAST BITTERN

Ixobrychus exilis   11–14in/28–35cm

IDENTIFICATION Very small heron that clings to tops of bushes or reeds, but spends most of its time inside deep cover. Male has black crown and back with bold, warm, buffy wing patches, that are particularly obvious in flight. Female and immature similar, but more dully colored.
VOICE Quiet coo-ing.
HABITAT Marshes, reed-beds.
RANGE Absent from most mountain states, otherwise widely spread across US.
MOVEMENTS Migratory wintering only in Florida, southern Texas and southern California.
BREEDING Marshes with extensive growths of cattails and bushes; May-June.
NEST AND EGGS A flimsy nest of vegetation suspended above water; the 4 to 6 eggs are white, washed blue.
INCUBATION Lasts 17 or 18 days and is performed by both members of the pair.
COMMENT A summer visitor that is frequently overlooked, though there is much flying in early summer.

GREAT BLUE HERON

Ardea herodias   39–52in/99–132cm

IDENTIFICATION Large, mainly gray heron with white head marked by fine black crest. Pale, streaked foreneck. Flies on huge arched, dark wings with neck tucked back in "shoulders".
VOICE Harsh squawks.
HABITAT Ponds, lakes, marshes, estuaries.

RANGE Widespread resident over most of temperate North America.

MOVEMENTS Northern birds move southward in winter.

BREEDING Deciduous and coniferous woods near water; April–May.

NEST AND EGGS A large platform of twigs and sticks near the top of a tree; the 3 to 7 eggs are pale green.

INCUBATION The eggs take some 28 days to hatch and are incubated by both sexes.

COMMENT These are colonial birds that frequently re-use the same nest year after year creating quite a substantial structure.

GREAT EGRET

Casmerodius albus   35–41in/89–104cm

IDENTIFICATION Largest, all-white egret marked by large, yellow bill and dark legs. Neck mostly held in distinctly kinked manner when at rest. The white form of the Great Blue Heron found in Florida is larger and has yellowish legs (*see* Snowy Egret).

VOICE Croaks.

HABITAT Marshes, pools, estuaries.

RANGE Breeds over much of the US except the grassland and mountain interior.

MOVEMENTS Moves southward to winter on south-eastern Gulf and southern Pacific coasts.

BREEDING Marshside thickets and reeds; April–May.

NEST AND EGGS A platform of sticks and/or reeds placed in a tree, but also among reeds over water; the 3 to 5 eggs are pale blue.

INCUBATION Lasts 23 to 26 days and is shared between the sexes.

COMMENT One of the world's most widespread birds with a consequent confusion of common and scientific names.

SNOWY EGRET

Egretta thula   20–27in/51–68cm

IDENTIFICATION Slim, elegant egret with white plumage, black bill, black legs and yellow feet. When feeding in mud the feet may appear black, even in flight afterwards. Young Little Blue Heron is also white, but has heavier gray bill and paler legs.

VOICE Mostly silent.

HABITAT Marshes, lake margins, estuaries.

RANGE Widespread over western, eastern and southern states.

MOVEMENTS Migrates southward in winter to South America, though some overwinter in California and from Florida north to North Carolina.

IDENTIFICATION Adult is dark, slate-gray with maroon neck. The bill is gray, tipped black, the legs gray. It thus bears a superficial resemblance to the larger Reddish Egret. Common in areas of south. Young birds are white – beware confusion with other egrets.

VOICE Croaks while breeding.

HABITAT Marshes, lagoons, often near coast.

RANGE Breeds along Gulf Coast and northward up the major river systems. Also in Florida and along the Atlantic coast to New England.

MOVEMENTS A post-breeding wanderer, as far north as Maritime provinces and as far west as northern California. Winters coastally along Gulf and as far north as mid-Atlantic states.

BREEDING Marshes and coastal islands with dense surrounding vegetation; April-May.

NEST AND EGGS A collection of sticks forms a platform in a low bush; the 3 to 6 eggs are greenish blue.

INCUBATION The eggs take 22 to 24 days to hatch and are incubated by both members of the pair.

COMMENT Birds in transition from immature (white) to adult (blue) plumage, are boldly blotched white and gray.

BREEDING Thickets and trees adjacent to marshes; April-May.

NEST AND EGGS A platform of twigs is placed in a tree or tall bush; the 3 to 6 eggs are pale blue.

INCUBATION Lasts 20 to 24 days and is shared by both members of the pair.

COMMENT When ladies fashion decreed plumes, this species was hunted mercilessly. It has since recovered.

LITTLE BLUE HERON

Egretta caerulea   25 – 30in/63 – 76cm

TRICOLORED HERON

Egretta tricolor   25 – 30in/63 – 76cm

IDENTIFICATION A slate-blue heron, with white underparts and rufous plumes at the base of the neck and on the back. The foreneck is white, streaked and with a rufous wash. The dagger-like bill is black, the legs dull yellow. Always appears more slender and longer necked than other herons and egrets.

VOICE Various croaking calls.

HABITAT Marshes, mangrove swamps, estuaries, backwaters.

RANGE From Gulf Coast to Florida northwards to New England.

MOVEMENTS Resident south of mid-Atlantic states.

BREEDING Marshes of various types near the coast with adjacent trees; April-May.

NEST AND EGGS A platform of sticks placed in a bush or sometimes on the ground among marshland vegetation; the 3 to 7 eggs are greenish blue.

INCUBATION Lasts 21 days and is shared between the pair.

COMMENT Some books refer to this species as Louisiana Heron.

REDDISH EGRET

Egretta rufescens   27½−31½in/70−80cm

IDENTIFICATION Dark egret usually found on salty or brackish lagoons. Slate-gray body, with bold rusty head, neck and breast that is held fluffed-up to produce an ill-kempt appearance. The legs are black, the bill dark pink, with a black tip. A white phase also occurs, but the bill and legs are colored as normal birds. Active feeder.

VOICE Croaks.

HABITAT Saline lagoons, estuaries.

RANGE Florida and Texas coastlines.

MOVEMENTS Resident.

BREEDING Shallow waters, often brackish, with mangroves and other shoreline shubbery; March-April.

NEST AND EGGS A mass of sticks placed in low shoreline vegetation; the 3 to 7 eggs are blue green.

INCUBATION The eggs are incubated by both members of the pair.

COMMENT The erratic rush-and-grab feeding tactics of the Reddish Egret are recognizable at a considerable distance.

CATTLE EGRET

Bubulcus ibis   19−21in/48−53cm

IDENTIFICATION Small, robust, white egret that associates with domestic animals and agricultural machinery. Neck mostly held tucked into shoulders; upright walking stance; yellow bill and black legs. In breeding season bill becomes orange, legs become pink and there is a warm wash of buff on head, back and breast.

VOICE Usually silent.

HABITAT Marshes, grasslands, arable.

RANGE Colonist this century from Old World via South America. Has spread northward through southern and eastern states as far as New England and as far west as California. Has been recorded across southern Canada.

MOVEMENTS Largely resident south of Carolinas and in southern California.

BREEDING Thickets and trees adjacent to rivers or marshes; April-May.

NEST AND EGGS A bulky cup of twigs placed in a bush or low tree, the 3 to 5 eggs are pale blue.

INCUBATION Is shared by both sexes and lasts 21 to 25 days.

COMMENT This is one of the most gregarious of the herons forming dense colonies with several nests in the same tree.

GREEN-BACKED HERON

Butorides striatus   15−22in/38−56cm

IDENTIFICATION Small, bittern-like heron of dense thickets and aquatic vegetation. Adult has chestnut face, neck and breast with dark green upperparts. There is a black crest and it has reddish legs. Usually seen flying on rounded wings between one patch of cover and another like dark Least Bittern.
VOICE Sharp croaks.
HABITAT Marshes and lake margins with dense vegetation.
RANGE Breeds in western and eastern states, absent from Rockies.
MOVEMENTS Winters southern California and Florida, otherwise migratory from remainder of range.
BREEDING Waterside thickets of many types; April-May.
NEST AND EGGS A platform of twigs hidden in a bush; the 3 to 5 eggs are greenish blue.
INCUBATION Both sexes share the incubation of 19 to 21 days.
COMMENT Though these small herons sometimes nest close together they are much less colonial than most other egrets and herons.

BLACK-CROWNED NIGHT-HERON

Nycticorax nycticorax   23−28in/58−71cm

IDENTIFICATION A crepuscular heron most active at dawn and dusk. Always holds itself hunched up, disguising its length of neck. Adult has black crown and back, gray wings and white underparts. The bill is decidedly chunky, the legs a yellow-orange. Immatures are streaked in gray brown. In flight, the chunky effect is enforced.
VOICE Various croaks.
HABITAT Flooded thickets, riversides.
RANGE Breeds over much of US northward into southern Canada.
MOVEMENTS Winters along west and east coasts of US.
BREEDING Marshes and wetlands with a substantial growth of tall trees; April-May.
NEST AND EGGS The nest is a substantial structure of sticks placed at some height in a tree; the 3 to 8 eggs are pale blue.
INCUBATION Lasts 24 to 26 days and is shared between the pair.
COMMENT Night-Herons frequently spend the day motionless

YELLOW-CROWNED NIGHT-HERON

Nycticorax violacea   22−27in/56−68cm

IDENTIFICATION Adult is gray on neck and underparts with boldly black and white upperparts and a unique striped head. A yellow crest extends behind crown. The black bill is chunky. Stands upright and hunts both by day and night. Immature closely resembles young Black-crowned Night Heron, but grayer with less spotting.
VOICE Various barking notes.
HABITAT Marshes and thickets.
RANGE Breeds along Gulf and Atlantic coasts of US and inland in Mississippi basin.
MOVEMENTS Winters along Gulf Coast and in Florida.

BREEDING Marshes with thickets and copses of trees; April-May.

NEST AND EGGS A nest of sticks and twigs is constructed in a waterside tree; the 2 to 6 eggs are greenish blue.

INCUBATION The incubation is shared by both sexes for 21 to 25 days.

COMMENT The colonies of this bird vary in size and sometimes pairs will nest in solitary isolation.

WHITE IBIS

Eudocimus albus   23−27in/58−68cm

IDENTIFICATION Large, all-white bird marked by black wing tips; red face, decurved red bill, red legs. Juvenile is brown above, white below with brown neck. Like other ibises, flies with neck extended.

VOICE Various grunting calls.

HABITAT Marshes, lagoons, estuaries.

RANGE Breeds along Gulf Coast through Florida, north to Carolina.

MOVEMENTS Mostly resident.

BREEDING A colonial nester, often in huge numbers in association with other long-legged waterbirds; April-June.

NEST AND EGGS Builds a loose structure of twigs of variable size in a low bush over water; the 4 eggs are creamy white, spotted with brown.

INCUBATION Lasts 21days and is performed by both parents.

COMMENT Night-Herons frequently spend the day motionless in a large tree where they are easily overlooked.

GLOSSY IBIS

Plegadis falcinellus   22−25in/56−63cm

IDENTIFICATION Glossy-purple and bronze bird with long legs and long decurved bill. Very similar to White-faced Ibis, especially in winter.

VOICE Croaks and grunts.

HABITAT Marshes with thickets and reeds.

RANGE Expanding northward to Great Lakes and westward to Texas from stronghold in Florida. Probably colonized New World only a hundred years or so ago as, equally probably, did the White-faced Ibis hundreds of years earlier.

MOVEMENTS Mostly migrates to Florida to winter.

BREEDING Nests in colonies among marshland bushes over water often mixed with other species, though the largest are single species colonies; May-June.

NEST AND EGGS Platform of sticks, often 10−15 feet above water; 3 or 4 eggs are pale green blue.

INCUBATION Male and female share the duty which lasts 21 days and the chicks fledge after 2 weeks.
COMMENT Believed to be an Old World colonist. Range now expanding north along east coast.

WHITE-FACED IBIS

Plegadis chihi   22−25in/56−63cm

IDENTIFICATION A bronzy-purple, glossy-plumaged bird, with long legs, long neck and long decurved bill. Very similar to Glossy Ibis of the east, but with bold white line around the eye and bill to form an enclosed area in summer. When this white area is lost in winter it becomes virtually impossible to separate from Glossy Ibis.

VOICE Quacking calls.
HABITAT Marshes with thickets and reeds.
RANGE From California inland to Idaho and along Texas and Louisiana coasts. Steadily contracting.
MOVEMENTS Winters Mexico, Texas coast, and California.
BREEDING Breeds colonially, sometimes among herons; May-June.
NEST AND EGGS A neat cup of reeds situated in a low bush in marshland; 3 or 4 pale green-blue eggs.
INCUBATION Male and female share incubation for 21−22 days; the young fledge in about 2 weeks.
COMMENT Doubtless derived from an early colonization by the Old World Glossy Ibis from which it is now specifically distinct. Widespread in New World.

ROSEATE SPOONBILL

Ajaia ajaja   30−32in/76−81cm

IDENTIFICATION Large pink bird with white neck and large, spatulate gray bill. Immature is white, with yellow bill and legs. Flies ibis-like with neck extended. Side-to-side sweeping of bill facilitates picking it out at great range.
VOICE Croaks.
HABITAT Mangrove swamps.
RANGE Florida and Texas coasts, but very local.
MOVEMENTS Resident.
BREEDING Breeds colonially in association with herons, storks and ibises in mangroves or trees, often on a marshy island; April-June.
NEST AND EGGS The well constructed twig nest is lined with leaves and placed some 10−15 feet high; 2 to 4 white eggs are speckled with brown.
INCUBATION Lasts 23 days and is performed by both sexes.
COMMENT Once abundant in Florida and the Gulf Coast, the Spoonbill was virtually extirpated in the US by 1920. Recovery under protection is a slow process.

WOOD STORK

Mycteria americana   40−44in/102−112cm

IDENTIFICATION Still widely called "Wood Ibis". Large white bird with bare, black head and upper neck, and long, thick, decurving black bill. The long legs trail prominently in flight when the white body and wing linings contrast with the flight feathers. Soars like other storks and nests in large colonies.

VOICE Croaks when breeding.

HABITAT Marshes with trees.

RANGE Breeds from Gulf Coast to Florida and North to South Carolina.

MOVEMENTS A post-breeding wanderer into mid-Atlantic states and California. Winters in Gulf coast states.

BREEDING Nests in colonies from 20 to 10,000 pairs in tall trees in swamp; April-June.

NEST AND EGGS Platform of sticks lined with moss; 3 white eggs.

INCUBATION Male and female share incubation for 28−32 days; young take about one month to fledge.

COMMENT Has suffered a serious decline due to drainage activities.

SWANS, GEESE & DUCKS

THE birds in this group are often referred to collectively as "wildfowl," not to be confused with "waterfowl," which title includes several other groups of birds. Wildfowl are numerous, widespread, and well known throughout North America, where 40 of the world's 153 species breed. In general they are easily recognized and of straightforward identification. For generations they have, along with the grouse, been a prime target for hunters, and several species have suffered a serious decline as a result. Most dramatic of all was the extermination of the Labrador Duck, which was formerly found from northeastern Canada as far south as Chesapeake Bay. From being on regular sale in markets during the middle of the nineteenth century, this well-marked bird declined to extinction by 1875. A similar fate almost befell the Trumpeter Swan which, by the 1930s, seemed doomed to extinction. Fortunately, conservationists recognized what was happening in time and effective measures have ensured the survival of one of the world's heaviest flying birds. Today there are several thousand individuals in the west.

Three distinct species of swans occur in North America, though one, the Mute Swan, is the result of an introduction from Europe. All are large, white birds that are separated by the color of the bill. Though they are capable of up-ending to reach food in water, the two native species are predominantly grazers.

Many North American geese are also dependent on grasslands though, unlike the swans, they often gather in the most spectacular numbers on migration and at their winter quarters. The flocks of Canada Geese and Snow Geese in particular may number tens of thousands – enough to send any hunter rushing off to the store for more shells.

Fortunately, conservation interests have established a network of waterfowl refuges where these huge populations can safely gather and where food is provided. The safety of wild geese is intimately connected with the maintenance of this refuge network, for these are long-distance migrants that favor particular stop-overs during their length-of-the-continent flights in spring and fall.

Duck, too, take advantage of refuges, though never in such numbers as the geese. No less than 34 distinct species breed in North America and, not surprisingly, each has evolved a different lifestyle. Most numerous are the surface-feeders such as the Mallard. These birds find their food on the surface of water or on dry land and though several species regularly up-end to reach underwater food, they do not regularly dive. Among the surface-feeding ducks, most species show a clear-cut sexual dimorphism; that is a difference between males and females. They are also unusual in that the males have a special "eclipse" plumage usually bearing a strong resemblance to that of the female; this is adopted during the period of moult in late summer when they are all but flightless.

North America is also blessed with a wide variety of diving ducks such as the widespread Ring-necked Duck and Lesser Scaup. As their name implies, these birds find their food underwater. Some eat only vegetation, while others take mainly animate food. A special branch of the diving ducks spend the winter, at least, on the sea and are commonly known as seaduck. This group includes the totally marine eiders, as well as birds like the Greater Scaup, which nest inland and resort to the sea only in winter. North America is well served by the eiders, no less than four species of which can be seen in Alaska. These are all well-marked birds, and the eiderdowns of yesteryear are the result of eider farms at some of the largest colonies.

The sawbills are a strange group of highly specialized fish hunters. Their narrow bills are equipped with hard, tooth-like serrations along the bill margins that are ideally suited to grasping slippery fish. Both the Red-breasted and Common Mergansers take quantities of young sporting fish, but do little harm to the populations.

Waterfowl are an integral part of the North American heritage, and although one species has been lost and many others seriously reduced, there seems little chance of a major disaster in the future. In fact, it was this group of birds that was responsible for the beginnings of the North American conservation movement with Ducks Unlimited and the US Fish and Wildlife Service.

FULVOUS WHISTLING-DUCK

Dendrocygna bicolor   18–21in/46–53cm

IDENTIFICATION A gregarious, upright-standing duck that, despite its alternative name, only rarely perches in trees. Head, neck and underparts are barred brown and black. The long neck has a bold white slash. The tail is short, the black legs long and trail in flight.
VOICE Whistling.
HABITAT Marshes, ponds.

RANGE In US along Mexican border to Texas and Louisiana Gulf Coast.
MOVEMENTS Summer post-breeding wanderer northward.
BREEDING Marshes and shallow backwaters, often with scattered trees; March-April.
NEST AND EGGS A cup of grasses and rushes hidden among emergent vegetation over water, but also a tree hole or old nest of another bird; the 6 to 16 eggs are white.
INCUBATION Lasts 24–26 days and is shared between the pair.
COMMENT Despite its old name "Tree-Duck", this species does not regularly perch in trees.

BLACK-BELLIED WHISTLING DUCK

Dendrocygna autumnalis   20–21in/51–53cm

IDENTIFICATION Gregarious, upright-standing duck with bright red bill and black belly forming distinct band with buffy-chestnut breast. Legs pink, face gray.
VOICE Whistles.
HABITAT Marshes, ponds.
RANGE Breeds southern Texas and southern Arizona.
MOVEMENTS Resident near coast, summer visitor inland.

TUNDRA SWAN

Cygnus columbianus   47–58in/119–147cm

IDENTIFICATION Most common and widespread of the swans. Adult is white with long neck usually held straight and a black bill. There is usually a small spot of yellow in front of the eye. Juvenile is light gray-brown with dull, pinkish bill.
VOICE Goose-like high-pitched call.
HABITAT Marshy tundra ponds in summer; coastal marshes and inland floods in winter.
RANGE Breeds on western Canadian and Alaskan tundra.
MOVEMENTS Migrates southward to winter at traditional sites on Atlantic and Pacific coasts and at a few inland sites in the west.
BREEDING Shallow marshes and lakes of tundra; June-July.
NEST AND EGGS Gathers a mound of grasses and moss near water; the 3 to 5 eggs are creamy white.
INCUBATION The eggs take 32 to 40 days to hatch and are incubated by the female alone.
COMMENT Now usually regarded as conspecific with the Eurasian Bewick's Swan.

TRUMPETER SWAN

Cygnus buccinator   59–71in/150–180cm

IDENTIFICATION Very large swan with proportionately longer neck than Whistling Swan. Neck mostly held straight; bill black with narrow, orange-margin to lower mandible. Juvenile is gray-brown with pink bill marked by extensive black areas.
VOICE Loud trumpeting calls.

HABITAT Wild and remote marshes.

RANGE Once in danger of extinction but has now increased in two native areas on Alaska-Canada border and in Montana. A reintroduction programme has re-established former populations in west.

MOVEMENTS Winters on breeding areas or ice-free areas to the south.

BREEDING Shallow lakes and marshes; May-June.

NEST AND EGGS A large collection of aquatic vegetation on a marshy island or lake margin; the 5 to 8 eggs are white.

INCUBATION Lasts 33 to 40 days and is performed by the female alone.

COMMENT Various reintroduction schemes seem to be helping this species back from the brink of extinction.

Mute Swan

Cygnus olor   57–63in/145–160cm

IDENTIFICATION A huge, white swimming bird with a long neck often held curved. Adults are white with an orange bill and a bare black knob at the base – larger in the male. The wings are often raised over the back. Juvenile is gray-brown becoming white over two or three years.

VOICE Silent except for hisses of aggression.

HABITAT Ponds and lakes.

RANGE Introduced from Europe to north-eastern US. Mostly found on Long Island and in New Jersey, New England and Maryland.

MOVEMENTS Resident, hard weather visitor to coastal bays.

BREEDING Lakes, ponds and marshes; April-May.

NEST AND EGGS A huge mound of vegetation is assembled among plants growing at the water's edge, or on an island; the 5 to 7 eggs are white.

INCUBATION Lasts from 34 to 38 days and is performed mainly by the female.

COMMENT These are aggressive birds that are intolerant towards other large birds that try to share their living space.

Greater White-Fronted Goose

Anser albifrons   25½–30in/65–76cm

IDENTIFICATION A small, gray goose that is easily identified. Basically, barred brown and buff above, with buffy underparts marked by bold black smudges. The base of the bill and forehead are white, the bill pink and the legs orange. Juvenile lacks white forehead and black belly smudging. Birds from Greenland have orange bills.

VOICE High-pitched honking.
HABITAT Breeds on tundra; winters on grasslands near coast.
RANGE Western Canadian Arctic tundra and Alaska.
MOVEMENTS Migrates to west coast and through Central Flyway to Gulf Coast.
BREEDING High Arctic tundra with bogs and open marshes; June-July.
NEST AND EGGS A scrape beside a bog or in a thicket is lined with down; the 5 or 6 eggs are white.
INCUBATION Lasts 27 or 28 days and is by the female alone.
COMMENT This species varies not only in the color of the bill (orange in Greenland birds, pink in Canadian breeders), but also in head and neck coloration. Taiga breeders are darker than those that breed on the tundra.

HABITAT Tundra in summer; winters on marshes.
RANGE From northern Alaska through Canadian Arctic to Baffin Island.
MOVEMENTS Uses all three flyways to winter on Pacific, Atlantic and Gulf coasts. Also inland in California and elsewhere.
BREEDING Tundra coasts with grassy plains and deltas; June-July.
NEST AND EGGS Constructs a neat pile of mosses and lichens lined with down; the 3 to 5 eggs are creamy white.
INCUBATION Lasts 20 to 25 days and is performed by the female.
COMMENT Highly colonial in summer with hundreds of pairs nesting in comparatively small areas.

SNOW GOOSE

Chen caerulescens   25−31in/64−79cm

IDENTIFICATION A small goose that is abundant in major breeding and wintering grounds. Adult is pure white with black wing tips and pink bill and legs. Dark phase birds are found in the eastern part of the breeding range and are known as the Blue Goose. They have white head, but slate-gray body and wings.
VOICE Nasal, muffled honking.

ROSS'S GOOSE

Chen rossii   21−25½in/53−65cm

IDENTIFICATION Very similar to Snow Goose with all-white plumage, black wing tips, pink bill and legs. Much, much smaller and daintier with smaller bill.
VOICE Various cackling calls.
HABITAT Breeds on tundra; winters on marshes.
RANGE Breeds in restricted area of Canadian tundra west of Hudson's Bay.
MOVEMENTS Follows narrow path southward to winter in the central valleys of California occasionally eastward.
BREEDING Islands of lakes, deltas and boggy tundra; June-July.

NEST AND EGGS Often a hollow lined with down, but also may construct quite a mass of vegetation to form a mound; the 2 to 9 eggs are white.

INCUBATION Lasts 24 days and is performed by the female alone.

COMMENT The wide range in number of eggs produced by this bird is probably an adaptation to the variable success enjoyed from year to year in its high Arctic breeding grounds.

EMPEROR GOOSE

Chen canagica   25−27in/63−68cm

IDENTIFICATION Arctic relative of Snow Goose and similar to blue phase of that bird. Head and hind-neck white, remaining upperparts and underparts barred gray except chin and throat which are black. Bill pink, legs yellow.

VOICE Nasal honking.

HABITAT Breeds on marshes, winters along coasts.

RANGE Breeds western coastal Alaska.

MOVEMENTS Winters Aleutians, rare southward along Pacific coast.

BRANT

Branta bernicla   23−26in/58−66cm

IDENTIFICATION Small, dark goose with black breast, neck and head, broken by white slash on side of neck. Bill small and delicate. Essentially a gregarious, shoreline bird in winter. This bird breeds right around the northern pole in the tundra zone. In North America, the western subspecies once treated separately as Black Brant. It differs in having a black belly with pale flanks.

VOICE A soft *rank-rank*.

HABITAT Tundra in summer; shores, bays and adjacent marshes in winter.

RANGE High Canadian and Alaskan Arctic.

MOVEMENTS Moves southward to winter along Pacific and Atlantic coasts.

BREEDING Arctic islands and coastal swamps among tundra; June-July.

NEST AND EGGS A depression is lined with mosses and down; the 3 to 5 eggs are pale cream.

INCUBATION Lasts from 22 to 26 days and is performed by the female alone.

COMMENT Gregarious on migration and in winter, these geese also form colonies on their breeding grounds.

CANADA GOOSE

Branta canadensis   22−36in/56−92cm

IDENTIFICATION Highly variable in size. Brown and buff body, with long, black neck and head, with white area on side extending from chin. Abundant, noisy, well-known.

VOICE Loud honking, especially in flight.

HABITAT Marshes, lakes, bays.

RANGE Breeds right across Alaska and Canada extending southwards through the prairies and Rockies. Small race of Alaska-Yukon known as 'Cackling Goose'.

MOVEMENTS Migrates throughout Canada and US to winter along Pacific and Atlantic coasts and in temperate US.

BREEDING A huge variety of wetland situations from tundra to city parks; April-June.

NEST AND EGGS A hollow near water, lined with vegetation and down; the 4 to 6 eggs are white.

INCUBATION The eggs take 24 to 33 days to hatch and are incubated by the female alone.

COMMENT These birds usually mate for life and are particularly caring in defense of their young.

WOOD DUCK

Aix sponsa   17−20in/43−51cm

IDENTIFICATION A woodland duck with bold, multi-colored plumage. Male has harlequin-patterned head in purple and white with red bill and eye. The upperparts are an iridescent green, but with chestnut and blue in the wing. Female is spotted below with a gray head broken by white markings, particularly around the eye. In flight, the tail is longer than most other duck.

VOICE Whistling *woo-eek*.

HABITAT Woodland ponds and rivers.

RANGE Resident in far western and southern US and summer visitor to north-eastern part of the country northward into southern Canada.

MOVEMENTS Eastern birds migrate to winter in Florida and Gulf Coast.

BREEDING Lakes and streams in wooded country; April-May.

NEST AND EGGS The nest is placed in a hollow or hole in a tree, or in a nest box; the 8 to 15 eggs are creamy.

INCUBATION Lasts 28 to 34 days and is performed by the female alone.

COMMENT The ducklings climb from the nesting chamber using their sharp claws; they then drop to the ground uninjured.

GREEN-WINGED TEAL

Anas crecca   13½−15in/34−38cm

IDENTIFICATION Common and widespread duck, normally found in flocks. Male has chestnut head broken by green slash through eye, bordered by broken yellow line. Breast is spotted and separated from flanks by vertical white wedge. Rear end is black and cream. Female is like other surface-feeding ducks, but with green speculum, bordered white, like male. In flight, white border forms a narrow bar across the wing.

VOICE Quacking, whistling.

HABITAT Marshes, lakes, estuaries.

RANGE Breeds through Canada and western half of US.

MOVEMENTS Migrates throughout US to winter on both coasts and in southern two-thirds of US.

BREEDING Shallow freshwaters from lake margins to overgrown marshes; April-June.

NEST AND EGGS A neat cup of grasses lined with down is well hidden on the ground, occasionally some distance from the nearest water; the 8 to 12 eggs are whitish.

INCUBATION Lasts 21 to 24 days and is performed by the female.

COMMENT Now considered conspecific with the Eurasian Teal and soon to be universally referred to by its American name.

AMERICAN BLACK DUCK

Anas rubripes   21–24in/53–61cm

IDENTIFICATION A widespread and common, surface-feeding duck in the eastern half of North America. Both sexes resemble female Mallard, but are much darker, with yellow, not orange, bills. The paler head contrasts with the darker body, the speculum is purple with only the narrowest of white margins. In flight, pale underwing contrasts with dark body.

VOICE Loud quacking.

HABITAT Ponds, marshes, sea bays.

RANGE Breeds over eastern half of Canada and north-eastern US.

MOVEMENTS Winters throughout eastern US to southern Texas.

BREEDING Fresh and saltwater marshes, often among woodland; April-May.

NEST AND EGGS The nest is a hollow lined with twigs, grasses and down; the 6 to 12 eggs are gray green.

INCUBATION Lasts for 27 to 33 days and is performed by the female alone.

COMMENT Now seen in the west as a result of introductions by sportsmen. Declining in east, partially due to competition with Mallard.

MOTTLED DUCK

Anas fulvigula   21–24in/53–61cm

IDENTIFICATION Easily confused with Black Duck and with female Mallard. The sexes are similarly clothed in mottled browns and buffs with a paler head and dark crown. The bill is yellow, the feet orange, and the speculum green. Not as dark as Black Duck, or as pale as female Mallard. The black-bordered green speculum is a clear field mark.

VOICE Loud quacking.

HABITAT Coastal marshes

RANGE Breeds in Florida and along the Gulf coast westwards from the Mississippi.

MOVEMENTS Resident.

BREEDING Lagoon margins; February-July.

NEST AND EGGS A cup of grasses lined with down is hidden among vegetation near the shoreline; the 8 to 12 eggs are washed green.

INCUBATION Lasts 26 to 28 days by female alone.

COMMENT This species does not overlap with either Mallard or Black Duck during the breeding season. It has been regarded as no more than sub-species of the Mallard by some ornithologists.

MALLARD

Anas platyrhynchos   21½–24½in/55–62cm

IDENTIFICATION Widespread and common duck over much of North America. Male has bottle-green head, white neck ring and brown throat. Upperparts are gray, underparts a pale silver with a black rear end. In flight, there is a blue speculum bordered white. Female is mottled in shades of brown with orange bill.

VOICE Loud quacking.

HABITAT Ponds, lakes, rivers, marshes, estuaries.

RANGE Breeds through most of boreal and temperate Canada south through the US except the south-east.

MOVEMENTS Much of the northern part of the breeding range is abandoned as birds move southward to winter throughout US.

RANGE Breeds across Canada to Alaska and southward through most of western and central states.
MOVEMENTS Winters on coasts and in southern US.
BREEDING Shallow lakes, ponds and marshes; April-June.
NEST AND EGGS A hollow lined with down placed on the ground, often near water; the 7 to 10 eggs are white, variably washed green or buff.
INCUBATION Lasts 22 to 26 days and is performed by the female alone.
COMMENT The long neck of this bird enables it to feed in deeper water than other dabbling duck.

BREEDING Wide variety of wetland types from dry river banks to marshes; April-June.
NEST AND EGGS A hollow lined with down on the ground serves as a nest; the 8 to 12 eggs are white.
INCUBATION Lasts 25 to 31 days and is by the female alone.
COMMENT Highly adaptable duck that has the ability to take advantage of all sorts of human activity.

NORTHERN PINTAIL

Anas acuta   21−27½in/53−70cm

IDENTIFICATION A slim, elegant duck with extended central tail feathers. Male is delicately colored with a chocolate-brown hood extending to the neck and with various shades of gray on the body terminating in a black and white rear end. The central tail feathers form the pin-tail. Female is mottled in shades of gray-brown. Both sexes have delicate blue bills, long necks and pointed tails.
VOICE Quacks.
HABITAT Marshes, estuaries.

BLUE-WINGED TEAL

Anas discors   14−15½in/36−40cm

IDENTIFICATION Small duck, marked in the male by a slate-blue head with bold white crescent before the eye. Heavily spotted brown on buff below. Female like female Green-winged Teal, but has pale blue inner wing like the male.
VOICE Quiet quacking.
HABITAT Ponds, marshes.
RANGE Breeds over western Canada and US, but not in southern states.
MOVEMENTS Migrates through US to winter in southern California along the Gulf and south-east coasts.
BREEDING A wide variety of shallow freshwaters; April-June.
NEST AND EGGS A hollow lined with grasses and down and

situated near water; the 9 to 12 eggs are pale buff.
INCUBATION Lasts 23 to 27 days and is performed by the
female alone.
COMMENT Highly migratory duck that winters mainly along
southern coasts.

CINNAMON TEAL

Anas cyanoptera   14½−17in/37−43cm

IDENTIFICATION Small duck that looks dark at a distance.
Male is, in fact, a deep cinnamon-brown on head and
underparts. Upperparts are darkly mottled. Female is mottled
in shades of brown. In flight, both show a pale forewing like a
Blue-winged Teal and pale wing linings contrasting with dark
body.
VOICE Quacking.
HABITAT Marshes, ponds.
RANGE Breeds over much of western US, extending
northward into adjacent Canada.
MOVEMENTS Moves southward to winter in south Texas and
across Mexican border.
BREEDING Marshes and shallow freshwater lakes and ponds
preferably with plentiful emergent vegetation; April-May.
NEST AND EGGS In a hollow near water, but well hidden
among vegetation; the 6 to 13 eggs are white.
INCUBATION The eggs hatch after 24 or 25 days of incubation
by the female.
COMMENT This bird is known to hybridize with the
Blue-winged Teal.

NORTHERN SHOVELER

Anas clypeata   18½−21in/47−53cm

IDENTIFICATION Both sexes have large spatulate bill. Male
has green head, chestnut belly and flanks and boldly white
breast that is often best feature when resting. Female is like
other surface-feeding ducks, but huge bill always apparent. In
flight, pale blue inner wing is useful.
VOICE Quacking.
HABITAT Shallow marshes, ponds, estuaries.
RANGE Breeds from Alaska and western Canada through
west-central US.
MOVEMENTS Migrates through US to winter on all coasts and
in southern states.
BREEDING Marshes and other shallow freshwaters; April-
June.
NEST AND EGGS A cup of grasses is lined with down and
placed on the ground near water; the 7 to 14 eggs are grayish
buff.
INCUBATION Lasts 22 to 25 days and are incubated by the
female.
COMMENT Extensive muddy margins of marshes are essential
to this sift-feeding duck.

GADWALL

Anas strepera   19−21½in/48−54cm

IDENTIFICATION At a distance, male resembles female of
other surface-feeding ducks, but a close approach reveals a
fine pattern of vermiculated grays. Most obvious feature is
black rear end and white speculum. Female similar to female
Mallard with orange bill; but white speculum separates when
seen. Smaller more round-headed than Mallard.

VOICE Quacks.

HABITAT Marshes, lakes, estuaries.

RANGE Breeds in western US through prairies and north-central states.

MOVEMENTS Migrates through the US to winter on both coasts and southern half of the country.

BREEDING Marshes and shallow lakes with plentiful emergent vegetation; April-May.

NEST AND EGGS On dry land, but usually near water, a hollow lined with down and well hidden by vegetation; the 8 to 12 eggs are creamy.

INCUBATION Lasts 25 to 27 days and is performed by the female.

COMMENT Though widespread, the Gadwall is nowhere numerous.

EURASIAN WIGEON

Anas penelope   16–19in/41–48cm

IDENTIFICATION Male is gray with chestnut head and golden crown slash. White flank slash and black rear end resemble American Wigeon. Female similar to female American Wigeon.

VOICE Whistles.

HABITAT Coastal marshes and adjacent wet grasslands.

RANGE Regular winter visitor in small numbers to east and west coasts.

MOVEMENTS Migrant from Iceland and eastern Asia.

AMERICAN WIGEON

Anas americana   17–19½in/44–50cm

IDENTIFICATION Common duck that forms large flocks at favored areas. Male has creamy-gray head with bold slash of dark green extending from the eye. Underparts are rufous and separated from the brown upperparts by a bold white lateral line. Female is more subdued and lacks green eye slash. Both have small, gray bills. Spends much time grazing. White inner wing only on male in flight.

VOICE Soft whistling.

HABITAT Coastal and inland marshes and floods.

RANGE Breeds from Alaska, through central western states and east to Ontario, occasionally on east coast.

MOVEMENTS Migrates through whole of US to winter on all coasts and in southern states.

BREEDING Freshwater margins of lakes, ponds and marshes; May-June.

NEST AND EGGS A nest of grass stems is lined with down and hidden on the ground among grass; the 7 to 12 eggs are creamy.

INCUBATION The eggs take some 24 to 25 days to hatch and are incubated by the female.

COMMENT Highly gregarious outside the breeding season forming flocks thousands strong during the winter.

CANVASBACK

Aythya valisineria   19½–24in/50–61cm

IDENTIFICATION Very similar to Redhead in plumage pattern, though male is paler gray on body and female grayer throughout. Longer neck and elongated wedge-shaped head with all-black bill are best identification features.

IDENTIFICATION A common diving duck. Male has chestnut-red head, black breast and tail and is gray between the two. The head is rounded and the bill gray with a black tip. It resembles the Canvasback, but is darker gray, has a smaller bill and lacks the wedge-shaped head of that bird. Female is similarly shaped, but patterned in gray browns with pale eye-ring.

VOICE Distinct mewing in breeding season.

HABITAT Lakes and ponds; estuaries in winter.

RANGE Breeds among prairies in Canada and US. Occasionally in east.

MOVEMENTS Migrates throughout temperate North America to winter in southern US and along Atlantic coast.

BREEDING Shallow margins of freshwater lakes; May-June.

NEST AND EGGS A large structure lined with down is usually placed among emergent vegetation; the 10 to 15 eggs are buffy.

INCUBATION Lasts 22 to 24 days and is performed by the female alone.

COMMENT There are good reasons to believe that the Redhead is expanding its range to the east, one of the few ducks that appears so successful.

VOICE Cooing during breeding season.

HABITAT Lakes and marshes; winters along sheltered shorelines and bays.

RANGE Breeds either side of the US-Canada border in the west, extending further northward than Redhead.

MOVEMENTS Migrates throughout US to winter in all but centralmost US.

BREEDING Marshes and shallow margins with plentiful vegetation; May-June.

NEST AND EGGS Mostly a down-lined cup of vegetation among densely vegetated shallows; the 7 to 10 eggs are olive gray.

INCUBATION Lasts 23 to 28 days and is performed entirely by the female.

COMMENT A serious decline in numbers is almost certainly due to habitat deterioration.

RING-NECKED DUCK

Aythya collaris   15½–18in/40–46cm

IDENTIFICATION Male is a boldly black and white duck, with purple sheen on head and green sheen on breast. The back is black and the flanks gray with a white vertical wedge forwards. It bears a strong resemblance to the scaup, but the dark back, white flank wedge and strongly peaked crown distinguish. Female is mottled in browns, has a white eye-ring and resembles female Redhead; peaked crown of present species separates at reasonable distance. In flight both sexes show gray wing-bar.

VOICE Whistle or purr.

HABITAT Lakes and ponds.

RANGE Breeds across southern Canada and adjacent northern US states.

MOVEMENTS Migrates throughout US to winter near all coasts and throughout the southern states.

BREEDING Bogs and marshes with plentiful vegetation along margins; May-June.

REDHEAD

Aythya americana   18–22in/46–56cm

BREEDING Freshwaters of varying size among forests; May-June.

NEST AND EGGS A depression lined with vegetation is placed on an island or shoreline; the 8 to 10 eggs are shades of olive.

INCUBATION Lasts 23 to 27 days and is performed by the female alone.

COMMENT In some areas these birds may breed colonially and are always highly gregarious in winter.

NEST AND EGGS A mass of vegetation is pulled together in the shallows and lined with down; the 6 to 14 eggs are olive brown.

INCUBATION The eggs take 25 to 29 days to hatch and are incubated by the female.

COMMENT Its preference for acidic waters on which to breed singles this species out from the other diving ducks.

LESSER SCAUP

Aythya affinis   15−18½in/38−47cm

GREATER SCAUP

Aythya marila   15−20in/39−51cm

IDENTIFICATION Marine duck outside the breeding season. Male has black head and breast marked bottle green, whitish flanks, gray back and black tail. Female is brown with bold white area at base of bill. In flight, both show white wing-bar extending across whole of wing. *See* Lesser Scaup.

VOICE Soft coos in breeding season.

HABITAT Tundra lakes; coastal in winter.

RANGE Breeds Alaska and neighboring Canada.

MOVEMENTS Migrates through whole of North America to winter along all coasts.

IDENTIFICATION Similar to Greater Scaup. Head and breast of male washed with purple, not green, sheen; flanks grayer. Female closely resembles female Greater Scaup. In both sexes the white wing-bar is more obvious on the inner wing, rather than extending across the whole wing as in the Greater Scaup. Additionally the black nail on the bill is tiny.

VOICE Cooing in summer.

HABITAT Marshes; winters lakes, marshes and estuaries. Far less marine than Greater Scaup.

RANGE Breeds from Alaska across western Canada into the prairie states.

MOVEMENTS Migrates throughout to winter on all coasts and inland along river systems and ponds of the south.

BREEDING Lakes, ponds and marshy margins of freshwater; May-June.

NEST AND EGGS A hollow on the ground is lined with down near water; the 8 to 12 eggs are buffy.

INCUBATION The eggs take some 23 to 26 days to hatch and are incubated by the female alone.

COMMENT Though confined to freshwater in the northern parts of its range, it will use saltwater in the south.

COMMON EIDER

Somateria mollissima   21½ – 24in/55 – 61cm

IDENTIFICATION Chunky, heavily built seaduck. Male has white head with black cap and dull green nape. The breast and back are whitish, the underparts black. Female is mottled and barred brown. Both sexes have wedge-shaped head with base of bill extending toward the eye.
VOICE Loud cooings when breeding.
HABITAT Coasts.
RANGE Breeds on coasts from British Columbia through Alaska and among the Canadian Arctic to Newfoundland, Nova Scotia and Maine.
MOVEMENTS Winters on Pacific coasts as far south as Vancouver and on Atlantic coasts to Carolina.
BREEDING Low lying and rocky shorelines, islands; May-June.
NEST AND EGGS A hollow in the ground, often quite open, is lined with down; the 4 to 6 eggs are buffy.
INCUBATION Lasts 28 or 29 days and is by the female alone.
COMMENT 'Eiderdown' is gathered from the nests of these colonial birds before the eggs are laid, the birds then replace the down and continue the breeding process.

KING EIDER

Somateria spectabilis   21 – 23in/53 – 59cm

IDENTIFICATION An Arctic breeding duck that is rare in temperate waters. Male is white on breast and black on flanks, back and underparts. The head is a unique pattern of white, blue and orange with an orange bill. Female is mottled brown, but with a much smaller bill than female Common Eider and a more rounded head.
VOICE Various croaks or cooing.
HABITAT Coasts.
RANGE Breeds Arctic coasts.
MOVEMENTS Winters on ice-free coasts as far south as British Columbia in the west and New England in the east.
BREEDING Freshwater pools and lakes among the tundra; June-July.
NEST AND EGGS A hollow among the tundra is lined with down, often some distance from water; the 4 to 7 eggs are buffy.
INCUBATION Lasts 22 or 23 days and is performed by the female alone.
COMMENT Though this is not a colonial nester, the young ducklings often form crèches consisting of several broods.

SPECTACLED EIDER

Somateria fischeri   20 – 22in/51 – 56cm

IDENTIFICATION Elusive Arctic species. Male is white above and black below with pale green head and black-bordered, white eye patch. Female is like female Common Eider, but with smaller bill and large gray eye patch.
VOICE Cooing when breeding.
HABITAT Coasts.
RANGE Breeds western coasts of Alaska.
MOVEMENTS Winters Bering Sea; moves northward through Straits in spring.

STELLER'S EIDER

Polysticta stelleri   16–17cm/41–43cm

IDENTIFICATION Male is warm cream on flanks with cascading scapulars in black and white. White head marked by black eye patch and pale green spots. Female mottled browns, but with less wedge-shaped head and bill than other eiders.
VOICE Cooing on breeding grounds.
HABITAT Coasts and coastal marshes.
RANGE Breeds west and north coasts of Alaska.
MOVEMENTS Winters Aleutians eastward to Central Alastea coast; scarce southward along Canadian coast.

HARLEQUIN DUCK

Histrionicus histrionicus   16–17½in/41–45cm

IDENTIFICATION Unique "torrent" duck that is at home among inland rapids and coastal breakers. Male is gray blue, broken by harlequin pattern of bold white slashes; flanks rust red. Female brownish, with three pale patches on sides of head. Could be confused with female White-winged Scoter and Surf Scoter, but has rounded head and tiny bill.

VOICE Squeak or whistle.
HABITAT Torrents in rivers in summer; rocky coasts in winter.
RANGE From Alaska southward through Rockies; and in north-eastern Canada.
MOVEMENTS To the nearest coast in the west, moves southward in the east to New England.

BREEDING Powerful rivers and torrents; May-June.
NEST AND EGGS The nest is a hollow lined with grass and down, hidden beneath a riverside bush or among rocks; the 5 to 7 eggs are creamy.
INCUBATION Lasts 27 to 29 days and is by the female alone.
COMMENT Though there have been reports of these duck nesting in tree holes, confirmation is required.

OLDSQUAW

Clangula hyemalis   16–23in/41–58cm

IDENTIFICATION Attractive sea duck with extended central tail feathers, particularly in the male. Unusual in having distinctive summer and winter plumages. Male, black and white in summer; white and black in winter. Female, blotched brown, with smudgy appearance. Rounded head, short bill and overall shape identify in all plumages.
VOICE Yodelling calls in summer.
HABITAT Tundra pools; winters along coasts.
RANGE Canadian Arctic in breeding season.
INCUBATION Lasts 24 to 29 days and is by the female alone.
COMMENT These birds arrive early on the breeding grounds and will gather in flocks offshore to wait for pools to thaw.

BLACK SCOTER

Melanitta nigra   18–20in/46–51cm

IDENTIFICATION An all-black seaduck. Male, uniformly black with yellow knob at base of bill. Female, dark brown with paler cheek patches. In mixed flocks at a distance at sea, the pale cheeks of the female are often the only detail visible.

VOICE Croaking or whistles.

HABITAT Tundra lakes; at sea in winter.

RANGE Breeds in western Alaska and Labrador.

MOVEMENTS Migrates along Pacific coast and across Canada to winter on east coast as far south as the Carolinas.

BREEDING Freshwater lakes and seashores among tundra and forest; July.

NEST AND EGGS A hollow lined with grasses and down on the ground near water; the 6 to 10 eggs are creamy buff.

INCUBATION Lasts for 30 or 31 days and is performed by the female.

COMMENT When diving for food offshore these birds regularly remain submerged for up to 50 seconds at a time.

SURF SCOTER

Melanitta perspicillata   17–21in/43–53cm

IDENTIFICATION Male similar to other scoter at any distance, but close approach reveals patches of white on crown and nape, and boldly colored orange, red and white bill. Female very closely resembles female White-winged Scoter with similar pale patches on sides of head. Both sexes lack white in wing of that bird.

VOICE Croaks in summer.

HABITAT Tundra in north-western Canada and in Alaska.

RANGE Breeds Alaska and north-western to north-eastern Canada.

MOVEMENTS Winters on all coasts.

BREEDING Pools and lakes among tundra and taiga; May-June.

NEST AND EGGS A hollow in the ground is lined mainly with down and hidden among low dense vegetation; the 5 to 7 eggs are buffy.

INCUBATION By the female.

COMMENT The isolation of the breeding grounds in Labrador has long been a matter of conjecture.

WHITE-WINGED SCOTER

Melanitta fusca   21–23in/53–59cm

IDENTIFICATION At any distance male closely resembles other scoter, but has white "eye" and bold white patch in wing. Female brown, with two pale patches on side of head and similar white in wing.

VOICE Croaks in summer.

HABITAT Lakes; coastal in winter, but some inland on lakes.

RANGE Breeds from Alaska in broad band through Manitoba and North Dakota.

MOVEMENTS Migrates to winter on both east and west coasts and occasionally in Great Lakes.

BREEDING Freshwater lakes and larger rivers, coastlines; June.

NEST AND EGGS A hollow lined with grass and down is well hidden among dwarf vegetation; the 8 to 14 eggs are pale pinkish.

INCUBATION The eggs take 27 or 28 days to hatch and are incubated by the female.

COMMENT Though this species shares a winter range with the Black Scoter, there is little overlap during the breeding season.

COMMON GOLDENEYE

Bucephala clangula   15½–19in/40–48cm

IDENTIFICATION Neatly proportioned diving duck with distinct, wedge-shaped head. Male has bottle-green head with white spot before the eye. Underparts are white, upperparts black, separated by an area that is white, striped black. Female has dark chocolate-colored head and is mottled gray above and below. Both sexes show white inner wing in flight. *See* Barrow's Goldeneye.

VOICE Whistles in summer.

HABITAT Marshes and lakes in boreal forest; lakes and coasts in winters.

RANGE Northern conifer forests across Canada.

MOVEMENTS Winters on all coasts and inland throughout the US.

BREEDING Lakes and pools among conifer forests; May-June.

NEST AND EGGS A tree hole serves as a nest, but it will readily take to nest boxes where provided; the 6 to 15 eggs are blue green.

INCUBATION Lasts 28 to 30 days and is performed by the female.

COMMENT Females may parasitize each other's nests, resulting in large clutches (up to 30).

BARROW'S GOLDENEYE

Bucephala islandica   16½–20in/42–51cm

IDENTIFICATION Highly localized relative of Goldeneye. Male similar to Common Goldeneye, but has purple, not green, sheen on head and white crescent, not spot, before eye. Black back and white flanks are separated by black area with white spots – not a white area with black lines. The overall effect is to make this a much darker bird than the Common Goldeneye. Female very similar to female Common Goldeneye. Both sexes have steep forehead.

VOICE Various notes when breeding.

HABITAT Lakes in forest; coastal in winter.

RANGE Breeds from Alaska through mountains to Wyoming and another population in northern Labrador.

MOVEMENTS Winters along west coast to California and in east as far as Long Island. More common in west.

BREEDING Ponds and lakes among conifers; May-June.

NEST AND EGGS Tree hollows, woodpecker holes or crevices among rocks; the 6 to 15 eggs are blue green.

INCUBATION Lasts 30 to 34 days, by female alone.

COMMENT The strangely disjointed distribution of this species is probably the result of the last Ice Age.

BUFFLEHEAD

Bucephala albeola   13–15in/33–38cm

IDENTIFICATION Dainty duck of wooded areas. Male is black above, white below, with black head showing broad white slash extending from eye to nape. Female is browner with white oval behind the eye. Large rounded head and small bill.

VOICE Whistles and quacks.

HABITAT Pools among conifers; winters on lakes, estuaries.

RANGE Breeds Alaska and across most of Canada, extending southward in Rockies.

MOVEMENTS Winters on all coasts and throughout ice-free US.

BREEDING Lakes and ponds among open mature woodland; May-June.

NEST AND EGGS A woodpecker or similar hole in a tree, even a nest box, lined with down; the 7 to 12 eggs are creamy buff.

INCUBATION Lasts 29 to 31 days and is by the female alone.

COMMENT Up to sixteen eggs have been found in a single nest, but these are generally regarded as having been laid by two females, doubtless because of the scarcity of suitable nest holes.

HOODED MERGANSER

Lophodytes cucullatus 15½–19in/40–48cm

IDENTIFICATION Smallest of the sawbills with large, erectile crest. Male has black head with broad, white wedge extending from the eye to the nape in a crest that can be raised or lowered. The breast is white with two narrow bands. Female is like diminutive female Red-breasted Merganser, but crest forms a fan rather than two points. Rather browner above than other female sawbills.

VOICE Croaking calls in summer.

HABITAT Lakes among woods; winters mostly on fresh water near coast.

RANGE Breeds from coast to coast in a broad area north and south of the US-Canada border excluding Great Plains. Locally into Mississippi Valley.

MOVEMENTS Winters near all three coastlines.

BREEDING Freshwater lakes and rivers among wooded country; May-June.

NEST AND EGGS A tree hole lined with down, often an old woodpecker hole; the 8 to 12 eggs are white.

INCUBATION Lasts for 29 to 37 days and is performed by female alone.

COMMENT Where nesting holes are in short supply two ducks will sometimes nest in the same hole, often mixing up their clutches to produce over twelve eggs.

COMMON MERGANSER

Mergus merganser 22½–27in/57–69cm

IDENTIFICATION Larger and stouter than Red-breasted Merganser. Male is black above, white below with bottle-green head that extends into rounded hind crest. Female similar to female Red-breasted Merganser, but with rounded, down-pointing crest and contrast between head and neck.

VOICE Croaks and cackles in summer.

HABITAT Freshwater pools and rivers; mostly freshwater in winter.

RANGE Breeds through conifer belt of Canada extending southward through much of west.

MOVEMENTS Migrates southward to winter throughout US.

BREEDING Lakes and rivers among well-forested areas; May-June.

NEST AND EGGS A tree hole or cavity, but also a hole among rocks or even a well sheltered spot among dense vegetation, is lined with down; the 8 to 11 eggs are creamy.

INCUBATION Lasts for 28 to 32 days and is by the female alone.

COMMENT The ability to nest in a wide variety of locations is a feature of this species.

RED-BREASTED MERGANSER

Mergus serrator   20–22in/51–56cm

IDENTIFICATION A slim, sawbill duck with ragged crest. Male has bottle-green head, white neck, a speckled brown breast, black and white upperparts and gray flanks. The bill is long, thin and red. Female has rufous head, gray body and dusky neck. In all plumages the spiked crest points horizontally to the rear. Male separated from Common Merganser at any distance by speckled, not white, breast.

VOICE Various purring and croaking calls while breeding.
HABITAT Rivers; in winter on creeks and sea.
RANGE Breeds among tundra from Alaska through northern Canada.
MOVEMENTS Migrates through much of US to winter on all three coastlines.
BREEDING Freshwater pools, lakes and rivers, also coastal bays; May-June.
NEST AND EGGS The nest is a hollow on the ground well-hidden among bushes or under rocks or tree roots. It is lined with grasses and down; the 7 to 12 eggs are buffy.
INCUBATION Lasts for 28 to 35 days and is performed by the female.
COMMENT These birds often hunt in packs swimming towards the shore in lines to drive fish before them.

RUDDY DUCK

Oxyura jamaicensis   14–17in/36–43cm

IDENTIFICATION Small, dumpy duck with curious, weight-forward appearance. Tail often held vertical or hidden in water surface. In summer, male is rich chestnut on body, with white face, black cap and bright blue bill. In winter, the colors are lost and it is clothed in shades of brown. Female mottled brown with distinctive horizontal stripe across "face".
VOICE Various croaking calls in summer.
HABITAT Marshes and ponds.
RANGE Breeds through prairies north and south of US-Canada border, as well as valleys of Rockies. Small population on east coast.
MOVEMENTS Migrates throughout US to winter on ice-free waters near all coasts.
BREEDING Shallow freshwater lakes and marshes; May-June.
NEST AND EGGS A well-hidden construction of aquatic vegetation placed in the shallow margins over water; the 5 to 10 eggs are white.
INCUBATION Lasts from 25 to 27 days and is performed by female only.
COMMENT Successfully introduced to Europe where it appears to be spreading.

BIRDS OF PREY

A VAST number of birds are predators, dependent on other animate life for their existence, yet this group of birds is well defined and self contained. It includes the vultures, eagles, buteos, accipiters, and falcons, all of which take fairly large prey. Largest of all is the California Condor, a bird that found its final refuge among the hills in crowded southern California – not the best place for an endangered species to make its last stand. After generations of hovering on the verge of extinction (concern over its future was being expressed over a hundred years ago), the final condors were taken into captivity in 1987. Though there was much disagreement between conservationists, including a courtroom drama, the future of this huge and magnificent bird now rests in captive breeding. The first chick was hand-reared in 1988, but it is far too early to say whether or not the program will succeed.

If the story of the California Condor gives little room for hope, that of the Bald Eagle is less gloomy. Once widespread throughout North America, this large and powerful fish-eating eagle was adopted as the national symbol of the embryonic United States. Within two centuries the Bald Eagle had almost been wiped out except for a few traditional strongholds. At one of these, in the Alaskan panhandle, there is one of the largest gatherings of eagles in the world every fall. Since the ban on DDT, the Bald Eagle's diet has been made safer and its numbers have recovered somewhat. But this does not mean that the eagle is secure.

Though there are some 280 species of birds of prey in the world, North America can boast only about 30 regular breeding species. These include the vultures, which are confined to the New World and quite unrelated to the Old World vultures that range from Europe to Africa and Asia. While both Turkey and Black Vultures are now scavengers at garbage dumps and around human settlements, this must be a relatively recent form of behavior. Originally, no doubt, they were dependent on wild carrion.

The light-winged kites are well represented, but most are on the edge of their range and are found in the southern states. One species, the Snail Kite, is found only in a few localities in southern Florida and was formerly known as the Everglade Kite. Sadly, North America boasts only one harrier, the Northern Harrier, formerly known as the Marsh Hawk. These flap-and-glide merchants are widespread breeders, though they are not always as popular as they deserve. Similarly, the accipiters are far from popular in many areas, especially where pheasant-rearing is a part of the local economy. Nevertheless, the three species can hardly have a dramatic effect on the population of game in any area.

With the buteos, on the other hand, North America is well endowed both in species and numbers. The gatherings of birds and their watchers at Hawk Mountain, Pennsylvania, each fall is spectacular, with huge flocks of Broad-winged Hawks, accompanied by other species, being the main diet. Buteos are a confusing group of birds that are not only subtly differentiated, but also highly variable in plumage characteristics within the species.

Some of the more spectacular birds of prey are the falcons, five species of which regularly breed in North America. They vary from the diminutive, but widespread American Kestrel, to the huge and powerful Gyrfalcon of the tundra zone. As dramatic as any is the magnificent Peregrine, a deadly aerial killer that specializes in preying on city pigeons, wherever they are found. Thus, Peregrines are regularly seen on office blocks in city centers in winter, and frequently stay on to breed in some regions. Sadly, the pesticide

fiasco of the 1960s exterminated this bird from many areas and it will be a long, slow process before they return to many of their former haunts.

Being at the top of the food chain and being seen as competitors by man may have caused an initial decline in American populations of birds of prey, but the decline continues in most areas as wild habitats progressively disappear under brick and concrete. Sadly, there seems no real hope of regenerating the populations of these birds, even in the long term.

BLACK VULTURE

Coragyps atratus   23 − 23½in/58 − 59cm

IDENTIFICATION All-black bird of prey. The Black Vulture is entirely black, though a silvery sheen shows on the folded wings. The face is bare and black, the bill thin and pointed – not chunky like juvenile Turkey Vulture. In flight the base of the primaries is a bold white. These are gregarious birds that soar on flat wings.

VOICE Silent.

HABITAT Open country, roadsides and, in the south, shorelines and villages.

RANGE Resident in south-eastern states.

MOVEMENTS May leave northern part of Mid-West in winter.

BREEDING Mostly open landscapes; April-May.

NEST AND EGGS A bare hollow on the ground sheltered by vegetation, log or rock serves as a nest; the 2 eggs are white, blotched brown.

INCUBATION Lasts 32 to 41 days and is shared between the pair.

COMMENT Common at refuse dumps and along shorelines where fish waste can be found.

TURKEY VULTURE

Cathartes aura   26 − 32in/66 − 81cm

IDENTIFICATION Large, dark bird of prey. Plumage basically black with brownish wings. In the air, the flight feathers are paler than the wing linings and the body. Head is bare, wrinkled and red; gray in immatures. Soars and glides on wings held in shallow "V". One of the largest birds of prey in America.

VOICE Silent.

HABITAT Open country, roadsides.

RANGE Breeds virtually throughout US and across Canadian border in prairies.

MOVEMENTS Leaves most of northern and central states in winter.

BREEDING Wide range of landscapes; April.

NEST AND EGGS There is no nest, the eggs being laid on bare ground or cliffs, in caves or among rocky ground; the 2 eggs are pale yellow, blotched brown.

INCUBATION Lasts 38 to 41 days and is shared by both members of the pair.

COMMENT Most commonly associated with refuse tips and carrion, though they also feed on small animals.

OSPREY

Pandion haliaetus   21 − 24½in/53 − 62cm

IDENTIFICATION Lightly-built, gray and white bird of prey that is a pure "fisherman". Gray-brown above with small white head marked by black eyestripe. Underparts white. In flight, shows black barring across white underwing and bold, black carpal patches. The wings are long and narrow and held arched, like a gull. Hovers and plunges to catch prey.

VOICE High-pitched whistles.

HABITAT Shorelines, estuaries, lakes, rivers.

RANGE Breeds over much of North America, though absent from central US.

MOVEMENTS Winters southern California, Florida and southward.

BREEDING Near fresh or saltwater; April-June.

NEST AND EGGS A huge mound of twigs is placed usually atop a tree and often on a coastal structure, but sometimes on a cliff; the 2 to 4 eggs are creamy, heavily spotted brown.

INCUBATION Lasts 35 to 38 days and is performed almost entirely by the female.

COMMENT Though declining is some areas, there are good grounds for optimism about this species' future in others.

NEST AND EGGS The nest of sticks and twigs is placed at some height in a large tree; the 2 to 4 eggs are cream colored, speckled brown.

INCUBATION Lasts 28 days and is performed mostly by the female.

COMMENT These are often gregarious birds while hunting. Sadly there has been a decline during the twentieth century.

BLACK-SHOULDERED KITE

Elanus caeruleus   15—17in/38—43cm

AMERICAN SWALLOW-TAILED KITE

Elanoides forficatus   22—24in/56—61cm

IDENTIFICATION A well-marked bird of prey with easy, masterful flight. Upperparts, wings and tail black, head and underparts white. Flattened head and bold red eye. In the air, the tail is deeply forked and the long, pointed wings are black with white linings. Mostly aerial, soaring effortlessly for hours at a time.

VOICE Whistles and high-pitched calls.

HABITAT Marshes, thickets, damp woodland.

RANGE Gulf Coast, Florida and South Carolina.

MOVEMENTS Migrates to South America.

BREEDING Marshes and swamps with adjacent woodland; March-April.

IDENTIFICATION Medium-sized bird of prey. Adult is gray above with black "shoulder" patches. Head, underparts and square-cut tail are white. The head is rather large and flat-topped, marked by large eye. In flight the wings are pointed and the bird hovers when hunting.

VOICE High pitched yelps.
HABITAT Parkland, fields, grasslands with trees.
RANGE Once rare, now re-established in California, also in southern Texas.
MOVEMENTS Resident.
BREEDING Parkland and other open areas with trees; March.
NEST AND EGGS A well-constructed nest of twigs lined with softer vegetation is placed in a tree or large bush; the 3 to 5 eggs are white, spotted brown.
INCUBATION Lasts some 30 days and is by the female alone.
COMMENT A highly adaptable species, benefiting from agricultural expansion in past 30 years.

VOICE High-pitched whistles.
HABITAT Woodland, usually near water.
RANGE South-eastern states into southern Great Plains and west to Arizona.
MOVEMENTS Migrates south to South America.
BREEDING Scrub and park-like woodland near water; April.
NEST AND EGGS A large nest of sticks and twigs is placed at variable heights in a tree; the 1 to 3 eggs are white.
INCUBATION The eggs take some 30 days to hatch and are incubated by both sexes.
COMMENT These are gregarious birds that frequently hunt together and also form loose colonies during the breeding season.

SNAIL KITE

Rostrhamus sociabilis   16−18in/41−46cm

IDENTIFICATION An all black-brown bird of prey marked by white tail base, small head and deeply curved, thin bill.
VOICE Generally silent.
HABITAT Marshes.
RANGE Rare breeder southern Florida.
MOVEMENTS Resident.

BALD EAGLE

Haliaeetus leucocephalus   30−43in/76−109cm

MISSISSIPPI KITE

Ictinia mississippiensis   12−14in/30−35cm

IDENTIFICATION Gray above with paler gray head and underparts and a black tail; large, flattened head and bold eyes. In the air appears dusky, with buoyant easy flight. Usually gregarious, catching and consuming insects as it flies.

IDENTIFICATION Large brown eagle with white head and neck and white tail. Immatures are all brown, but feathers of tail usually show white bases at centers. Large yellow bill.
VOICE Loud yelping.
HABITAT Coasts, rivers, lakes.
RANGE Recently confined to Alaska, northern Canada, some remote areas of US, and Florida. Now increasing.
MOVEMENTS Winters along Pacific coast and uncommonly through much of US.

BREEDING Rivers, lakes and coasts with woodland; April-June.

NEST AND EGGS A large structure of sticks is placed near the top of a large tree; the 1 to 3 eggs are white.

INCUBATION Lasts about 35 days and is shared by both members of the pair.

COMMENT Only along the coasts of Alaska and British Columbia can large congregations of this splendid bird now be seen.

NORTHERN HARRIER

Circus cyaneus   17–20in/43–51cm

IDENTIFICATION A long-winged, long-tailed bird of prey that flaps and glides low over the ground with slightly up-raised wings. Male is gray above and white below, with bold white rump band. Female is mottled brown and buff, but has same white rump.

VOICE Sharp *kee-kee-kee* when breeding.

HABITAT Marshes, rough grassland.

RANGE Breeds over much of Alaska, Canada and the northern US.

MOVEMENTS Winters virtually throughout US, but only locally in southern Canada.

BREEDING Bogs and marshes, but also rough, dry ground; April-May.

NEST AND EGGS The nest is a platform of vegetation well hidden on the ground among reeds or grasses; the 4 or 5 eggs are white, or washed blue with spots of brown.

INCUBATION Lasts 29 to 39 days and is performed by the female alone.

COMMENT Formerly called the "Marsh Hawk" for it is quite distinct from the true "hawks". All members of the genus are called "harriers" in Europe.

SHARP-SHINNED HAWK

Accipiter striatus   10–14in/25–35cm

IDENTIFICATION Smallest of the accipiters. Gray above and barred rusty below. Rounded wings and long-tailed which is square-eendded (Cooper's is rounded) and shows four or five clear dark bands. Agile flier in pursuit of small birds.

VOICE High-pitched *ka-ka-ka*.

HABITAT Conifer and deciduous forests; virtually any woodland or wooded country in winter.

RANGE From Alaska through boreal Canada to most of the US except the extreme south.

MOVEMENTS Leaves northern part of range and most of Canada; winters through most of the US.

BREEDING Extensive woodlands, usually mixed but sometimes pure conifer; May-June.

NEST AND EGGS A large, well-built shallow cup of twigs placed high in a conifer and frequently well hidden; the 3 to 6 eggs are white, blotched brown.

INCUBATION Lasts 34 or 35 days and is shared between members of the pair.

COMMENT Now the most widespread and common of the accipiters in North America.

COOPER'S HAWK

Accipiter cooperii   14—20in/35—51cm

IDENTIFICATION Medium-sized accipiter with rounded wings and long tail. Gray above, barred rusty below with rounded tail showing four or five clear bands. Fast and agile flier that soars with series of fast wing beats interrupting still-winged gliding.

VOICE High-pitched, repetitive *kee-kee-kee*.
HABITAT Deciduous woods, sometimes also conifers.
RANGE Virtually throughout US and into adjacent Canada, but serious decline and disappearance from many areas of US.
MOVEMENTS Leaves central and northern parts of range in winter.
BREEDING Woods and forests, both deciduous and coniferous; April-May.
NEST AND EGGS A nest of twigs is placed at considerable height in a large tree; the 3 to 5 eggs are off white, lightly spotted brown.
INCUBATION Lasts 34 to 36 days and is performed primarily by the female.
COMMENT Less frequently found in open countryside than the Sharp-shinned Hawk and, therefore, occupies more extensive woodlands.

NORTHERN GOSHAWK

Accipiter gentilis   19—23in/48—58cm

IDENTIFICATION Large, dashing accipiter mainly confined to northern forests. The smaller male is gray above and streaked on white below. A bold, white eyebrow creates a fierce expression. Female is larger and browner with heavily barred underparts. These are magnificent and powerful birds that are agile fliers among trees. They soar easily and show a white powder-puff under the tail in diving display.
VOICE High-pitched *kee-kee-kee*.
HABITAT Conifer forests, but also deciduous forests to the south.
RANGE Boreal forests of Canada and conifers in Rockies and north-western US. Extending southwards to deciduous forests recently.
MOVEMENTS Moves southwards as winter visitor to central US.

BREEDING Extensive forests, preferably mixed deciduous and coniferous; April-May.
NEST AND EGGS A large nest of twigs is placed high against the trunk of a tall tree; the 2 to 4 eggs are white, washed with blue.
INCUBATION Lasts 36 to 38 days and is performed mainly by the female.
COMMENT Goshawks often use the same nest for several successive years decorating it afresh with sprigs of green vegetation.

COMMON BLACK-HAWK

Buteogallus anthracinus   20–22in/51–56cm

IDENTIFICATION Similar to more widespread Zone-tailed Hawk but with single, broad white bar, not multiple-gray, tail band. Broad wings and short tail create characteristic shape in flight.
VOICE Harsh *ka-ar*.
HABITAT Frequents watercourses in dry regions.
RANGE Southern Arizona and adjacent New Mexico.
MOVEMENTS Summer visitor.

HARRIS'S HAWK

Parabuteo unicinctus   18–22in/46–56cm

IDENTIFICATION Adult is dark gray on body with rust-red "shoulders", "thighs" and, in flight, wing linings. The tail has a white base, a broad, black band, is narrowly tipped white and is longer than most other buteos.
VOICE A scream.
HABITAT Scrub, mesquite, brushland, semi-desert.
RANGE Penetrates US in south-west.
MOVEMENTS Resident.
BREEDING Dry open countryside, with trees often along dry river courses; March-April.
NEST AND EGGS A nest of twigs is placed in a tree or yucca; the 2 to 5 eggs are white.

INCUBATION The eggs take 28 days to hatch and are incubated by both sexes.
COMMENT This is often a confiding bird that will allow a close approach when perched.

GRAY HAWK

Buteo niditus   16–17in/41–43cm

IDENTIFICATION An accipter-like buteo. Gray above, heavily barred gray below, with banded tail.
VOICE Whistles.
HABITAT Streamside woods.
RANGE Rare breeder southern Arizona.
MOVEMENTS Rare wanderer to Mexican border states.

RED-SHOULDERED HAWK

Buteo lineatus   15½–24in/40–61cm

IDENTIFICATION Well-marked buteo with rusty "shoulders". Upperparts brown, underparts closely barred rufous. In the air the upperwing is clearly banded black and white across the flight feathers, and the tail is equally clearly barred with broad black and narrow white bands. Below, the rusty body and wing linings contrast with pale flight feathers and the tail is barred black and white as above. Longer and more slender wings than Red-tailed Hawk.

VOICE Screams.

HABITAT Wet woodland.

RANGE Breeds over most of eastern US and into neighboring Canada. Also in California.

MOVEMENTS North-eastern part of range abandoned in winter.

BREEDING Woodland among open farming country; April-May.

NEST AND EGGS A nest of twigs placed high in either a deciduous or coniferous tree; the 2 to 4 eggs are white, spotted brown.

INCUBATION Lasts 25 to 28 days and is shared between the pair.

COMMENT Often associated with moist woodlands. Its California range is a thousand miles from the nearest eastern birds.

BROAD-WINGED HAWK

Buteo platypterus   13–15in/33–38cm

IDENTIFICATION A woodland buteo with short, rounded wings. Adult is brown above with clearly barred, rust-red underparts like an accipiter. In flight the rufous body contrasts with the white wings and neatly banded black and white tail. Migrates in huge flocks.

VOICE High-pitched whistle.

HABITAT Deciduous forests.

RANGE Breeds throughout eastern US northward into Canada as far as the Gulf of St Lawrence.

MOVEMENTS Winters in South America; some in south Florida.

BREEDING Decidedly a forest-dwelling bird; April-May.

NEST AND EGGS A small, untidy cup of twigs is placed in a tree; the 2 to 4 eggs are whitish, spotted brown.

INCUBATION The eggs take 23 to 25 days to hatch and are incubated by both members of the pair.

COMMENT This species will often use the old nest of a crow or another bird rather than construct its own, poorly-built, nest.

SHORT-TAILED HAWK

Buteo brachyurus   15–16in/38–41cm

IDENTIFICATION Compact and small hawk, dark above with white or black underparts. Tail banded black and white in both color phases.

VOICE Generally not vocal.

HABITAT Open-wooded country.

RANGE Florida.

MOVEMENTS Found only in southern Florida in winter.

SWAINSON'S HAWK

Buteo swainsoni   17½–22in/45–56cm

IDENTIFICATION A large buteo that makes the longest of migrations. Brown above and white below, marked by a broad, brown breast band. The tail is white, finely barred, and with a broad, subterminal, black band. A dark phase is brown below with no obvious breast band, but retains the pale tail pattern. Migrates in great swirling flocks.

VOICE Whistles.

HABITAT Plains, prairies, open grasslands.

RANGE From Alaska southward through most of western and central US.

MOVEMENTS Migrates south as far as Argentina, but some birds move across the US to winter in Florida.

BREEDING Highly variable open country from dry valleys to tundra; April-June.

NEST AND EGGS A large nest of twigs is placed in a tree or bush; the 2 or 3 eggs are white, washed blue and spotted brown.

INCUBATION Lasts 28 days and is shared between the pair.

COMMENT The extraordinary range of this species extends from arid northern Mexico to the tundra near the Mackenzie River delta.

WHITE-TAILED HAWK

Buteo albicaudatus   22–24in/56–61cm

IDENTIFICATION Long-winged buteo, with dark gray upperparts marked by chestnut wing patches, and white underparts. Tail white with black sub-terminal band.

VOICE Shrill *ke-ke-ke* repeated.

HABITAT Open country.

RANGE Southern Texas.

MOVEMENTS Resident.

ZONE-TAILED HAWK

Buteo albonotatus   18 1/2–22 1/2in/47–55cm

IDENTIFICATION A very dark, virtually black buteo marked by black and white-barred flight feathers, from below, and by a black and white-barred tail. There are two or three clear-cut, black bands on the tail. The similar, but rarer,

Common Black-Hawk, has only one broad, black band on a shorter tail.

VOICE Loud whistles.

HABITAT Scrub and semi-desert.

RANGE Arizona, New Mexico and western Texas.

MOVEMENTS May move across border into Mexico.

BREEDING Dry country with woodland, but also open semi-deserts; April-May.

NEST AND EGGS A bulky platform of twigs placed in a tree or on a cliff face; the 1 to 3 eggs are white, variably speckled brown.

INCUBATION The eggs take 35 days to hatch and are incubated by both sexes.

COMMENT A decidedly scarce and localized bird that is often found along dry and all-but-dry rivers.

RED-TAILED HAWK

Buteo jamaicensis   19–25in/48–64cm

IDENTIFICATION The typical phase is brown above and paler below, with a narrow dark band across the belly and a plain rufous tail. A dark phase has brown body and wing linings contrasting with pale primaries. There is much plumage variation including birds with white tails. Young birds have

VOICE Raucous cries.
HABITAT Open brush, prairies.
RANGE Breeds in central-western US and adjacent Canada.
MOVEMENTS Northernmost birds move southward to winter in western US and beyond. Casual as far east as Wisconsin and Florida.
BREEDING Open plains, prairies and other bare areas; April-May.
NEST AND EGGS A nest of sticks is placed on a ledge, river bank or tree; the 3 to 5 eggs are white, spotted brown.
INCUBATION Lasts 28 days and is shared by both sexes.
COMMENT This hawk will use a wide variety of nest sites depending totally on what is available in the open landscapes it prefers.

finely-barred, brown tails. "Harlan's Hawk" is regarded as a phase of this species.
VOICE High-pitched *kee-argh*.
HABITAT Virtually any open area with adjacent woods – very widespread.
RANGE Virtually everywhere in North America except open tundra.
MOVEMENTS Most Canadian birds move south in winter.
BREEDING Open country with woods as well as pure forest landscapes; March-April.
NEST AND EGGS A heavy mass of twigs and sticks placed high in a deciduous or coniferous tree; the 2 to 4 eggs are white, speckled brown.
INCUBATION Lasts 28 to 32 days and is shared by both sexes.
COMMENT Where trees are unavailable this species will breed on cliff sites.

FERRUGINOUS HAWK

Buteo regalis   22−25in/56−64cm

IDENTIFICATION This is the largest of the buteos and is typically a western bird of arid brush country. Mottled in buffs and browns, but with rufous at bend of wing, on uppertail band and on legs. Rare, dark phase birds are brown with white flight feathers and all-white tail. Pale phase birds are white below, with only rufous patches on carpals, legs and tail.

ROUGH-LEGGED HAWK

Buteo lagopus   19−24in/48−61cm

IDENTIFICATION A typical buteo, with broad wings and medium-length, white tail, with broad terminal band. Black belly and dark carpal patches are the best field marks. There is much plumage variation and dark birds may show only the characteristic tail. Hovers more than most buteos and soars on flat wings.
VOICE Whistling.
HABITAT Tundra and thin forests; winters on marshes.
RANGE Tundra Canada.

NEST AND EGGS A huge structure of sticks on a cliff, sometimes in a tree; the 2 eggs are white, blotched reddish brown.

INCUBATION Lasts 43 to 45 days and is usually performed by the female alone.

COMMENT Re-use of a nest year after year creates a huge pile of sticks at a favored nest site.

MOVEMENTS Migrates to winter over most of the US except the extreme south. Migrant through temperate Canada.

BREEDING Tundra ridges and rocky outcrops, but also trees; May-June.

NEST AND EGGS A cup of twigs is placed on a cliff or outcrop or in a tree; the 2 to 7 eggs are white washed green and spotted brown.

INCUBATION Lasts 28 to 31 days and is performed by the female, sometimes with the assistance of her mate.

COMMENT Though the normal clutch of this species is two to four eggs, larger clutches are laid when lemmings are plentiful.

GOLDEN EAGLE

Aquila chrysaetos   30−35½in/76−90cm

IDENTIFICATION Huge, magnificent eagle confusable only with Bald Eagle in juvenile plumage. Adult is brown above and below, with wash of "gold" on crown and nape. Juvenile and immatures have white base to tail and white bar along underwing. Soars on huge flat wings, glides over hillsides. Eagles have large prominent heads compared with buteos.

VOICE Quiet mewing – mostly silent.

HABITAT Tundra, mountains.

RANGE Northern Canada and western US.

MOVEMENTS Northern birds move southward over much of US.

BREEDING Open mountainsides, hillsides, grasslands; April-May.

CRESTED CARACARA

Polyborus plancus   22−24in/56−61cm

IDENTIFICATION A long-legged bird of prey that spends much time on the ground. Large head accentuated by black cap and large, red-based bill. Upperparts black, white sides of face becoming barred on breast.

VOICE Various cackling calls.

HABITAT Open country.

RANGE Southern and eastern Texas, central Florida.

MOVEMENTS Resident, probably declining.

AMERICAN KESTREL

Falco sparverius   9−11in/23−28cm

IDENTIFICATION A dainty, well-marked falcon, common over much of North America. Male has rusty, black-barred back with dark-blue inner wings. The head is boldly marked with patches of rust, white and black. The rusty tail is long and banded black at tip. Female is browner, with more barring and has only a rudimentary head pattern. Frequently hovers.

VOICE High-pitched *kee-kee-kee*.

HABITAT Open country.

RANGE Breeds everywhere except tundra.

MOVEMENTS Canadian and mountain birds move southward.

BREEDING A wide variety of open landscapes with suitable nest sites; April-June.

NEST AND EGGS A bare cavity from a tree hole to a cavity in a building serves as a nest: the 3 to 7 eggs are white, heavily blotched reddish brown.

INCUBATION Lasts 27 to 29 days and is performed almost entirely by the female.

COMMENT Specializes in large insects during the summer, but switches to small mammals in winter.

MERLIN

Falco columbarius   10½−12½in/27−32cm

IDENTIFICATION Small, stocky falcon that takes mainly small birds. Male is slate-gray above with striped breast and only a hint of a moustachial streak. Female is brown and similarly marked. Flies low over ground, perches openly at dawn and dusk waiting to hunt.

VOICE *Ki-ki-ki* when breeding.

HABITAT Open tundra, moors, mountains; plus coasts in winter.

RANGE Breeds from Alaska across Canada and southward into the Rockies in the US.

MOVEMENTS Migrates southward to western, eastern and southern states.

BREEDING Rolling, untended hillsides usually with trees; May-June.

NEST AND EGGS Usually in an old nest of another species, but sometimes on the ground; the 4 or 5 eggs are pale cream, spotted with brown.

INCUBATION Lasts 28 to 32 days and is performed by both members of the pair.

COMMENT Occupies a wide range of countryside, though bare, open areas are necessary for hunting.

PEREGRINE FALCON

Falco peregrinus   15−18½in/38−48cm

IDENTIFICATION Medium-sized, powerful falcon. Slate-gray above, white below, closely barred black. The black moustache against a white "face" is a prominent field mark. The wings are long and angular, the tail relatively short. Juvenile is brown and streaked, rather than barred, below.
VOICE Loud *kek-kek-kek*.
HABITAT Cliffs on coasts, rivers, mountains.

RANGE Virtually extirpated in east by pesticide poisoning. Confined to western localities and to far north – some reintroductions in east.
MOVEMENTS Northern birds migrate through Canada and northern states. Uncommon in winter in US.
BREEDING Cliffs, both inland and coastal; April-June.
NEST AND EGGS A depression on a cliff ledge serves as a nest; the 3 to 5 eggs are pale cream, heavily spotted brown.
INCUBATION Lasts 29 to 32 days and is shared between the sexes.
COMMENT A catastrophic decline due to pesticide poisoning in the 1960s has turned this into a decidedly scarce bird.

GYRFALCON

Falco rusticolus   20−25in/51−64cm

IDENTIFICATION A bird of the high Arctic that only rarely wanders to US. Three distinct color phases occur, as well as intermediate plumages. Long, pointed wings, shortish tail and streamline shape pick it out as a falcon. Most spectacular is white phase which is white, lightly speckled black. A gray phase is very pale, but more heavily speckled black, especially above. A dark phase is slate-gray above and heavily speckled below. The latter resembles a Peregrine, but lacks a prominent moustache.
VOICE Slow *ka-ka-ka*.
HABITAT Tundra, cliffs; in winter mainly coastal.
RANGE Alaskan and Canadian tundra including the archipelago.
MOVEMENTS Irregular movements south to just beyond US border.
BREEDING Remote cliffs among the tundra; May-July.
NEST AND EGGS A ledge is decorated with a few twigs; the 3 or 4 eggs are pale cream with pale blotches of brown.
INCUBATION The eggs take about 28 to 29 to hatch and are incubated almost entirely by the female.
COMMENT When one of these splendid falcons moves south of its normal range, listers have a field day.

PRAIRIE FALCON

Falco mexicanus   17–20in/43–51cm

IDENTIFICATION Brown falcon of the west, that is common where found. Upperparts, brown, edged buffy to produce a "scaled" appearance. Underparts, white, streaked brown. Head shows narrow, moustachial streak that is repeated toward rear of head. Pale crown. In flight, shows narrow black axillaries – armpits.

VOICE Shrill *kree-kree-kree*.

HABITAT Mountains, prairies.

RANGE The west from British Columbia, east to Prairies and into Mexico.

MOVEMENTS Moves southward from northern half of North American range.

BREEDING Dry cliffs and canyons in grassland country; April-June.

NEST AND EGGS A bare ledge or old nest of another species serves to hold the eggs; these are white, spotted reddish brown and number from 3 to 6.

INCUBATION Lasts for 29 to 31 days and is performed by the female alone.

COMMENT This falcon specializes in feeding on ground-dwelling mammals such as ground squirrels.

M.J.PLEDGER

PARTRIDGES, PHEASANTS, GROUSE, TURKEYS & QUAILS

I F any group of birds has close association with man, it must surely be these. They are often referred to collectively as "gamebirds" because they have long been hunted for sport. But the shotgun arrived with the early settlers and free food was doubtless irresistible, leading to a huge onslaught on these birds that continues to the present day, particularly on those birds that are good to eat.

Yet, despite all the gamebirds that were found in North America, man could not resist the temptation to introduce a few more. Ring-necked Pheasant, Gray and Red-legged Partridges, Chukar, Black Francolin, and even Japanese Quail have all been introduced with varying degrees of success. To date, only the Ring-necked Pheasant, Gray Partridge, and Chukar have managed to establish themselves permanently. And even these populations are augmented by regular releases in most years.

Largest of the North American native gamebirds is the Wild Turkey, which can still be found patchily distributed throughout much of the U.S. Widely domesticated and generating a huge industry, these birds prove perfect for Thanksgiving and Christmas feasts. The well-known strutting display of the male with spread tail and full "war-painted" wattles is impressive, but most other male gamebirds have similar displays.

The so-called Prairie-Chicken gathers at special "leks," where males joust like medieval knights to impress their would-be mates. As in the days of chivalry, the dominant male gets the hen, but in this case, the male may get all the hens in the district.

Other grouse also display to attract a mate, making much of their boldly colored tails and breasts. Like the Greater Prairie-Chicken, the male Blue Grouse has inflatable sacs on either side of its neck that are puffed out to show a colorful area of bare skin surrounded by a bold patch of feathers that is at other times invisible. Though the visual effect is quite stunning, and doubtless impresses the female, the sacs also act as sounding boxes to amplify the bird's hooting calls.

The boreal forests of the north and west hold a wide variety of specialized birds. A Blue Grouse displays in the foreground, while a Ruffed Grouse beats its wings at a female. Above, a Sharp-shinned Hawk watches as a Merlin chases off a Golden Eagle.

In the case of the Ruffed Grouse of the northern forests, the bird produces its calls by rapidly beating its wings while standing on a hollow log – an interesting form of instrumentalism similar to the drumming of a woodpecker on a dead tree branch. Ptarmigan, in contrast, are purely vocal producing a series of cackling calls which assert their dominance over a particular territory. Living in the far north or among high mountains, these birds are camouflaged in shades of brown and gray in summer, but become white in winter when snow covers the ground.

With the exception of the Northern Bobwhite, quails are of decidedly western distribution. Most have bold face patterns topped by a distinctive crest and are superficially similar. Some, like Gambel's Quail and California Quail, are clearly closely related and should be separated with great care. Generally, however, each species has either its own range, own habitat preference, or both. Certainly, they are seldom found together.

Not surprisingly, several grouse have suffered a serious decline in numbers and some populations have actually been exterminated completely. Sadly, some of the distinct forms of the Greater Prairie-Chicken have disappeared mainly as a result of hunting and habitat loss. Tautological as it may seem, a lost species is lost forever and there seems no need for North America to add any of its indigenous birds to the list of those that have disappeared for ever.

PLAIN CHACHALACA

Ortalis vetula   21−22in/53−56cm

IDENTIFICATION An all-brown and buff, tree-dwelling "game bird" with long, broad, white-tipped tail. Small head, long neck, with bare, red skin on throat.
VOICE *Cha-cha-lac.*
HABITAT Woods.
RANGE Lower Rio Grande valley.
MOVEMENTS Resident.

GRAY PARTRIDGE

Perdix perdix   11½−12½in/29−32cm

IDENTIFICATION Chunky gamebird with orange face, brown streaked upperparts and gray breast. Underparts show smudgy chestnut "horseshoe". Gregarious bird of open areas.
VOICE A fast *krikri-kri-kri-krikri.*
HABITAT Fields, grasslands.
RANGE Either side of US-Canada border right across the continent. Introduced from Europe.
MOVEMENTS Resident.
BREEDING Arable fields with rough areas and thickets; May-June.
NEST AND EGGS A depression lined with grasses and hidden in longer dead grass; the 9 to 20 eggs are dark olive.

INCUBATION Lasts 23 to 25 days and is performed by the female alone.
COMMENT The success of this species, following multiple introductions from Europe, is quite remarkable.

CHUKAR

Alectoris chukar   13−15in/33−39cm

IDENTIFICATION Substantial gamebird with distinctive face pattern of black enclosing a creamy bib. Bold series of black and white stripes along flanks. Red legs and bill.
VOICE Distinct *choo-kar* repeated.
HABITAT Arid mountain and barren areas.
RANGE Dry areas of far west. Introduced from Europe.
MOVEMENTS Resident.
BREEDING Dry areas among stony hillsides; March-April.
NEST AND EGGS A hollow lined with grass and feathers is hidden among rocks; the 7 to 15 eggs are buff, spotted brown.
INCUBATION Lasts 24 to 26 days and is by the female alone.
COMMENT This introduced bird has prospered and spread in the arid mountains of the west.

RING-NECKED PHEASANT

Phasianus colchicus   20½–35½in/52–90cm

IDENTIFICATION Large colorful gamebird introduced from Europe. Male boldly colored in rich browns and golds, liberally spotted and barred in black and white. Blue head with bare red area around eye, often white neck ring. Female, subdued shades of brown and buff, with paler area around eye. Both sexes have long, pointed tails.

VOICE Deep, resonant crowing.

HABITAT Fields, thickets, woodland edges.

RANGE Widespread across northern US and southern Canada.

MOVEMENTS Resident.

BREEDING Farmland fields with hedges and woodland; March-May.

NEST AND EGGS A hollow lined with leaves; the 8 to 15 eggs are a dark olive color.

INCUBATION Lasts 22 to 25 days and is performed by the female alone.

COMMENT Successfully introduced from Europe where, in turn, it was successfully introduced from Asia.

SPRUCE GROUSE

Dendragapus canadensis   15–17in/38–43cm

IDENTIFICATION Common grouse of conifer forests. Male has black chin enclosed by white border and black on breast and central belly. There is a red wattle above the eye. Female heavily barred, but with black tail tipped rufous.

VOICE Low-pitched booming.

HABITAT Conifer forests.

RANGE Boreal zone from Alaska to Nova Scotia.

MOVEMENTS Resident.

BREEDING Mostly conifers, but also mixed woodland; April-May.

NEST AND EGGS A depression on the ground beneath a small tree lined with grasses; the 7 to 10 eggs are deep cream, spotted brown.

INCUBATION Lasts 17 to 24 days and is performed by the female alone.

COMMENT The female of this grouse is tenacious while nesting and is easily approached.

BLUE GROUSE

Dendragapus obscurus   15–21in/39–53cm

IDENTIFICATION Large grouse of woodland. Male is uniform gray below with white, mottled flanks and brown upperparts. The tail is square and mainly dark. Female is brown with barring on foreparts and a boldly spotted belly. The dark tail is a useful feature.

VOICE Booming calls of male.

HABITAT Forests.

RANGE Breeds west in mountains.

MOVEMENTS Resident.

BREEDING Forest margins, clearings, hillsides, meadows; May-June.

NEST AND EGGS A hollow lined with leaves and grasses; the 7 to 10 eggs are cream, spotted brown.

INCUBATION Lasts 24 or 25 days and incubated by the female alone.

COMMENT Strangely, this bird breeds among low altitude, deciduous forest moving up into conifers for the winter.

WILLOW PTARMIGAN

Lagopus lagopus   11−17in/28−43cm

IDENTIFICATION Stocky grouse of open country. Male is rich rufous, with red comb and white wings and feet. In winter, whole plumage becomes white, when confusion with closely-related Rock Ptarmigan is likely.

VOICE Crowing *koc-koc-koc*

HABITAT Tundra, open moors.

RANGE Alaska, northernmost Canada to Newfoundland.

MOVEMENTS Some birds move a short distance south in winter.

BREEDING Open country beyond the tree line, either on tundra or higher mountain slopes; May-June.

NEST AND EGGS A hollow lined with grasses and leaves; the 5 to 17 eggs are rich buff, spotted brown.

INCUBATION Lasts 22 to 26 days and is performed by the female alone.

COMMENT The males contribute more to the care of the young than any other species of ptarmigan or grouse.

ROCK PTARMIGAN

Lagopus mutus   13−14in/33−36cm

IDENTIFICATION Similar to Willow Grouse, but mottled gray rather than red. Also white in winter, but dark mark between bill and eye creates an "angry" expression.

VOICE A rolling *karr*.

HABITAT Found at higher altitudes and higher latitudes than Willow Grouse; tundra and mountain tops.

RANGE Extreme north Canada and archipelago from Alaska to Newfoundland.

MOVEMENTS Some southward movement in winter.

BREEDING Open arctic and mountain areas where lichens and mosses cover the ground; May-June.
NEST AND EGGS A hollow, near a rock, lined with grasses and feathers; the 3 to 12 eggs are cream, spotted dark brown.
INCUBATION Lasts 21 to 26 days by the female alone.
COMMENT Inhabits higher latitudes and altitudes than the Willow Ptarmigan with less ground cover.

WHITE-TAILED PTARMIGAN

Lagopus leucurus   12–13in/30–33cm

IDENTIFICATION Smaller than other ptarmigan. Similar to Rock Ptarmigan being mottled gray with white below and white wings. In flight, shows white, not black, tail and in winter is pure white with no dark mark between bill and eye. Thus even in winter the white tail is diagnostic.
VOICE Low chuckle.
HABITAT Mountain slopes.
RANGE From Alaska southward through the Rockies to New Mexico.
MOVEMENTS Resident.
BREEDING High mountains in higher latitudes; May-June.
NEST AND EGGS A hollow in the ground lined with whatever vegetation is available; the 4 to 15 eggs are buffy, spotted brown.
INCUBATION Lasts 22 to 23 days, and is performed by female alone.
COMMENT Though it would seem to inhabit really inhospitable areas, it frequently occurs among meadows and the lower slopes in winter.

RUFFED GROUSE

Bonasa umbellus   16–19in/41–48cm

IDENTIFICATION Secretive bird of forest edges. There are two color phases: red and gray. "Red" birds are rufous above with brown barring below. The tail is large and heavily banded rust and black. "Gray" birds are gray rather than rusty. Both phases have a dark mark on the side of the neck and fan their tail in flight and in display on a hollow log.
VOICE Drumming sound produced by beating wings.
HABITAT Forests, both deciduous and conifer.
RANGE The boreal zone extending southward in Rockies and Appalachians and elsewhere.
MOVEMENTS Resident.
BREEDING Deciduous scrub and regenerating woodland; May-June.
NEST AND EGGS A hollow next to a tree or rock is lined with leaves and grass; the 9 to 12 eggs are buff, lightly speckled brown.
INCUBATION Lasts 24 days and is performed by the female alone.
COMMENT The male's "drumming" is used for display and usually occurs on a log.

SAGE GROUSE

Centrocercus urophasianus   22−30in/56−76cm

IDENTIFICATION Largest of the grouse. Male is mottled buff and black above, and marked by black on throat, breast and belly, below. Most of the breast is whitish and, in display, this is puffed up and shows two yellow air sacs. The long tail is fanned to show a series of spikes. The female is smaller, duller, but also has a black belly.

VOICE Popping sounds by male in display.

HABITAT Arid sage brush country, plains.

RANGE From Southern Alberta and Saskatchewan.

MOVEMENTS Resident.

BREEDING Sagebrush country; March-April.

NEST AND EGGS A hollow on the ground lined with grass and sheltered by a sagebrush or other low vegetation; the 7 to 13 eggs are dull buff, speckled brown.

INCUBATION Lasts 26 days and is performed by the female alone.

COMMENT Very much a western bird that just extends northwards across the Canadian border.

GREATER PRAIRIE-CHICKEN

Tympanuchus cupido   15½−18in/40−46cm

IDENTIFICATION Once widespread, now decidedly rare bird of open plains. Heavily barred brown and black bird with elaborate display using orange neck sacs and extended crest. Square cut, black tail. The paler Lesser Prairie-Chicken of the Texas panhandle and vicinity, has red neck sacs.

VOICE Booming.

HABITAT Prairies.

RANGE Remnants of former range from Dakotas to Texas.

MOVEMENTS Resident.

BREEDING Prairies and other natural grasslands with or without bushes; April-May.

NEST AND EGGS A hollow on the ground lined with grasses and hidden among tall grass or bush; the 7 to 17 eggs are greenish, spotted brown.

INCUBATION Lasts 21 to 28 days and is performed by the female.

COMMENT Decidedly scarce and highly localized. In some areas, it cross-breeds with Sharp-tailed Grouse.

LESSER PRAIRIE-CHICKEN

Tympanuchus pallidicinctus   15−17in/38−43cm

IDENTIFICATION Very similar to Greater Prairie-Chicken, but less contrasting barring creating a paler effect. Displaying male shows orange-yellow neck sacs.

VOICE Booming.

HABITAT Arid grasslands and sagebrush.

RANGE Northern Texas and adjacent areas.

MOVEMENTS Resident, endangered.

SHARP-TAILED GROUSE

Tympanuchus phasianellus   15−20in/38−51cm

IDENTIFICATION Grassland grouse. Rather dully colored in shades of buff and brown in both sexes. Tail is pointed, larger in the male, and is fanned in display, when male shows violet patch on neck.

VOICE Cooing in courtship.

HABITAT Clearings in forest, open country.

RANGE Breeds from Alaska through north, west and central Canada as far east as Hudson Bay and southward into the prairies.

MOVEMENTS Resident.

BREEDING Grasslands and prairies, forest clearings; April-June.

NEST AND EGGS A well-hidden hollow is lined with grasses and leaves; the 10 to 15 eggs are buff, sometimes speckled.

INCUBATION Lasts 21 to 24 days by the female alone.

COMMENT A typical 'lek' species in which males gather at traditional jousting grounds.

WILD TURKEY

Meleagris gallopavo   36−48in/91−122cm

IDENTIFICATION Large, ground bird with blue and red head wattles, iridescent black plumage and large tail, fanned in display.

VOICE Loud gobbling.

HABITAT Woodland clearings, scrub.

RANGE Scattered through US, once more widespread.

MOVEMENTS Resident.

BREEDING Deciduous woodland with dense ground cover and clearings; March-April.

NEST AND EGGS A bare scrape on the ground hidden among dense cover serves as a nest; the 8 to 15 eggs are gray, speckled darker gray.

INCUBATION Lasts for 28 days by the female alone.

COMMENT The size of the bird plus the large clutch laid made this an obvious candidate for domestication by the earliest human settlers.

MONTEZUMA QUAIL

Cyrtonyx montezumae   8−9½in/20−24cm

IDENTIFICATION Small, dark, chunky quail. Male is dark, chocolate-brown below, heavily spotted white on flanks. Head shows intricate pattern of interlaced black and white lines. Female, brown and buff with broken dark lines extending from eye to enclose chin.

VOICE Soft whistling.

HABITAT Semi-arid oak and pine forest floors.

RANGE South-western US.

MOVEMENTS Resident.

BREEDING Undergrowth in pine-oak woods; April-May.

NEST AND EGGS A hollow lined with grasses; the 8 to 14 eggs are white.

INCUBATION Some confusion about the roles of the sexes in this respect. The eggs hatch in 25 to 26 days.

COMMENT Whatever the truth about the roles of the sexes in incubation, it is clear that the male shares in the care of the freshly hatched chicks.

NORTHERN BOBWHITE

Colinus virginianus   8−11in/20−28cm

IDENTIFICATION Virtually the only small gamebird that is at all common in the eastern US. Male is brown above, scaled white below, with distinctive white face enclosed by black. Female is similar, but has creamy face with less black. Best located by call.

VOICE Distinctive *bob-white*.

HABITAT Grasslands, farms.

RANGE Virtually the eastern half of the US to foothills of Rocky Mountain system. Introduced in the west.

MOVEMENTS Resident.

BREEDING Brush, arable field margins, overgrown pastures; March-April.

NEST AND EGGS A depression lined with grasses concealed among overhanging ground vegetation; the 7 to 20 eggs are white.

INCUBATION Lasts 23 or 24 days and is shared between the pair.

COMMENT Introduced in many areas, including the Old World.

SCALED QUAIL

Callipepla squamata   10−12in/25−30cm

IDENTIFICATION A distinctive western quail with a pale crest that gives it its country name of "cotton-top". Gray-brown above, rufous below and heavily "scaled" over most of foreparts. Gregarious, runs rather than flies.

VOICE A twanging *be-cos*, *be-cos*.

HABITAT Semi-desert.

RANGE South-west US.

MOVEMENTS Resident.

BREEDING Dry desert and grassland areas, often with yucca; March-April.

NEST AND EGGS A hollow, lined with grass, hidden among prickly desert vegetation; the 9 to 16 eggs are buff, speckled brown.

INCUBATION Lasts 21 days and is performed by the female alone.

COMMENT A great running bird whose numbers vary from year to year depending on the prevalent rainfall pattern.

GAMBEL'S QUAIL

Callipepla gambelii   10–12in/26–30cm

IDENTIFICATION Very similar to California Quail, but found in drier, near desert country. Face pattern, crest and blue breast as California Quail, but underparts creamy with bold black patch on belly. Female lacks black patch.
VOICE Similar to California Quail, but shorter.
HABITAT Desert scrub.
RANGE South-western US.
MOVEMENTS Resident.
BREEDING Dry arid country with thickets; April-May.
NEST AND EGGS A hollow in the ground, usually well protected by spiky vegetation; the 10 to 14 eggs are buffy, speckled brown.
INCUBATION Lasts 21 to 24 days and is performed by the female.
COMMENT Though up to 20 eggs have been found in a single nest, there is a strong chance that these are the work of two females.

CALIFORNIA QUAIL

Callipepla californica   9–11in/23–28cm

IDENTIFICATION One of series of western quails. Male is boldly marked with black and white on head, has a chocolate crown and a "comma" shaped crest. The breast is blue and the underparts heavily barred. The latter, in both male and more subdued female, is best means of distinquishing from very similar Gambel's Quail.
VOICE Loud *ka-ka-kow*.
HABITAT Chaparral, brush, scrub.
RANGE Washington to Baja California.
MOVEMENTS Resident.
BREEDING Thickets with open clearings, gardens and parks; April-May.
NEST AND EGGS A depression lined with grass and leaves hidden among dense vegetation; the 10 to 18 eggs are buffy, spotted brown.
INCUBATION The eggs take 18 days to hatch and are incubated by the female.
COMMENT Native to California, this bird has been introduced northwards as far as British Columbia and Vancouver Island.

Mountain Quail

Oreortyx pictus   10½–11½in/27–29cm

IDENTIFICATION Resembles other western quails, but foreparts less boldly patterned, with blue on breast extending over nape and crown. Chestnut bib enclosed by white, crest longer and straighter. Rusty belly shows bold pattern of white spots on flank. Has distinctive head plumes.

VOICE Low *whook*.

HABITAT Brushy mountain slopes.

RANGE South-western US.

MOVEMENTS Resident, but leaves higher slopes in winter.

BREEDING Dry mountain slopes with thickets and chaparral; March-April.

NEST AND EGGS A depression on the ground is lined with leaves and grass and hidden among rocks or ground cover; the 8 to 12 eggs are dull pink.

INCUBATION Lasts 21 days and may well be shared between the pair.

COMMENT Like the California Quail, this species has been introduced to British Columbia and Vancouver Island.

RAILS, GALLINULES, COOTS, LIMPKINS & CRANES

THIS is a varied group of predominantly aquatic birds, most of which are found on fresh water of one kind or another. They vary considerably in size, with most rails being rather small, while the cranes are among the largest of all birds. Of the world's 130 species of rails, only nine are found in North America, while of 15 species of cranes, two breed within the continent. Clearly, rails are poorly represented within these shores, but this is less surprising when it is realized that they are rather poor fliers, with many species existing in glorious isolation on remote oceanic islands.

In general, rails are dull-colored, secretive birds that spend most of their time among dense, aquatic vegetation. They have thin, laterally compressed bodies that pass easily through grasses and reeds, and most have long probing bills. Though they are short-winged, many species perform lengthy migrations, though the Clapper Rail is resident among marine habitats that remain free of ice on both Atlantic and Pacific coasts. Being so secretive, the presence of rails at a particular site is often betrayed only by their calls, many of which are decidedly unbird-like. Such calls are essential to facilitate contact between birds in well-vegetated habitats.

The gallinules, a term used here to include the Moorhen and Coot, are more frequently seen swimming than the rails proper, though they are closely related and share similar habitats. Like those birds, they are usually solitary, though coots regularly form large flocks in winter. Coots are also unusual among the rails in having adopted a diving habit by which they frequently feed.

North America is blessed by two of the world's 15 species of cranes. They are large,

gregarious birds that make long migrations in noisy, goose-like skeins. Their calls are a reminder of the wild and it is a sad condemnation of the approach to wildlife that the magnificent Whooping Crane has been reduced to its present precarious state.

These are birds of the great northern marshes, where they trumpet and dance as part of their courtship rituals. Until quite recently, they were confined to Canada's Wood Buffalo National Park in Alberta from where, every fall, they would make a length-of-the-continent flight to the Texas coast to winter at Aransas National Wildlife Refuge. During the present century, their numbers fluctuated, but showed an overall decline until they seemed doomed to extinction. We can only guess at their previous abundance and the sight and sound of large migrant flocks of these magnificent birds.

In order to create an alternate population, an operation involved establishing a captive breeding and reintroduction program in Idaho, and there is now a small population that summers at Grays Lake National Wildlife Refuge and migrates to winter quarters in New Mexico. Slowly, the Whooping Crane seems to be recovering, but it will be a long, long time before Americans can thrill to the sight and sound of large flocks of these birds.

The final member of this group, the Limpkin, is so unusual that it is placed in a family by itself. It is a large, long-legged, long-billed wading bird with a superficial resemblance to a curlew. It inhabits the swamps of the extreme southeast, being virtually confined to Florida, but is widespread southward through Central and South America. Though something of a snail specialist, it is not averse to frogs and insects.

YELLOW RAIL

Coturnicops noveboracensis   6–8in/15–20cm

IDENTIFICATION Small buff and brown rail marked by yellow legs and bill and smudgy, dark mark through eye. Banded on undertail coverts. Shows bold white patch on trailing edge of inner wing when flushed.

VOICE Click notes in series of twos and threes – like tapping two stones together.

HABITAT Floods, damp grasslands.

RANGE Breeds across much of central and eastern Canada, as well as in adjacent areas across the US border.

MOVEMENTS Winters California, Gulf and Atlantic coasts and Florida.

BREEDING Breeds secretively in densely vegetated marshes; May-June.

NEST AND EGGS A neat cup of grasses among emergent vegetation; the 8 or 9 eggs are buffy, spotted red brown at the larger end.

INCUBATION Lasts 18 days, and is performed by female.

COMMENT One of the most secretive of all North American birds usually located by five-note clicking call.

BLACK RAIL

Laterallus jamaicensis   5–6in/13–15cm

IDENTIFICATION Tiny black rail that mainly frequents brackish coastal marshes. Foreparts blue-black; back and hindparts black with fine white vertical bars. Patch of chestnut at top of back. Bill short and conical. Very difficult to see.

VOICE High-pitched *kic-ki-doo*, the last note being quieter and lower pitched.

HABITAT Salt, brackish and sometimes fresh marshes.

RANGE Breeds Pacific and Atlantic coasts of US and in some places inland.

MOVEMENTS Winters Florida, Gulf coast, and southern California.

BREEDING Breeds among the plants of saltings along estuaries; April-June.

NEST AND EGGS Cup of grasses hidden beneath canopy of vegetation; the 4 to 10 eggs are buffy, spotted brown.

INCUBATION Lasts 17 days, and is performed by both sexes.

COMMENT A tiny, highly secretive rail that lives among coastal marshes and is seldom seen.

CLAPPER RAIL

Rallus longirostris   14–15½in/35–40cm

IDENTIFICATION A large pale rail, similar to King Rail, but largely confined to salt marshes. Upperparts gray-brown, lightly streaked; underparts gray on breast, banded gray and white on flanks and undertail. Bill long and yellowish, legs pinkish.

VOICE Loud *kek-kek-kek-kek*.

HABITAT Salt marsh.

RANGE Most coasts of US, though less continuous along rocky Pacific.

MOVEMENTS Resident.

BREEDING Found among coastal salt marshes; April-June.

NEST AND EGGS A mass of plant material among emergent vegetation; the 8 to 11 eggs are cream colored, lightly spotted red-brown.

INCUBATION Lasts for 21 days and is shared by both sexes.

COMMENT Though a secretive bird, the loud raucous calls of this species are a common estuary sound.

KING RAIL

Rallus elegans   15−19in/38−48cm

IDENTIFICATION Freshwater equivalent of Clapper Rail. Slightly larger and much more clearly marked with warm rufous breast being the major feature. Upperparts streaked brown and black, undertail and flanks finely barred black and white.

VOICE Deep *kep-kep-kep* similar to Clapper Rail, but more musical.

HABITAT Fresh marshes.

RANGE Breeds over eastern half of US.

MOVEMENTS Most birds migrate, but some winter along Atlantic and Gulf coasts, in Florida and in the Mississippi basin.

BREEDING Found in fresh marshes and adjacent fields; April-June.

NEST AND EGGS A shallow structure or well-lined depression in or near marshland; the 6 to 14 eggs are buff, spotted brown.

INCUBATION Lasts for 21 days and is shared by both sexes.

COMMENT Elusive, but not as secretive as many other members of the family.

VIRGINIA RAIL

Rallus limicola   9−11in/23−28cm

IDENTIFICATION Colorful, long-billed rail. Upperparts streaked black and brown, underparts warm rust with undertail black, finely barred white. Legs reddish; bill reddish, slightly decurved. Immature is dusky, streaked gray and black, with black and white barred undertail. Skulking and seldom seen.

VOICE Characteristic *kickit-kickit-kickit*.

HABITAT Marshes with dense vegetation.

RANGE Breeds right across US, save for southern states, northward into Canada.

MOVEMENTS Winters Pacific coast, Florida and Gulf and south Atlantic coasts.

BREEDING Frequents freshwater marshes with a strong growth of emergent vegetation; April-June.

NEST AND EGGS Creates a neat cup of aquatic vegetation, lined with grass, just above the water level and attached to a marshy clump; the 7 to 12 eggs are pale buffy to creamy, lightly spotted with red brown.

INCUBATION The eggs take 19 to 20 days to hatch and are incubated by both sexes.

COMMENT Even when disturbed, the Virginia Rail will run rather than fly and is forced into the air only in extreme circumstances. Nevertheless, it is a long distance migrant, flying mainly by night.

SORA

Porzana carolina   8−10in/20−25cm

IDENTIFICATION Common but secretive rail. Adult is streaked brown above and plain gray below, with black and white striped undertail. A dark crown, black "face" and central breast make identification easy, if seen. Bill and legs yellow. Immature has dusky face, yellow bill, green legs.

VOICE A pleasant, descending trill.

HABITAT Marshes.

RANGE Throughout northern US and southern Canada.

MOVEMENTS Winters California, Gulf and Atlantic coasts and Florida. Most birds leave North America.

BREEDING Breeds in freshwater or brackish marshes, often alongside the lower reaches of rivers; May-June.

NEST AND EGGS Builds a cup of marsh vegetation attached to a sapling, or a heavier structure in a marshy clump; the 8 to 15 eggs are arranged in two or three layers so that the bird can cover them; they are buffy with brown spots.

INCUBATION By both sexes, last 16 to 20 days.

COMMENT The most abundant of North American rails that benefits from its ability to lay a large clutch of eggs often among brackish marshes.

PURPLE GALLINULE

Porphyrula martinica   11−13in/28−33cm

IDENTIFICATION Shape and size as Common Moorhen, but vividly blue, with bronze-green upperparts and white frontal shield. Bill red with yellow tip; legs long and yellow. Swims less than its more widespread relative.

VOICE Harsh crackling.

HABITAT Marshes with plentiful vegetation.

RANGE Florida, Gulf coast and adjacent Atlantic coasts.

MOVEMENTS Winters along Gulf coast and in Florida.

BREEDING Found in marshes and ditches with emergent vegetation; April-May.

NEST AND EGGS Platform constructed in isolated tussock; the 6 to 10 eggs are a warm buff, spotted brown.

INCUBATION Lasts 23 to 25 days, and is shared by both sexes.

COMMENT A confiding and colorful bird that is easily seen within its southern breeding grounds.

COMMON MOORHEN

Gallinula chloropus　　12–14in/31–35cm

IDENTIFICATION Medium-sized waterbird that swims well and is often confiding, even tame. Back is dark brown, separated from the black underparts by a bold, white, flank slash. The undertail is white and frequently cocked when walking. The remaining plumage is black with a bold, red, frontal shield. The legs are green-yellow, with long toes; the bill red, tipped yellow.

VOICE Loud *currick*.

HABITAT Pond and lake margins.

RANGE Breeds over most of eastern US and resident in California.

MOVEMENTS Migrates southward to Gulf and south Atlantic coasts.

BREEDING Frequents ponds, river margins and marshes; 2 or even 3 broods reared April-June.

NEST AND EGGS Substantial structure among emergent vegetation, but occasionally in a low bush; the 5 to 11 buffy eggs are spotted black.

INCUBATION Shared by the pair and lasts 19 to 22 days.

COMMENT One of the least secretive members of the rail family.

AMERICAN COOT

Fulica americana　　14–15in/35–39cm

IDENTIFICATION All-black waterbird that spends much time swimming. Runs over water to avoid danger and may then show white trailing edge to the wing. Otherwise white bill

and frontal shield, plus white outer feathers of undertail coverts are the best field marks.

VOICE Sharp *kuk-kuk-kuk*.

HABITAT Ponds, lakes, coastal bays.

RANGE Breeds over most of temperate North America northward into the Canadian prairies.

MOVEMENTS Leaves much of the interior in winter.

BREEDING Frequents open waters, but breeds among emergent vegetation at margins; April-June.

NEST AND EGGS A bulky cup of vegetation situated in marginal cover; the 6 to 9 buffy eggs are spotted black.

INCUBATION Lasts 21 to 24 days and is shared by male and female.

COMMENT A familiar and successful species that takes a wide range of foods.

L IMPKIN

Aramus guarauna   25−28in/64−71cm

IDENTIFICATION Superficial resemblance to a curlew. A medium-sized waterbird with brown plumage spotted white. Long legs and heavy, decurved bill. Labored flight with neck extended.

VOICE Loud *krrow*.

HABITAT Marshes with pomacea snails.

RANGE Florida and adjacent Georgia.

MOVEMENTS Resident.

BREEDING Breeds in extensive swamps with a thick growth of emergent vegetation; January-May.

NEST AND EGGS A mass of marshland vegetation attached to a growing stem above the water level, but may also build a thin platform of twigs several feet high in dense waterside vegetation; the 5 or 6 eggs are buff-colored, spotted with brown.

INCUBATION Is shared by both members of the pair.

COMMENT This Florida speciality feeds largely on the huge pomacea snails which it hunts during the hours of darkness.

S ANDHILL CRANE

Grus canadensis   34−48in/86−122cm

IDENTIFICATION Gray crane, with droopy gray "tail" and white "face" topped by red crown. Like other cranes, flies with neck extended.

VOICE Loud rolling rattle.

HABITAT Marshes, ponds and tundra.

RANGE Breeds over large areas of Canadian and Alaskan tundra as well as on prairies westward to Pacific coast. Also in Florida.

MOVEMENTS Spectacular migrations southward to Mexico, California and Texas. Resident Florida.

BREEDING Frequents marshes, bogs and thawing tundra pools; April-July.

NEST AND EGGS The nest is a mass of aquatic vegetation, lined with twigs of willow and grass, situated in a marsh or on a hummock; the 2 eggs are buffy, blotched with shades of brown.

INCUBATION By both members of the pair for 29 to 32 days.

COMMENT Despite their size, these birds are still reasonably plentiful over much of their range. Some pairs have played foster parents to young Whooping Cranes as part of the effort to save the larger species from extinction.

WHOOPING CRANE

Grus americana   45—50in/114—127cm

IDENTIFICATION Spectacular, large, white waterbird that may still recover from the verge of extinction. Whole plumage is white save for black wing tips. Cascading "tail" plumes are actually extended tertial wing feathers. Head with black through eye and bright red crown.

VOICE Rolling, trumpeting calls.

HABITAT Breeds in bogs; winters in marshes.

RANGE Breeds only in Wood Buffalo National Park, Canada, though a separate population has been established artificially in recent years at Gray's Lake Refuge, Idaho.

MOVEMENTS Migrates south to winter at Aransas National Wildlife Refuge, Texas. New population winters New Mexico.

BREEDING Breeds only in huge marshy wildernesses; May-July.

NEST AND EGGS The nest is a platform of marsh vegetation heaped together in the middle of an extensive wetland and surrounded by open water; the 2 eggs are clay colored with brown blotches.

INCUBATION By both sexes, lasting 34 or 35 days.

COMMENT This splendid bird may yet be saved from the extinction that seemed almost inevitable only 30 years ago.

SHOREBIRDS

THIS is a medium-sized group of birds that is particularly well represented in North America. The vast majority are long-distance migrants that exploit food-rich northern marshes in summer, and winter, as their collective name implies, along shorelines and estuaries. They vary in size from the tiny Least Sandpiper, a little under 6in/15cm in length, to the large Long-billed Curlew, at 20–26in/50–65cm. Most are clothed in shades of brown and buff and have well-developed bills and longish legs. They are generally birds of mudflats and marshland, regularly wading in shallow water in search of their food, though some have abandoned wetlands in favor of a dry-land existence.

Shorebirds are readily divided among several families. The oystercatchers are large, chunky, black, or black and white, birds with heavy, orange-red bills. Though it would be reasonable to assume that they are major predators of oyster beds they are, in fact, mussel specialists. They live between the tides on muddy ooze and along rocky shorelines, where they are often found in company with turnstones. Two distinct species – the stilts and avocets – occur in North America, and are among the longest-legged of all shorebirds. The appropriately named Black-necked Stilt has the longest legs of all and in flight its "stilts" trail behind like an extended pink tail. The American Avocet has an uptilted "awl" of a bill that is swept from side to side over soft mud in its search for small, animate food items. Phalaropes are, perhaps, the most extraordinary of all shorebirds. They spend the summer among shallow northern marshes, where they frequently swim in search of food. Two species, the Red and Red-necked Phalaropes, regularly spin while swimming to bring minute food particles to the water's surface where they are delicately picked up. These same two birds spend their winters at sea, often hundreds of miles from the nearest land. Wilson's Phalarope is the largest and least aquatic of the three species and breeds much farther south than the others. It frequents marshlands at all times and is less frequently seen swimming.

By far the largest group of shorebirds are the sandpipers of the family Scolopacidae. There are some 90 species of these birds in the world, no less than 35 of which are found in North America. Some can be conveniently divided into groups such as the plovers, godwits, curlews, and peep, but others are more difficult to describe. The two major "tribes" are the genus *Tringa* and the genus *Calidris*; the former includes the shanks, the latter the peep. In general terms, *Tringa* sandpipers are slim, elegant, long-legged birds, whereas *Calidris* birds are squat, dumpy, and

bustling in character.

To the layman, the sandpipers are a bewildering array of remarkably similar birds which inhabit areas that are only seldom visited. To the birder they are the bread and butter of any shoreline or marshland outing. The plovers are a well-marked group of birds, with long legs and short bills that spend much of their time on marshland edges and nearby dry land. They pick their food from the surface rather than probe like the larger-billed species, and have the curious habit of alternating fast runs with immobile stops. The "ringed" plovers are marked with black breast bands of varying degrees of completeness and prominence. One species, the Killdeer, has a double breast band and has abandoned marshes to become a bird of grassland throughout the interior of North America. Its distinctive call is known to all country dwellers and is the source of its name.

The various curlews have long legs and long, decurved bills ideally suited to probing deep into soft mud. Most are, therefore, estuarine birds that feed on marine worms, though they are not averse to picking soft crabs and other creatures from the surface. Both the Long-billed Curlew and the Whimbrel are fairly common, but both were once outnumbered by the Eskimo Curlew. During the last century, these tundra-breeding birds literally poured out of the sky along the coasts of Labrador. They would then feed up prior to a long migration over the Atlantic to South America. For the "sportsman" of yesteryear they made an ideal target and were shot in their thousands. Within a couple of decades they were rare, and by early this century regarded as extinct. Then the occasional individual started to appear in spring along the coast of Texas, the species' normal return route. Clearly, a few pairs survived but no one knows where they breed, or where they winter, which is probably just as well.

The most abundant of North American shorebirds are the peep – dainty little waders that often form huge flocks. Most numerous of all is the Semipalmated Sandpiper, which breeds in the Canadian Arctic and migrates through the center of the continent and along the east coast. In fall, in particular, the peep can present formidable identification problems, particularly when one is trying to pick out a European Little Stint, or Asiatic Rufous-necked or Long-toed Stint. Altogether, there are eight peep-stints, and considerable care is required to pick out one from the other.

Fortunately, not all shorebirds are as tricky. The long-legged *Tringa* sandpipers are often well marked, with the Greater and Lesser Yellowlegs presenting few problems for the experienced birder. Similarly, it is not difficult to pick out a dowitcher, though there may be problems in deciding whether the bird is a Long-billed or a Short-billed variety, especially as bill length is a poor indicator.

BLACK-BELLIED PLOVER

Pluvialis squatarola   11–12in/28–31cm

IDENTIFICATION Similar to golden plovers, but in all plumages spangled black and white above. In summer, "face" and belly are black, bordered by white line. In winter, underparts mottled gray. Shows white wing bar and black axillaries (armpits) in flight.
VOICE Whistled *tlee-oo-ee*.
HABITAT Tundra; in winter, estuaries and shorelines.
RANGE Breeds far northern Alaska and Canada.
MOVEMENTS Migrates to winter all coasts as far north as Washington and New England.
BREEDING High Arctic tundra is its nesting ground; June-July.
NEST AND EGGS A depression on the ground is lined with a little moss; the 4 buffy eggs are spotted with black.
INCUBATION 23 to 27 days of incubation are shared between members of the pair.
COMMENT Outside the breeding season these are essentially maritime birds of estuary and shoreline, where they frequently associate with Red Knot.

LESSER GOLDEN-PLOVER

Pluvialis dominica   9½–11in/24–28cm

IDENTIFICATION Typical round-headed, short-billed plover. In summer black face and underparts are separated from golden-spangled upperparts by broad, white line. In winter, dull buffy-gray below, but with a touch of gold on upperparts. *See* Pacific Golden-Plover.
VOICE Fast *teu-ee*
HABITAT Tundra, grassland.
RANGE Breeds Alaskan and Canadian tundra to Baffin Island.
MOVEMENTS Migrates southward over Atlantic to winter in South America. Returns in spring through Central Flyway.
BREEDING Found among tundra slopes of the far north; May-July.
NEST AND EGGS A simple depression lined with grass; the 4 eggs are buffy, blotched with black.
INCUBATION Shared between members of the pair for the 26 days the eggs take to hatch.
COMMENT Drastically reduced in number by hunting, these birds are showing a welcome increase under a more protective climate.

PACIFIC GOLDEN-PLOVER

Pluvialis fulva   9−10in/23−26cm

IDENTIFICATION A well-marked form of Lesser Golden-Plover, and may be a separate species. Smaller, slimmer and with shorter wings than that bird. Tends to be more coastal. More pronounced white on flank may be first clue to identification.
VOICE Fast *teu-ee*.
HABITAT Tundra, grassland.
RANGE Breeds western Alaska.
MOVEMENTS Migrates westward to Hawaii, Oceana and California.
BREEDING Frequents dry areas of tundra; May-July.
NEST AND EGGS A depression lined with grasses serves as a nest; the 4 eggs are buffy, blotched black.
INCUBATION Lasts 26 days and is shared by male and female.
COMMENT Only recently separated from the American Golden Plover, by European ornithologists, and accorded specific status but not yet by American ornithologists.

SNOWY PLOVER

Charadrius alexandrinus   6−6½in/15−17cm

IDENTIFICATION Small sandy plover marked in summer and winter by dark marks at sides of breast. Immature shows no more than a smudge. Legs black. Wing-bar and white, outer tail show in flight.
VOICE *Wit-wit-wit*.
HABITAT Sandy wastes and margins of saline and fresh

marshes, open shorelines.
RANGE Breeds locally throughout the west, and along the Pacific and Gulf coasts. Declining.
MOVEMENTS Migrates southward and to the Pacific coast to winter. Resident in Gulf.
BREEDING Shorelines with sandy beaches, both maritime and inland; April-May.
NEST AND EGGS Bare scrape with a few decorative shells or stones acts as a nest; the 3 pale buffy eggs are spotted black.
INCUBATION The eggs hatch after 24 days of incubation shared by male and female.
COMMENT One of the most widespread of the world's birds, breeding in every major region, though it is uncommon, and declining in North America.

WILSON'S PLOVER

Charadrius wilsonia   6½−8in/17−20cm

IDENTIFICATION Similar to Semipalmated Plover but with more prominent white eyebrow and black eye stripe, and much broader breast band. Bill is black and heavy, the legs a dull pink.
VOICE *Quit-quit*.
HABITAT Sandy and muddy shorelines.

RANGE Gulf and Atlantic coasts to Virginia.
MOVEMENTS Winters Florida and Gulf coast.
BREEDING A coastal plover that finds a home between the sea and backing dunes; April-June.
NEST AND EGGS A bare scrape among sandy shingle acts as a nest; the 3 eggs are buff and spotted with black.
INCUBATION The pair share the incubation which lasts for 24 days.
COMMENT Formerly called the Thick-billed Plover, a name that picks out its major identification feature.

SEMIPALMATED PLOVER

Charadrius semipalmatus   6½−8in/17−20cm

IDENTIFICATION Common along shorelines. Brown above and white below marked by neat head pattern of black and white, and bold, black breast band. Orange bill tipped black; orange or yellowish legs.
VOICE Pleasant *chur-lee*.
HABITAT Breeds tundra; winters, sandy shores and estuaries.
RANGE Alaskan and Canadian tundra.
MOVEMENTS Migrates to winter in California and along Atlantic and Gulf coasts.
BREEDING A wide variety of open, aquatic habitats is used by this plover including shoreline beaches and river margins; April-June.
NEST AND EGGS A simple depression, often devoid of lining and decoration acts as a nest; the 4 buffy eggs are spotted brown.
INCUBATION The eggs hatch after 23 to 26 days of incubation by both parents.
COMMENT Breeding pairs are aggressively territorial and will display vigorously at any intruders.

PIPING PLOVER

Charadrius melodus   6−6½in/15−17cm

IDENTIFICATION Small sandy plover with narrow, black breast band, wider at side of neck in summer. In winter, only smudge at side of neck remains. Yellow legs separate from similar Snowy Plover. Broad wing-bar and white rump show in flight.
VOICE Whistling *peep-lo*.
HABITAT Sandy wastes.
RANGE From prairies through Great Lakes to Atlantic and Gulf coasts. Declining.
MOVEMENTS Migrates to winter on south Atlantic and Gulf Coasts.
BREEDING Frequents sandy shorelines of sea and large inland lakes; May-June.
NEST AND EGGS A shallow scrape, with a few largely decorative stems, serves as a nest; the 4 eggs are pale buff, lightly spotted black.
INCUBATION Lasts for 27 to 31 days and is shared by both sexes.
COMMENT In all cases this plover is intolerant of vegetation and soon abandons sites once colonized by plants. This is an endangered species.

KILLDEER

Charadrius vociferus   9−11in/23−28cm

IDENTIFICATION Common and widespread plover of fields and grasslands. Easily picked out by black face pattern and double, black breast bands. Rusty rump and pointed tail most visible in flight.

VOICE *Kill-dee*, repeated.

HABITAT Fields and grasslands.

RANGE Breeds throughout US and temperate Canada.

MOVEMENTS Leaves northern and central parts of range in winter.

BREEDING An inland plover that frequents bare or closely cropped fields, shores and grasslands; April-June.

NEST AND EGGS A depression is lined with a few pieces of vegetation and perhaps small stones; the 4 eggs are pale buffy blotched with black.

INCUBATION 24 to 26 days shared between the male and female.

COMMENT This is one of the first birds to return to the interior at the end of the winter and frequently begins courtship while there is still snow on the ground.

BREEDING Frequents dry prairies during the breeding season; May-June.

NEST AND EGGS A shallow depression among grassland; the 3 eggs are greenish buff, spotted black.

INCUBATION Lasts 29 days and is shared by both sexes.

COMMENT Drastic decline in numbers due to intensive cultivation of the prairies.

AMERICAN OYSTERCATCHER

Haematopus palliatus   17−21in/43−53cm

IDENTIFICATION Large, chunky, pied shorebird, black above and white below. Shows bold, white wing-bar in flight. Long, thick bill is red; strong legs are pink.

MOUNTAIN PLOVER

Charadrius montanus   8−9½in/20−24cm

IDENTIFICATION Brown plover with white underparts in summer. Sandy smudges at sides of breast, black crown, white forehead and eyebrow are main features. In winter, face and breast are washed sandy. White wing-bar and tail margins in flight.

VOICE *Krrr* in flight.

HABITAT Grassy plains at altitude.

RANGE Breeds in US east Rockies to western Nebraska.

MOVEMENTS Moves southward to winter, but regular as far north as southern California.

VOICE Loud *kleep*.

HABITAT Mud flats, shorelines.

RANGE Breeds from New England southwards along Atlantic coast and at a few spots on the Gulf coast.

MOVEMENTS Leaves northern coasts in winter.

BREEDING Frequents coastlines and breeds on open beaches; April-May.

NEST AND EGGS The nest is a bare scrape above high water mark; the 3 eggs are buffy, spotted and blotched with black.

INCUBATION Male and female share the 22 to 24 days that the eggs take to hatch.

COMMENT The US bird's close relative, the European Oystercatcher, has prospered under protection and colonized inland areas in northern Britain. Will the American Oystercatcher follow suit?

BLACK OYSTERCATCHER

Haematopus bachmani   17−17½in/43−45cm

IDENTIFICATION All-black shorebird of stout build, with large, red bill and pink legs.

VOICE Loud *wee-wee-wee*.

HABITAT Rocky shorelines.

RANGE Pacific coast from Alaska to Baja California.

MOVEMENTS Resident.

BREEDING Even in the breeding season this remains a bird of rocky shorelines; May-June.

NEST AND EGGS A depression on either an open beach or bare rock; the 2 or 3 eggs are buff, spotted black.

INCUBATION Lasts 26 or 27 days and is shared between the pair.

COMMENT A resident, Pacific coast speciality that is unmistakable.

BLACK-NECKED STILT

Himantopus himantopus   13−16in/33−41cm

IDENTIFICATION Extremely long-legged wader; black above, white below with long neck and needle-like bill. Pink legs trail in flight.

VOICE Loud repeated *keep-keep*.

HABITAT Fresh and saline pools and shallow marshes.

RANGE Western US and, in the south, along the Gulf coast through Florida to mid-Atlantic states.

MOVEMENTS Migrant, but winters California; Gulf states in east.

BREEDING Frequents shallow, often alkaline, waters where it forms loose colonies; April-June.

NEST AND EGGS Often a substantial structure on a small island; the 4 eggs are buffy, spotted blackish.

INCUBATION Lasts for 25 or 26 days and is shared by male and female.

COMMENT These birds virtually collapse on to their nests as their long legs buckle under them during incubation.

AMERICAN AVOCET

Recurvirostra americana   16–20in/41–51cm

IDENTIFICATION Slim, elegant shorebird with long, blue legs and black, recurved bill. Feeds with side-to-side motion, sifting soft mud. Black and white plumage with rusty wash on head and neck.

VOICE Loud *kleep*.

HABITAT Fresh and saline lakes.

RANGE Breeds western half of US northward into Canada. Also mid-Atlantic coasts.

MOVEMENTS Moves to coasts in winter, southward in east.

BREEDING Frequents shorelines and the margins of alkaline lakes where it breeds colonially in April-May.

NEST AND EGGS No more than a collection of grass-stems line a shallow depression; the 3 to 5 eggs are olive, spotted dark brown.

INCUBATION Lasts 22 to 24 days and is shared between the pair.

COMMENT Formerly a more widespread breeder (to the Atlantic coast), that could expand its range again, with suitable encouragement.

GREATER YELLOWLEGS

Tringa melanoleuca   12½–15in/32–38cm

IDENTIFICATION Mottled black and white above to produce a gray impression; white below with some streaking on neck and breast. Long, thickish, slightly upturned bill; long, yellow legs. In flight, shows uniform wing, white rump and trailing legs. *See* Lesser Yellowlegs.

VOICE Loud *keu-keu-keu*.

HABITAT Breeds between boreal and tundra zones – taiga; winters, fresh marshes, lakes.

RANGE Breeds in band from southern Alaska to Newfoundland.

MOVEMENTS Winters across southern US and along all three coasts, southward to South America.

BREEDING Bogs and marshes among northern forests; May-June.

NEST AND EGGS A well-lined scrape in a marsh or among woodland debris; the 4 eggs are buffy, spotted brown.

INCUBATION About 21 days by the female, though the male may also participate.

COMMENT Surprisingly little is known of this common bird's breeding routines.

LESSER YELLOWLEGS

Tringa flavipes   9½–11in/24–28cm

IDENTIFICATION Superficially similar to Greater Yellowlegs, but much more lightly and more elegantly built. Gray above, white below, but with proportionately shorter, pencil-thin, straight bill. Legs yellow and proportionately longer. Uniform wing and white rump in flight.

VOICE *Yoo-yoo*.

HABITAT Tundra and taiga marshes and bogs in summer; winters fresh marshes.

RANGE More northerly than Greater Yellowlegs from Alaska and Canadian Arctic to Hudson Bay.

MOVEMENTS Winters California, Gulf coast and Florida southward.

BREEDING Open marshes in conifer forests; June-July.

NEST AND EGGS Hollow lined with stems among forest debris; the 4 eggs are buffy, spotted with brown.

INCUBATION By both parents for about 20 days.

COMMENT As with the Greater Yellowlegs, the nesting routine is poorly known.

SOLITARY SANDPIPER

Tringa solitaria   8–8½in/20–22cm

IDENTIFICATION A bird of ponds and streams rather than open marshes and estuaries. Taller, slimmer and more elegant than Spotted Sandpiper. Upperparts very dark, liberally

spotted white. Streaked on sides of neck, breast, and lightly barred on flanks. Long neck, rounded head, medium-length, thin bill. Legs long and black, trail beyond tail in flight. Dark rump, black and white barred tail and uniform dark wings show in flight. Has bold white eye ring.

VOICE *Weet-weet-weet*.

HABITAT Ponds, streams, breeds on boggy pools.

RANGE Mainly boreal zone from Alaska across Canada.

MOVEMENTS Winters southward in Central and South America.

BREEDING Margins of lakes and marshes in wooded country are the breeding zone; June-July.

NEST AND EGGS The disused nest of a tree-nesting species is re-used; the 4 eggs are greenish buffy, spotted brown.

INCUBATION The eggs take 28 days to hatch. The female is thought to perform the incubation.

COMMENT Uses the nests of birds as variable as Cedar Waxwing, Grackle and American Robin, though few are actually found.

WILLET

Catoptrophorus semipalmatus   14–17in/36–43cm

IDENTIFICATION A large gray shorebird that is heavily barred and streaked in summer, but gray and white in winter. Strong, gray legs and long, somewhat thickly-based bill give an impression of solidity. Black and white wings diagnostic at all times.

VOICE *Pee-wee-wee*.

HABITAT Damp grasslands and pond shores; winters on lagoons, estuaries.

RANGE Breeds in central Rockies and northern prairies into Canada. Also eastern and Gulf coasts.

MOVEMENTS Migrates to all temperate coasts to winter and into South America.

BREEDING From estuarine marshes to interior lakes and marshes; May-June.

NEST AND EGGS A hollow lined with stems; the 4 eggs are buffy olive, spotted brown.

INCUBATION By both sexes, for 22 days.

COMMENT A large and conspicuous bird that is surprisingly little-known on its breeding grounds.

MOVEMENTS Migrates to winter around Pacific including California.

BREEDING Fond of hilly streams and adjacent grassy fields; June-July.

NEST AND EGGS On shingle island lined with grasses; 4 olive green eggs, spotted brown.

INCUBATION Both sexes participate for a 24-day incubation period.

COMMENT Few nests of this Arctic breeding species have been described.

SPOTTED SANDPIPER

Actitis macularia   7½in/19cm

IDENTIFICATION Brown above, white below, evenly spotted with black in summer. In winter, underparts are white and best field mark is wedge of white between breast and wing. Bobs body continuously, flies low on jerky wings.

WANDERING TATTLER

Heteroscelus incanus   10½–11½in/27–29cm

IDENTIFICATION In summer this is a gray bird, uniform above, heavily barred below. In winter the barring disappears and the breast and flanks are gray, the belly white. At all seasons the legs are yellow, the bill medium and thick based. In flight, the upperparts show no wing bar or tail pattern.

VOICE Rapid whistles.

HABITAT Breeds mountains; winters, rocky shorelines.

RANGE Mountains of Alaska.

VOICE High-pitched *weet-weet*.

HABITAT Running streams, ponds, lakesides, marshes.

RANGE Breeds over most of North America except extreme tundra and all southern US.

MOVEMENTS Winters Florida, Texas and California southwards.

BREEDING Frequents the margins of tumbling streams and other freshwater areas; April-June.

NEST AND EGGS A depression, thinly lined with vegetation and usually not too far from water; the 4 eggs are buff, spotted brown.

INCUBATION The eggs take 20 to 22 days to hatch and the male performs most of the incubation.

COMMENT Though decidedly territorial, bare river islands will often attract many pairs to nest in close proximity.

UPLAND SANDPIPER

Bartramia longicauda   11–12½in/28–32cm

IDENTIFICATION A shorebird that is most at home on grassland. Streaked brown and black above, streaked and arrowed brown below, with contrasting white belly. Long yellow legs, long thin neck with curiously emaciated look to head. Medium-length, thin bill and long, wedge-shaped tail. The shape, buffy coloration and habitat preference make this an easily identified bird.

VOICE *Quip-ip-ip-ip*.

HABITAT Grasslands.

RANGE From Alaska through prairies eastwards to the Great Lakes, the Mid-West and infrequently to north-eastern states.

MOVEMENTS Leaves North America to winter.

BREEDING Grassy upland areas including meadows and prairies; May-June.

NEST AND EGGS A well-hidden depression lined with grasses; the 4 pale buffy eggs are spotted brown.

INCUBATION Lasts 21 days by both male and female.

COMMENT Formerly called Upland Plover, a name that reflects its habits and habitats rather than its relationships.

WHIMBREL

Numenius phaeopus   15–17in/39–43cm

IDENTIFICATION Large shorebird with striped crown and longish, decurved bill. Similar to Long-billed Curlew, but smaller, shorter bill curves more toward the tip. Rare Bristle-thighed Curlew of west Alaska is very similar but has rusty rump.

VOICE Seven high-pitched whistles form a trill.

HABITAT Tundra, shorelines and marshes in winter.

RANGE Breeds coastal Alaska and Canadian Arctic.

MOVEMENTS Migrates mostly along coasts to winter in California, south Atlantic and Gulf coasts.

BREEDING Tundra and the margins of freshwater marshes are the breeding grounds of this species; May-July.

NEST AND EGGS A hollow or heart of a marshy tussock is lined with vegetation; the 4 eggs are olive green, blotched with brown.

INCUBATION The eggs are incubated for 27 or 28 days by both sexes.

COMMENT Very much a northern breeder, but a long-distance migrant through much of North America.

LONG-BILLED CURLEW

Numenius americanus   20—26in/51—66cm

IDENTIFICATION Unmistakable, large, brown shorebird with huge, decurved bill. Young birds have shorter bills. Cinnamon underwing is diagnostic.

VOICE Clear *coo-lee*.

HABITAT Prairies in summer; winters on estuaries, shorelines.

RANGE Western states from high plateaux to upland prairies extending northward into Canada and south to Texas.

MOVEMENTS Migrates south to western Gulf coast and California.

BREEDING A grassland species that is equally at home on prairie or in mountain valleys; May-June.

NEST AND EGGS A depression is variably lined with grasses; the 4 eggs are olive brown, spotted with darker markings.

INCUBATION Is shared between members of the pair and lasts 28 days.

COMMENT Though solitary when nesting, outside the breeding season these birds, like so many other shorebirds, are highly gregarious.

HUDSONIAN GODWIT

Limosa haemastica   14—15in/36—39cm

IDENTIFICATION Smaller than Marbled Godwit and marked at all times by black and white rump and tail pattern, and white wing-bar. In summer, chestnut breast is closely barred black. In winter, is brown above and buff below. Bar-tailed Godwit, which breeds in Alaska, occasionally seen along both US coasts, shows black and white banded tail.

VOICE *Quit-quit*.

HABITAT High Arctic tundra, estuaries in winter.

RANGE Northernmost Canada and Alaska to western shores of Hudson Bay.

MOVEMENTS Passes out over Atlantic on way to South American wintering grounds. Returns via Central Flyway.

BREEDING Spends the summer on the tundra, usually adjacent to a lake or marsh; June-July.

NEST AND EGGS An unlined scrape beneath dwarf vegetation or in a marshy tussock; the 4 eggs are olive, spotted brown.

INCUBATION Both sexes incubate and 22 to 24 days are required before the eggs hatch.

COMMENT Little is really known about the breeding of this highly localized, Arctic bird.

BAR-TAILED GODWIT

Limosa lapponica   14−16in/35−41cm

IDENTIFICATION In summer, head and underparts rich chestnut. In other plumages, heavily streaked above, buffy on breast, whitish below. Relatively short-legged compared with other godwits and bill distinctly uptilted. In flight shows barred tail.

VOICE Harsh *kerrick* repeated.

RANGE Breeds western Alaska.

MOVEMENTS Occasional along Pacific coast; rare on Atlantic coast.

MARBLED GODWIT

Limosa fedoa   16−20in/41−51cm

IDENTIFICATION Large, long-billed, long-legged shorebird. Brown, spangled with black and white above; buff, barred brown below. Long, pinkish bill, tipped black and slightly uptilted. Legs gray, trail in flight. No prominent marks in flight. *See* Hudsonian Godwit.

VOICE *Kar-rack*.

HABITAT Grasslands; in winter, near coasts or along shorelines.

RANGE Prairies of US-Canada border.

MOVEMENTS Migrates southward to winter in California, south Atlantic and Gulf coasts.

BREEDING Frequents lakes in dry prairie country; May-June.

NEST AND EGGS A depression lined with grass may be at variable distances from water; the 3 to 5 eggs are buffy, lightly spotted brown.

INCUBATION 22 days, shared by both sexes.

COMMENT During the period of breeding these birds are largely insectivorous, but change to a diet of aquatic animals in late June.

RUDDY TURNSTONE

Arenaria interpres   8½−9½in/22−24cm

IDENTIFICATION Stocky wader, found only along shorelines, with short bill and stone-turning habits. In summer, has a "harlequin" "face" pattern in black and white with rich-chestnut and black wings. In winter, smudgy "face" pattern and grayish upperparts; legs, short and red. In flight, shows white "braces" and wing-bar.

VOICE Sharp *tuk-a-tuk*.

HABITAT Rocky and muddy coasts; breeds on tundra islands.

RANGE Far northern Canada and archipelago and coastal Alaska.

MOVEMENTS Winters on all coasts of US.

BREEDING Coastal tundra and islands with marshy pools; June-July.

NEST AND EGGS A scrape on the ground with little or no lining; 4 olive-green eggs are blotched with brown.

INCUBATION The eggs hatch after 21−23 days and are incubated by both sexes, though mainly the female.

COMMENT A true globe-spanner that, at one time of the year or another, can be found along virtually every coastline in the world.

BLACK TURNSTONE

Arenaria melanocephala   8½–9½in/22–24cm

IDENTIFICATION Similar in size, shape and habits to Ruddy Turnstone, but essentially a western bird. In summer, black above, white below with white spot between eye and bill. Dull-sooty above in winter with uniform face. Boldly black and white in flight.

VOICE As Ruddy Turnstone but higher.

HABITAT Tundra coasts in summer; rocky coasts in winter.

RANGE Breeds western coastal Alaska.

MOVEMENTS Winters Pacific coasts.

BREEDING Confined to the coastline throughout the year; June-July.

NEST AND EGGS Scrape on ground; 4 white eggs.

INCUBATION By both sexes, for 21 days.

COMMENT Much remains to discover about this species, though it is generally thought its breeding cycle closely resembles that of the more widespread Ruddy Turnstone.

SURFBIRD

Aphriza virgata   9½–10in/24–26cm

IDENTIFICATION Robust, short-billed shorebird of rocky coastlines. Always appears plump with short, orange bill, tipped black, and short, yellow legs. In summer is heavily spotted above and below. In winter, much duller with uniform gray 'face' and breast, like Purple Sandpiper. In flight, shows very bold, white wing-bar and white tail with black terminal band.

VOICE Whistle of three notes.

HABITAT Tundra mountains.

RANGE Breeds interior Alaska and neighboring Canada.

MOVEMENTS Winters along Pacific coast.

BREEDING Mountain slopes above tree line; June-July.

NEST AND EGGS A bare hollow on rocky ground with scant vegetation; the 4 eggs are buffy with large black spots.

INCUBATION Probably by both sexes.

COMMENT The first nest of this species was found only in 1926 and its breeding biology remains one of the least known in North America.

RED KNOT

Calidris canutus   9½–10½in/24–27cm

IDENTIFICATION Stocky shorebird that may occur in large numbers at favored sites. In summer, underparts are pure chestnut. In winter, gray above, white below rather like large, rotund, short-billed Dunlin.

VOICE Dull *nut*.

HABITAT Arctic tundra; winters on shorelines and estuaries.

RANGE Central Canadian archipelago.

MOVEMENTS Winters coasts of California, Gulf coast, Florida and Atlantic.

BREEDING High Arctic tundra with strong growth of dwarf ground cover; June-July.

NEST AND EGGS A substantial cup of twigs and grasses in a depression in marshy or dry tundra; the 4 eggs are buffy, spotted brown.

INCUBATION Lasts 20 to 25 days and is shared by both members of the pair.

COMMENT Though restricted in its breeding range, this chunky shorebird is abundant in winter at favored estuaries.

SANDERLING

Calidris alba   7 ½–8½in/19–22cm

IDENTIFICATION A neat little shorebird, most often seen in small flocks running up and down beaches following the movements of the surf. In winter, pale gray plumage with black at bend of wing is diagnostic. In summer, rich chestnut head, back and breast are heavily spotted black. Shortish, black bill.

VOICE Rippling, *kip-kip*.

HABITAT Tundra; sandy beaches in winter.

RANGE Canadian archipelago.

MOVEMENTS Winters along all coasts.

BREEDING Tundra hills and dry rocky areas; June-July.

NEST AND EGGS A neat hollow on the ground lined with grass; the 4 eggs are olive green, spotted with brown.

INCUBATION This is shared by members of the pair and takes 23 or 24 days.

COMMENT One of the most northerly breeders of all birds, nests as far north as there is ice-free land.

SEMIPALMATED SANDPIPER

Calidris pusilla   5½–6in/14–16cm

IDENTIFICATION Common, small, shorebird with partially webbed feet that are virtually impossible to see in the field. Short, straight bill with thick base and blunt tip. Upperparts with feathers edged buff to create a regular, uniform pattern. This latter feature is important when comparing with easily confused Western Sandpiper.

VOICE An abrupt *chirk*.

HABITAT Tundra; on passage, marshes, pools, sheltered bays.

RANGE Breeds northern Alaska across Canada to Labrador.

MOVEMENTS Passes through center and east coast on way to South America to winter.

BREEDING Occupies a wide variety of tundra habitats; June-July.

NEST AND EGGS A hollow, lined with grasses and leaves, in a marshy tussock or ridge; the 4 eggs are creamy white, spotted and blotched in shades of brown.

INCUBATION The eggs take 18 or 19 days to hatch and are incubated by both members of the pair.

COMMENT North America's most abundant shorebird over most of its range.

WESTERN SANDPIPER

Calidris mauri   6−6½in/15.5−17cm

IDENTIFICATION Of all the "peep" (small sandpipers) this is the longest legged and longest billed, but it is still easy to confuse with the Semipalmated Sandpiper. In summer, this bird has chestnut on crown, ear coverts and back and is marked by extensive streaking on breast with "arrow-like" markings on sides of neck and flanks. Juvenile has chestnut on scapulars and an irregular feather pattern on folded wings: compare with uniform, scaly upperparts of Semipalmated Sandpiper. Also has less pronounced eyebrow.

VOICE High-pitched *jeet*.

HABITAT Breeds tundra; winters marshes, bays.

RANGE Breeds north and west coastal Alaska.

MOVEMENTS Winters all southern coasts, often common on passage.

BREEDING Moist tundra with marshes and bogs; May-June.

NEST AND EGGS A hollow, lined with grasses, is situated in a variety of areas from marshes to dry, grassy slopes; the 4 eggs are creamy, blotched brown.

INCUBATION The eggs take 21 days to hatch and are incubated by both members of the pair.

COMMENT Very similar to Semipalmated Sandpiper and only separated from that species a little over a hundred years ago.

RUFOUS-NECKED STINT

Calidris ruficollis   6−6 ½in/16cm

IDENTIFICATION Tiny, peep-like shorebird marked in summer by rufous on sides of face and neck. Similar to Semipalmated Sandpiper and European Little Stint outside breeding plumage. Dark legs.

VOICE A sharp *prip*.

HABITAT Shores and tidal flats.

RANGE Irregular breeder on west coast of Alaska.

MOVEMENTS Migrates westward through Asia; rare anywhere south of Alaska.

LEAST SANDPIPER

Calidris minutilla   5−5½in/13.5−14.5cm

IDENTIFICATION Tiny sandpiper with short, thin bill slightly downcurved and yellow legs: the latter may be muddy and appear dark. In summer and winter, breast-streaking forms a band; juvenile has buffy breast with streaking at sides. Upperparts with rich, buffy feather margins; hint of pale inverted "V" on back.

VOICE High-pitched *kreep*.

HABITAT Tundra; on passage and, in winter, marshes, pools, lagoons.

RANGE In summer from Alaska across Arctic Canada to Labrador.

MOVEMENTS On passage throughout North America to winter through southern states and along all coasts.

BREEDING Northern marshes or bogs with extensive growth of emergent vegetation; June-July.

NEST AND EGGS A hollow lined with grasses and leaves; the 4 creamy eggs are spotted in shades of brown.

INCUBATION The eggs take 19−22 days to hatch and the male plays the largest role in incubation.

COMMENT One of the few "peeps" (along with Western Sandpiper) that can be found wintering in the U.S.A.

WHITE-RUMPED SANDPIPER

Calidris fuscicollis   6–7in/16–18cm

IDENTIFICATION A little shorebird with shortish, black legs and short, straight bill. Slimline accentuated by long wings projecting beyond tail. Generally grayish, with streaking on breast extending as "arrowheads" along flanks, particularly in breeding plumage. Juvenile has chestnut wash on back and crown. In flight shows white rump.

VOICE Shrill *jeet*.

HABITAT Tundra; passage and winters, marshes and estuaries.

RANGE Northern and archipelago coasts of Alaska and Canada.

MOVEMENTS Moves mainly south and east to winter in South America.

BREEDING Marshes and swamps with emergent vegetation in tundra; June-July.

NEST AND EGGS A shallow depression is lined with a few grasses and often located in a marshy tussock; the 4 eggs are olive green, blotched with brown.

INCUBATION Probably entirely by the female for a period of 21 days.

COMMENT In spring, this sandpiper migrates mainly through the interior; in fall, it will move south over the Atlantic. It is uncommon elsewhere.

VOICE Harsh *kreep*.

HABITAT Tundra; on passage or marshes and pond-edges.

RANGE Breeds northern Alaska and Canada, extending northward into the archipelago.

MOVEMENTS Migrates mainly through the Central Flyway to South America.

BREEDING Tundra ridges, usually on dry ground; June-July.

NEST AND EGGS A cup of grasses and leaves well hidden on the ground; the 4, occasionally 3, eggs are buff, spotted brown.

INCUBATION Lasts 21 days and is shared between the sexes.

COMMENT Despite being relatively uncommon on the east coast, this is one of the more regular vagrants to Europe in autumn.

BAIRD'S SANDPIPER

Calidris bairdii   6½–7½in/17–19cm

IDENTIFICATION A short-legged and billed sandpiper with long wings accentuating slim, elongated appearance. In all plumages, warm, buffy wash over scaly upperparts and streaked breast creates impression of a "brown" rather than "gray" bird.

PECTORAL SANDPIPER

Calidris melanotos   7–8½in/18–21cm

IDENTIFICATION Stocky shorebird marked by large, plump body with short, thin neck and small head and shortish, orange-yellow legs. In all plumages, shape, plus uniformly streaked neck and breast ending abruptly to form clear-cut pectoral band, are best field marks. The Sharp-tailed Sandpiper from Siberia, seen along Pacific coast and rarely in the east in fall, has brighter eyebrows and no well-defined breast-ending.

VOICE Far carrying *kreet*.

HABITAT Summer tundra; passage and winter fresh marshes, pond margins.

RANGE Breeds northern coasts of Alaska and Canada.

MOVEMENTS Mainly a migrant, especially on east coast. Winters South America.

BREEDING Tundra, mainly coastal marshes with plentiful low vegetation; May-June.

NEST AND EGGS A well-constructed cup of grasses hidden in a tussock or beneath dwarf vegetation; the 4 eggs are greenish, blotched with brown.

INCUBATION The eggs hatch after 21 to 23 days of incubation by the female.

COMMENT The species' south-easterly orientation in autumn takes it out over the Atlantic and makes it particularly prone to transatlantic vagrancy.

SHARP-TAILED SANDPIPER

Calidris acuminata   8−9in/20−23cm

IDENTIFICATION Very similar to Pectoral Sandpiper, but separated by less clear-cut, streaked breast band and virtual absence of streaking in juvenile.

VOICE Double whistle.

HABITAT Tidal grassy areas, shores.

RANGE Regular in fall Alaska.

MOVEMENTS Migrant from Asia, scarce along Pacific coast; very rare elsewhere.

PURPLE SANDPIPER

Calidris maritima   8−8½in/20−22cm

IDENTIFICATION A rocky coast shorebird that is easily overlooked in dull winter plumage. In summer is heavily spotted above and below with short, orange legs and orange-based bill. In winter, foreparts more uniform gray

with spotting below. At all times dumpy shape is important feature.

VOICE Quiet *wut-wut*.

HABITAT Tundra in summer; winters rocky coasts.

RANGE Breeds central Canadian tundra.

MOVEMENTS Winters east coast as far south as Carolinas.

BREEDING Coastal and mountain tundra with open shorelines nearby; June-July.

NEST AND EGGS A hollow, lined with leaves, serves as a nest; the 4 eggs are greenish, blotched with brown.

INCUBATION The eggs hatch after 21 or 22 days and are incubated mainly by the male.

COMMENT The construction of harbor walls and jetties has enabled this rocky coastline specialist to occupy otherwise unsuitable coastlines.

ROCK SANDPIPER

Calidris ptilocnemis   8½−9½in/22−24cm

IDENTIFICATION The western equivalent of the east coast Purple Sandpiper. In summer, spots boldly merging on lower breast to form "Dunlin-type" patch. In winter, head and breast uniformly dull gray.

VOICE Repeated *ticker*.

HABITAT Breeds tundra; winters rocky shores.

RANGE Breeds western Alaska.

MOVEMENTS Winters west coasts as far south as northern California.

BREEDING Breeds along tundra and Arctic shorelines; June-July.

NEST AND EGGS A simple hollow with a little lining; the 4 eggs are olive, blotched with brown.

INCUBATION 20 days by both members of the pair.

COMMENT Though published, the breeding data needs to be checked.

DUNLIN

Calidris alpina   6−7½in/16−19cm

IDENTIFICATION Stocky little shorebird marked by black belly in summer. In winter, gray above, white below with streaking on breast. In all plumages relatively long, slightly decurved bill tip are good features. Juvenile is warm-buffy above and on breast, but is always streaked.

VOICE Nasal *tree*.

HABITAT Breeds tundra; passage and winter coastal marshes, shorelines, estuaries.

RANGE Alaskan and Canadian tundra east to Hudson Bay.

MOVEMENTS Winters all coasts.

BREEDING Frequents hillsides, moors, bogs, tundra and even quite temperate coastal marshes in some areas; May-July.

NEST AND EGGS A hollow lined with grasses; the 4 greenish eggs are spotted brown.

INCUBATION The eggs take 21 or 22 days to hatch and are incubated by both members of the pair.

COMMENT This species breeds right around the northern polar region and is, in many areas, the most abundant of the shorebirds.

CURLEW SANDPIPER

Calidris ferruginea   7−8in/18−20cm

IDENTIFICATION Rich chestnut in breeding plumage; mottled buffs on migration, gray in winter. This is a slim and elegant *Calidris* with long neck and long, decurved bill, quite unlike the dumpy character of other species. A white rump separates from all but White-rumped Sandpiper.

VOICE *Churrip*.

HABITAT Tidal flats, shorelines.

RANGE Scarce, mainly east coast.

MOVEMENTS Eurasian breeder from Siberia.

STILT SANDPIPER

Calidris himantopus   8−8½in/20−22cm

IDENTIFICATION In summer, brown above with heavily and completely barred underparts. Also chestnut ear coverts. In winter, is gray above and white below with light eyebrow. At all times, long, grayish legs and long, slightly drooping bill are useful, giving the bird a peculiar, if not unique, shape. White rump shows in flight.

VOICE *Tu-tu.*

HABITAT Tundra in summer; freshwater shores in winter.

RANGE Breeds on central Canadian and Alaskan tundra.

MOVEMENTS Migrates mainly through plains. Winters South America, though small numbers remain in southern part of California, Texas and Florida.

BREEDING Frequents tundra, especially lake and pond margins and marshes; June-July.

NEST AND EGGS A shallow depression, thinly lined with grasses and moss; the 4 creamy-buff eggs are spotted brown.

INCUBATION By both sexes, for about 20 days.

COMMENT The remoteness of the breeding grounds accounts for the lack of definite knowledge of this species' breeding routines.

BUFF-BREASTED SANDPIPER

Tryngites subruficollis   7½–8½in/19–21cm

IDENTIFICATION Uniformly warm-buff underparts and plain face pick this bird out easily. Upperparts darkly streaked, thin bill, yellow legs.

VOICE *Preet.*

HABITAT Breeds tundra, passage and winter on short-grass meadows and fields.

RANGE Breeds only north Canadian Arctic west of Hudson Bay to north-east Alaska.

MOVEMENTS Migrant through Great Plains. A few reach either coast in fall.

BREEDING Though a grassland bird, during the breeding season this is a dry or wet tundra species; June-July.

NEST AND EGGS A shallow depression lined with grasses is the nest; the 4 eggs are dull creamy, spotted with brown.

INCUBATION By female.

COMMENT A high Arctic breeder that is well known on migration, but whose life history remains something of a mystery.

RUFF

Philomachus pugnax   10–12in/25–30cm

IDENTIFICATION Summer male has ruff of feathers around head and neck that vary in color. At other times resembles female. Small head and long neck reminiscent of Upland Sandpiper, but underparts plain buff and upperparts with distinctive pattern of pale edges to feathers. Medium length bill, long legs yellow, orange or red.

VOICE *Chuck-uck.*

HABITAT Freshwater or brackish marshes.

RANGE Erratic breeder Alaska.

MOVEMENTS Eurasian species that rarely wanders to mainly North American coasts.

SHORT-BILLED DOWITCHER

Limnodromus griseus   10–12in/26–30cm

IDENTIFICATION Very similar to Long-billed Dowitcher and to be distinguished at all seasons with the greatest of care. These are chunky, large-bodied waders that have long, straight bills and feed with a vigorous probing motion. In summer they are spangled chestnut and black above; chestnut with spots (Short-billed) or bars (Long-billed) below. Short-billed has lighter chestnut belly. The length of bill is of little value in the field and there is considerable overlap. In flight, both species show a narrow, white wing-bar on the secondaries and a white "V" extending up the rump. Both have green legs. The Short-billed has a white tail with dark bars, lighter than the Long-billed.

VOICE Melodic *tu-tu-tu*.

HABITAT Boreal marshes; winters, estuaries.

RANGE Breeds south coastal Alaska, central northern Canada.

MOVEMENTS Winters all coasts southward of Oregon and Virginia.

BREEDING Marshy areas of conifer forests and dwarf vegetation; June-July.

NEST AND EGGS A hollow lined with grass and moss in a marsh; the 4 eggs are olive, spotted with brown.

INCUBATION The eggs are incubated for probably 21 days by the female and possibly also by the male.

COMMENT Though its breeding distribution is poorly known, there are three clear-cut subspecies distributed across North America.

LONG-BILLED DOWITCHER

Limnodromus scolopaceus   10½–12½in/27–32cm

IDENTIFICATION A chunky, long-billed shorebird, very similar to Short-billed Dowitcher. For distinctions see that species. Generally darker, with a darker tail than that bird.

VOICE Shrill *keek*.

HABITAT Tundra bogs; winters found more often on fresh marshes than Short-billed Dowitcher.

RANGE Breeds western Alaska and adjacent north coast of Canada.

MOVEMENTS Winters, coastal US south from Washington and North Carolina.

BREEDING Found only on northern tundra marshes; June-July.

NEST AND EGGS Depression, lined with grasses and moss; 4 creamy-buff eggs, spotted brown.

INCUBATION By both sexes, though mostly the male, for 20 days.

COMMENT Very little is known about the breeding of this species in its extreme north tundra habitat.

COMMON SNIPE

Gallinago gallinago   10–10½in/25–27cm

IDENTIFICATION Highly camouflaged marshland bird, heavily streaked in brown, black and buff with bold, double "V" in cream on back. Long, straight bill is probed vigorously while feeding. When flushed, towers with zig-zag flight into the air. Nuptial flight consists of series of aerial dives with stiff outertail feathers vibrating to produce a bleeting sound.

VOICE Harsh *scarp*.

HABITAT Wide variety of marshes.

RANGE Throughout Alaska and Canada, except northernmost tundra, southward through northern US.

MOVEMENTS Winters in east, west and southern states.

BREEDING Marshes, moors and damp, neglected fields; April-June.

NEST AND EGGS A neat cup of grasses is constructed among marshside grass; the 4 eggs are buffy brown with extensive brown markings.

INCUBATION Lasts 18 to 20 days and is said to be by both sexes.

COMMENT The same species occurs in Europe where incubation is performed solely by the female.

AMERICAN WOODCOCK

Scolopax minor   6–11in/16–28cm

IDENTIFICATION A rotund, round-winged bird that is found in moist woodlands. Most often seen when flushed, or at dawn and dusk in spring when performing its nuptial flight. Chunky shape with rounded wings and long, straight, downward-pointing bill are best features. If seen in daylight, black bars on crown and streaked, black back contrast with brown wings. Highly camouflaged.

VOICE A repeated *peent*.

HABITAT Damp woods.

RANGE Eastern half of US and adjacent Canada.

MOVEMENTS Abandons northern half of US range.

BREEDING Forests with open glades and boggy places; April-June.

NEST AND EGGS A simple depression is variably lined with dead leaves; the 4 eggs are a warm-buff, lightly spotted brown.

INCUBATION The eggs take 19 to 21 days to hatch and are incubated by the female.

COMMENT Often seen in spectacular display flights at dusk and dawn in springtime.

WILSON'S PHALAROPE

Phalaropus tricolor   8½–10in/22–26cm

IDENTIFICATION Less inclined to swim than other phalaropes. In summer, female has bold chestnut "S" extending from the eye, along the side of the neck to trail over the back. Male is similar, but duller and darker. In winter, pale gray above, white below with thin, needle-like bill 1½ times length of head. No black comma behind eye as in other phalaropes.

VOICE A croak.

HABITAT Marshes.

RANGE Breeds over much of western North America extending eastward through Great Lakes and increasing in eastern Canada.

MOVEMENTS Winters in South America, moving southward mainly along west coast.

BREEDING Frequents marshes and shallow lakes with some emergent vegetation; May-June.

NEST AND EGGS A variably lined hollow; the 4 eggs are creamy-buff, blotched with dark brown.

INCUBATION The eggs take some 20 days to hatch and are incubated totally by the male.

COMMENT The least aquatic of the three phalaropes.

RED-NECKED PHALAROPE

Phalaropus lobatus   6½−7½in/17−19cm

IDENTIFICATION Small, delicate phalarope. In summer, gray with white chin and red neck patch. In winter, gray, with black comma behind eye. Shortish, needle-like bill. Juvenile much darker above.
VOICE Quiet *tit*.
HABITAT Tundra pool; winters at sea.
RANGE Alaskan and Canadian tundra.
MOVEMENTS Migrates along coasts to winter at sea.
BREEDING Shallow lakes and their margins beyond the tree-line; May-June.
NEST AND EGGS A hollow is lined with grass and leaves situated near a lake or marsh; the 4 eggs are greenish buff, spotted with brown.
INCUBATION Incubation lasts 18 or 21 days and is entirely by the male.
COMMENT The typical spinning phalarope of the northern marshes of summer.

RED PHALAROPE

Phalaropus fulicaria   7½−8½in/19−21cm

IDENTIFICATION A swimming shorebird that spends the winter at sea. In summer, rich chestnut underparts and white "face" preclude confusion. In winter, gray above, white below with dark comma extending from eye. Bill, thick, and yellow-based compared with other phalaropes' needle-thin ones.
VOICE High *twit*.
HABITAT Tundra, on passage along coasts; winters at sea.
RANGE Tundra coasts of Alaska, Canada and archipelago.
MOVEMENTS Mostly seen on passage wind-blown to coasts.
BREEDING Marshes and shallow lakes in the tundra, often very near the coast; June-July.
NEST AND EGGS A tussock or bank of a pond is chosen as a nest site and a hollow is lined with grasses; the 4 olive-buff eggs are spotted with brown.
INCUBATION Lasts 18 or 19 days and is by the male alone.
COMMENT The most pelagic of the three phalaropes.

Jaegers, Gulls, Terns & Skimmers

T HIS family can be divided quite neatly into three easily distinguished main groups — the gulls proper, the terns, and the jaegers. All are long-winged, masterful fliers of coastal or pelagic distribution. In fact, the layman usually refers to them as "seagulls," even though several may hardly see the sea at all during their entire lifespan.

Gulls proper are generally white bodied and gray- or black-winged birds. They are gregarious, forming huge breeding colonies, and gather in even larger winter roosts. Typical gulls, like the Herring Gull, are plunge-divers and shoreline scavengers, but over the years they have learned to exploit other food sources associated with man. As a result, many species have enjoyed a population explosion and may actually be a menace. Mostly they pose a threat to other bird species near whom they breed. The Atlantic Puffin, for example, is under threat from the huge Great Black-backed Gull wherever the two species share a breeding habitat. But gulls in number may also pose a threat to the modern jetliner, and there have been several crashes due to "bird strikes" between gulls and aircraft.

Though most gulls are coastal in origin, some are decidedly oceanic, while others are inland birds. Franklin's Gull, for example, breeds only among the marshes of the prairies, while the Black-legged Kittiwake spends its summers along sea-girt cliffs and its winters roaming the oceans. Some, like Sabine's Gull, make huge migrations to the southern hemisphere, while others, like the Western Gull, are virtually resident. The variety of gulls reflects the variety of lifestyles that they have adopted and, indeed, the variety of niches that are available to them.

The jaegers are closely related to gulls and bear a superficial resemblance to young gulls in having brown plumage. There, however, the resemblance ends, for these are fast-flying pirates that have all the power and grace of a falcon. There are four species in the northern hemisphere, plus one that visits from the south, all of which are seen regularly in North America. Though they breed on tundra marshes and feed on lemmings through the summer, their normal method of feeding involves pursuing other seabirds to make them drop or disgorge their meal. Terns are particularly prone to their attacks, but

even birds as large as a Gannet may be attacked by the huge Great Skua.

The larger species are marked by white flashes in the wing that are very distinctive, and three species have extended tail feathers which are the surest means of identification during spring and summer. Two species also occur in both a pale and a dark phase as adults.

Terns, so often the victims of jaeger attacks, are lightly built, long-winged birds that find their food over water. Mostly they are pale, with black caps and colorful bills and feet, and dive for food at sea. Others are darker and snatch food from the surface, like the noddies over the sea, or Black Tern over marshland. Terns vary greatly in size from the Least to the Caspian. While the tiny birds specialize in small fry, the larger birds can handle quite sizable fish. Both Black and Gull-billed Terns feed inland, snatching insects from water or dry land.

These are generally gregarious birds that breed in colonies. Some may be scattered along a beach, while others, like the Sandwich Tern, nest cheek by jowl, tightly packed together. In either case the scene is one of continual action and bustle. The tropical Sooty Tern often nests in enormous colonies of over a million pairs. America's largest colony is on Florida's Dry Tortugas, but there are a few others in the south.

Though placed in a separate family, the Black Skimmer bears a strong resemblance to the terns. It is a large bird, marked by a black cap and short, red legs. It is, however, black above and white below, and has an extraordinary red and black bill in which the lower mandible is longer than the upper. Its peculiar method of feeding involves skimming the water's surface with the lower mandible to strike the fish and clamp down on the prey with the upper half of the bill.

POMARINE JAEGER

Stercorarius pomarinus   17−21in/43−53cm

PARASITIC JAEGER

Stercorarius parasiticus   15−19in/38−48cm

IDENTIFICATION Summer adult has extended central tail feathers, blunt-tipped and twisted. In autumn, heavy build and, in pale phase birds, prominent breast band are best features. In all, plumages has more white in wing flashes than other jaegers.

VOICE Silent at sea.

HABITAT Tundra in summer; at sea in winter.

RANGE Breeds north coasts of Alaska, Canada and archipelago.

MOVEMENTS Moves southward along west coast, rather scarce off east coast.

BREEDING Usually among coastal tundra intersected by rivers and pools; June-July.

NEST AND EGGS An unlined hollow on a ridge; the 2 eggs are olive brown, spotted with darker brown.

INCUBATION The eggs take 26 or 28 days to hatch and are incubated by both sexes.

COMMENT This is very much an offshore migrant that is seldom seen through most of North America.

IDENTIFICATION Dark, athletic seabird that pursues other seabirds to rob them of food. In summer, adult has two extended tail feathers projecting in flight, but these are often broken by the fall. At all times this is a narrow-winged, angular jaeger that is smaller than Pomarine Jaeger and heavier than Long-tailed Jaeger. Pale phase birds have dark cap and pale underparts with ill-defined dark breast band. Dark phase birds are uniform brown. Both show white flashes in dark wings.

VOICE High-pitched *kee-ow* on breeding grounds.

HABITAT Arctic tundra; passage and winter at sea.

RANGE Breeds Alaska, northern Canada and in archipelago.

MOVEMENTS Migrates along west coast, less numerous off east coast, to winter at sea off South America.

BREEDING A variety of open tundra from marshes to stony ridges; May-June, often semi-colonial.

NEST AND EGGS A simple, unlined depression on a ridge or hillside; the 2 eggs are olive brown with variable amounts of brown blotching.

INCUBATION Lasts 24 to 28 days and is performed by both members of the pair.

COMMENT Jaegers tend to breed successfully only during years when small mammals are plentiful in the Arctic.

LONG-TAILED JAEGER

Stercorarius longicaudus   15–22in/38–56cm

IDENTIFICATION Smallest and most lightly built of the jaegers, more tern-like than others. Summer adult has long tail streamers. In fall, shows little, if any, white wing flash; but contrast between grayish upperparts and all-black flight feathers. Juvenile shows white wing flashes on under surface. At all times, size and build are best features.

VOICE Silent at sea.

HABITAT Summer, tundra; winter, sea.

RANGE Western and northern Alaska, northern Canada and archipelago; winters off South America.

MOVEMENTS Scarcest of jaegers on passage, more regular west than east coast.

BREEDING Tundra, often on dry, stony hillsides, but also beside rivers and pools; June-July.

NEST AND EGGS A simple, unlined depression on dry ground; the 2 eggs are olive, blotched with brown.

INCUBATION Lasts 23 days and is shared between the sexes.

COMMENT Totally dependant on the population of small mammals during the breeding season.

GREAT SKUA

Catharacta skua   22–24in/56–61cm

IDENTIFICATION Heavily-built, all-brown seabird with broad wings marked by bold, white flash. Body has rufous wash and is heavily streaked, creating a subtle contrast with darker, more uniformly brown wings.

VOICE Nasal *skeer*.

HABITAT Bare hills in summer; winters at sea.

RANGE Breeds in northern Europe.

MOVEMENTS Winters offshore, off east coast.

BREEDING Grassy slopes and moors at no great distance from the sea; May-June, often semi-colonial.

NEST AND EGGS An unlined hollow on dry ground; the 2 eggs are olive, spotted with brown.

INCUBATION The eggs take 28–30 days to hatch and are incubated by both sexes.

COMMENT A regular visitor to North America that has its breeding quarters in the eastern Atlantic.

SOUTH POLAR SKUA

Catharacta maccormicki   20−22in/51−56cm

IDENTIFICATION Very similar to Great Skua, but lacks streaking of that bird. Pale phase has gray head, neck and body with brown wings.
VOICE Harsh *uk*, but generally silent.
HABITAT Seas and coasts.
RANGE Scarce spring and summer visitor mostly to west coast.
MOVEMENTS Breeds Antarctic.

LAUGHING GULL

Larus atricilla   14½−16in/37−41cm

IDENTIFICATION A black-hooded gull with dark-gray upperparts and extensive black tips to wings. Bill is large, red and droopy; legs are black. A narrow, white eye-ring is present in all plumages. In winter, hood is lost and replaced by dark around eye and on hind crown. Immatures have dusky breast.

VOICE Low chuckles.
HABITAT Coasts.
RANGE Atlantic coast southward from Maine to Mexico.
MOVEMENTS Northern breeders move southward.
BREEDING Coastal marshes, estuaries and saltings; April-May, colonial.
NEST AND EGGS Grasses and other vegetation lining a hollow; the 3 eggs are olive brown, spotted with brown.
INCUBATION The eggs take about 20 days to hatch; incubation is shared between the pair.
COMMENT A coastal species that may be declining due to predation by the booming population of Herring Gulls.

FRANKLIN'S GULL

Larus pipixcan   13−14in/33−36cm

IDENTIFICATION Black-hooded, summer visitor to prairies. In summer, upperparts are slate-gray marked by a white bar and black and white wing tips. Underwing, uniform silver. Red bill and legs; bold white eye-ring. In winter, has remnant hood, particularly noticeable on ear coverts; shows white eye-ring prominently. Immatures similar to winter adult, with white breast and brownish, mottled wing. Often hawks insects in air.
VOICE High-pitched chuckle.
HABITAT Lakes and marshes.
RANGE Breeds prairies and upland grasslands.
MOVEMENTS Migrates through interior and Gulf coast; rare winter visitor there and California.
BREEDING Inland lakes and marshes with plentiful low emergent vegetation; April-May, colonial.
NEST AND EGGS A floating platform of aquatic vegetation anchored to growing marsh plants; the 3 eggs are buffish and spotted with shades of brown.
INCUBATION Lasts from 18 to 20 days and is shared by male and female.
COMMENT These highly gregarious gulls are a feature of the prairies where they consume enormous numbers of agricultural pests.

LITTLE GULL

Larus minutus   10−11in/25−28cm

IDENTIFICATION Tiny, tern-like gull that frequently feeds by picking food from the water's surface in flight. Adult has black hood, replaced by spot behind eye outside breeding season. Wings pale gray with white margins, underwing very dusky. Immatures have black "W" across wings.
VOICE Generally silent outside breeding season.
HABITAT Shores and freshwaters.
RANGE Breeds western Great Lakes.
MOVEMENTS Scarce migrant and winter visitor east coast from Europe and North American breeding range; quite rare elsewhere.

COMMON BLACK-HEADED GULL

Larus ridibundus   13−14½in/33−37cm

IDENTIFICATION Similar to Bonaparte's Gull with white fore-wing and black tips to primaries. Underwing dusky, not white, on primaries. Red bill, dirty orange-yellow with black tip in juvenile, separates from smaller, black-billed Bonaparte's.
VOICE Harsh *kee-arr*.
HABITAT Shores, docks, dumps, farmland.
RANGE Scarce winter visitor east coast, colonizing eastern Canada.
MOVEMENTS Transatlantic vagrant.

BONAPARTE'S GULL

Larus philadelphia   12−13in/30−33cm

IDENTIFICATION Smallest regular gull marked by black head in summer and black spot behind the eye in winter. In flight, shows bold white forewing, both above and below, with trailing wing edge of black primary tips. Small, black bill, short, red legs.
VOICE Chattering.
HABITAT Tundra and muskeg ponds and marshes.

RANGE In broad band from Alaska through Canada almost to the Great Lakes.
MOVEMENTS Winters, Great Lakes and all coasts of US.
BREEDING Frequents marshes, ponds and lakes among conifer forests; May-June.
NEST AND EGGS A neat cup of twigs, grasses and mosses in a tree; the 3 buffy eggs are spotted brown.
INCUBATION Takes 23 or 24 days and is apparently by the female alone, though the male may help.
COMMENT A neat and attractive little gull that is unusual in nesting in forest trees.

HEERMANN'S GULL

Larus heermanni   18−20in/46−51cm

IDENTIFICATION Dusky, west coast gull. Adult in summer is dusky on back and wings, gray below with paler neck and white head. Bill is red, tipped black; legs black. In winter, head becomes gray, streaked black.

Immatures are dusky all over. In flight, adult shows gray tail with broad, black terminal band.

VOICE *Whee-oo*.

HABITAT Breeds on offshore islands; winters, coasts.

RANGE Breeds west coast of Mexico.

MOVEMENTS Disperses northward after breeding, to California and beyond.

BREEDING Coastal and offshore islands; March-April.

NEST AND EGGS The nest is a scrape; the 2 or 3 eggs are buffy, spotted brown.

INCUBATION About 28 days, and by both sexes.

COMMENT Unusual in that it breeds in the south (Mexico) and migrates northwards along Pacific coasts.

MEW GULL

Larus canus   15−17in/38−43cm

IDENTIFICATION Gray-backed gull with black wing tips and large white mirrors. Gentle appearance, with rounded head, smallish yellow bill and yellow legs. Immatures have pink bills with black tips and grayish legs. First winter birds confusable with similar aged Ring-billed Gull, but head and bill shape distinct.

VOICE High-pitched *kee-ar*.

HABITAT Tundra marshes in summer; coasts in winter.

RANGE Breeds Alaska and north-western Canada into Northern Manitoba.

MOVEMENTS Winters Pacific coast.

BREEDING Found on inland marshes, lakes and rivers; May-June, colonial.

NEST AND EGGS The nest is a bulky structure, of available materials, on the ground, but sometimes in trees; the 2 or 3 eggs are buffy, spotted and blotched brown.

INCUBATION The eggs take 22 to 27 days to hatch and are incubated by both sexes.

COMMENT Colonies of this species are usually small, and solitary nesting is quite common.

RING-BILLED GULL

Larus delawarensis   17−18½in/43−47cm

IDENTIFICATION Pale-gray gull with black wing tips and white mirrors. Bill, yellow with clear, black vertical bar; legs yellow. In winter, spotted on crown and nape. From second winter, eye is pale creating fierce expression. Immature, brown with grayish legs and dark eye, may be difficult to separate from Mew Gull, but has larger bill and head and is more spotted.

VOICE Loud *kyow*.

HABITAT Marshes and lakes in summer; in winter also along coasts.

RANGE Breeds in western prairies and eastward through Great Lakes. Also Maritime provinces.

MOVEMENTS Winters all coasts and inland especially in southern and eastern states.

BREEDING Islands of freshwater lakes and marine coastal islands; April-June, colonial.

NEST AND EGGS A pile of grasses and other available material; the 3 buffy eggs are spotted brown.

INCUBATION Lasts 21 days, and is shared by the pair.

COMMENT This is a highly successful gull and is increasing in numbers and extending its North American range.

CALIFORNIA GULL

Larus californicus   19½–21½in/50–54cm

IDENTIFICATION Like smaller, darker Herring Gull with less massive, more rounded head and yellow bill with black and red spots. Legs are greenish yellow. Gray mantle, black wing tips with white mirrors. First-winter bird is dark with pinkish legs.

VOICE Yelping *kyow*.

HABITAT Breeds on inland marshes and lakes; winters, coasts.

RANGE Breeds on western prairies as far east as North Dakota.

MOVEMENTS Pacific coast from southern British Columbia to Mexico.

BREEDING Inland lakes together with marshes and river systems; April-June, colonial, often associated with Ring-billed Gulls.

NEST AND EGGS A depression variably lined with whatever material is at hand; the 3 eggs are buffy, boldly marked with brown.

INCUBATION 24 to 27 days of incubation are shared by both sexes.

COMMENT This is an inland nesting gull that is found on the west coast (thus its name) on migration and in winter.

HERRING GULL

Larus argentatus   21½–23½in/54–60cm

IDENTIFICATION Gray-mantled, medium-sized gull with contrasting black wing tips marked by white mirrors. Bill, yellow with red spot, legs pink. Immature is mottled in shades of brown and, in flight, has pale inner primaries with dark terminal tips.

VOICE Loud *kyow-kyow*.

HABITAT Coasts.

RANGE Breeds over much of northern Canada, Alaska and extending southward through the eastern US. Most abundant coastal gull in most areas.

MOVEMENTS Winters along Pacific coasts of Canada and US, on Atlantic and Gulf coasts and inland on Great Lakes and southern and eastern US.

BREEDING Variable from cliffs and islands to dune coastlines and saltings, inland marshes, lakes and moorlands; April-June, colonial.

NEST AND EGGS Usually a mass of marine debris, but often a simple depression; the 2 or 3 eggs are pale green, blotched with brown.

INCUBATION Lasts from 25 to 33 days and is performed mainly by the female.

COMMENT One of the most successful of all gulls and a committed scavenger at all times.

ICELAND GULL

Larus glaucoides   20–22½in/51–57cm

IDENTIFICATION Very similar to Glaucous Gull with white flight feathers and pale gray mantle. Slightly smaller, with rounded head and more gentle expression. Plumge sequence of immatures similar to Glaucous, but first-winter has all-black bill.

VOICE Shrill *kyow*.

HABITAT Breeds tundra coasts; winters coasts.

RANGE Breeds eastern Baffin Island.

MOVEMENTS Winters, east coast from Newfoundland to Virginia.

BREEDING Coastal cliffs and islands in the Arctic; June-July, colonial.

NEST AND EGGS A collection of grasses and seaweeds; the 2 or 3 eggs are olive buff, spotted with brown.

INCUBATION Undescribed.

COMMENT A highly localized Arctic breeder that is decidedly scarce away from its Arctic home.

LESSER BLACK-BACKED GULL

Larus fuscus   20–22in/51–56cm

IDENTIFICATION Similar to Herring Gull, but with darker gray back and wings and yellow legs. Immatures like Herring Gull, but more contrasted plumage and dark ends to all flight feathers creating a bar along trailing edge of wing. Similar bar of Herring Gull is broken by pale inner primaries.

VOICE Loud *ky-ow*.

HABITAT Coasts, dumps.

RANGE Scarce east coast.

MOVEMENTS Vagrant from Europe

WESTERN GULL

Larus occidentalis   23½–25in/60–64cm

IDENTIFICATION Dark-backed gull with heavy, yellow bill, spotted red, and pink legs. Southern birds are very dark, almost black with white terminal mirrors; northern birds are paler, but still very dark. Hybrids with Glaucous-winged Gull are widespread and confusing. The yellow-footed Gull of Mexico is sometimes seen at Salton Sea in California and has yellow legs.

VOICE Loud *owk*.

HABITAT Coasts.

RANGE West coast southward from Vancouver.

MOVEMENTS Resident.

BREEDING Coastal headlands, stacks and offshore islands; April-May, colonial.

NEST AND EGGS Depression well lined with grass or seaweed; the 3 buffy eggs are blotched with brown.

INCUBATION Lasts for 24 to 29 days and is shared between the pair.

COMMENT Closely related to the Glaucous-winged Gull with which it probably shares a common ancestry.

GLAUCOUS-WINGED GULL

Larus glaucescens   23½−26in/60−66cm

IDENTIFICATION Large, west coast gull marked by gray mantle extending to wing tips, broken only by white terminal mirrors. Bill is yellow with red spot and decidedly deep and heavy. First-winter bird has all-black bill like young Iceland Gull, but is buffy across wings rather than creamy.
VOICE Harsh *kyow*.
HABITAT Tundra coasts.
RANGE Breeds coastal Alaska southward along coasts of Canada.
MOVEMENTS Alaskan birds move southward. Winters Pacific coast to Mexico.
BREEDING Coastal cliffs and islands; May-June, colonial.
NEST AND EGGS Mass of marine vegetation on cliffs or low offshore islands; the 2 or 3 eggs are buffy, spotted with brown.
INCUBATION The eggs take 26 to 28 days to hatch and are incubated by both sexes.
COMMENT This voracious gull is often seen on salmon rivers of the Pacific coast where bears and eagles catch the fish.

GLAUCOUS GULL

Larus hyperboreus   23−27in/58−69cm

IDENTIFICATION Large, pale-gray gull, with broadly white-tipped flight feathers, that lacks contrasting wing tip pattern of most other pale gulls. Adult has yellow bill with red spot, a pale "fierce" eye, and pink legs. First-winter bird is spotted buffy, has pale, creamy wings, and pink base to bill. Second-winter bird is whitish throughout.
VOICE Harsh *kyow*.

HABITAT Breeds tundra; winters, coasts and some inland waters.
RANGE Breeds coastal Alaska, Canada and to Labrador.
MOVEMENTS Winters ice-free coasts in north-east and north-west and among Great Lakes.
BREEDING Frequents Arctic cliffs and small islands; June-July, colonial.
NEST AND EGGS A mass of available vegetation often on the base of previous year's nest; the 2 or 3 eggs are olive buff, spotted brown.
INCUBATION The eggs take 27 or 28 days to hatch and are incubated by both members of the pair.
COMMENT A coastal species of the far north that is only seldom seen inland at any time of the year.

GREAT BLACK-BACKED GULL

Larus marinus   25−27in/63−69cm

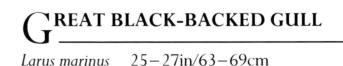

IDENTIFICATION Huge gull with equally huge, heavy bill. Adult is all-black across upperparts to wing tips, broken only by white terminal mirrors. Immature spotted brown and buff appearing paler-headed and more contrasty than other eastern, immature, large gulls. Bill yellow with red spot, legs pale pink.

VOICE Hard *owk*.

HABITAT Coasts.

RANGE Breeds eastern Canada southwards along adjacent US coasts.

MOVEMENTS Resident, though some birds move southward as far as Florida.

BREEDING Rocky offshore islands and stacks; April-June, semi-colonial.

NEST AND EGGS Varies from an unlined hollow to a mass of marine vegetation; the 2 or 3 eggs are olive brown, blotched with dark brown.

INCUBATION The eggs take 26 to 28 days to hatch and are incubated by both sexes.

COMMENT A large, fearsome gull that is a predator on adult and young seabirds that share its breeding zone. Its range is expanding.

BLACK-LEGGED KITTIWAKE

Rissa tridactyla   15–17in/38–43cm

IDENTIFICATION Gray-backed gull with long, narrow wings and pure black wing tips. Legs black and short, bill yellow. In winter, adult has dark smudge on nape. Immature has black

"W" across wings and black bar across nape. Abundant at cliff breeding colonies.

VOICE Repeated *kitti-waak*.

HABITAT Cliffs in summer; at sea in winter.

RANGE Breeds Alaska, Canadian archipelago, Newfoundland and Gulf of St Lawrence.

MOVEMENTS Disperses over northern Pacific and Atlantic, but regularly seen off both coasts.

BREEDING Sheer, precipitous cliffs often of islands; June-July.

NEST AND EGGS A well-structured mass of marine vegetation placed on a tiny ledge; the 2 eggs are creamy, speckled with brown.

INCUBATION The eggs take 25 to 30 days to hatch and incubation is shared between the pair.

COMMENT An oceanic gull that has a strangely broken distribution in eastern and northern Canada and Alaska.

ROSS'S GULL

Rhodostethia rosea   13–14in/33–35cm

IDENTIFICATION Breeding adult is washed pink with black ring around neck and nape. In winter all gray-white, perhaps hint of neck ring, with long, wedge-shaped tail, tiny black bill and short red legs. Immatures with blackish flight feathers.

VOICE Generally silent outside breeding season.

HABITAT Tundra marshes, winters at sea.

RANGE Breeds Arctic Canada at two or three sites.

MOVEMENTS Mostly breeds Siberia, winters off pack ice. Extremely rare farther south.

SABINE'S GULL

Xema sabini   12½–13½in/32–34cm

IDENTIFICATION Adult in summer has black outer primaries, white inner primaries and secondaries, contrasting with warm gray wing coverts and forming a unique flight pattern. Slate-gray hood, bordered by narrow, black line, and black bill with yellow tip, are best features at rest, though primaries show white mirrors that are never obvious in flight. Hood lost in winter though some dusky on head and partial border remains. Black legs. Tail neatly notched. Flashes black and white in flight.

VOICE Tern-like.

HABITAT Tundra coasts; winters at sea.

RANGE Western and northern coasts of Alaska, north and archipelago coasts of Canada.

MOVEMENTS Reasonably common off Pacific coast. Northern and eastern birds head eastward over Atlantic to coasts of south-western Europe.

BREEDING Coastal tundra lakes and marshes; June-July, colonial, sometimes in association with Arctic Tern.

NEST AND EGGS A hollow lined with grasses, usually on a lake or marsh island; the 2 or 3 eggs are olive brown, spotted with darker brown.

INCUBATION Lasts 21 to 26 days and is performed by both members of the pair.

COMMENT This remarkable Arctic gull migrates across the Atlantic to Africa, as well as along the Pacific coast.

IVORY GULL

Pagophila eburnea   16−18in/41−46cm

IDENTIFICATION Curiously short-legged, short-billed and round-headed gull that resembles a pigeon. Adult is pure white with black legs and yellow-tipped gray bill. Immature is speckled black with dirty-looking face.

VOICE Generally silent when not breeding.

HABITAT Arctic seas.

RANGE Breeds on Arctic islands, including Canada.

MOVEMENTS Winters pack ice, rare farther south.

GULL-BILLED TERN

Sterna nilotica   14−15in/35−39cm

IDENTIFICATION Large, pale gray tern with thick, bull-necked appearance and large, deep-black bill. As pale as Sandwich Tern, but distinctive heavy shape. Legs black and long for a tern. Hawks insects over dry land and wetlands.

VOICE Harsh *ka-wak*.

HABITAT Coastal marshes.

RANGE Breeds, Atlantic and Gulf coasts of US, rarely southern California.

MOVEMENTS Winters, Florida and Gulf coast.

BREEDING Islands in coastal marshes, shingle flats, beaches; May-June, colonial.

NEST AND EGGS A bare scrape often lined with shell fragments; the 2 or 3 eggs are buffy, spotted brown.

INCUBATION The eggs hatch after 22 or 23 days and incubation is shared by both parents.

COMMENT These 'marsh' terns nest on low islets that are often left high and dry as the surrounding saltmarsh dries out in summer.

CASPIAN TERN

Sterna caspia   19−22in/48−56cm

IDENTIFICATION Huge, gray tern with massive, coral-red bill. Black cap when breeding, mottled other times. Legs black.

VOICE Hard *kraa*.

HABITAT Coasts, lakes, rivers.

RANGE Locally along all coasts and inland as far north as tundra; very disjointed.

MOVEMENTS Winters, Gulf coast, Florida and adjacent Atlantic coast.

BREEDING Sandy or rocky islands of coasts and large inland

lakes; May-June, colonial.

NEST AND EGGS A simple depression, sometimes well lined with vegetation; the 2 or 3 eggs are buffish, lightly spotted with brown.

INCUBATION The eggs take some 20 to 22 days to hatch, they are incubated by both members of the pair.

COMMENT This large tern is colonial and, where the ranges overlap, is often found in company with Ring-billed Gulls.

ROYAL TERN

Sterna maxima   17½−20in/45−51cm

IDENTIFICATION Similar to Caspian Tern, but with thinner, orange-red bill. Out of breeding season, black crest starts behind (not at) black eye. Legs, black.

VOICE High-pitched *chirrip*.

HABITAT Coasts.

RANGE Breeds on Gulf and Atlantic coasts.

MOVEMENTS Winters, southern California, Gulf and Atlantic coasts and Florida.

BREEDING Islands along sandy shorelines; April-May, highly colonial.

NEST AND EGGS A bare scrape serves as a nest; the 1 or 2 creamy eggs are spotted with brown.

INCUBATION Lasts 28 to 35 days, incubation by both sexes.

COMMENT A large, well-built tern that is common along the southern coasts of US.

ELEGANT TERN

Sterna elegans   15½−17in/40−43cm

IDENTIFICATION Large gray tern with prominent, ragged crest and long, thin, orange-red to yellowish bill. Legs, black. In winter, crest encompasses eye and extends over hind crown. *See* Royal Tern.

VOICE Harsh *kee-rick*.

HABITAT Coasts.

RANGE Breeds, coastal, western Mexico to southernmost California.

MOVEMENTS California coasts in fall.

BREEDING Low-lying offshore or lagoon islands; April-May, highly colonial.

NEST AND EGGS A bare scrape among sand serves as a nest; the single egg varies enormously in color.

INCUBATION Estimated at 20 days.

COMMENT Began nesting in San Diego, California in 1959. Variable egg color enables the adult to locate its otherwise featureless nest.

SANDWICH TERN

Sterna sandvicensis   15−17in/38−43cm

IDENTIFICATION Large, pale tern with long, pointed, black bill, tipped yellow. Adult in summer is pale gray, as pale as Roseate and Gull-billed Terns, with ragged black crest. Legs are black, tail forked. Breeds in dense colonies. In winter, black confined to rear crest.

VOICE Harsh *kee-rick*.

HABITAT Shorelines, coastal marshes, sand bars.

RANGE Breeds mid-Atlantic and Gulf coasts of US.

MOVEMENTS Winters, Gulf coast and Florida.

BREEDING Coastal dunes and islands; April-May, highly colonial.

NEST AND EGGS A bare scrape serves as a nest; the 2 eggs are buffy, speckled with brown.

INCUBATION Lasts from 20 to 24 days and is shared between the sexes.

COMMENT Nests much closer together than most other terns and will often totally abandon a colony that has been used for many years.

ROSEATE TERN

Sterna dougallii   12½–15½in/32–40cm

IDENTIFICATION Smaller than Common and Arctic Terns, but with longer tail. Summer adult very pale gray above with white underparts washed with warm, pinkish flush. Bill, black, red base (when breeding); legs, red.

VOICE Quiet *kee-aa*.

HABITAT Beaches, islands, coasts; winters at sea.

RANGE Scarce breeder east coast US.

MOVEMENTS Winters to the south.

BREEDING Frequents coastlines and low islands; May-June, colonial.

NEST AND EGGS A bare scrape, sometimes with a little lining; the 2 or 3 eggs are buffy olive, speckled with brown.

INCUBATION Lasts from 21 to 26 days and is shared by both sexes.

COMMENT Generally a scarce and declining species that does not compete effectively with Common and Arctic Terns for nest sites.

COMMON TERN

Sterna hirundo   12–14in/30–36cm

IDENTIFICATION Pale gray above, paler below with black cap, but no contrasting white cheek patch. Bill orange-red with black tip (sometimes absent); legs orange-red. First winter, has dark trailing edge to wing contrasting with paler mid-wing panel. *See Arctic Tern.*

VOICE A drawn-out *kee-arr*.

HABITAT Marshes, pools, lagoons, beaches.

RANGE Mainly across southern Canada eastward of Rockies, but southward across the US border and along north-east coast.

MOVEMENTS Common migrant along US coasts. Winters on coasts of South America.

BREEDING Beaches, islands in lakes and marshes; May-June; colonial.

NEST AND EGGS A hollow or scrape with a scant lining of available material; the 2 to 4 eggs are buffy olive, speckled with brown.

INCUBATION Lasts 20 to 23 days and is shared between members of the pair.

COMMENT Where their ranges overlap these birds will nest in mixed colonies with Arctic and Roseate Terns.

ARCTIC TERN

Sterna paradisaea   12–15in/30–39cm

IDENTIFICATION Summer adult is pale gray above and below with black cap and white cheeks. Bill is blood-red, legs short and red. Tail deeply forked. First winter has white trailing edge to inner wing. To be distinguished with care from Common Tern.

VOICE *Key-rrr.*

HABITAT Tundra marshes; winters at sea.

RANGE Breeds across whole of northern Canada and Alaska and, in the east, south to Nova Scotia.

MOVEMENTS Long-distance migrant to southern oceans.

BREEDING Frequents a variety of aquatic habitats including shorelines, sand spits, lake and marsh islands, offshore islands; May-June, colonial.

NEST AND EGGS A simple unlined scrape; the 2 or 3 eggs are buffy, spotted dark brown.

INCUBATION Lasts 20 to 22 days and is performed by both members of the pair.

COMMENT Nesting Arctic Terns are among the few birds that will actually attack and make contact with intruders.

FORSTER'S TERN

Sterna forsteri   13½–15in/34–38cm

IDENTIFICATION Like Common Tern, gray above and white below. Red bill with black tip; longer red legs. Tail, long and forked. In flight, shows white primaries and white edges to tail. In winter, black cap becomes bold black mark behind eye, bill all black.

VOICE *Ky-aar.*

HABITAT Marshes, scarce on coasts.

RANGE Breeds on western prairies; also on Gulf coast marshes and locally on Atlantic coast.

MOVEMENTS Winters, Gulf coast, Florida, Atlantic coast as far north as the Carolinas.

BREEDING A marshland tern that frequents saltwater habitats in the east and freshwater ones in the west, in Canada it is found inland; April-June.

NEST AND EGGS Floating structure in shallow marshes; the 2 to 4 eggs are buffy, spotted brown.

INCUBATION Lasts 23 days and is shared between the sexes.

COMMENT Generally found further north along the coasts in winter than other terns.

LEAST TERN

Sterna antillarum   9–10in/23–26cm

IDENTIFICATION Smallest tern marked by gray upperparts, white below with black cap and peaked white forehead. Bill and feet yellow, the former tipped black. Long, narrow wings, frequently hovers, dives for food.

VOICE High *ki-tik.*

HABITAT Shorelines, beaches, sand bars.

RANGE Breeds all US coastlines and along Mississippi River system.

MOVEMENTS Moves south in winter.
BREEDING Mostly shingle coastlines, but also along shingle banks of rivers; April-May, semi-colonial.
NEST AND EGGS A bare scrape among shingle serves as a nest; the 2 or 3 olive eggs are blotched with brown.
INCUBATION Lasts 19 to 22 days and is shared between the sexes.
COMMENT Nesting so close to the sea, colonies are often completely washed out by the highest tides.

ALEUTIAN TERN

Sterna aleutica   12–13in/30–33cm

IDENTIFICATION Dusky-gray above and below, with black cap and distinctive white forehead and cheek patch. Whitish underwing shows darker bar across secondaries. Bill and legs black.
VOICE A squeaky *twee-ee*.
HABITAT Coasts and islands.
RANGE Coastal Alaska and Aleutians.
MOVEMENTS Summer visitor, disperses at sea.

BRIDLED TERN

Sterna anaethetus   14–15in/35–38cm

IDENTIFICATION Brown above, white below with black cap separated from upperparts by white collar. Separated from similar Sooty Tern by smaller size and brown, not black, appearance.
VOICE Hard *wep-wep*.
HABITAT Seas.
RANGE Frequent summer visitor to Gulf, often driven inshore and northward by gales.
MOVEMENTS Breeds Caribbean.

SOOTY TERN

Sterna fuscata   15–17in/38–43cm

IDENTIFICATION Brown-black above, white below with black cap and bold, white forehead. Similar to Bridled Tern, but larger and blacker.
VOICE *Ker-wacky-wack*.
HABITAT Seas and isolated islets.
RANGE Breeds in colonies, along Gulf coast and most notably on Dry Tortugas off Florida Keys.
MOVEMENTS Storm-bound northward along Atlantic coast.

WHITE-WINGED TERN

Chlidonias leucopterus   9–10in/23–25cm

IDENTIFICATION Black body and wing linings contrast with white wings and tail in breeding plumage. In winter adult like Black Tern, but lacks smudge on chest at front of wing. Juvenile has dark saddle and white rump.
VOICE *Krip-krip*.
HABITAT Marshes.
RANGE Vagrant east coast.
MOVEMENTS Eurasian breeder winters in Africa.

BLACK TERN

Chlidonias niger   9–10in/23–26cm

IDENTIFICATION Adult in summer is black with slate-gray wings and white undertail. In winter, is white below, slate-gray above with black cap and dark smudge at side of breast. Hawks insects over water.

VOICE High-pitched *kik*.

HABITAT Marshes, lakes.

RANGE Breeds right across temperate Canada and throughout northern and western states.

MOVEMENTS Regular migrant to South America.

BREEDING Marshes and shallow lakes with plentiful emergent vegetation as well as open water; May–June.

NEST AND EGGS A floating platform is anchored to emergent vegetation; the 3 eggs are buffy, spotted with brown.

INCUBATION Lasts 14 to 17 days and is performed mainly by the female.

COMMENT The combination of habitat and feeding method makes this "marsh tern" one of the easiest of our birds to identify.

BLACK SKIMMER

Rynchops niger   16½–18in/42–46cm

IDENTIFICATION Black above, white below, with black crown extending to eye; white forehead. Huge, knife-like red and black bill. Skims over water.

VOICE Deep *oow*.

HABITAT Coastal bays and marshes.

RANGE Breeds, Atlantic and Gulf coasts, uncommonly in southern California.

MOVEMENTS Leaves northern parts of Atlantic coast in winter.

BREEDING Coastal bays, sand bars, tidal lagoons; May–June, colonial.

NEST AND EGGS A bare scrape among sand and shells; the 2 to 5 eggs are variable in ground color from pale blue to buff and are speckled with dark brown.

INCUBATION Incubation is by the female alone, for about 22 days.

COMMENT These birds are intolerant of vegetation on their breeding sites and move away when sandy tracts are colonized by plants.

AUKS OR ALCIDS

T HERE are some 90 species of gulls and their allies in the world, of which about 40 are found in North America. In contrast, there are 22 species of auks, or alcids, of which no less than 20 are North American. Thus, while the continent is a good place to be a gull-watcher, it is an absolutely perfect place for an auk-watcher.

The reasons for the unique position of North America in the world of auks are relatively easy to explain. These are all committed seabirds that come to land only to breed, and they are confined to the northern hemisphere, where there are only two major oceans – the Pacific and the Atlantic. North America is the only continent with extensive coastlines along both oceans. Thus, in the Atlantic there are Atlantic Puffin, Dovekie, and Razorbill, while the Common Murre, Thick-billed Murre, and Black Guillemot are found in both the Atlantic and the Pacific. All the other auks are confined to the Pacific, and most to the northern area around the Bering Straits and the Aleutians.

Auks are relatively small, dark birds with short wings and bills, webbed feet set well back on the body, and with color, if it exists at all, confined to the head and bill. They are expert swimmers that spend most of their lives at sea, where they catch their prey by diving. Underwater, they use their wings for propulsion. In fact, the auk wing is a compromise between a flipper and a proper wing. They are not as fast or agile underwater as the penguins, and the wings have to be beaten immensely fast to become airborne. The penguins have abandoned flight altogether, while the auks have maintained their flying ability. Despite being unrelated, these two groups of birds share a very similar lifestyle. Indeed, the penguins of the southern hemisphere were named after a now extinct northern auk – the Great Auk, *Penguinus impennis*, which was flightless and finally exterminated in 1844.

The auks come to land only to breed, or when forced to do so by storm, illness, or oil pollution. With their legs set at the rear of their bodies to act as a rudder at sea, they are decidedly awkward on land, and many are easy prey to the larger gulls. Most breed on steep sea cliffs, or uninhabited offshore stacks and islands. They are gregarious and often form huge colonies; indeed, the Dovekie is arguably the most numerous bird in the northern hemisphere. Most spectacular are the murres, which may number tens of thousands packed tightly together on a single cliff. Most other auks seek some protection by hiding their nests in a burrow or crevice, though some nest in tree-holes some distance from the sea.

DOVEKIE

Alle alle   8−8½in/20−22cm

IDENTIFICATION Only tiny auk of Atlantic coast. Dumpy shape, narrow, rounded wings, and tiny, stubby bill added to size preclude confusion. Neck and breast, black in summer, white in winter. Breeds in enormous colonies in far north.
VOICE Silent at sea.
HABITAT Tundra screes; winters at sea.
RANGE Breeds on coasts of Greenland.
MOVEMENTS Winters over Atlantic and may be seen off north-east coasts, particularly after storms.
BREEDING Screes and stony mountains on high Arctic islands; June-July, highly colonial.
NEST AND EGGS An unlined crevice or hole among rocks acts as a nest; the single egg is blue, spotted with brown.
INCUBATION Lasts some 24 days and is shared by male and female.
COMMENT Despite its rarity further south, the Dovekie breeds in enormous numbers at its Arctic strongholds.

COMMON MURRE

Uria aalge   15½−17in/40−44cm

IDENTIFICATION Chunky, short-winged seabird with blackish upperparts washed with dark brown. Bill is pointed. In summer, dark upperparts extend to breast; in winter, only to sides of head. A varying proportion of Atlantic birds have a bridle of white eye-ring and line across cheek.

VOICE Growls.
HABITAT High cliffs, winters at sea.
RANGE Breeds from Labrador to Gulf of St Lawrence in east; and from western Alaska to coast of California in west.
MOVEMENTS Winters at sea near breeding colonies.
BREEDING Sea cliffs and stacks; May-June, highly colonial.
NEST AND EGGS A small space on a cliff ledge acts as a nest; the single egg is highly variable in color, but blotched black.
INCUBATION The egg hatches after 28 or 35 days and incubation is shared by both sexes.
COMMENT These auks nest tightly-packed on sea cliff ledges or atop an offshore stack.

THICK-BILLED MURRE

Uria lomvia   16−18in/41−46cm

IDENTIFICATION Very similar to Common Murre, but blacker with thicker bill and pale line along base of upper mandible. In winter, shows darker face than Common Murre.
VOICE Growls.
HABITAT Cliffs; winters at sea.
RANGE Overlaps with, but breeds farther north than Common Murre. Abundant among Canadian archipelago, in Alaska and locally in Labrador.
MOVEMENTS Seldom progresses much farther south than breeding grounds, though may be commonest murre off east coast of US.

INCUBATION Lasts from 25 to 35 days and is shared between the pair.

COMMENT Because of its nest sites this is a remarkably difficult seabird to count accurately.

BREEDING Sea cliffs of northern seas; May-June, highly colonial.

NEST AND EGGS A simple bare ledge acts as a nest; the single egg is variable in color, spotted and scrawled with browns.

INCUBATION The egg is incubated for 30 to 35 days by both sexes.

COMMENT Like that of the Common Murre, the egg of the present species is pear-shaped and spins rather than rolls on its precarious nest site.

RAZORBILL

Alca torda   15–17in/39–43cm

IDENTIFICATION Chunky seabird, similar to Common Murre, but with deep-black bill marked by white, vertical line. Black above extends to breast in summer, but only to sides of head in winter. Flies with fast wing beats.

VOICE Grunts.

HABITAT Broken cliffs in summer; offshore in winter.

RANGE Breeds on coasts of Labrador southward to Maine.

MOVEMENTS Winters near breeding grounds and as far south as New York.

BREEDING Cliffs and stacks of headlands and islands; May-June, colonial.

NEST AND EGGS The nest is a bare cleft or niche in a rocky cliff face; the single egg is of variable color, blotched with brown.

BLACK GUILLEMOT

Cepphus grylle   13–14in/33–35cm

IDENTIFICATION All-black auk marked by white ovals on wings. In winter, head, neck and underparts are white, wings black with white ovals, upperparts barred dark gray. In flight, shows white underwings in all plumages and white on inner wing above.

VOICE Various whistles.

HABITAT Broken bases of cliffs; winters inshore.

RANGE Breeds from Canadian archipelago eastwards to St Lawrence and Nova Scotia. Also in northern Alaska.

MOVEMENTS Winters near breeding colonies.

BREEDING Rocky debris at the foot of tall seabird cliffs; June-July.

RANGE Breeds from Alaska to California.
MOVEMENTS Winters near breeding stations.
BREEDING Debris of rocks and boulders at foot of sea cliff; May-June.
NEST AND EGGS A rock crevice or burrow, sometimes excavated by the birds themselves; the 2 eggs are white, speckled with black.
INCUBATION Lasts 28 days and is shared by male and female.
COMMENT Very similar to Black Guillemot, but confined to the Pacific coast.

NEST AND EGGS A hole among fallen boulders acts as a nest; the 2 eggs are white, lightly spotted with black.
INCUBATION Lasts from 21 to 30 days and is shared by both members of the pair.
COMMENT This auk tends to remain in the vicinity of its breeding colonies throughout the year.

MARBLED MURRELET

Brachyramphus marmoratus   8½–10in/22–25cm

IDENTIFICATION In summer, marbled brown and chestnut above, brown and buff below, with pale, broken eye-ring. In winter, slate-gray above, white below. There is a white patch on the wing (scapulars) and the dark cap extends below the white-rimmed eye. The similar Kittlitz's Murrelet, confined to Alaska, is paler, lacks white eye-ring in summer, and has dark cap terminating well above the dark eye in winter.
VOICE Repeated *keer* notes.
HABITAT Inland screes and trees; winters, coasts.
RANGE Pacific coast southward to California.
MOVEMENTS Mainly resident.
BREEDING Forests within a few miles of the coast; May-June.
NEST AND EGGS A hollow high up in a tree lined with moss; the number of eggs is unknown, but presumed one, which is pale green and heavily marked.
INCUBATION Probably by both sexes for about 27 days.
COMMENT The first nest of this species was found only in 1963 in Kamchatka, USSR. The first North American nest was discovered in a Douglas fir in California in 1974.

PIGEON GUILLEMOT

Cepphus columba   13½–14in/34–36cm

IDENTIFICATION Very similar to Black Guillemot, but with white patch on wing divided by black wedge. Underwing dark in all plumages. In winter is darker on head and neck.
VOICE Whistles.
HABITAT Broken cliffs; winters inshore.

[139]

KITTLITZ'S MURRELET

Brachyramphus brevirostris   9–10in/23–25cm

IDENTIFICATION Similar to Marbled Murrelet in all plumages. Separated in summer by shorter bill and slightly paler plumage, in winter by shorter bill and white extending to above eye.
VOICE Generally silent.
HABITAT Rocky islands.
RANGE Breeds along Alaskan coast.
MOVEMENTS Disperses at sea.

XANTUS' MURRELET

Synthliboramphus hypoleucus   9–10in/23–25cm

IDENTIFICATION Black above, white below with distinctive white eye-ring and white underwing.
VOICE Silent at sea.
HABITAT Rocky islands.
RANGE Breeds California.
MOVEMENTS Disperses along California coast.

CRAVERI'S MURRELET

Synthliboramphus craveri   10in/25cm

IDENTIFICATION Virtually identical to Xantus' Murrelet, black above and white below. Separated by gray, not white, underwing.
VOICE Silent at sea.
HABITAT Rocky islands.
RANGE Breeds off Western Mexico.
MOVEMENTS Moves northward to Californian waters in late summer and fall.

ANCIENT MURRELET

Synthliboramphus antiquus   8½–10in/22–25cm

IDENTIFICATION In summer black head and breast is broken by white crown plumes. The back is gray, separated from the white underparts by a black lateral slash. The small bill is yellow. In winter is similarly, but less boldly, marked. In flight, the black, flank-slash separates white underparts from white wing linings.
VOICE Whistles.
HABITAT Islands; coasts in winter.
RANGE Alaska to British Columbia in summer.
MOVEMENTS Winters, from Alaska south to California.
BREEDING Wooded coastal islands; May–June, colonial.
NEST AND EGGS The nest of grass is placed in a burrow, rock crevice, or niche beneath a rock or tree; the 1 or 2 eggs are white, washed with blue or buff and spotted brown.
INCUBATION By both sexes for about 35 days.
COMMENT Young birds leave the nest at a very early age and join adults on the sea.

CASSIN'S AUKLET

Ptychoramphus aleuticus   8–9in/20–23cm

IDENTIFICATION A dull, sooty auklet marked by short, black bill with a yellow spot at the lower base and a bold, broken white eye-ring. Undertail and belly white.
VOICE Repeated croaks.
HABITAT Islands; winters at sea.
RANGE From Alaska to Southern California.
MOVEMENTS Often out of sight of land south of breeding range.
BREEDING Coastal islands with grassy slopes; May-June.
NEST AND EGGS The nest is a pad of vegetation placed in a burrow excavated by the birds themselves; the single egg is white with a blue-green wash.
INCUBATION By both sexes, for 38 days.
COMMENT One of the few auklets that lacks any breeding adornments and even a distinctive summer plumage.

PARAKEET AUKLET

Cyclorrhynchus psittacula   10in/25cm

IDENTIFICATION Large auklet with gray-black upperparts and white underparts, marked by tuft of white feathers extending behind pale eye. Huge red bill.
VOICE A trill when breeding; silent at sea.
HABITAT Rocky islands.
RANGE Aleutian, and Bering Sea islands, and western coastal Alaska.
MOVEMENTS Disperses off Alaskan coast.

LEAST AUKLET

Aethia pusilla   6−6½in/16cm

IDENTIFICATION Tiny, Dovekie-like auk, slate-gray above, white below, mottled gray in breeding season to create a white bib and dark breast band. Pale scapulars, tiny reddish bill.
VOICE Twittering while breeding.
HABITAT Rocky islands.
RANGE Breeds islands of Bering Straits.
MOVEMENTS Disperses south to Aleutians and coasts of Siberia. Vagrant southward.

WHISKERED AUKLET

Aethia pygmaea   7½−8in/19−20cm

IDENTIFICATION All slate-gray auklet marked by triple white plumes around eye and black, quail-like crest in summer. In winter plumes much reduced. Bill red.
VOICE Silent at sea.
HABITAT Rocky islands.
RANGE Breeds on a few Aleutian islands.
MOVEMENTS General dispersal throughout Aleutians.

CRESTED AUKLET

Aethia cristatella   10−11in/25−28cm

IDENTIFICATION An all slate-gray auk with bold crest of dark feathers extending from forehead and a single white tuft behind eye. Bill large and red. In winter crest reduced and tuft all but absent.
VOICE Grunting while breeding, silent at sea.
HABITAT Rocky islands.
RANGE Breeds on islands in the Bering Sea.
MOVEMENTS Disperses at sea in Bering region.

RHINOCEROS AUKLET

Cerorhinca monocerata   14−15in/35−38cm

IDENTIFICATION A large, bulky auklet with a chunky bill. Upperparts are blackish; underparts slaty brown. In summer, there is a "rhino-like" horn at the base of the yellow bill, plus two tufty plumes on the side of the head. In winter, the horn disappears and the plumes are reduced to two pale lines.

VOICE Growls.

HABITAT Coastal islands; winters, inshore.

RANGE Breeds from Alaska to southern California.

MOVEMENTS Large flocks gather along coasts of British Columbia and the Pacific coast of the US.

BREEDING Coastal islands with grassy or wooded slopes; May-June, colonial.

NEST AND EGGS Excavates a long tunnel with a nest of grasses and leaves at the end chamber; the single egg is white, usually spotted with gray or buff.

INCUBATION Lasts for 21 to 31 days (probably nearer the latter) and is shared between the sexes.

COMMENT This is the largest of the auklets, but is more closely related to the similar fish-eating puffins.

TUFTED PUFFIN

Fratercula cirrhata   14−15in/35−38cm

IDENTIFICATION Similar to other puffins, but plumage black above and below. In summer, face is white, long golden tufts extend from the eye and the huge bill is orange red with a creamy-buff base to the upper mandible. In winter, tufts are lost, whole head is black and bill is slightly reduced.

VOICE Growls.

HABITAT Sea cliffs; winters at sea.

RANGE Pacific coast from Alaska to California.

MOVEMENTS Winters offshore at sea.

BREEDING Coastal islands with cliffs and grassy slopes; April-June, colonial.

NEST AND EGGS Mostly nests in rock crevices, but also in burrows, a lining of leaves and grasses is added; a single white egg, lightly marked grayish.

INCUBATION Lasts for some 30 days and is shared by both sexes.

COMMENT Often abundant, especially at its northern colonies.

ATLANTIC PUFFIN

Fratercula arctica   11½−12in/29−31cm

IDENTIFICATION Only Atlantic puffin. Upperparts, black extending to crown and breast, with silvery-white face; underparts, white. Large red, yellow and black bill in summer. Legs, red. In winter, "face" becomes gray and bill becomes less colored. Juvenile has narrower, pointed bill.

VOICE Deep *arr-arr*.

HABITAT Cliff tops and cliff sides in summer; in winter at sea.

RANGE Breeds from Labrador to Massachusetts.

MOVEMENTS Winters near breeding colonies and at sea. Seldom seen south of New England.

BREEDING Offshore islets, sea cliff landslides with a good covering of earth and grass; June-July, colonial.

NEST AND EGGS A burrow is excavated or adopted as the nest; the single egg is white.

INCUBATION The egg hatches after 40 to 43 days of incubation by the female alone.

COMMENT The increase in the numbers of the larger gulls has seriously reduced the numbers of this attractive auk at many of its colonies.

Horned Puffin

Fratercula corniculata   14—15in/35—38cm

IDENTIFICATION This puffin has clear white underparts and a large red and yellow bill. In winter, depth of bill creates a notch between bill and forehead. Horn extending upwards from eye invisible except at extreme close range.

VOICE Various *arrs*.

HABITAT Crumbling cliffs in summer; at sea in winter.

RANGE Confined to coasts of Alaska.

MOVEMENTS Local dispersal, but mostly stays near breeding colonies. Irregularly straggles to California.

BREEDING Sea cliffs, offshore stacks and islands; June-July.

NEST AND EGGS A bare crevice among rocks forms a nest, though occasionally this species will excavate a burrow; the single white egg is finely spotted black.

INCUBATION Shared between the sexes, for about 40 days.

COMMENT A replacement of the Atlantic Puffin in the Pacific where it is usually outnumbered by the Tufted Puffin.

PIGEONS, DOVES, PARROTS, CUCKOOS & ROADRUNNERS

THESE birds belong to quite distinct families that are regularly placed in a systematist's no man's land between the auks and the owls. Though there are nearly 300 species of pigeons and doves in the world, only 11 breed in North America. In general, the word "pigeon" is reserved for the larger species, the word "dove" for the smaller ones.

Pigeons are well-developed flying birds, with pointed wings and substantial flight muscles. They fly extremely fast and have remarkable powers of endurance. In several parts of Europe, Rock Dove derivatives are used for racing and these same birds are used in many homing experiments concerned with avian navigation. During the pre-electronic age, pigeons were used to carry messages, often during times of war; in fact, during the Second World War the British government even fought the pigeon's arch enemy, the Peregrine Falcon, to ensure that crucial messages from the front were not lost along the way.

The Rock Dove is among the world's most successful species for, having been domesticated for food, it subsequently established the feral flocks that now frequent every large city in the world. Sadly, America was also home to the Passenger Pigeon, probably the New World's most abundant land bird at the beginning of the last century. At that time flocks of these birds were said to number millions and darken the sky as they passed overhead. Shooting was so easy that a single shot might bring down a dozen birds. Inevitably, the Passenger Pigeon was shot out of existence by frontiersmen and the last individual, named Martha, died in Cincinnatti Zoo in 1914.

Pigeons usually nest in trees and construct a flimsy nest of a few twigs pushed together. Their eggs are white and hatch remarkably quickly for such large birds. The chicks are fed, quite uniquely, on the broken-down linings of the parents' crop – the so-called pigeon's milk. This substance compares in its nutritional value with mammals' milk and is a remarkable adaption to feed its young by a bird that eats seeds throughout the year.

If pigeons and doves seem somewhat boring, cuckoos, in contrast, are among the most interesting. Several Old World species are brood parasites, that lay their eggs cowbird-fashion in the nests of other birds, and that have given their name to unfaithfulness via the word "cuckhold." North America's two most widespread cuckoos are the Yellow-billed and Black-billed. These are very similar in appearance and overlap in distribution over much of the east. In the southwest the Roadrunner is a remarkable, ground-dwelling cuckoo that lives in desert country and builds its nest among the thorns of cactus. Renowned for its ability to capture snakes, the Roadrunner is, in fact, virtually omnivorous. Denizens of the deep south, the two species of ani, the Smooth-billed and Groove-billed, are all black members of the family that have adopted a strange co-operative form of nesting. Several females lay their eggs in the same nest and then share the duties of incubation and care of the young.

Though parrots are widespread and abundant members of the avifauna of South America, only a handful of species can even remotely be considered North American birds. The Red-crowned Parrot now lives a feral existence in southern Florida and in the area around Los Angeles. Other species have established themselves elsewhere. The only real native parrot to North America, the Carolina Parakeet of the southeastern U.S.A., was

hunted for sport, trapped for sale and slaughtered as "an agricultural pest." It became extinct by the 1920s, though it was doomed much earlier.

ROCK DOVE

Columba livia 11½−12½in/29−32cm

IDENTIFICATION The town pigeon with a wide variety of plumages. Pure wild birds are gray with two black wing bars and white rump.
VOICE *Ooo-roo-coo*, repeated.
HABITAT Cliffs, cities.
RANGE Whole of temperate North America.
MOVEMENTS Resident.
BREEDING Sea and inland cliffs and city centers that offer suitable nest holes; March-August.
NEST AND EGGS A hole in cliff or building is lined with twigs and grasses; the 2 eggs are pure white.
INCUBATION The eggs hatch after 17 to 19 days of incubation shared by both sexes.
COMMENT Introduced from Europe where it is widespread as a feral bird.

WHITE-CROWNED PIGEON

Columba leucocephala 12−13in/30−33cm

IDENTIFICATION A large, uniformly dark pigeon that looks black at any distance. Males have bold, white crown, females and immatures are gray.
VOICE *Coora-coo* repeated.
HABITAT Mangroves and adjacent orchards.
RANGE Florida.
MOVEMENTS Summer visitor to US that winters in Caribbean.

RED-BILLED PIGEON

Columba flavirostris 14−15in/35−38cm

IDENTIFICATION A large and very dark pigeon with a vinous head and red and yellow bill.
VOICE *Upp-coop-a-coo* repeated.
HABITAT Woodland.
RANGE Rio Grande valley, Texas.
MOVEMENTS Uncommon resident that is rare in winter.

BAND-TAILED PIGEON

Columba fasciata 14−14½in/35−37cm

IDENTIFICATION Large dark pigeon with purple head and breast, white half collar and iridescent hind neck. In flight, appears uniformly dark, though gray on inner wing and on banded tail may be useful features.
VOICE *Coo-cooo*.
HABITAT Conifer and mixed woods, gardens.
RANGE Breeds, Pacific coast and south-western states.
MOVEMENTS Winters, California.
BREEDING Open woods of deciduous and coniferous trees; April-May.
NEST AND EGGS A platform of twigs at variable height; the single egg (occasionally 2) is white.
INCUBATION The egg hatches after 18 to 20 days of incubation by both members of the pair.
COMMENT This is fast becoming a familiar garden and parkland bird along the Pacific coast.

RINGED TURTLE-DOVE

Streptopelia risoria   11in/28cm

IDENTIFICATION Pale creamy dove marked by a narrow, black half collar and white tail corners.
VOICE *Koo-krr-oo*.
HABITAT Suburbs.
RANGE Feral populations around cities from Florida to California.
MOVEMENTS Resident, introduced.

SPOTTED DOVE

Streptopelia chinensis   11−12in/28−30cm

IDENTIFICATION Brown-gray above with pinkish breast, pale gray head and white-spotted, black collar. In flight shows white margins to wedge-shaped tail.
VOICE *Oo-oo-rupp*.
HABITAT Suburbs and agricultural land.
RANGE Southern California.
MOVEMENTS Resident, introduced.

WHITE-WINGED DOVE

Zenaida asiatica   10½−11½in/27−29cm

IDENTIFICATION A sandy-buff dove with bold, white wing patches, obvious both at rest and in flight. White-tipped tail shows well.
VOICE *Hooo-hooo-hoo-hooo*.
HABITAT Dry woods, orchards, semi-desert.
RANGE Mexican-US border, locally abundant.
MOVEMENTS Winters Mexico and Gulf coast to Florida.
BREEDING Thick bush country with plentiful undergrowth and dense shrubs; March-May.
NEST AND EGGS A platform of twigs placed in a shrub at no great height from the ground; the 2 eggs are buffy.
INCUBATION Lasts 14 days, and is performed by both sexes.
COMMENT These doves may nest in huge colonies numbering hundreds of pairs.

MOURNING DOVE

Zenaida macroura   11½−12in/29−31cm

IDENTIFICATION Brown upperparts spotted black; rich-pinkish on breast. In flight, appears uniformly dark, but long, pointed tail has white margins.
VOICE *Oooh-oo-oo-oo*.
HABITAT Farms, towns, cities.
RANGE Most widespread pigeon. Breeds throughout US and southern Canada.
MOVEMENTS Northern birds move southward in winter.
BREEDING Wooded and agricultural land, parks, wind breaks, neglected land; February-September.

NEST AND EGGS A platform of twigs at variable height in a tree, though ground nests are not unknown; the 2 eggs are white.

INCUBATION Lasts for 14 to 15 days with incubation by both sexes.

COMMENT A successful species that lives happily alongside man and has evolved an extremely lengthy breeding season that may allow three or four broods to be reared.

INCA DOVE

Columbina inca   7½−8½in/19−22cm

IDENTIFICATION Similar to Common Ground-Dove, but heavily marked with scaly crescents above and below. Shows chestnut in wing, particularly in flight, but also has long, gray tail with black and white margins.

VOICE *Coo-coo*.

HABITAT Dry semi-desert, often near buildings.

RANGE Mexican border country.

MOVEMENTS Resident.

BREEDING Semi-arid areas of brush, with low trees and open ground; March-August.

NEST AND EGGS A platform of twigs in a thick tangle; the 2 eggs are creamy white.

INCUBATION The eggs take 14 days to hatch and are incubated by both sexes.

COMMENT A typical 'ground dove' that rears four or five broods during an extended breeding season.

COMMON GROUND-DOVE

Columbina passerina   6−7in/16−18cm

IDENTIFICATION Gray-brown above with black spots on folded wings. Male has gray crown and pinkish breast, heavily scaled. Female is grayer. In flight, shows rusty outer wing. *See* Inca Dove.

VOICE *Hoo-ah* rising.

HABITAT Brush country and open ground.

RANGE Mexican border country and across Gulf coast states to Florida.

MOVEMENTS Resident.

BREEDING Dry, open ground, gardens, parks, even beaches; March-September.

NEST AND EGGS A hollow in the ground often serves as a nest, but a low twig platform may be constructed among vegetation near the ground; the 2 eggs are white.

INCUBATION The eggs hatch after 13 days of incubation by both sexes.

COMMENT An aptly named species that spends most of its time walking with nodding head.

WHITE-TIPPED DOVE

Leptotila verreauxi   11−12in/28−30cm

IDENTIFICATION Chunky brown and pinkish dove with pale forehead and bib; shows white tips to outer tail in flight.

VOICE Deep flute-like whistle.

HABITAT Woodland thickets.

RANGE Lower Rio Grande, Texas.

MOVEMENTS Resident.

BUDGERIGAR

Melopsittacus undulatus   7−7½in/18−19cm

IDENTIFICATION A highly variable, escaped cage-bird. Yellow head, barred upperparts and green breast is dominant form, but there is great variation. Long, pointed tail.
VOICE Various warblings and loud screams.
HABITAT Suburbs and parks.
RANGE Widespread, but well-established in south-western Florida.
MOVEMENTS Resident, introduced from Australia.

CANARY-WINGED PARAKEET

Brotogeris versicolurus   8½−9in/21−23cm

IDENTIFICATION An all-green parakeet marked by a bold patch of yellow and white in wing.
VOICE High-pitched series of calls.
HABITAT Suburbs.
RANGE Florida coast and Los Angeles.
MOVEMENTS Resident; a South American bird.

RED-CROWNED PARROT

Amazona viridigenalis   12−13in/30−33cm

IDENTIFICATION Chunky green parrot with ivory bill and red crown.
VOICE Loud, raucous calls.
HABITAT Suburbs.
RANGE Rare visitor to southern Texas.
MOVEMENTS Escaped birds resident in Florida and Los Angeles.

BLACK-BILLED CUCKOO

Coccyzus erythrophthalmus   10½−11½in/27−29cm

IDENTIFICATION Similar shape, size and coloration as Yellow-billed Cuckoo. Separated by having no rust in wing, dark bill and only tips of tail feathers marked black and white.
VOICE *Co-co-co.*
HABITAT Streamside woods.
RANGE Northern, eastern and central US, together with southern Canada.
MOVEMENTS Summer visitor.
BREEDING Woodland, damp thickets; May-June.
NEST AND EGGS A platform of twigs lined with grasses and roots placed low in a tree or bush; the 2 to 4 eggs are blue-green.
INCUBATION The eggs hatch after 10 to 13 days and incubation is shared between the sexes.
COMMENT Occasionally lays eggs in nests of other species which, together with the short incubation period, indicates a species with the potential to become a brood parasite.

YELLOW-BILLED CUCKOO

Coccyzus americanus   10½–11½in/27–29cm

IDENTIFICATION Slim, long-tailed bird; brown above and white below. Distinguished by bill with yellow lower mandible, rust in wings, and boldly-barred, black and white undertail. The Mangrove Cuckoo of Florida lacks rufous in wings and has buffy belly and dark mask.
VOICE Sharp *kuk-kuk-kuk*.
HABITAT Woodland, groves.
RANGE Throughout US, but scarce or absent California and north-west states. Barely penetrates southernmost Canada.
MOVEMENTS Summer visitor.
BREEDING Woodland, damp thickets; April-June.
NEST AND EGGS The nest is a platform of twigs with a lining of bents placed low in a tree or shrub; the 3 or 4 eggs are greenish blue.
INCUBATION Both male and female, mainly the latter, participate in incubation that takes 10 to 13 days.
COMMENT This bird occasionally lays its eggs in the nests of other species.

MANGROVE CUCKOO

Coccyzus minor   12in/30cm

IDENTIFICATION Typical slim, long-tailed cuckoo, with buffy underparts and black mask. Lacks rufous in wing of similar Yellow-billed Cuckoo.
VOICE Harsh *ga-ga-ga*.
HABITAT Mangroves.
RANGE Southern Florida, resident.
MOVEMENTS Rare vagrant from Mexico to Texas Gulf coast.

GREATER ROADRUNNER

Geococcyx californianus   22–23in/56–59cm

IDENTIFICATION Well-known, ground-dwelling bird with heavily spotted upperparts, bold crest, large, black bill and extremely long, black tail. A great runner.
VOICE Pigeon-like cooing.
HABITAT Mesquite and semi-desert.
RANGE South-western US.
MOVEMENTS Resident.

BREEDING Desert scrub, chaparral, cactus; March-May.
NEST AND EGGS Constructs a neat, saucer-shaped nest in a shrub or cactus; the 3 to 6 eggs are white.
INCUBATION Lasts 18 days, by both sexes.
COMMENT This unusual bird adopts the tactic of hatching its young at intervals like a bird of prey.

SMOOTH-BILLED ANI

Crotophaga ani   14–15in/35–38cm

IDENTIFICATION Large, all-black bird with very long fan-shaped tail and deep, parrot-like black bill. Separated from Groove-billed Ani by bill bulging upwards above level of crown.
VOICE *Kee-lick.*
HABITAT Farmland.
RANGE Southern Florida.
MOVEMENTS Resident.

GROOVE-BILLED ANI

Crotophaga sulcirostris   13–14in/33–35cm

IDENTIFICATION Slightly smaller than Smooth-billed Ani, with more regular, wedge-shaped bill. Otherwise black and similar in shape.
VOICE *Kee-ho.*
HABITAT Farmland.
RANGE Rio Grande and adjacent Texas coastlands.
MOVEMENTS Wanders eastward to Louisiana coastlands in winter.

OWLS

THERE are some 142 species of owls in the world, of which 19 breed in North America. This is a well-defined group of birds that share common features and whose members are all easily recognized as owls. Though they vary enormously in size, all owls are fierce predators. These are the nocturnal birds of prey that have several significant adaptions to their night-time lifestyle. Most obviously, they have "flat" faces with both eyes pointing forward, offering excellent binocular vision. Their eyes are exceptionally large with great light-gathering power, enabling them to "see in the dark" when the human eye can barely distinguish anything. Though they have such excellent vision, owls also hunt by sound and their ears are placed asymmetrically on the head to enable sounds to be located by both direction and distance. One of the essentials of nocturnal hunting is silence, and the flight feathers of owls are fringed with soft margins that muffle the sound of their wings through the air. Finally, and like the diurnal birds of prey, they have sharp talons and hooked bills suitable for grasping and tearing their "catch."

While sharing these common features, owls vary enormously in their modes of living. Some are forest birds, some birds of open countryside. Some are secretive and totally nocturnal, while others actually prefer to hunt by day. Some take large prey, whereas others are earthworm or insect specialists. In the tropics there are even owls that plunge into water in pursuit of fish. All owls do, however, suffer from the attentions of small birds during the hours of daylight and all are, in some way or another, camouflaged to hide their presence. Many are clothed in shades of mottled browns that make them difficult to see when perched against the trunk of a tree in dappled light. The Snowy Owl, however, is a tundra bird that spends much of its life among bare rocks and snow where its white plumage makes it less conspicuous. Even the white-breasted Barn Owl is easily overlooked, as it perches in a weathered tree-hole looking, for all the world, like a dead stump.

Being so geared to a nocturnal existence, owls communicate with one another by calls rather than visual signals. Thus, the familiar hooting and shrieking is particularly noticeable when establishing the territories that will be used for nesting. Fortunately, the calls of owls are relatively distinct and the would-be owl-watcher can locate a particular species by listening rather than watching.

Though deserts often appear quite lifeless, they hold a highly specialized population of birds. The Prairie Falcon and Elf Owl differ enormously in size, but both are expert predators. A male Sage Grouse displays quite openly, while a Gila Woodpecker and a Cactus Wren explore a saguaro. Below, a roadrunner has a lizard for its young.

Of all of the North American owls, the Short-eared is the most likely to be seen during the day. Frequenting open country, this long-winged owl has smaller eyes than most other species. Like a Northern Harrier, it quarters the ground, turning this way and that, and hovering in its search for voles. In a good year it may rear six or seven young, while in a poor year, none at all. The Northern Hawk Owl is also diurnal in habits, frequently being seen perched atop an Arctic conifer at any time of the day. The rounded wings and long tail are reminiscent of an accipiter, which is not surprising as the Northern Hawk Owl lives a very similar lifestyle among the trees as those birds.

Like the diurnal birds of prey, owls breed early in the year, and the number of eggs laid depends on the quantity of food available. Incubation commences as soon as the first egg is laid and the chicks hatch over a lengthy period. Indeed, by the time the last egg hatches, the eldest chick will be well grown and active. This is usually bad news for late hatchers, for owls do not share food among the brood equally, but simply feed the most demanding of their young. Thus, only if food is superabundant is there any chance of late hatchers receiving anything other than the "crumbs" from the table. Many late hatchers do not survive, but this does mean that every year the parents will raise some young, rather than having their entire brood starve for some human sense of fairness.

Owls are a fascinating group of highly specialized birds about which we still know comparatively little. There are new species in the world to be discovered, as well as much to find out about those we do know.

BARN OWL

Tyto alba   13–14in/33–36cm

IDENTIFICATION Ghost-like, white-breasted owl with cinnamon upperparts. Often hunts late in the day or in the early morning. Breast color varies from white to pale cinnamon. Has heart-shaped face.

VOICE Hissing and snoring calls.

HABITAT Farmland, suburbs, woodland, parks.

RANGE Breeds across US, though absent from central, northern states.

MOVEMENTS Largely resident.

BREEDING Old buildings, barns, old broken trees; March-May.

NEST AND EGGS A hole or hollow in a tree, or the loft of a barn serves as a nest; the 4 to 7 eggs are white.

INCUBATION Lasts for 32 to 34 days and is performed by the female alone.

COMMENT Though they have excellent night vision, these owls are most active at dawn and dusk. Their vision is aided by an excellent sound location system.

FLAMMULATED OWL

Otus flammeolus   6–7in/16–18cm

IDENTIFICATION Small, heavily barred and streaked owl. Small ear tufts, dark eyes. Appears in rufous and gray phases. Has rufous-edged facial disc.

VOICE Series of single mellow hoots.

HABITAT Extensive woods.

RANGE Western mountain states.

MOVEMENTS Summer visitor.

BREEDING Virtually confined to forests of conifers; May-June.

NEST AND EGGS A natural tree hole, or disused woodpecker hole serves as a nest; the 3 or 4 eggs are white.

INCUBATION Probably by the female for about 22 days.

COMMENT As with other species of this genus, the male is the hunter while the female tends and cares for the young.

EASTERN SCREECH OWL

Otus asio   8½–9in/21–23cm

IDENTIFICATION Variably colored, small owl that is found in two plumages – rusty and gray. Yellow eyes, prominent ear tufts, bold white spots across folded wing, pale bill and black-edged, facial disc are all good features.

VOICE Wavering trills.

HABITAT Woods, parks, suburbs.

RANGE Throughout eastern US.

MOVEMENTS Resident.

BREEDING Woods with open glades, orchards, parks, gardens; March-May.

NEST AND EGGS An unlined tree hole or woodpecker hole at variable height from the ground; the 4 or 5 eggs are white.

INCUBATION Lasts 26 days, probably by the female alone.

COMMENT A widespread nocturnal owl that responds well to bird houses wherever suitable ones are erected.

WESTERN SCREECH-OWL

Otus kennicottii   8−9in/20−23cm

IDENTIFICATION Formerly regarded as subspecies of *Otus asio*, the Eastern Screech Owl, and very similar in markings. The present species has a dark bill.
VOICE Series of whistles and a trill.
HABITAT Woods, parks, suburbs.
RANGE Western US extending northward through western British Columbia to the Alaskan panhandle.
MOVEMENTS Resident.

WHISKERED SCREECH-OWL

Otus trichopsis   7−7½in/18−19cm

IDENTIFICATION Similar to, but smaller than, gray screech owls, with ear tufts, yellow eyes and heavily streaked and mottled plumage.
VOICE Regular, repeated whistles and hoots.
HABITAT Forests usually at altitude.
RANGE South-eastern Arizona.
MOVEMENTS Resident.

GREAT HORNED OWL

Bubo virginianus   22−23in/53−58cm

IDENTIFICATION Huge, powerful owl, with large, rounded wings. Upperparts are mottled and barred brown; underparts streaked and closely barred. Prominent ear tufts, white at throat, facial disc and yellow eyes.
VOICE Deep *hooo-hoo-hoo*.
HABITAT Forests, mountains, suburbs, parks.
RANGE Throughout North America save extreme northern tundra.
MOVEMENTS Resident.
BREEDING Conifer and deciduous woods, cliffs and canyons; March-June.
NEST AND EGGS Uses a wide variety of sites as long as a hole, cave, or other form of shelter is available; old nests of other species are often used; the 2 or 3 eggs are white.

INCUBATION The eggs hatch after 30 days having been incubated by the female.
COMMENT One of the largest and most powerful of avian predators, it is remarkable that this bird has managed to survive so well in North America.

SNOWY OWL

Nyctea scandiaca   21−26in/53−66cm

IDENTIFICATION Large white owl of tundra. Smaller male is white with variable black spotting on wings and flanks. Female is more heavily spotted and barred all over. Rounded head appears small.
VOICE Deep hooting.
HABITAT Tundra.

RANGE Northernmost Alaska and Canada, including archipelago.

MOVEMENTS Irregular in irruptive movements southward across Canada to northern states.

BREEDING Tundra with rolling ridges and rocky outcrops; May-July.

NEST AND EGGS A shallow depression with little or no lining; the 5 to 7 eggs are white.

INCUBATION Lasts 32 or 33 days and is performed by the female.

COMMENT The Snowy Owl lays a variable number of eggs dependent on the availability of small mammalian prey.

NORTHERN HAWK-OWL

Surnia ulula   15−16½in/39−42cm

IDENTIFICATION Long-tailed owl of northern forests that is often seen perched openly on a tree top in daylight. Dark-gray, heavily spotted white above; heavily barred black below. White facial disc with yellow eyes, boldly bordered black. Long, barred tail.

VOICE Falcon-like *ki-ki-ki*.

HABITAT Conifer forests.

RANGE Boreal Canada and Alaska from coast to coast.

MOVEMENTS Resident.

BREEDING Conifer woods with clearings and regenerating secondary growth; April-May.

NEST AND EGGS An old nest of crow or hawk or an old woodpecker hole in a dead tree serves as a nest; the 3 to 10 eggs are white.

INCUBATION The eggs are incubated by the female (possibly with help from the male) for 25 to 30 days.

COMMENT One of the easiest of all northern owls to locate because of its diurnal habits.

NORTHERN PYGMY-OWL

Glaucidium gnoma   6−7in/16−18cm

IDENTIFICATION Small owl with rounded head, long tail, spotted facial disc and yellow eyes. Underparts streaked. Some birds are brown (red phase), some gray (gray phase). Flies fast and direct, often during daylight.

VOICE *Hoo-hoo*.

HABITAT Woodlands.

RANGE Breeds in Rocky Mountain system and foothills.

MOVEMENTS Resident.

BREEDING Clearings and edges of conifer woodland; April-May.

NEST AND EGGS Old woodpecker holes are almost universally used as nests; the 2 to 7 eggs are white.

INCUBATION The eggs are incubated for 28 days by the female alone.

COMMENT Despite sharing a similar English name, the Northern Pygmy Owl is a different species to that found in Europe. In fact there are "pygmy owls" in most parts of the world.

FERRUGINOUS PYGMY-OWL

Glaucidium brasilianum   6−7in/15−18cm

IDENTIFICATION Very similar to Northern Pygmy-Owl, but with rusty-barred tail.
VOICE Rythmically repeated *took*.
HABITAT Semi-desert woodland.
RANGE Southern Arizona and lower Rio Grande, Texas.
MOVEMENTS Resident.

ELF OWL

Micrathene whitneyi   5½−6in/14−15cm

IDENTIFICATION Tiny, desert owl, barred and spotted in browns, buffs and chestnut. Rounded head with black-bordered facial disc, short tail and yellow eyes. Roosts and nests in trees and saguaros; active dawn and dusk.
VOICE Repeated chirrups.
HABITAT Deserts and dry woods.
RANGE Mexican border country.
MOVEMENTS Summer visitor.
BREEDING Deserts and scrub, particularly saguaro; April-May.
NEST AND EGGS An old woodpecker hole in a saguaro or tree forms the nest; the 3 or 4 eggs are white.
INCUBATION The eggs hatch after 21 days and are incubated by both members of the pair.
COMMENT This diminutive owl is virtually insectivorous in its diet.

BURROWING OWL

Athene cunicularia   9−10in/23−25cm

IDENTIFICATION Small, ground-dwelling owl with remarkably long legs. Upperparts brown, spotted white; underparts white, neatly barred brown. Head seems small and rounded with prominent white eyebrows and black chin patch. Often perches openly during day.
VOICE Quick *coo-cooo*.
HABITAT Dry, open grassland.
RANGE Breeds over western half of US northwards just into Canada. Also found in southern Florida.
MOVEMENTS Migrates southward; winters along Mexican border.
BREEDING Open prairies and other dry country without trees; March-May.
NEST AND EGGS Utilizes a lengthy burrow that has been excavated by a mammal; the 6 to 10 eggs are white.
INCUBATION The eggs take 28 days to hatch and incubation is shared by male and female.
COMMENT A combination of habitat, nest site and long, bare legs make this an easy species to identify.

SPOTTED OWL

Strix occidentalis   17−18in/43−46cm

IDENTIFICATION Similar to Barred Owl, but brown plumage is boldly spotted white above and especially below. Black-edged facial disc, ringed face and dark eyes.

Voice Various barking notes.
Habitat Wooded gullies and damp forests.
Range Pacific coast of US and inland in south-western states.
Movements Resident.
Breeding Extensive conifer forests and adjacent cliffs; April-May.
Nest and eggs A hole in a tree or cliff forms the usual nest, but it will also occupy a disused hawk's nest; the 2 or 3 eggs are white.
Incubation By female, lasting about 30 days.
Comment A scarce species that is quite intolerant of disturbance.

Barred Owl

Strix varia 20 − 21½in/51 − 54cm

Identification Medium-sized owl, heavily barred above and streaked below. Black-bordered facial disc with ringed face and dark eyes.

Voice *Oo-oo-ooo-oooo.*

Habitat Conifer and other dense woodlands.
Range Breeds across eastern US and Canada extending north and west to British Columbia; colonizing westwards.
Movements Resident.
Breeding Extensive conifer forests and mixed woodland, often near water; May-June.
Nest and eggs A tree hole or the disused nest of another species is used; the 2 or 3 eggs are white.
Incubation The eggs hatch after 28 days of incubation by the female.
Comment An elusive species that must be searched for by using its distinctive call as a means of location.

Great Gray Owl

Strix nebulosa 25½ − 27½in/65 − 70cm

Identification Large gray owl, spotted, barred and streaked black. Huge head with facial disc prominently ringed. Small, yellow eyes. Hunts dawn and dusk.
Voice Deep *who* repeated.
Habitat Boreal and mountain conifer forests.
Range Boreal forests of Canada eastward to Great Lakes, southward into US Rockies and to northern California.
Movements Mainly resident, but some birds do wander a little southward.

BREEDING Extensive conifer and mixed woodlands; April-May.

NEST AND EGGS The old nest of another large bird, a hawk or crow, is used; the 2 to 5 eggs are white.

INCUBATION The eggs take 30 days to hatch and are incubated by the female alone.

COMMENT This owl frequently hunts during daylight and can be intimidating in its attacks on intruders.

LONG-EARED OWL

Asio otus   13½–14½in/34–37cm

IDENTIFICATION Medium-sized owl with heavy streaking above and below and prominent, close-set ear tufts, facial disc and yellow-orange eyes. Totally nocturnal. Appears tall and slim when discovered perched.

VOICE A low *hoo*.

HABITAT Forests and woods.

RANGE Breeds throughout North America south of the tree line, though absent from southern states.

MOVEMENTS Many boreal-zone birds migrate south. Winters throughout US, including areas of south where it does not breed.

BREEDING Conifer and deciduous/mixed woodland; February-May.

NEST AND EGGS Uses a disused tree nest of another species; the 4 or 5 eggs are white.

INCUBATION The eggs take 25 to 30 days to hatch and are incubated throughout by the female.

COMMENT In winter, this owl regularly forms communal roosts in dense woodland.

SHORT-EARED OWL

Asio flammeus   14–15in/36–39cm

IDENTIFICATION Long-winged, diurnal owl that mostly frequents rough ground and marshes. Buffy and heavily streaked above and below, with clear-cut facial disc and yellow eyes. Glides and hovers in search of prey.

VOICE Barking in breeding season.

HABITAT Marshes, rough ground, tundra.

RANGE Breeds throughout Alaska, Canada and the northern half of the US.

MOVEMENTS Migrates from Canada to winter over most of the US.

BREEDING Coastal and inland marshes, grassland, bogs and tundra; March-August.

NEST AND EGGS A hollow on the ground variably lined with grasses; the 4 to 9 eggs are white.

INCUBATION The eggs take 25 to 30 days to hatch and are incubated by the female alone.

COMMENT Like other owls, this bird lays white eggs, but this is unusual for a ground-nesting species.

BOREAL OWL

Aegolius funereus   9–10in/23–25cm

IDENTIFICATION Small, gray-brown owl, spotted white above and streaked brown below. Has yellow eyes, white face, boldly bordered facial disc. Spots are on forehead.

VOICE *Hoo-hoo-hoo* repeated.

HABITAT Conifer forests.

RANGE Boreal Canada to Alaska, also in several areas of Rockies.
MOVEMENTS Resident.
BREEDING Extensive conifer and mixed woodland; April-May.
NEST AND EGGS Tree holes and, particularly, old woodpecker holes are used to nest, but this bird will take to nest boxes where provided; the 3 to 7 eggs are white.
INCUBATION Lasts 27 days and is almost certainly by the female alone.
COMMENT The erection of suitable nest boxes can help to maintain the population of this species in areas that have been logged and replanted.

NORTHERN SAW-WHET OWL

Aegolius acadicus   7½−8½in/19−21cm

IDENTIFICATION Small owl with brown upperparts liberally spotted white; underparts white, boldly streaked rust. Facial disc is radially streaked rufous and brown. Pale streaks on forehead.

VOICE Repeated single whistle.
HABITAT Dense conifer and mixed forests.
RANGE Most of US and southern Canada extending northwards to Alaska along Pacific coast. Absent central and southern states.
MOVEMENTS Some movement to areas of center and south where it does not breed.
BREEDING Thick woodlands of a variety of types; April-May.
NEST AND EGGS Holes in trees, often disused woodpecker holes, are used as a nest; the 4 to 7 eggs are white.
INCUBATION Variously recorded as 21 to 28 days with the female incubating.
COMMENT The smallest owl over most of North America.

NIGHTJARS, SWIFTS & HUMMINGBIRDS

THOUGH these three groups of birds look so dissimilar and are placed in three quite distinct families, they are related and share several common characteristics. All, for example, are totally aerial feeders, with only tiny, rudimentary legs. Thereafter, they vary enormously. The nightjars are exceptionally well camouflaged and hunt only after dark; the swifts are totally aerial and come to "land" only to nest; the hummingbirds feed on the wing, though they could feed from a perch, and are boldly colored in iridescent hues.

Were it not for their distinctive calls, the nightjars, sometimes quaintly called "goatsuckers," would present baffling problems of identification. All are superbly camouflaged in shades of brown, buff, and gray mixed together to resemble the dead vegetation of the rough, broken landscapes they prefer. Several of their vernacular names reflect their calls and derive from the early settlers' wish to name all the new sounds of their new country. Thus we have Chuck-will's-widow and Whip-poor-will, both of which remain the standard renderings of these birds calls.

Nightjars feed after dark on flying insects, mostly moths, and are thus summer visitors over most of North America. Their bills are tiny, but their mouths are huge. They have soft margins to their flight feathers, like owls, and are totally silent in the air. Some have white marks in their tails and wings, but these can be seen only when they fly and are a visual means of communication between individual birds. The eggs are white and are laid quite openly on the ground, hidden by the sitting bird which remains quite stationary, even on a close approach. As a result many birders have never seen the nest of any nightjar.

Swifts — and there are over 70 species in the world, though only four breed in North America — are among the most aerial of all birds. Their wings are long and sickle-shaped, their bodies rounded and streamlined. They feed, drink, mate, gather nesting materials, and even bathe on the wing. Like the nightjars, they have small bills backed by large gapes which act as effective funnels for catching insects on the wing. Not surprisingly, all four species are summer visitors over most of their North American range. Most widespread and numerous is the Chimney Swift of the east, which has prospered by taking

to chimneys as nest sites. In the west it is replaced by three species – the Black, Vaux's, and White-throated Swifts. While the Black Swift is a large bird and the White-throated is marked by white underparts, Vaux's Swift is remarkably similar to the Chimney Swift. Though this bird occasionally nests in chimneys in the west, it usually prefers nesting in trees.

Hummingbirds are really tropical birds, some of which have managed to spread northward. Thus, of the 320 species in the world, only 14 have adapted to North America; the rest are confined to the New World south of the Mexican border. These are brightly colored birds that feed on nectar sucked from flowers through their tube-like bills. They are unique in obtaining lift on both the forward and backward strokes of their wings, and are the only birds in the world that can actually fly backward. They are named for the hum produced by their wings, and one species, the tiny Bee Hummingbird of Cuba, beats its wings between 50 and 80 times per second. The metabolism of such tiny birds is remarkable and many species pass the night by turning off all their life-support systems and entering a state of torpor. Were all these systems to

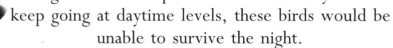

keep going at daytime levels, these birds would be unable to survive the night.

Despite their obvious tropical origins, some North American hummers can be found as far north as Alaska and Nova Scotia. While they then enjoy the long hours of the near-Arctic summer, they are also forced to make migrational journeys of several thousand miles to their wintering grounds. The Ruby-throated Hummingbird, the only one frequently found east of the Mississippi, regularly flies non-stop across the Caribbean. Physiologists investigating this remarkable feat and considering the energy requirements of such a flight by such a small bird concluded that it was impossible! Thus we learned that migrating birds have a far greater range than was previously realized.

Most North American hummers are found in the west where their identification can cause problems for those not well acquainted with this family. Though books show the colors in bright light, the angle between bird and sunlight can change the iridescent sheen from one color to another in a fraction of a second. As a result, calls take on a new significance.

LESSER NIGHTHAWK

Chordeiles acutipennis   8½–9in/21–23cm

IDENTIFICATION Similar to Common Nighthawk, but paler and with less clear-cut barring. Best distinctions are more rounded wings, with white primary patch nearer wing tip; and notched (not forked) tail with broad, white band and several smaller bands.
VOICE Rapid trilling.
HABITAT Dry scrub, semi-desert.
RANGE Mexican border states.
MOVEMENTS Summer visitor.
BREEDING Frequents arid scrub, dry grassland and desert; April-June.
NEST AND EGGS The 2 grayish eggs are spotted brown and laid on bare ground.
INCUBATION Lasts 18 to 19 days, by female only.
COMMENT This species may become torpid ("hibernates") when temperature cool, or if food unavailable.

COMMON NIGHTHAWK

Chordeiles minor   9–10in/23–25cm

IDENTIFICATION Dark, gray nightjar with white chin and closely barred black and white underparts. In flight, wings are long and pointed with bold, white patch across the primaries. The tail is distinctly forked, with a narrow, white band near the tip. Flies by day and night. Similar but buffier Antillean Nighthawk is local in south Florida, and calls, *killy-ka-dick*.
VOICE Nasal *peent*.
HABITAT Grasslands, woods, towns.
RANGE Virtually whole of sub-tundra North America.
MOVEMENTS Summer visitor.
BREEDING A variety of open areas from open woodland to flat-topped city buildings; March-June.
NEST AND EGGS A bare hollow is used as a nest, flat roofs are preferably gravel covered; the 2 eggs vary from creamy to olive buff and are also variably speckled.
INCUBATION The eggs take 19 days to hatch and are incubated by the female.
COMMENT The adaption to nesting on buildings is quite unique among the nightjars.

ANTILLEAN NIGHTHAWK

Chordeiles gundlachii   9–10in/23–25cm

IDENTIFICATION Similar to Common Nighthawk, but much more rufous below.
VOICE *Pti-pi-pit*.
HABITAT Sandy scrub.
RANGE Vagrant to Florida, regular breeder on keys.
MOVEMENTS Summer visitor from Caribbean.

COMMON PAURAQUE

Nyctidromus albicollis   11in/28cm

IDENTIFICATION Large, sandy-colored nightjar with long, rounded tail, margined black and white in the male and with a neat, obscured white frontal collar. Rounded wings marked by bold white patches across primaries.
VOICE *Per-weeeer*.
HABITAT Scrub.
RANGE Lower Rio Grande and adjacent areas of Texas.
MOVEMENTS Resident.

COMMON POORWILL

Phalaenoptilus nuttallii   7½−8½in/19−21cm

IDENTIFICATION Small nightjar, mottled in shades of gray and brown, with white-tipped tail and rounded wings. White throat-crescent contrasts with dark chin and black breast.
VOICE *Poor-will*.

HABITAT Dry, open country.
RANGE Western half of US.
MOVEMENTS Summer visitor, resident along Mexican border.
BREEDING Dry, arid areas, sagebrush, clearings in dry woodland; March-June.
NEST AND EGGS A bare depression on the ground, even on a rock, acts as a nest; the 2 eggs are white, washed with pink.
INCUBATION Shared between male and female.
COMMENT It was this bird that was discovered hibernating in the California desert, thus reopening the 'hibernate-migrate' debate.

CHUCK-WILL'S-WIDOW

Caprimulgus carolinensis   11½−12in/29−31cm

IDENTIFICATION Typical nightjar, mottled and barred in browns and buffs. More rufous than other species and substantially larger. Creamy crescent on throat contrasts with blackish breast and rufous chin.
VOICE *Chuck-will's-widow*.
HABITAT Woods and groves.
RANGE South-eastern third of US.

MOVEMENTS Summer visitor, but resident Florida.
BREEDING Woodland clearings and margins, adjacent arable fields; April-June.
NEST AND EGGS A shallow depression on the ground, either bare or lined with a few leaves, serves as a nest; the 2 eggs are pale creamy, marked with brown.
INCUBATION By the female, for 20 days.
COMMENT Best located by characteristic rhythmic calls.

BUFF-COLLARED NIGHTJAR

Caprimulgus ridgwayi   8½−9in/21−23cm

IDENTIFICATION Compact, short-tailed nightjar clothed in grays, with white frontal collar, extending on hind-neck in sandy buff.
VOICE A repeated *cuck-cuck-cuck* ending in a flourish.
HABITAT Scrubby desert.
RANGE Southern Arizona and New Mexico.
MOVEMENTS Probably summer visitor, but rare and poorly known.

WHIP-POOR-WILL

Caprimulgus vociferus   9½–10in/24–26cm

IDENTIFICATION Grayish nightjar, considerably smaller than Chuck-will's-widow. Black chin and white throat-crescent more prominent in male, which has white tail corners in flight.
VOICE *Whip-poor-will.*

HABITAT Conifer and mixed woods.
RANGE Breeds most of eastern and south-western US.
MOVEMENTS Migrates south, but winters in Florida and along Gulf Coast.
BREEDING Open woodlands, clearings and margins of various types including pure conifers; May-June.
NEST AND EGGS A bare depression among dead leaves acts as a nest; the 2 eggs are white, blotched with gray.
INCUBATION The eggs take 19 to 21 days to hatch and are incubated almost entirely by the female.
COMMENT As with the other 'nightjars' this species is best located by its call.

BLACK SWIFT

Cypseloides niger   6½–7in/17–18cm

IDENTIFICATION An all-black swift with notched tail; largest of our regular swifts. Breeds among cliffs in west; decidedly scarce.
VOICE Repeated *plik-plik.*
HABITAT Sheltered cliffs and canyons.
RANGE From southern Alaska through British Columbia and sporadically through far-western states.
MOVEMENTS Summer visitor.

BREEDING Mountain or sea cliffs, often in canyons; June-July.
NEST AND EGGS A crevice in a cliff wall holds the few bits of vegetation that act as a nest; the single egg is white.
INCUBATION About 23 days and probably by both members of the pair.
COMMENT Not many nestings have been studied and there is no full account of the species' breeding routine.

CHIMNEY SWIFT

Chaetura pelagica   4½–5in/12–13cm

IDENTIFICATION Dark brown above and below, with paler gray, buffy throat and upper breast. Tail short and cut abruptly square. Only swift in the east and confused only with Vaux's Swift of the west.
VOICE Loud chatter.
HABITAT Breeds in chimneys, trees.
RANGE US and southern Canada east of Rockies.

MOVEMENTS Summer visitor.
BREEDING Mostly towns and suburbs; May–June.
NEST AND EGGS Originally nested in cliffs and tree hollows, but has now changed almost entirely to house chimneys; the nest itself is a shelf of twigs glued to the chimney side with saliva; the 4 or 5 eggs are white.
INCUBATION Lasts 19 days and is shared between members of the pair.
COMMENT The Chimney Swift has increased and spread as a result of human construction of chimneys providing nest sites in otherwise unsuitable areas.

VAUX'S SWIFT

Chaetura vauxi   4½/11–12cm

IDENTIFICATION Similar to Chimney Swift, but slightly shorter in the wing and paler on breast. Short, square-cut tail.
VOICE Soft chattering.
HABITAT Nests in hollow trees, sometimes chimneys.
RANGE Pacific Canada, Alaska and sporadically in western states.
MOVEMENTS Summer visitor. Note that Chimney Swift and Vaux's Swift can occur together on migration in southern California.
BREEDING Wide variety of habitats providing that suitable nest sites are available; May–June.
NEST AND EGGS Consists of twigs or bents glued together to form a ledge inside a hollow tree or, less frequently, a chimney; the 4 to 6 eggs are white.
INCUBATION The eggs take 18 to 20 days to hatch and are incubated by both sexes.
COMMENT Though it may nest in chimneys, this swift has shown little interest in abandoning its natural nesting sites, unlike the Chimney Swift.

WHITE-THROATED SWIFT

Aeronautes saxatalis   6–6½in/16–17cm

IDENTIFICATION Large swift marked by bold black and white pattern above and below. Only swift with white on underparts. Tail distinctly forked.
VOICE Shrill chattering.

HABITAT Cliffs and canyons.
RANGE Mountains of the western US.
MOVEMENTS Migrates, but resident in Mexican border states.
BREEDING Mountain areas, cliffs and canyons; May–June.
NEST AND EGGS A neat cup of feathers and plant material glued to the inside of a crevice on a cliff; the 4 or 5 eggs are white.
INCUBATION Undescribed.
COMMENT The inaccessibility of the nests of this species leave its breeding routine something of a mystery.

BROAD-BILLED HUMMINGBIRD

Cynanthus latirostris   4in/10cm

IDENTIFICATION Male is green with a blue throat and white undertail coverts. The bill is long, red and black tipped. The large tail is black and distinctly notched. Female has buffy-gray underparts and a lengthy, pale eyestripe.
VOICE *Jerdit*.
HABITAT Semi-deserts and hillside woods.
RANGE South-eastern Arizona.
MOVEMENTS Summer visitor from Mexico.

WHITE-EARED HUMMINGBIRD

Hylocharis leucotis   4in/10cm

IDENTIFICATION A purple-headed hummer marked by a bold white slash behind the eye. The upperparts and breast are bright green, the bill red with black outer half. Female is similar though bronzy green rather than purple headed. The broad, notched tail has green central feathers.
VOICE Loud *chink-chink*.
HABITAT Mountain-sides.
RANGE South-eastern Arizona.
MOVEMENTS Summer visitor from Mexico.

BERYLLINE HUMMINGBIRD

Amazilia beryllina   4¼in/11cm

IDENTIFICATION A green hummingbird with brown tail and boldly rufous wings. Bill reddish.
VOICE High-pitched.
HABITAT Mountains.
RANGE South-eastern Arizona.
MOVEMENTS Summer visitor from Mexico.

BUFF-BELLIED HUMMINGBIRD

Amazilia yucatanensis   4¼in/11cm

IDENTIFICATION Bronzed back, dark forehead and green breast contrast with plain, buff underparts. Bill bright red, wings dark brown.
VOICE High-pitched calls.
HABITAT Lowland scrub.
RANGE Rio Grande valley, Texas.
MOVEMENTS Wanders eastward along Gulf coast in fall.

VIOLET-CROWNED HUMMINGBIRD

Amazilia violiceps   4½in/11cm

IDENTIFICATION Bronzy-green upperparts and bright violet crown contrast with completely white underparts. Bill red, tipped black.

VOICE High-pitched *tis-tis*.
HABITAT Streamside vegetation in semi-desert country.
RANGE Southernmost borders of Arizona and New Mexico.
MOVEMENTS Summer visitor.

BLUE-THROATED HUMMINGBIRD

Lampornis clemenciae   5in/13cm

IDENTIFICATION Green above, dull gray below marked by blue throat in the male. Distinctive face pattern of white lines through and below eye. Dark blue tail, broadly tipped white.
VOICE *See-see*.
HABITAT Mountain streamsides.
RANGE South-eastern Arizona and adjacent New Mexico.
MOVEMENTS Summer visitor.

MAGNIFICENT HUMMINGBIRD

Eugenes fulgens   5in/13cm

IDENTIFICATION Green above with bright purple crown patch, green chin and black breast. Bill long and black, tail green and notched.
VOICE Repeated *chip-chip*.
HABITAT Mountains.
RANGE South-east Arizona.
MOVEMENTS Summer visitor.

PLAIN-CAPPED STARTHROAT

Heliomaster constantii   5in/13cm

IDENTIFICATION Bronzy-green upperparts, including tail, with dull-gray underparts marked by bright red throat and white flank tufts.
VOICE High-pitched calls.
HABITAT Deserts and foothills.
RANGE South-east Arizona.
MOVEMENTS Scarce wanderer north from Mexico.

LUCIFER HUMMINGBIRD

Calothorax lucifer   3½in/9cm

IDENTIFICATION A tiny, greenish hummer, with a long, decurved bill, brilliant purple throat and buffy underparts. Female and young male lack purple throat and instead are buffy.
VOICE Repeated *chip-chip*.
HABITAT Mountains.
RANGE Western Texas and more uncommonly in south-east Arizona.
MOVEMENTS Summer visitor.

RUBY-THROATED HUMMINGBIRD

Archilochus colubris   4in/10cm

IDENTIFICATION Male is green above, white below, with metallic ruby-colored throat patch. The latter changes to black in some lights. Female lacks ruby throat and is white on underparts. This is virtually the only hummingbird in the east, but beware Black-chinned Hummingbird where ranges meet. Females virtually inseparable.
VOICE Squeaky *chip*.
HABITAT Woodland edges, gardens.
RANGE Eastern half of US northward across southern Canada.

MOVEMENTS Summer visitor.
BREEDING Wide variety of vegetated areas with trees; April-June.
NEST AND EGGS A neat little cup placed on a branch and decorated with lichens; the 2 eggs are white.
INCUBATION The eggs hatch after 16 days and are incubated solely by the female.
COMMENT As with other hummingbirds, the nest is held together with spiders' webs which provide an elastic and expandable structure.

BLACK-CHINNED HUMMINGBIRD

Archilochus alexandri   4in/10cm

IDENTIFICATION Male has violet throat, becoming black on chin, though in most lights the "bib" looks totally black. Female very similar to female Ruby-throated Hummingbird of the east.

VOICE Quiet *tu*.
HABITAT Dry scrub, open woods, suburbs.
RANGE Western and south-western US.
MOVEMENTS Summer visitor; some winter in south-eastern states.
BREEDING Frequents a variety of habitats from mountain meadows to orchards and thickets; April-June.
NEST AND EGGS Plant down and lichens bound together with spiders' webs; the 2 eggs are white.
INCUBATION Lasts about 15 days and is performed by the female.
COMMENT Closely related to the more widespread Ruby-throated Hummingbird which it replaces in the west. Sometimes hybridizes with other hummers.

ANNA'S HUMMINGBIRD

Calypte anna   4in/10cm

IDENTIFICATION Metallic-green above, whitish below. In male, whole head has a pale, rosy-ruby color; female has rosy speckles on white chin; juvenile has neat, black streaking.
VOICE A hard *tic*.
HABITAT Lowland woods, gardens, mountains.
RANGE Pacific coast south to Arizona, north to British Columbia.

MOVEMENTS Largely
resident.
BREEDING Dry areas
of brushy woodland,
gardens; January-
June.
NEST AND EGGS A neatly woven cup of vegetation perched
saddle-like on a horizontal branch; the 2 eggs are white.
INCUBATION Lasts 16 days and is performed by the female.
COMMENT Though mainly confined to the lowlands of the
Pacific coast as a breeding bird; in winter, these hummers also
occur on dry, mountain areas and deserts.

COSTA'S HUMMINGBIRD

Calypte costae   3½in/9cm

IDENTIFICATION Tiny hummer with violet head, in male
extending along sides of neck. Female, green above, white
below with all but center feathers of tail gray, tipped black
and white.
VOICE Penetrating *tink*.
HABITAT Dry, arid hillsides and scrub.
RANGE Southern California and Arizona.
MOVEMENTS Migrant, but some winter in breeding areas.
BREEDING Dry areas of chapparal and semi-desert; March-
June.
NEST AND EGGS The typical neat cup is built astride a low
branch of a bush of leaves and lichens; the 2 eggs are white.
INCUBATION Lasts about 17 days and is performed by the
female.
COMMENT The known preference
of hummingbirds for red flowers
correlates with the association
of this bird with red
beardtongue.

CALLIOPE HUMMINGBIRD

Stellula calliope   3in/8cm

IDENTIFICATION Tiny hummingbird with green upperparts
and white below. Male has red-purple throat streaks; female
has spotted throat with pale, rufous wash on flanks.
VOICE *See-ree*.
HABITAT Mountain glades, canyons.
RANGE Rocky Mountains and foothills.
MOVEMENTS Summer visitor.
BREEDING Woodland with clearings, either conifer or
deciduous; May-June.
NEST AND EGGS The neat cup is placed on a branch and is
made of plant material and mosses bound together with
spiders' webs; the 2 eggs are white.
INCUBATION After 15 days of incubation by the female, the
eggs hatch.
COMMENT Though primarily a nectar feeder like other
hummingbirds, the Calliope Hummingbird also takes insects
and even catches them in mid-air.

BROAD-TAILED HUMMINGBIRD

Selasphorus platycercus   4in/10cm

IDENTIFICATION Green above, with metallic, ruby-colored
throat in male. Thus very similar to Ruby-throated
Hummingbird which it replaces in the west. One of best
features is that wing beats produce a loud whistle. Female has
white throat and pale, rufous wash on flanks.

VOICE Hard *chip*.
HABITAT Mountain thickets, glades.
RANGE Southern and central Rockies and Great Basin mountains.
MOVEMENTS Summer visitor.
BREEDING Tree and bushy areas in mountains; May-June.
NEST AND EGGS A neat cup of bents and spiders' webs placed on a branch and decorated with lichens, often in the same tree year after year; the 2 eggs are white.
INCUBATION The eggs hatch after about 15 days of incubation by the female.
COMMENT Despite its name the broad tail of this species is of dubious use for identification in the field.

Rufous Hummingbird

Selasphorus rufus   4in/10cm

IDENTIFICATION Adult male is reddish on body, with green wings and ruby-colored throat. At all ages, the tail is reddish, tipped black. Female is green above with ruby spots on throat. Only Allen's Hummingbird can be confused.
VOICE An abrupt *chup*.
HABITAT Woodland edges and glades.
RANGE From southern Alaska southwards through British Columbia to northern California.

MOVEMENTS Summer visitor.
BREEDING Occupies a wide variety of areas from coasts to mountains; April-June.
NEST AND EGGS The well-woven cup of plant down and lichens is usually placed on a low, conifer branch; the 2 eggs are white.
INCUBATION Lasts about 16 days and is performed by the female.
COMMENT The extraordinary altitudinal range of this species, together with its migrational pattern, indicates that it may follow the flowering season up the mountain sides.

Allen's Hummingbird

Selasphorus sasin   4in/10cm

IDENTIFICATION Male has green back and crown, ruby throat and rufous underparts and tail. Female not reliably separated from female Rufous Hummingbird.
VOICE *Chup*.

HABITAT Wooded ravines, parks, gardens.
RANGE Breeds coastal California.
MOVEMENTS Summer visitor.
BREEDING Found in dry, bushy country and forest margins; February-June.
NEST AND EGGS The usual hummer cup, placed on a branch and bound with spiders' webs and decorated with lichens; the 2 eggs are white.
INCUBATION Lasts from 16 to 22 days, and is performed by the female.
COMMENT Though territories may be small, they are defended vigorously through the breeding cycle.

KINGFISHERS & TROGONS

THOUGH there are no less than 86 species of kingfisher in the world, North America can claim only three. Even so, two of these only just cross the Mexican border, while the third, the Belted Kingfisher, is one of North America's most widespread and well-known birds. It would be easy to think that kingfishers were the "kings of fishermen," and, indeed, many species are excellent fishers. But many other members of the family do not fish at all, finding their food by a wait-and-pounce technique similar to that of a shrike. They may take insects, reptiles, worms or centipedes, but never fish. In fact, even proper kingfishers are not averse to supplementing their fishy diet with the odd insect or two.

The three North American birds all feed on fish. They frequent streams, rivers, and ponds where they obtain their food by diving head-first into the water, sometimes directly from a perch, but also by hovering. Prey is caught underwater and the bird then carries it to a favored perch where, after a quick beating, it is swallowed head-first.

Kingfishers are hole nesters that lay uncamouflaged white eggs which are easier to see in dark confines. The North American species all excavate a tunnel in a riverside bank and create a rounded nest chamber at the end. They use no nesting material, but a debris of odd fishbones soon creates a rather smelly lining. Though they seem rather colorful and well-marked birds, they are dull compared to the brightly colored kingfishers that can be found in the tropics.

Though the trogons are not closely related to the kingfishers, this is a convenient place to mention this mainly tropical family of 35 species, which ranges from South and Central America to Africa and Asia. Just one species, the Elegant Trogon, has managed to breed in the U.S.A. along the border region of southern Arizona. Despite their large size and often brightly colored plumage, these are remarkably difficult birds to locate, frequently perching stock-still in the shady lower or middle branches of a tree. Birders heading southward into Central America invariably have a trogon, the Resplendent Quetzel, national bird of Guatemala, high on their "wanted" list.

ELEGANT TROGON

Trogon elegans   12–13in/30–33cm

IDENTIFICATION Male is green above, with gray wings and a bronze-buff tail, terminating in a black band. The breast is green, with a white breast band and red belly and undertail. The female lacks green and is buffy brown with red on lower belly and undertail. Both sexes show pale bills. Sits motionless in trees.
VOICE Repeated *oo-ah*.
HABITAT Mountain woodlands.
RANGE South-eastern Arizona.
MOVEMENTS Summer visitor, rare in adjacent states.

RINGED KINGFISHER

Ceryle torquata   15–17in/38–43cm

IDENTIFICATION Larger than Belted Kingfisher, but similar, with brick-red underparts in male and female. Female has gray and white breast bands.
VOICE Loud rattle.
HABITAT Rivers, ponds.
RANGE Lower Rio Grande, Texas.
MOVEMENTS Resident.

BELTED KINGFISHER

Ceryle alcyon   12½–13½in/32–34cm

IDENTIFICATION The only widespread North American Kingfisher. Male has blue-gray upperparts, crown and crest, and breast band. Breast and collar are white. Female differs in having a rich-chestnut breast band. The long bill is gray. This is a great hovering bird that dives to catch fish. Larger Ringed Kingfisher of south Texas has chestnut underparts.
VOICE Loud rattle.
HABITAT Ponds, rivers, lakes, creeks.
RANGE Breeds throughout sub-tundra North America except south-western US.
MOVEMENTS Northern and central birds are migratory.

BREEDING A steep bank of earth often, but not always, near water; April-May.
NEST AND EGGS A tunnel is excavated, usually near the top of a bank, no lining is provided; the 5 to 8 eggs are white.
INCUBATION Lasts 23 or 24 days and is performed mainly by the female, though her mate sometimes assists.
COMMENT Like kingfishers elsewhere in the world, both male and female combine to excavate the nesting tunnel and chamber.

GREEN KINGFISHER

Chloroceryle americana   8½–9in/21–23cm

IDENTIFICATION Emerald green above, black-spotted white below. Only male has broad, chestnut breast band.
VOICE *Tic-tic* repeated.
HABITAT Rivers, ponds.
RANGE South-western Texas.
MOVEMENTS Resident.

WOODPECKERS

WHEN it comes to woodpeckers, North America is decidedly well off, boasting no less than 20 of the world's 210 species. While most bear the name "woodpecker," there is one quite distinct group called "sapsuckers." All are ideally suited for a life among the trees, and all are agile and well-equipped climbers. All have sharp, chisel-like bills for hacking at tree bark to seek the wood-boring insects that hide beneath. They have long, bristle-covered tongues with which to seek out their food through the maze of tunnels that these creatures create beneath the surface.

The woodpecker foot is unusual in having two toes pointing forward and two back, each armed with a strong, sharp claw. Such an arrangement is ideally suited to climbing — a sort of avian climbing iron. Additionally, the tail feathers have extremely well-developed shafts to support the bird as it hacks at tree trunks. Finally, but quite remarkably, the structure of the skull is reinforced to enable these often prolonged and ferocious attacks on hard surfaces to be performed without damaging the brain.

Having said all of this, some woodpeckers feed predominantly on the ground, often on ants, and bore holes only in the softest of wood. Others, in contrast, are totally arboreal and excavate their nest holes in the hardest of living trees. Largest and most spectacular of all North American woodpeckers was the Ivory-billed, nearly 20in/150cm in overall length. This magnificent bird, boldly marked black and white, with a bright red crest in the male, formerly inhabited the large swamp forests that bordered the rivers of the southeastern U.S.A. Sadly, each pair required about 3000 acres of such woodland as a territory, and extensive logging, especially prior to the First World War, virtually wiped out the entire habitat. By the outbreak of the Second World War there were no more than 24 birds left, and 30 years later there were only six. Though the whereabouts of these birds has been kept a well-guarded secret, there have been no reliable reports for a decade or more, so the Ivory-bill can be presumed to be extinct in the U.S.A. The Cuban subspecies is barely holding on, so yet another bird may join the gone-forever list.

The almost as large and spectacular Pileated Woodpecker was always more abundant and widespread, having a more catholic choice of habitat. Similar in plumage to the Ivory-billed, this bird is probably responsible for all reports of Ivory-bills over the past 20 years. Its success stems from its ability to live in open woods, in parklands, and even in semi-isolated forest clumps. Unlike the Ivory-billed, it regularly feeds on ants rather than on wood-boring insects.

Many smaller woodpeckers inhabit the forests and woods of North America. Most are colored black and white, like the remarkable Acorn Woodpecker of the far west. This bird has the unusual habit of boring small holes in trees and inserting an acorn in each as a store of winter food. As these birds will use the same tree year after year, some are riddled with tiny holes. Its habits have done little to endear it to telephone companies whose poles make fine storage "trunks" for these unique little birds.

The three species of sapsucker have also evolved a curious method of feeding. Using their sharply pointed bills, these birds drill a series of holes in a tree trunk, returning later to feed on the sap and the insects that have been attracted by it.

The ability of woodpeckers to excavate large chambers inside dead and living trees to act as their nests offers them great security against predators. However, the birds do like to excavate a new nest each season and this means that a wood well stocked with these birds will offer a range of nest sites to other hole-nesting birds. In this alone, the woodpeckers form an integral part of the ecology of North American woodlands.

LEWIS'S WOODPECKER

Melanerpes lewis   10–11in/26–28cm

IDENTIFICATION Very dark, metallic-green woodpecker with dark-red face, grayish-pink belly and pale-gray collar, that is particularly obvious in flight. Often catches insects in air; gregarious in winter.

VOICE Mostly silent.

HABITAT Open woods.

RANGE Throughout western states northward into British Columbia and east to South Dakota.

MOVEMENTS Northern birds migrate southwards.

BREEDING Open woodland together with areas devastated by fire or man; April-June, colonial.

NEST AND EGGS A hole is excavated usually in a dead tree; the 6 or 7 eggs are white.

INCUBATION The eggs hatch after 14 days and are incubated by both male and female.

COMMENT Though a true woodpecker, this bird finds its food by catching flying insects rather than climbing trees. It also stores nuts and acorns.

RED-HEADED WOODPECKER

Melanerpes erythrocephalus   9–10in/23–25cm

IDENTIFICATION Boldly black, white and red woodpecker. Adult has whole head red, upperparts black, with white rump and white secondaries.

VOICE *Querk.*

HABITAT Woods, parks, gardens.

RANGE US and southern Canada east of the Rockies.

MOVEMENTS Northern and western birds are migrants.

BREEDING Open woodland, parkland and burned-over woods; April-June.

NEST AND EGGS Excavates a hole in a dead tree, telegraph pole or post; the 4 to 7 eggs are white.

INCUBATION Lasts about 14 days and is shared between members of the pair.

COMMENT Though it feeds in typical woodpecker fashion this species also consumes nuts, fruit and even takes insects on the wing.

ACORN WOODPECKER

Melanerpes formicivorus   8½–9½in/22–24cm

IDENTIFICATION Shiny black above, white below with red crown, black around base of bill and broad, black breast band becoming streaky on belly. Prominent white rump. Stores acorns in holes in bark of trees or telegraph poles.

VOICE Harsh *ja-cob.*

HABITAT Oak woods, or mixed woods with oaks.

RANGE California and south-western states.

MOVEMENTS Resident.

BREEDING Oak and other woodlands, usually open with clearings; April-June.

NEST AND EGGS Colonial, all members joining in excavating a hole in the branch of a tree; the 4 to 6 eggs are white.

INCUBATION The eggs are incubated by male and female, together with other members of the colony for about 15 days.

NEST AND EGGS The nest hole is excavated in a low tree or in a saguaro cactus; the 3 to 5 eggs are white.

INCUBATION The eggs take some 21 days to hatch and are incubated by both members of the pair.

COMMENT One of the primary providers of nest holes in giant saguaro, later used by the Elf Owl.

COMMENT The behavior of this bird is remarkable in many ways. The co-operative nesting behavior and reuse of previous years' nesting holes is a special characteristic.

GILA WOODPECKER

Melanerpes uropygialis   9–10in/23–25cm

IDENTIFICATION Medium-sized woodpecker with buffy underparts and black and white "ladder-back". Male has red on top of crown; female has plain, buffy head.

VOICE *Churr*.

HABITAT Dry scrub, saguaro scrub, towns.

RANGE Arizona and neighboring California.

MOVEMENTS Resident.

BREEDING A bird of dry, open country with cactus or trees for nesting; April-May.

GOLDEN-FRONTED WOODPECKER

Melanerpes aurifrons   9½–10in/24–26cm

IDENTIFICATION Similar to Red-bellied Woodpecker with black and white "ladder-back". Male has top of crown red, with golden nape and base of bill. Female lacks red on crown. Tail black, not barred.

VOICE *Churr*.

HABITAT Woods, groves.

RANGE Central Texas.

MOVEMENTS Resident.

BREEDING Dry, open woodland, riverside scrub and town gardens; April-May.

NEST AND EGGS A nest hole is excavated in a tree, but also in a telegraph pole or fence post; the 4 to 7 eggs are white.

INCUBATION The eggs are incubated for 12 days by both male and female.

COMMENT Often quite common in parts of its range, especially in town parks.

RED-BELLIED WOODPECKER

Melanerpes carolinus   9½–10in/24–26cm

IDENTIFICATION Clearly barred, black and white upperparts create "ladder-back". Underparts, buffy with red wash on belly. Male has whole crown red, female only hind-crown.

VOICE *Churr.*
HABITAT Open woods, suburbs.
RANGE Breeds through eastern US.
MOVEMENTS Leaves northern states in winter.
BREEDING A wide variety of woodland types including garden trees; April-May.
NEST AND EGGS A hole at variable heights excavated frequently in a dead tree; the 4 or 5 eggs are white.
INCUBATION The eggs take some 14 days to hatch and are incubated by both members of the pair.
COMMENT Like its relative the Acorn Woodpecker, this species is one that stores food for the winter.

YELLOW-BELLIED SAPSUCKER

Sphyrapicus varius   8½in/21—22cm

IDENTIFICATION Yellow underparts, white rump and wing patch, and red forehead distinguish this Sapsucker. Female lacks red throat and chin. Excavates series of holes in trees to feed on sap and insects attracted by it. Similar Red-naped Sapsucker of Rocky Mountain states has a red patch on nape, while the Red-breasted Sapsucker of the Pacific coast has a red head, nape and breast.

VOICE Mostly silent.
HABITAT Deciduous and conifer forests.
RANGE Most of boreal Canada and north-east US.
MOVEMENTS Whole population migrates south to winter in southern states and Mexico.
BREEDING Usually in deciduous or mixed woodland with birch or poplar; April-June.
NEST AND EGGS A hole excavated in a dead or dying tree; the 4 to 7 eggs are white.
INCUBATION The eggs hatch after 14 days of incubation by both members of the pair.
COMMENT Despite their name and obvious inclination to take sap, these birds are still largely dependent on insects taken woodpecker-fashion from tree bark.

RED-NAPED SAPSUCKER

Sphyrapicus nuchalis   8½in/21cm

IDENTIFICATION Similar to and, until recently, regarded as conspecific with eastern Yellow-bellied Sapsucker. Both male and female have red patches on hind crown; additionally male has red throat, the female a white throat.
VOICE Mostly silent.
HABITAT Deciduous and conifer woods.
RANGE Western North America, away from coast.
MOVEMENTS Mostly a summer visitor, some winter along Mexican border.

RED-BREASTED SAPSUCKER

Sphyrapicus ruber   8½in/21cm

IDENTIFICATION Like Yellow-bellied and Red-naped Sapsuckers, but whole of head, nape and breast is bright red.
VOICE Mostly silent.
HABITAT Conifer and mixed woods.
RANGE Pacific coast from Alaska to California.
MOVEMENTS Northern birds move southward in winter.

WILLIAMSON'S SAPSUCKER

Sphyrapicus thyroideus   8½−9in/22−23cm

IDENTIFICATION Male is mainly black with white lines on face, a red chin, white wing coverts and a yellow belly. Female quite different with black and white "ladder-back", brown head and black- and white-barred underparts. Both sexes have a white rump.
VOICE Nasal *cheer*.
HABITAT Pine forests.
RANGE Western mountain states from Canadian border to Mexico.

MOVEMENTS Northern birds migrate.
BREEDING Conifer woodland with clearings; May-June.
NEST AND EGGS A hole excavated in a dead or dying tree acts as a nest; the 5 or 6 eggs are white.
INCUBATION Both sexes share the incubation.
COMMENT Confined to mainly pine forests of the west, this bird frequents mountains in the south of its range and lower elevations farther north.

LADDER-BACKED WOODPECKER

Picoides scalaris   6½−7½in/17−19cm

IDENTIFICATION Typical black and white woodpecker with black-and white-barred upperparts producing "ladder-back". Underparts buffy, spotted black. Male has red crown and distinctive black line across side of head enclosing the "cheeks". Female has similar face pattern and black crown.
VOICE Sharp *pic*.
HABITAT Dry semi-desert, towns.
RANGE States bordering Mexico.
MOVEMENTS Resident.
BREEDING Dry, semi-desert areas, brushland, adjacent to dry woodland; April-May.

NEST AND EGGS Hole excavated in the dead stem of an agave, sometimes in other trees; the 2 to 6 eggs are white.
INCUBATION The eggs take some 13 days to hatch and are incubated by both members of the pair.
COMMENT Largely dependent on the larvae of the agave beetle.

NUTTALL'S WOODPECKER

Picoides nuttallii   7−7½in/18−19cm

IDENTIFICATION Similar to "Ladder-backed" Woodpecker, but with ladder not extending to black nape. Male has red hind-crown and black cheeks, making it the darkest "faced" of the group. Female lacks red on crown.
VOICE *Week*.
HABITAT Wooded canyons.
RANGE California.
MOVEMENTS Resident.

BREEDING Dry areas of oak woods and scrub; March-May.
NEST AND EGGS Excavates a hole in the branch of a tree or in a thin stem of a shrub; the 3 to 6 eggs are white.
INCUBATION The eggs take 14 days to hatch and incubation is shared between the sexes.
COMMENT Generally a bark picker rather than avid tree borer. The thin branches used for nesting are doubtless less resilient than heavy tree trunks.

DOWNY WOODPECKER

Picoides pubescens   6–6½in/16–17cm

IDENTIFICATION Similarly marked, but much smaller than Hairy Woodpecker with white back, barred wings and red spot on hind-crown of male. Tiny bill is diagnostic.

VOICE *Pik*.

HABITAT Woods, parks, gardens.

RANGE Virtually whole of sub-tundra North America.

MOVEMENTS Resident.

BREEDING Deciduous or mixed woodland with a strong undergrowth of regenerating trees, also parks and orchards; April-May.

NEST AND EGGS A hole excavated in a dead tree; the 4 or 5 eggs are white.

INCUBATION The eggs take some 12 days to hatch and incubation is by both male and female.

COMMENT Though basically a woodland bird, this species is a regular visitor to suburban feeding stations.

HAIRY WOODPECKER

Picoides villosus   9–10in/23–25cm

IDENTIFICATION Medium-sized, pied woodpecker marked by white back and white barring on black wings. Black and white face pattern with red on rear crown of male. *See* Downy Woodpecker.

VOICE *Peek*.

HABITAT Dense forests.

RANGE Most sub-tundra areas of North America.

MOVEMENTS Resident.

BREEDING Generally mixed or deciduous forests with mature trees, also forest margins; April-May.

NEST AND EGGS A hole is excavated in a dead or living tree; the 3 to 5 eggs are white.

INCUBATION Lasts 14 days and is shared between members of the pair.

COMMENT Prefers climax forest with a heavy canopy and little secondary growth.

STRICKLAND'S WOODPECKER

Picoides stricklandi   7–8in/18–20cm

IDENTIFICATION Upperparts dark brown, devoid of spots and bars save for a hint of barring on the wings. White lines outline dark ear coverts. Underparts evenly spotted.

VOICE Sharp calls.

HABITAT Mountain forests.

RANGE South-eastern Arizona and adjacent New Mexico.

MOVEMENTS Resident.

RED-COCKADED WOODPECKER

Picoides borealis   8½−9in/21−23cm

IDENTIFICATION Woodpecker with black and white barring on back. Has large white cheek patch. Red in male confined to tiny dash at rear of ear coverts.

VOICE Rasping *srip*.

HABITAT Old pine woods.

RANGE South-eastern states, declining.

MOVEMENTS Resident.

BREEDING Confined to pine woods; April-May.

NEST AND EGGS The nest is excavated in a long leaf pine with heartwood disease or other old pine; the 3 to 5 eggs are white.

INCUBATION Lasts 11 days and is performed by both sexes.

COMMENT Small holes are drilled in nearby trees to produce a sticky resin that may act as a repellant to predators.

WHITE-HEADED WOODPECKER

Picoides albolarvatus   9−10in/23−25cm

IDENTIFICATION All-black woodpecker marked by white head, red spot on hind-crown and white in outer wing, particularly obvious in flight. Feeds on pine cones.

VOICE *Chick*.

HABITAT Pine forests.

RANGE Pacific US.

MOVEMENTS Resident.

BREEDING Conifer forests of pines and firs; April-May

NEST AND EGGS Excavates a hole in the stump of a broken conifer; the 3 to 5 eggs are white.

INCUBATION The eggs take some 14 days to hatch and are incubated by both members of the pair.

COMMENT Generally a quiet woodpecker that is difficult to locate.

THREE-TOED WOODPECKER

Picoides tridactylus   8½in/21−22cm

IDENTIFICATION Similar to Black-backed Woodpecker, but has white and black "ladder-back" (sometimes pure white) and widening, white stripe extending behind eye.

VOICE *Pik*.

HABITAT Conifer forests.
RANGE Boreal Canada southward through Rockies.
MOVEMENTS Resident.
BREEDING Conifer forests and areas that have been burned, with standing trees; May-June.
NEST AND EGGS A hole excavated in a conifer, often a dead tree; the 4 or 5 eggs are white.
INCUBATION The eggs take 14 days to hatch and are incubated by both male and female.
COMMENT This species breeds right around the world in the northern hemisphere.

BLACK-BACKED WOODPECKER

Picoides arcticus   9−9½in/23−24cm

IDENTIFICATION Black above, white below, heavily barred black. Face pattern consists of fine white line behind eye and bold, black, zig-zag line across white cheek and neck. Male has golden crown, lacking in female.

VOICE Hard *kip*.
HABITAT Conifer forests.
RANGE Boreal Canada southward through northern US Rockies.
MOVEMENTS Resident.
BREEDING Conifer forests together with burnt-out areas with dead trees; May-June.
NEST AND EGGS A hole excavated usually in a dead or living conifer; the 4 or 5 eggs are white.
INCUBATION Lasts 14 days and is performed by both sexes.
COMMENT The association of this species with burned-out forests is far from complete, but such areas within its range often hold this bird.

NORTHERN FLICKER

Colaptes auratus   12−13in/30−33cm

IDENTIFICATION North American flickers were, until recently, regarded as three separate species: Yellow-shafted, Red-shafted and Gilded. All are brown on back and wings spotted with black; white below, similarly spotted black with a black breast-crescent and white rump. Western birds have a red malar stripe; eastern birds a black one. In flight, the underwing is rufous (Red-shafted) or yellow (Yellow-shafted). These are expert climbers that are also frequently seen on the ground.

VOICE *Wik-wik-wik*.
HABITAT Woods, suburbs, but also remote areas.
RANGE From tundra southwards throughout North America, but absent central Texas.
MOVEMENTS Most Canadian birds move southward.
BREEDING Frequents a wide variety of areas, even treeless plains; March-June.
NEST AND EGGS Excavates a hole in a tree, often dead; the 6 to 9 eggs are white.
INCUBATION The eggs take 11 or 12 days to hatch and are incubated by both members of the pair.
COMMENT This successful bird will excavate a nest hole in telegraph pole or fence post and will even nest in a building or use a nest box.

PILEATED WOODPECKER

Dryocopus pileatus   15½−17in/40−43cm

IDENTIFICATION Large, black woodpecker with white facial lines and red chest. Male also has red malar stripe. In flight, underwing has white linings. Confusable only with the presumed extinct Ivory-billed Woodpecker which has white "V" on back and white secondaries forming a white "lower back" when perched. In flight, Ivory-billed Woodpecker has broad, white, trailing edge to wings, both above and below.

VOICE *Wucka-wucka-wucka*.

HABITAT Forests and parks.

RANGE Breeds through most eastern states and westwards across southern and central Canada. Also southward through Pacific states.

MOVEMENTS Resident.

BREEDING Mature woodland, preferably with dead trees; April-May.

NEST AND EGGS A hole excavated usually in a dead tree; the 3 to 5 eggs are white.

INCUBATION The eggs take some 18 days to hatch and are incubated by both sexes.

COMMENT With the apparent demise of the Ivory-billed Woodpecker, the Pileated Woodpecker excavates the largest tree hole in North America, sometimes in living trees.

TYRANT FLYCATCHERS

Of all the birds of the New World, the Tyrannidae, or tyrant flycatchers, are among the most abundant and confusing. Even the warblers do not pose problems on quite the same scale. There are, in fact, no less than 367 species in this family, of which 35 species breed in North America. These are robust, heavy-billed birds with a strong growth of rictal bristles. They feed on insects, largely taken in flight with sallies from a prominent perch. Though most species bear the name of "flycatcher," there are others that are called "kingbird," "kiskadee," "pewee," "wood-pewee," and "phoebe."

Many flycatchers are clothed in shades of brown or olive and are virtually devoid of field marks. Others are more boldly marked, with greenish-yellow breasts and gray heads that seem distinctive enough until it is realized that there is at least another handful of virtually identical birds. Only a tiny few are sufficiently distinct as to be identifiable on the spot. These include the vividly red and brown Vermilion Flycatcher, Black Phoebe, and Scissor-tailed Flycatcher. Otherwise one is continually looking for fine points.

Size of bill, the presence or absence of an eye ring, and a line from eye to bill through the lores are often significant features. So too is the presence or absence of a wing-bar, or double wing-bar. Thereafter, fine plumage characters need to be sought, some of which are so subtle that the birds need to parade up and down in perfect light for minutes at a time. Fortunately, many flycatchers have clear-cut habitat preferences, distinctive calls and songs, and differences in distribution. Thus, a dark olive, double wing-barred flycatcher breeding in Alaska is the Alder, whereas the "same" bird breeding in Ohio is the Willow. Both are, however, like most other flycatchers, long-distance migrants that need to be identified individually on passage. Frankly, unless the bird calls, one is completely lost in these circumstances. Imagine birding in South America where the other 330-odd tyrants are found! The members of the genus *Empidonax* are really something of a nightmare, even for experienced watchers, so beware.

No less than six flycatchers have managed to colonize Alaska, though so far as is known, none have yet colonized the Old World across the Bering Straits. These birds make huge migrations to winter in the tropics, where they are joined by ten species that have colonized southward as far as Tierra del Fuego.

Another summer visitor, and one that is widespread throughout North America, is the Eastern Kingbird, from which most other members of the genus *Tyrannus* get their name. The native Indians of the North American continent referred to this bird as "little chief" because of its fearlessness. Eastern Kingbirds will not only attack any intruder of their own species, as do most birds, but will attack with equal ferocity even an intruding hawk.

NORTHERN BEARDLESS-TYRANNULET

Camptostoma imberbe   4½in/11cm

IDENTIFICATION Small, secretive flycatcher, mostly located by its calls. Dull gray-green foreparts with stubby bill and short supercilium. Greenish-yellow belly, dark wings with bold, double wing-bar.
VOICE Flourishing *pre-yer*; series of *pee-pee-pee* notes.
HABITAT Waterside woods in desert country.
RANGE Southern Arizona and lower Rio Grande valley of Texas.
MOVEMENTS Some birds move southward to winter in Mexico.

OLIVE-SIDED FLYCATCHER

Contopus borealis   7–7½in/18–19cm

IDENTIFICATION Closely related to the wood-pewees. A chunky flycatcher with stout bill and short tail. Upperparts brown with white tufts sometimes visible on inner part of wing. Heavily streaked breast (suggesting a dusky vest) and white throat are best field marks.
VOICE A whistled *whip-three beers*.
HABITAT Conifer forests.
RANGE Boreal zone from Alaska to Newfoundland southwards through western mountains and Great Lakes areas.
MOVEMENTS Summer visitor.

BREEDING Frequents various areas with isolated dead trees, often conifers; May-July.
NEST AND EGGS A cup of twigs lined with plant fibres, usually at some considerable height in a tree; the 3 or 4 eggs are pale buff, spotted brown.
INCUBATION The eggs take some 16 or 17 days to hatch and are incubated by the female.
COMMENT The need for isolated dead, but still standing, trees, restricts this flycatcher to burnt-over, flooded and part-felled woodlands.

GREATER PEWEE

Contopus pertinax   7½–8in/19–20cm

IDENTIFICATION Large brown flycatcher with yellowish belly and hint of a crest. Double wing-bar very faint, bill heavy with pale lower mandible.
VOICE Likened to *josé-maria*.
HABITAT Mountain woods.
RANGE South-eastern Arizona.
MOVEMENTS Summer visitor.

WESTERN WOOD-PEWEE

Contopus sordidulus   6in/15–16cm

IDENTIFICATION Dull brown flycatcher with two wing-bars and an obscure eye ring. Bill dark but lower mandible may also be orange.

VOICE *Peer*; also three note *swee-tee-tee*.
HABITAT Deciduous woods.
RANGE Western North America from Alaska to westernmost Texas.
MOVEMENTS Summer visitor.
BREEDING Open woodland with clearings; May-July.
NEST AND EGGS A neat cup of grasses situated on a horizontal branch; the 2 to 4 eggs are white, spotted brown.
INCUBATION The eggs hatch after 12 days and the female performs the incubation.
COMMENT Where Eastern and Western Wood-Pewees overlap in range in the foothills of the Rockies, they do not interbreed.

EASTERN WOOD-PEWEE

Contopus virens   6in/15–16cm

IDENTIFICATION Dull brown flycatcher has only an obscure, pale eye-ring and narrow, pale, double wing-bar. Identical to Western Wood-Pewee, separated only by voice and distribution. Lower mandible orange.

VOICE *Pee-a-wee*.
HABITAT Woods, margins, suburbs.
RANGE Eastern US and adjacent Canada.
MOVEMENTS Summer visitor.
BREEDING Frequents mature deciduous woodland as well as well-treed suburbs; May-June.
NEST AND EGGS A neat, lichen-camouflaged cup placed on a horizontal branch at variable heights; the 2 to 4 eggs are white, spotted brown.
INCUBATION The eggs take some 12 or 13 days to hatch and are incubated by the female.
COMMENT The distinctive call is the main means of locating this self-effacing little bird.

YELLOW-BELLIED FLYCATCHER

Empidonax flaviventris   5–5½in/13–14cm

IDENTIFICATION One of highly confusing genus of small, mainly olive-colored flycatchers marked by bold eye-ring and pale, double wing-bar. Identification often rests on call and minor plumage features. This species has yellow throat, extensive olive breast, tiny bill with pale lower mandible.
VOICE *Per-wee* or *killek*.
HABITAT Northern conifer forests.
RANGE Boreal Canada and north-eastern US.
MOVEMENTS Summer visitor; scarce on migration.
BREEDING Dark, shady waterside thickets and woodland; May-June.
NEST AND EGGS A neat cup of mosses is placed on a bank; the 3 to 5 eggs are lightly spotted brown.
INCUBATION The eggs take some 12 to 14 days to hatch and are incubated by the female.
COMMENT Though mainly found on or near the ground, tall trees are often used as song posts.

ACADIAN FLYCATCHER

Empidonax virescens   5½–6in/14–15cm

IDENTIFICATION Very similar to Yellow-bellied Flycatcher. Pale eye-ring; bold, double wing-bar; lower mandible pale yellow; breast olive, separated from yellow belly by white on lower breast. Throat grayish.
VOICE *Peet-za*.
HABITAT Dense forests.
RANGE Only *Empidonax* flycatcher that breeds in eastern lowlands of US.
MOVEMENTS Summer visitor.

BREEDING Mature woodlands with dark interiors near streams; May-June.

NEST AND EGGS A large, suspended cup at no great height from the ground constructed of grasses; the 3 eggs are lightly spotted brown.

INCUBATION The eggs take 13 to 15 days to hatch, incubated by the female.

COMMENT The rather untidy nest of this species is often suspended over water.

ALDER FLYCATCHER

Empidonax alnorum   5½–6in/14–15cm

IDENTIFICATION Darkish flycatcher with medium-strength eye-ring and long, black tail. Very similar to Willow Flycatcher with which previously regarded as con-specific; rather greener above and eye-ring more obvious.

VOICE *Fee-bee-o.*

HABITAT Boggy woods of birch and alder in conifer zone.

RANGE Boreal Alaska and Canada to north-eastern US.

MOVEMENTS Summer visitor.

BREEDING Thickets in damp areas, often willow or alder; May-June.

NEST AND EGGS A ragged cup placed in a low bush; the 3 or 4 eggs are white, spotted with brown.

INCUBATION Lasts from 12 to 14 days and is performed by the female.

COMMENT Only recently separated from the Willow Flycatcher, both formerly regarded as a sub-species of Trail's Flycatcher.

WILLOW FLYCATCHER

Empidonax traillii   5½–6in/14–15cm

IDENTIFICATION Dark flycatcher, even darker than closely related Alder Flycatcher, from which it should be separated only with the greatest of care. Inconspicuous eye-ring and call are best field marks.

VOICE *Fitz-beu.*

HABITAT Meadows, streamsides, thickets.

RANGE Right across US, but absent from southern states.

MOVEMENTS Summer visitor.

BREEDING Thickets of willow and alder among marshside vegetation; May-June.

NEST AND EGGS A cup of loose grasses in a low bush; the 3 or 4 eggs are white, spotted brown.

INCUBATION The eggs take 12 to 14 days to hatch and are incubated by the female alone.

COMMENT Outside the breeding season, when not singing, these flycatchers pose enormous identification problems.

LEAST FLYCATCHER

Empidonax minimus 4½ − 5in/12 − 13cm

IDENTIFICATION Smallest member of this genus with large-headed appearance, bold eye-ring and dark olive, or olive-brown upperparts. White throat and gray breast are good features; bill appears small with pale base to lower mandible.

VOICE *Che-bek.*
HABITAT Open woodland, farmland, orchards.
RANGE From boreal zone southward into the northern US.
MOVEMENTS Summer visitor.
BREEDING Deciduous woods, parks, orchards and gardens; May-June.
NEST AND EGGS A well-constructed cup usually placed in the crotch of a tree or shrub; the 3 to 6 eggs are pale cream.
INCUBATION The eggs take 12 days to hatch and are incubated by the female alone.
COMMENT Size is of little help in identifying this bird, despite its name.

HAMMOND'S FLYCATCHER

Empidonax hammondii 5 − 5½in/13 − 14cm

IDENTIFICATION Small, western flycatcher with boldish eye-ring. Appears large headed, with small bill and short tail. Best field mark is gray head contrasting with olive-gray back and breast. Gray-edged tail and wings frequently flicked.

VOICE A busy, three-part *zuree.*
HABITAT Mountain conifers.
RANGE Mountains from central Alaska southward to California and New Mexico.
MOVEMENTS Summer visitor.
BREEDING Conifer and mixed forests at some altitude, often near the tree-line; May-June.
NEST AND EGGS A neatly constructed cup suspended in a horizontal fork of a conifer; the 3 or 4 eggs are plain white.
INCUBATION The eggs hatch after 15 days and are incubated probably by the female alone.
COMMENT As these birds nest up to 60 ft above the ground, relatively few have been fully studied.

DUSKY FLYCATCHER

Empidonax oberholseri 5½ − 6in/14 − 15cm

IDENTIFICATION Medium-sized, dully colored flycatcher. Brown above with white throat, olive-gray breast and pale lemon-yellow belly. Bill dark with pale base to lower mandible; tail long, black and narrowly edged gray white.
VOICE Three or four *slurpp* phrases.
HABITAT Bushy mountain slopes.
RANGE British Columbia to New Mexico, west.
MOVEMENTS Summer visitor.
BREEDING Mostly secondary growth such as willows in deciduous or conifer woodland; May-June.
NEST AND EGGS A neat cup placed low in a willow or similar shrub; the 3 or 4 eggs are white.
INCUBATION The eggs take 12 to 14 days to hatch and are probably incubated by the female alone.
COMMENT Very similar to Hammond's Flycatcher, but prefers undergrowth to tall trees during the breeding season.

GRAY FLYCATCHER

Empidonax wrightii   5½–6in/14–15cm

IDENTIFICATION Pale gray, washed-out flycatcher with pale head, white chin and belly and grayish breast. White eye-ring present, but not obvious on pale gray head. Has the habit of pumping tail downwards.
VOICE *Cha-bit, seeo.*
HABITAT Dry brushland and pines.
RANGE Great Basin and interior west.
MOVEMENTS Summer visitor, winters southern Arizona.

BREEDING Confined to Rocky Mountain plateau sagebrush and adjacent woodland; May-June.
NEST AND EGGS A loose, ragged cup of grasses is placed in a sagebrush or other low shrub; the 3 or 4 eggs are creamy white.
INCUBATION The eggs hatch after 14 days and are incubated by the female alone.
COMMENT The all-gray summer plumage of this flycatcher merges well with the dry, sagebrush country that it inhabits during the breeding season.

CORDILLERAN FLYCATCHER

Empidonax occidentalis   5–5½in/13–14cm

IDENTIFICATION Olive-brown above with very bold eye-ring, but relatively narrow wing-bars. Chin and belly both yellow, separated by extensive olive breast. Tail is long and lower mandible a clear orange. The very similar west-coast Pacific-slope Flycatcher has a different call (an upslurred *sweep*).
VOICE *Wee-seet.*
HABITAT Woods and forests.
RANGE Rocky Mountains and Great Basin regions.
MOVEMENTS Summer visitor.

BREEDING Occurs in mixed and conifer woodland, especially near water; May-June.
NEST AND EGGS The neat cup of grasses and other plant materials is located among rocks, roots and a variety of other situations; the 3 to 5 eggs are white, sparsely spotted brown.
INCUBATION The eggs take 12 to 15 days to hatch.
COMMENT This *Empidonax* of the Rockies commonly forages within the shaded and moist forest.

BUFF-BREASTED FLYCATCHER

Empidonax fulvifrons   5in/13cm

IDENTIFICATION Small flycatcher with bold white eye-ring, double wing-bar and sulphur-buff breast.
VOICE *Chew-lick.*
HABITAT Conifer and mixed woods.
RANGE South-eastern Arizona.
MOVEMENTS Summer visitor.

BLACK PHOEBE

Sayornis nigricans   6−6½in/16−17cm

IDENTIFICATION Boldly black and white bird with chunky body and longish tail, which is pumped up and down. Black upperparts, head and breast; white belly and outer tail feathers. Juvenile is browner above with rusty margins to wing coverts.

VOICE *Pee-wee.*
HABITAT Woodlands, suburbs, parks, canyons, usually near water.
RANGE California and south-western US, east to central Texas.
MOVEMENTS Resident over most of range.
BREEDING Frequents human settlements and dark, waterside areas; May-June.
NEST AND EGGS The nest is placed on a rock or building beam and consists of a cup of grasses and mud lined with soft material; the 3 to 6 eggs are white, lightly spotted.
INCUBATION Lasts 15 to 17 days and is performed by the female alone.
COMMENT Within an individual clutch, the eggs that are laid later are more speckled than those laid earlier.

EASTERN PHOEBE

Sayornis phoebe   6½−7in/17−18cm

IDENTIFICATION A rather dull little bird that is brown above (darker on head, tail and wings) and white below; with short, all-black bill. Pumps and spreads tail continuously when perched. In fall, a yellow wash covers belly. Pewees have generally large, pale-based bills.
VOICE *Fee-be.*
HABITAT Farms, suburbs, woods.

RANGE Breeds over most of eastern US extending northward through Canadian prairies and beyond.
MOVEMENTS Most birds are summer visitors, but winter along Atlantic and Gulf coasts and over much of south-eastern US.
BREEDING Usually near water and under bridges, but also around farmsteads; May-June.
NEST AND EGGS A substantial structure of grasses often bound together with mud; the 5 eggs are white, sometimes spotted.
INCUBATION Lasts 15 to 20 days and is performed by the female.
COMMENT An unusual species in the variation of time the eggs take to hatch. First broods take longer to hatch than second ones.

SAY'S PHOEBE

Sayornis saya   7–7½in/18–19cm

IDENTIFICATION Buffy brown above, with black tail and rusty belly and undertail coverts. Though rather nondescript, the black tail is wagged and spread like other phoebes.
VOICE *Pee-ee*.
HABITAT Dry, rocky areas, farmsteads.
RANGE Whole of western North America from Alaska to western Texas and into the prairies.
MOVEMENTS Summer visitor, though some birds winter in south-western US.
BREEDING Rocky outcrops, bridges and buildings; May-June.
NEST AND EGGS A shallow saucer of grasses well protected by an overhang; the 4 or 5 eggs are white, often with a few brown speckles.
INCUBATION The eggs hatch after 14 days of incubation by the female alone.
COMMENT An easily overlooked bird of dark, waterside areas of the west.

VERMILION FLYCATCHER

Pyrocephalus rubinus   5½–6in/14–15cm

IDENTIFICATION Adult male unmistakable with vividly red crown and underparts. Female is buff-brown above with dark ear coverts, streaked breast, and a warm, orange-red wash on the belly. Immature male has red belly and a few red feathers on throat and crown. Immature female has yellow wash on belly.
VOICE A pleasant *pit-a-see* repeated.
HABITAT Aquatic woods and tangles.
RANGE Mexican border states.
MOVEMENTS Northernmost birds move to Mexican border.
BREEDING Frequents dry, scrub areas with scant vegetation; April-May.
NEST AND EGGS Constructs a neat cup hidden in a shrub or tree; the 2 to 4 eggs are off-white, spotted brown.
INCUBATION Lasts 12 days and is performed mainly by the female, with some help from the male.
COMMENT Though a dry-ground bird, this flycatcher spends much of its time among the tops of trees and builds its nest often at considerable height.

DUSKY-CAPPED FLYCATCHER

Myiarchus tuberculifer   7–7½in/18–19cm

IDENTIFICATION Brown above with double, rusty wing-bar. Pronounced crest, gray breast and bright yellow underparts. Large dark bill. Separate carefully from other *Myiarchus* flycatchers.
VOICE Whistles.
HABITAT Woodlands.
RANGE South-eastern Arizona and adjacent New Mexico.
MOVEMENTS Summer visitor.

ASH-THROATED FLYCATCHER

Myiarchus cinerascens   8½in/21–22cm

IDENTIFICATION Brown upperparts, bushy crest, rust in tail and wings. Pale-gray throat and pale-yellow underparts are good clues. Bill thinner, generally paler than similar flycatchers.

VOICE Short *ka-wheer*.

HABITAT Western woods, scrub, semi-desert.

RANGE Breeds west of a line drawn from Texas to mid-way on the Gulf coast of Oregon.

MOVEMENTS Summer visitor, a few winter extreme south-west US.

BREEDING Woodland and scrub in dry country; May-June.

NEST AND EGGS A woodpecker or natural hole in a tree is lined with grasses and leaves; the 4 or 5 eggs are pale, creamy buff, spotted brown.

INCUBATION Lasts about 15 days and is performed by the female alone.

COMMENT These aggressive birds will take over a freshly excavated woodpecker hole by dispossessing the rightful owners.

GREAT CRESTED FLYCATCHER

Myiarchus crinitus   8½in/21–22cm

IDENTIFICATION Brown above with distinct crest, pale margins to wing coverts forming bold, white, double wing-bar. Rusty margins to flight feathers of wing and tail.

Easily confused with other flycatchers, but gray throat, finely streaked white, is darker than similar species and tail is more rusty.

VOICE Hard *wheep*.

HABITAT Deciduous woods.

RANGE Eastern US northward into adjacent Canada.

MOVEMENTS Summer visitor; a few winter southern Florida.

BREEDING Frequents the canopy area of deciduous and mixed woods and their environment; May-June.

NEST AND EGGS Uses a hole in a tree, often that of a woodpecker, and builds a loose structure of leaves, grasses and other material; the 4 to 6 eggs are pale buffy, spotted brown.

INCUBATION Lasts 13 to 15 days and is performed by the female.

COMMENT Though its hole-nesting habit is unusual, so is the strange habit of incorporating snake skins into its nest.

BROWN-CRESTED FLYCATCHER

Myiarchus tyrannulus   8½–9in/21–23cm

IDENTIFICATION Large, brown flycatcher with narrow double wing-bar, pale gray breast and yellow underparts. Heavy crest and large, dark bill.

VOICE *Wit*.

HABITAT Dry woodland.

RANGE South Texas, southern half of Arizona and into adjacent states.

MOVEMENTS Summer visitor.

GREAT KISKADEE

Pitangus sulphuratus   9½–10in/24–25cm

IDENTIFICATION Large, chunky flycatcher marked by black
and white stripes on large head. Chestnut in wings, yellow
underparts.
VOICE Penetrating *kiss-ka-dee*.
HABITAT Waterside woods.
RANGE Lower Rio Grande, Texas.
MOVEMENTS Resident.

SULPHUR-BELLIED FLYCATCHER

Myiodynastes luteiventris   8½–9in/21–23cm

IDENTIFICATION Heavily streaked black on buffy-yellow with
rusty tail and pale yellow undertail coverts.
VOICE Harsh, squeaking calls.
HABITAT Mountain woodland.
RANGE South-eastern Arizona.
MOVEMENTS Summer visitor.

TROPICAL KINGBIRD

Tyrannus melancholicus   9–9½in/23–24cm

IDENTIFICATION Similar to other kingbirds, but with large,
heavy bill; thus virtually identical to Couch's Kingbird. Dark
ear coverts, gray-green back, notched tail are all finer features
to look for.
VOICE *Pip-pip-pip*.
HABITAT Waterside woods.
RANGE South-eastern Arizona.
MOVEMENTS Summer visitor.

COUCH'S KINGBIRD

Tyrannus couchii   9–9½in/23–24cm

IDENTIFICATION Virtually identical to Tropical Kingbird, but
with slightly greener back and thicker bill.
VOICE *Kip-kip-kip*.
HABITAT Waterside woods.
RANGE Lower Rio Grande, Texas.
MOVEMENTS Some birds migrate.

CASSIN'S KINGBIRD

Tyrannus vociferans   8½–9in/22–23cm

IDENTIFICATION Very similar to Western Kingbird, but buffy
tips to tail and lack of white margins are good features. Gray
head marked by whiter chin and pale margins to wing
feathers are further distinctions. Separate with care.

VOICE *Chi-hew*.
HABITAT Usually denser thickets in dry country than
Western Kingbird.
RANGE From coastal California through adjacent western
states northwards to eastern Montana.
MOVEMENTS Summer visitor.
BREEDING Dry, open areas from desert and scrub with
scattered trees to mountains; May-June.
NEST AND EGGS The nest is constructed of twigs lined with
grasses and hair; the 3 to 5 eggs are white, spotted brown.
INCUBATION The eggs take 12 to 14 days to hatch and are
incubated by the female.
COMMENT This bird can be overlooked as it perches
immobile among the topmost branches of a tree.

THICK-BILLED KINGBIRD

Tyrannus crassirostris   9½in/24cm

IDENTIFICATION Bulky black and gray flycatcher with decidedly deep, gray bill. Uniform, unbarred upperparts are good feature in all plumages. In fall underparts are yellow.
VOICE High *wee*.
HABITAT Waterside woods.
RANGE South-eastern Arizona.
MOVEMENTS Summer visitor.

WESTERN KINGBIRD

Tyrannus verticalis   8½in/21–22cm

IDENTIFICATION Gray head and breast, yellow belly, olive-gray back combine with black wings and tail, the latter with white outer feathers. This is the widespread tyrant flycatcher of the west and forms a basis from which other "yellow" flycatchers should be separated with care. Perches openly, upright, with large bill and head prominent. Often appears nervous.
VOICE *Whit*.
HABITAT Open country with scrub and fences.
RANGE Common over western US northward into adjacent Canada.
MOVEMENTS Summer visitor, migrant through eastern US.

BREEDING Open agricultural land as long as there are trees, wires or houses to act as perches; May-June.
NEST AND EGGS A loose structure of a wide variety of materials placed in whatever is available: tree, post, building; the 3 to 5 eggs are white, spotted brown.
INCUBATION The eggs take 12 to 14 days to hatch and are incubated mainly by the female.
COMMENT A highly adaptable species that lives comfortably alongside farmers.

EASTERN KINGBIRD

Tyrannus tyrannus   8½in/21–22cm

IDENTIFICATION Black crown, dark-gray back and wings, with black tail, broadly tipped white. Underparts are dusky white, with subtle gray breast band. Generally perches openly.
VOICE *Zeet* repeated.
HABITAT Woodland edges, farms, usually near water.
RANGE Breeds over most of sub-tundra North America, but absent from far-west and south-west.
MOVEMENTS Summer visitor.
BREEDING Trees and windbreaks among open countryside; May-June.
NEST AND EGGS A substantial nest of twigs lined with bents and hair; the 3 or 4 white eggs are spotted brown.
INCUBATION The eggs take 12 or 13 days to hatch and are incubated by the female.
COMMENT A large bird that perches openly and is relatively easy to locate.

GRAY KINGBIRD

Tyrannus dominicensis   8½–9in/21–23cm

IDENTIFICATION Separated from Eastern Kingbird by larger size, heavier bill and lack of black crown and back. Crown and back, gray with darker area on lores and ear coverts. Underparts whitish, wings with large, gray margins; tail long and black.

VOICE *Pe-cherree.*

HABITAT Mangroves and scrub.

RANGE Common among Florida Keys, less so along adjacent mainland coasts.

MOVEMENTS Summer visitor.

BREEDING Confined to the south-east coast where it occurs among mangroves; May-June.

NEST AND EGGS A large structure of twigs, lined with grasses, placed over water in a mangrove; the 3 or 4 eggs are pinkish, blotched brown.

INCUBATION Lasts about 15 days, incubated by the female.

COMMENT Kingbirds get their name from their aggressiveness towards other birds, including birds of prey.

SCISSOR-TAILED FLYCATCHER

Tyrannus forficatus   12½–13½in/32–34cm

IDENTIFICATION Adult, marked by very long outer tail feathers creating extremely deep forked tail. Head and back pearl gray; wings black with feathers broadly edged white. Underparts, rich pink, extending to underwing linings. Juvenile lacks extreme tail length and pink on underside; wing linings show subdued pink.

VOICE *Ka-leep.*

HABITAT Farms, scrub, open country.

RANGE Texas and nearby south-central states.

MOVEMENTS Summer visitor, some winter southernmost Florida.

BREEDING Dry areas of open country; April-June.

NEST AND EGGS A shallow cup of twigs lined with grass is built in a low shrub; the 4 to 6 off-white eggs are lightly spotted.

INCUBATION The eggs take some 13 or 14 days to hatch and are incubated by the female alone.

COMMENT Though it inhabits sparsely populated areas, this bird is often obvious, using power wires and fences as perches.

ROSE-THROATED BECARD

Pachyramphus aglaiae   7–7½in/18–19cm

IDENTIFICATION Male is slate-gray above with black head and bright pink throat. Female brown and buff with black cap.

VOICE *See-you.*

HABITAT Woodlands.

RANGE Southern Arizona and rarely in Rio Grande valley of Texas.

MOVEMENTS Summer visitor.

EURASIAN SKYLARK

Alauda arvensis   6½−7in/16−18cm

IDENTIFICATION Chunky, ground-dwelling bird heavily streaked, above and below, in buffs and browns. Shows small crest and white outer tail feathers.
VOICE Melodic singing in high song-flight.
HABITAT Grasslands and fields.
RANGE Vancouver Island.
MOVEMENTS Introduced from Europe, resident.

HORNED LARK

Eremophila alpestris   7−7½in/17−18cm

IDENTIFICATION Brown and buff streaked above, with black crown patch and horns, black through eye and black breast crescent. Face usually yellow, flanks usually streaked chestnut. Though divided among several sub-species, the "face" pattern is distinctive. Horns often difficult to see.
VOICE A high-pitched *seee*.
HABITAT Breeds among tundra, bare plains, mountains; winters on bare fields and along shorelines.
RANGE Breeds over most of Alaska and Canada south throughout most of US.

MOVEMENTS Canadian birds move mainly into US; winter visitor only in south-east.
BREEDING A variety of locations with short grass from prairie to tundra; March-July.
NEST AND EGGS A simple cup of grasses on the ground; the 4 eggs are greenish, speckled brown.
INCUBATION The eggs hatch after 10 to 14 days and are incubated by the female.
COMMENT This is probably an Arctic bird by origin that has colonized the short grass prairies with their tundra-like habitat.

PURPLE MARTIN

Progne subis   7½−8in/19−20cm

IDENTIFICATION Large, chunky swallow with all-black plumage in metallic purple. Tail has distinct "V". Female has gray, mottled underparts. Glides on broader wings than other swallows.
VOICE Deep twittering.
HABITAT Common where multiple nest boxes are available.
RANGE Widespread in eastern US extending northward through Canadian prairies. Patchily distributed through Rockies, but widespread along Pacific coast.
MOVEMENTS Summer visitor.
BREEDING Previously nested in tree holes and cliff cavities, now mostly in martin boxes; April-June, colonial.
NEST AND EGGS In multiple nest boxes placed on poles and lined with grass and feathers; the 4 or 5 eggs are white.
INCUBATION Lasts 15 to 17 days and is performed probably entirely by the female.
COMMENT The provision of martin tenements has enabled this species to prosper, despite the attentions of House Sparrows.

TREE SWALLOW

Tachycineta bicolor   5½−6in/14−15cm

IDENTIFICATION Dark metallic-blue above, white below. Dark upperparts extend below eye; no white on rump. Flaps and glides in flight. Gregarious and widespread.
VOICE Twittering.
HABITAT Woodlands near water.

RANGE Breeds over most of Canada and northern US.
MOVEMENTS Summer visitor; winters along eastern, southern and western coasts; resident California.
BREEDING Often near water and frequently flooded, dead trees; May-June, colonial.
NEST AND EGGS A natural tree hole or woodpecker hole, occasionally a nest box, is lined with grass and feathers; the 4 to 6 eggs are white.
INCUBATION The eggs take 13 to 16 days to hatch and are incubated by both members of the pair.
COMMENT Colonies of this bird are very much dependent on the supply of suitable tree nest holes in relatively close proximity.

VIOLET-GREEN SWALLOW

Tachycineta thalassina   4½−5in/12−13cm

IDENTIFICATION A "black and white" swallow that shows an iridescent green on back and inner wing only on a close approach. Similar to Tree Swallow, but with white cheek extending above eye so that it stands out; and white rump divided by black center. Tail is square cut; flight more erratic than Tree Swallow.
VOICE A twittering.

HABITAT Woods, gardens.
RANGE Rocky Mountains to western coasts.
MOVEMENTS Summer visitor, resident central California.
BREEDING Frequents cliffs, holes in buildings and trees and bird boxes; May-June, colonial.
NEST AND EGGS Creates a bed of grasses and feathers inside a hole; the 4 or 5 eggs are white.
INCUBATION The eggs take some 15 days to hatch.
COMMENT These swallows rear only one brood and, soon after hatching, the family moves from altitude down into the valleys where the young are still fed by the female.

NORTHERN ROUGH-WINGED SWALLOW

Stelgidopteryx serripennis   5−5½in/13−14cm

IDENTIFICATION A chunky, longer-winged, less fluttering version of the Bank Swallow. Chin, throat and breast are dusky, lacking the well-defined band of the more abundant bird. Less gregarious than that species, not colonial.
VOICE A buzzing twitter.
HABITAT Cliffs, river banks.
RANGE Throughout US and southern Canada.
MOVEMENTS Summer visitor, resident southern California and Texas Gulf coast.
BREEDING Sand or gravel banks; May-June.
NEST AND EGGS A tunnel is excavated in a bank and lined with vegetation; the 6 or 7 eggs are white.
INCUBATION The eggs take 16 days to hatch and are incubated by the female, probably alone.
COMMENT These birds are nowhere near as colonial as the Bank Swallow and will even nest solitarily in old kingfisher holes.

NEST AND EGGS A large nest of twigs and other vegetation lined with grass and feathers placed in a conifer (usually); the 4 to 6 eggs are greenish-buff, spotted brown.
INCUBATION The eggs take 17 or 18 days to hatch and are incubated by both sexes.
COMMENT A widespread and vociferous bird in many parts of North America that is at home in the heart of the largest cities.

GREEN JAY

Cyanocorax yncas   10−11in/25−28cm

IDENTIFICATION Bright, multi-colored jay. Pale blue crown and nape broken with black on sides of head and chin. Green upperparts, pale green underparts, and yellow underside to blue tail form unique color combination.
VOICE Various squawks.
HABITAT Scrub.
RANGE Lower Rio Grande, Texas.
MOVEMENTS Resident.

BROWN JAY

Cyanocorax morio   16−17in/41−43cm

IDENTIFICATION Very large, all-brown jay, paler below, with large, black bill and rounded tail.
VOICE Various squawks.
HABITAT Woodlands.
RANGE Lower Rio Grande.
MOVEMENTS Resident.

SCRUB JAY

Aphelocoma coerulescens   10½−11½in/27−29cm

IDENTIFICATION Blue head, wings and tail are standard features, along with gray underparts. Color of back varies from pale to dark gray; that of chin from gray to white. Large bill and long tail are characteristic, as is a variably prominent breast band.
VOICE Rasping *shreep*.
HABITAT Suburbs, scrub, woods.
RANGE Most of Pacific states, interior west, plus Florida.
MOVEMENTS Resident.
BREEDING Woods and scrub areas with tall trees; May-June.
NEST AND EGGS A well-built cup of twigs placed among dense scrub; the 3 to 5 eggs are washed green or red and spotted with brown.
INCUBATION The eggs take some 16 days to hatch and are incubated by both members of the pair.
COMMENT Basically a western bird, there is an isolated population in Florida that exists in scrub oak and is colonial in breeding habits.

GRAY-BREASTED JAY

Aphelocoma ultramarina   11−12in/28−30cm

IDENTIFICATION Very similar to more widespread Scrub Jay but lacks white throat, pale supercilium and breast band of that species.
VOICE Loud *week*.
HABITAT Woodland.
RANGE South-eastern Arizona and extreme western Texas.
MOVEMENTS Resident.

PINYON JAY

Gymnorhinus cyanocephalus   10–10½in/25–27cm

IDENTIFICATION Rich, pale blue above and below with darker cap and white streaking on throat. Tail shortish and notched. Gregarious.
VOICE Loud mewing.
HABITAT Pinyon-juniper forests of western mountains.
RANGE Interior mountains and plateau of western states.
MOVEMENTS Resident.
BREEDING Mountain areas with pinyon-juniper woods, pines and oaks; March-October.
NEST AND EGGS Constructs a cup of twigs in a tree; the 3 or 4 eggs are white, washed with green.
INCUBATION The eggs take some 16 days to hatch and are incubated by both members of the pair.
COMMENT Like the other jays, these birds are great hoarders. They store pine nuts during the fall that then serve as winter food.

CLARK'S NUTCRACKER

Nucifraga columbiana   11½–12in/29–31cm

IDENTIFICATION Large, jay-like bird of mountain forests. Ash-gray above and below; black wings with white-tipped secondaries and black and white tail. Pointed black bill; flies with crow-like flaps.
VOICE Harsh *kra-a-a*.
HABITAT Conifer forests in mountains.
RANGE US Rockies and other mountain systems northward into adjacent Canada.

MOVEMENTS Resident, with periodic irruptions into lowland and desert areas.
BREEDING High altitude conifer forests with clearings or burnt-out areas; March-June.
NEST AND EGGS A well-structured cup of twigs in a conifer, lined with various softer materials; the 2 to 4 eggs are olive, spotted brown.
INCUBATION Lasts 16 or 17 days and is shared between the pair.
COMMENT This is a mountain bird that descends to valleys

only in winter. It often attends camp sites where it scavenges for scraps.

BLACK-BILLED MAGPIE

Pica pica   18–19in/46–48cm

IDENTIFICATION Large black and white bird with long, wedge-shaped tail and green-blue gloss on wings and tail. Large, black bill on strong head; black above broken by white ovals on folded wings; white below.
VOICE Laughing and chuckling calls.
HABITAT Woodland and brush country.
RANGE From southern Alaska southward through prairies and Rockies.
MOVEMENTS Resident.
BREEDING Hedgerows, thickets, woodland margins; April-June.
NEST AND EGGS A large structure of twigs bound together with mud and often domed; the 6 to 9 eggs are gray-green, spotted brown.

INCUBATION Lasts 16 to 18 days and is performed by the female alone.
COMMENT A colonizing species that is a major predator of the eggs and nestlings of small birds.

YELLOW-BILLED MAGPIE

Pica nuttalli   15½−16½in/40−42cm

IDENTIFICATION Plumage as Black-billed Magpie, but bill bright yellow and patch of bare yellow skin around the eye.
VOICE Chuckles and laughs.
HABITAT Foothills and fields.
RANGE Central Valley, California.
MOVEMENTS Resident.
BREEDING Streamside trees, oak groves, park-like suburbs with substantial trees; March-May, colonial.
NEST AND EGGS A heavy structure of twigs and mud with a twiggy dome; the 5 to 8 eggs are dull greenish, blotched brown.

INCUBATION The eggs take some 18 days to hatch, incubated by the female.
COMMENT Highly colonial bird that has adapted well to the urban environment.

AMERICAN CROW

Corvus brachyrhynchos   16−17½in/41−45cm

IDENTIFICATION Large, all-black bird with powerful bill and square-shaped tail in flight. The slightly smaller Northwestern Crow is sometimes treated as a separate species.
VOICE Familiar *caw-caw*.
HABITAT Very catholic, favoring wide range of habitats.
RANGE Most of sub-tundra North America. Northwestern Crow is found in coastal Alaska and British Columbia.
MOVEMENTS Most Canadian birds move southward in winter.
BREEDING Trees in a wide variety of situations, depending on availability; February-May.
NEST AND EGGS A well-constructed cup of twigs lined with whatever softer materials are to hand; the 4 to 6 eggs are greenish, blotched with brown.

INCUBATION The eggs take 17 to 20 days to hatch and are incubated by both members of the pair.
COMMENT An omnivorous bird that preys on the eggs and young of other species, is a scavenger and also takes large quantities of insects and beetles.

NORTHWESTERN CROW

Corvus caurinus   16–17in/41–43cm

IDENTIFICATION Virtually identical to American Crow. Best separated by range.
VOICE Lower-pitched than American Crow.
HABITAT Shorelines.
RANGE Coastal Alaska and British Columbia.
MOVEMENTS Resident.

MEXICAN CROW

Corvus imparatus   14–15in/35–38cm

IDENTIFICATION Similar to American Crow, but smaller with more glossy plumage.
VOICE Croaks.
HABITAT Open country.
RANGE Lower Rio Grande valley, Texas.
MOVEMENTS Has wintered in Texas since 1960s.

FISH CROW

Corvus ossifragus   14½–15in/37–39cm

IDENTIFICATION Very similar to American Crow, but smaller with thinner bill.
VOICE Nasal *cah* or *cah-cah*.
HABITAT Shorelines, rivers.

RANGE Mainly near coast from New England to Texas.
MOVEMENTS Inland populations tend to move to coast in winter.
BREEDING In trees near the coast in the north, but also adjacent to lake or swamp in the south; March-May.
NEST AND EGGS A cup of sticks is lined with various softer materials, both deciduous and coniferous trees are used; the 4 or 5 eggs are green with brown blotches.
INCUBATION The eggs take some 17 to 18 days to hatch and incubation is shared between the pair.
COMMENT The name stems from its habit of feeding on dead fish along the shoreline though, like other crows, it is virtually omnivorous.

CHIHUAHUAN RAVEN

Corvus cryptoleucus   19–19½in/48–50cm

IDENTIFICATION Larger than American Crow, but easily confused; slightly wedge-shaped tail, but smaller bill and head than Common Raven. Most easily distinguished by calls. Formerly called White-necked Raven, but the white bases of the neck feathers are usually obscured in the field.
VOICE Low croak, higher pitched than Common Raven.
HABITAT Arid lands.
RANGE South-western US.
MOVEMENTS More northerly birds move southward in winter.

BREEDING Dry, open plains with yuccas or other low vegetation; May-June.
NEST AND EGGS A large platform of twigs placed in low vegetation or on a telegraph pole; the 4 to 7 eggs are olive-green, blotched with brown.
INCUBATION The 21-day incubation is performed by both sexes.
COMMENT A gregarious bird that frequently uses the same nest year after year gradually creating a huge mass of sticks.

COMMON RAVEN

Corvus corax   23−24in/58−61cm

IDENTIFICATION Huge crow with heavy head, long and powerful bill and long, wedge-shaped tail that is particularly obvious in flight. Shaggy throat-feathers can be obvious both in flight and when perched.
VOICE Deep, croaking call.
HABITAT Mountains, forests, tundra.
RANGE Throughout Alaska and Canada, save the prairies, and in western US and along Appalachians.
MOVEMENTS Resident.

BREEDING Wild mountains, canyons and cliff-girt coastlines; March-May.
NEST AND EGGS Creates a large structure of twigs on a cliff ledge, but sometimes in a tree; the 3 to 5 eggs are green, blotched with brown.
INCUBATION The eggs hatch after 20 or 21 days and are incubated by the female alone.
COMMENT The most ferocious of the crows that regularly preys on other birds and their nests, and is quite fearless in defending its own.

CHICKADEES, TITMICE, BUSHTITS, NUTHATCHES & CREEPERS

THIS is a conglomerate of various bird families, all of which are essentially woodland or scrub birds which present few identification problems. The chickadees and titmice are small, active birds which find most of their food among the foliage of trees, but which have proved adaptable enough to exploit man-made gardens and parks. They are invariably the first to appear at a newly-created feeding station, and several bird photographers have reported these confiding birds returning to their nest while the photographer was still erecting the hide to enable him to make a close approach! All titmice and chickadees are members of the genus *Parus*, though they vary in appearance.

In general, the titmice are rather plain birds marked by crests, whereas the chickadees have bold black caps and bibs. Most familiar of all is the Black-capped Chickadee, which ranges right across North America from Alaska to Newfoundland, and southward to northern California and Virginia. In the southeastern U.S.A. it overlaps with the Carolina Chickadee and may then interbreed to produce hybrids. The Black-capped largely avoids competition by occupying the higher ground of the Appalachians. The two species should be separated with care, for even the songs are similar. To the north the Boreal Chickadee becomes dominant, while in the west the Rockies are home to the Mountain Chickadee. Similarly, among the titmice it is the Tufted Titmouse that is the common bird in the east, being replaced by the Plain Titmouse in the west.

Of the world's 22 species of nuthatches, four breed in North America. These are totally arboreal birds which are able to climb both up and down the trunks of trees. Though they share a similar plumage pattern, none are particularly difficult to identify. Surprisingly enough, there is considerable overlap in range between the North American species, though they are largely separated by distinctive habitats. Most are resident, though the Red-breasted Nuthatch sporadically appears in areas south and east of its normal range when the seed crop of conifers is poor. In 1989 these irruptive movements were responsible for sending one individual on a transatlantic journey that ended on the east coast of Britain — one of the most surprising examples of vagrancy ever recorded.

The three other families jointly treated here are all represented in North America by only a single species. The Verdin is a member of the largely Old World family of penduline tits and builds a large, suspended, spherical nest like most of its relatives. Nevertheless, it is a unique bird which has puzzled ornithologists for years.

BLACK-CAPPED CHICKADEE

Parus atricapillus   4½–5in/12–13cm

IDENTIFICATION This small bird has a gray back, black bib, black cap and white cheeks. Also note white margins to flight feathers forming a distinct, pale wing-panel, and ragged lower edge to black bib.
VOICE *Chick-a-dee-dee-dee*.
HABITAT Gardens, woods, forest clearings.
RANGE Boreal Alaska and Canada extending southward over northern half of US.
MOVEMENTS Resident.
BREEDING Scrub and woodland clearings with dead trees and stumps; April-June.
NEST AND EGGS A hole excavated in a rotten stump is lined with moss, hair and other soft materials; the 6 to 8 eggs are white, spotted with reddish brown.
INCUBATION The eggs take some 13 days to hatch and incubation is by the female.
COMMENT Though it prefers to excavate its own nest hole, the work being shared by both sexes, this bird will also use old woodpecker holes and nest boxes.

CAROLINA CHICKADEE

Parus carolinensis   4½in/11–12cm

IDENTIFICATION Similar to Black-capped Chickadee, but lacks pale panel in wing and has neat, square-cut, black bib.
VOICE High-pitched, fast *fee-bee, fee-bee*.
HABITAT Deciduous woods, clearings, suburbs.

RANGE South-eastern US.
MOVEMENTS Resident.
BREEDING Deciduous woodland and edges, suburbs with trees; April-May.
NEST AND EGGS A hole in a dead or rotting tree, or a nest box, is lined with feathers and soft plant fibres; the 6 to 8 eggs are white, speckled with reddish brown.
INCUBATION The eggs take 13 days to hatch, incubation is by the female.
COMMENT The southern equivalent of the more widespread Black-capped Chickadee.

MEXICAN CHICKADEE

Parus sclateri   5in/13cm

IDENTIFICATION Similar to Carolina Chickadee, but with larger black bib and gray flanks. Ranges do not overlap.
VOICE Whistled warbling.
HABITAT High conifer woods.
RANGE Borders of Arizona, New Mexico and Mexico.
MOVEMENTS Resident.

MOUNTAIN CHICKADEE

Parus gambeli   4½–5in/12–13cm

IDENTIFICATION Neat, gray chickadee. Whole body is pale gray above and also below. Black bib extends to upper breast, while black cap is separated from black eye-stripe by bold white eyebrow. The latter is the best distinguishing feature.

VOICE Harsh *chick-adee-adee-adee*.

HABITAT Mountain conifer forests.

RANGE Rocky and other mountain systems of the west.

MOVEMENTS Resident.

BREEDING During the breeding season, mostly conifer woods up to the mountain tree-line; April–June.

NEST AND EGGS Uses a natural or woodpecker hole in a conifer, but also a nest box where available; the 6 to 12 eggs are white, speckled reddish brown.

INCUBATION The eggs take 14 days to hatch.

COMMENT Though this bird often feeds away from conifers, it is essentially a canopy bird that seldom descends to eye height.

BOREAL CHICKADEE

Parus hudsonicus   5–5½in/13–14cm

IDENTIFICATION Chunky chickadee, marked by dusky-brown cap, back and flanks; sooty wings and tail; bib black. The overall impression is of a rather scruffy bird.

VOICE Nasal *seek-a-da-da*.

HABITAT Conifers.

RANGE Boreal Alaska and Canada.

MOVEMENTS Resident.

BREEDING Mostly found in conifers, but also in mixed woods; May–June.

NEST AND EGGS A natural or woodpecker hole at no great height is used, but the birds will excavate their own hole in a rotten stump; the 5 to 7 eggs are white, lightly spotted brown.

INCUBATION The eggs take about 14 days to hatch, incubated by the female.

COMMENT A canopy feeder that is often decidedly awkward to see well among dense leaves.

SIBERIAN TIT

Parus cinctus   5½in/14cm

IDENTIFICATION Similar to Boreal Chickadee, but with pale flanks, larger tail, and bolder white cheeks.

VOICE *Dee-der* notes.

HABITAT Dwarf conifers or willows.

RANGE Central Alaska and adjacent Canada.

MOVEMENTS Resident.

CHESTNUT-BACKED CHICKADEE

Parus rufescens   4½in/12cm

IDENTIFICATION The most obvious feature of this small chickadee is the patches of rich chestnut on back, rump and flanks. Rounded head with black cap is washed grayish; cheeks boldly white; underparts white. California birds lack chestnut on flanks.

VOICE Rapid *seek-a-dee-dee*.

HABITAT Coniferous forests, but also in deciduous woodland.

RANGE Pacific coast from Alaska to California.

MOVEMENTS Resident.

BREEDING Mostly coniferous woodland, but also in pure stands of deciduous trees; March-May.

NEST AND EGGS A hole in a dead tree, either excavated by these birds or by a woodpecker; the 5 to 9 eggs are white, spotted brown.

INCUBATION Undescribed.

COMMENT As with the Boreal Chickadee it is awkward to see well among dense leaves.

BRIDLED TITMOUSE

Parus wollweberi   5in/13cm

IDENTIFICATION A gray titmouse marked by bold gray and black crest, distinctive black and white face pattern and neat little bib.

VOICE High *chick-a-dee-dee*.

HABITAT Deciduous mountain woodland.

RANGE Southern Arizona and New Mexico.

MOVEMENTS Resident.

BREEDING Mountain deciduous woods as well as mixed woodland; March-May.

NEST AND EGGS Tree holes, both natural and created by woodpeckers; the 5 to 7 eggs are white.

INCUBATION Undescribed.

COMMENT Though mainly an occupant of natural tree holes, these birds will take to nest boxes where provided.

PLAIN TITMOUSE

Parus inornatus   6in/15cm

IDENTIFICATION A plain gray titmouse, darker above than below, and virtually devoid of field marks. A small crest extends from the rear crown and there is a patch of white at the base of the bill. Coastal birds are browner.

VOICE *Sic-a-dee-dee*.

HABITAT Mixed woodland.

RANGE From California to Colorado south.

MOVEMENTS Resident.

BREEDING A wide variety of deciduous and coniferous growth; April-June.

NEST AND EGGS A hole in a tree, building or even post, lined with grass and other soft materials; the 5 to 8 eggs are white, lightly spotted brown.

INCUBATION The eggs take 14 days to hatch and are incubated by the female alone.

COMMENT Interestingly, coastal birds of this species are markedly darker in coloration than those found in the mountains. The fact that the two color phases occupy ranges that are separated by a gap may indicate species in the making.

TUFTED TITMOUSE

Parus bicolor   6–6½in/16–17cm

IDENTIFICATION Gray above, white below, with a wash of warm rufous along the flanks. The plain face makes the dark eye a prominent feature as are the gray crest and black forehead patch. Birds from southern Texas have black crests and were formerly treated as a separate species.
VOICE Repeated *peeta*, *peeta*, *peeta*.
HABITAT Suburbs, parks, bush country.
RANGE Eastern US.
MOVEMENTS Resident.
BREEDING Mixed woodland and other areas with substantial trees, including suburbs; March-May.
NEST AND EGGS Tree cavity or woodpecker hole lined with moss and feathers; the 5 or 6 eggs are white, lightly speckled brown.
INCUBATION The eggs take 12 days to hatch, incubated by the female.
COMMENT Though the Black-crested Titmouse found in Texas was, for long, regarded as a separate species, recent studies have proved a 'gradation' between the two birds that are now regarded as conspecific.

VERDIN

Auriparus flaviceps   4½in/11cm

IDENTIFICATION Tiny, titmouse-like bird with fine, pointed bill. Adult is gray above, whitish below marked by yellow head and throat and a wedge of chestnut at the bend of the wing. Juvenile is browner above and lacks the distinguishing features of the adult.
VOICE *Chip-chip-chip* repeated.
HABITAT Dry scrubland.
RANGE All states bordering Mexico.
MOVEMENTS Resident.
BREEDING Desert shrubs and thickets; February-April.
NEST AND EGGS Constructs a hanging, globe-shaped nest with a side entrance among cactus or other prickly vegetation; the 3 to 5 eggs are green, spotted brown.
INCUBATION The eggs take 10 days to hatch, incubated by both sexes.
COMMENT A member of the small family of penduline tits, which is unusual in not building its suspended nest over water.

BUSHTIT

Psaltriparus minimus   4½in/11cm

IDENTIFICATION Tiny, titmouse-like bird that is usually seen in large flocks busily feeding as they pass. Upperparts are gray, underparts slightly paler. The ear coverts have a warm wash of pale brown, the bill is tiny and the tail long. Coastal

birds have a pale brown cap and juvenile males in the south-west have black ear coverts and were formerly regarded as a separate species.

VOICE Thin, high-pitched notes.

HABITAT Dry woodland, chaparral.

RANGE From southern British Columbia to western Texas.

MOVEMENTS Resident.

BREEDING A wide variety of wooded and bushy country including suburbs; February-May.

NEST AND EGGS Constructs a large, well-woven structure suspended from a branch with a side entrance; the 5 to 7 eggs are white.

INCUBATION The eggs take 12 days to hatch and are incubated by both members of the pair.

COMMENT The nest of the Bushtit is a surprisingly large affair intricately woven from vegetation bound together with spiders' webs and cocoons.

RED-BREASTED NUTHATCH

Sitta canadensis   4½in/11–12cm

IDENTIFICATION Equivalent of White-breasted Nuthatch in conifer forests, though the two do overlap. Smaller, with black cap broken by bold, white eyebrow and black stripe running through eye. Gray back, with black and white tail. Underparts a warm rust. Stripe through eye is best field mark.

VOICE Nasal *hank-hank-hank*.

HABITAT Conifer forests in north and in mountains of east and west.

RANGE Breeds from north-western Canada to California, through the Rockies and in narrow band across the border and Great Lakes region. Also southwards from Newfoundland to the Appalachians.

MOVEMENTS Irregular movements southward across US when food crops crash.

BREEDING Mostly conifers, but also mixed woodland in some areas; April-May.

NEST AND EGGS A hole is excavated in a rotting stump by the birds themselves; the 4 to 7 eggs are white, spotted with reddish brown.

INCUBATION The eggs take some 12 days to hatch, incubated by the female.

COMMENT The curious habit of smearing the entrance of the nest hole with resinous pitch from pine trees is not understood. Often birds become quite messy as a result.

WHITE-BREASTED NUTHATCH

Sitta carolinensis   5–6in/13–15cm

IDENTIFICATION Boldly-pied bird that climbs up and down trees with equal ease. Crown and nape are black, the remaining upperparts gray with black in wings and white corners to the tail. Underparts white with black eye standing out in contrast.

VOICE A repeated nasal whistle *wee-wee-wee*, also a single *hank*.
HABITAT Conifer, oak, juniper and other woodlands.
RANGE Resident US except where forests or woods absent. Just penetrates southern Canada.
MOVEMENTS Resident in native woodland.
BREEDING Deciduous and mixed woods, but also pure pines in some areas; April-May.
NEST AND EGGS A tree hole, either natural, woodpecker, or self-excavated lined with feathers, grass, and leaves; the 5 to 9 eggs are white, spotted brown.
INCUBATION The eggs take 12 days to hatch and are incubated by the female.
COMMENT Like other nuthatches this is a bird that is largely resident and remains on its breeding territory throughout the year.

PYGMY NUTHATCH

Sitta pygmaea   4½in/11cm

IDENTIFICATION Upperparts are blue gray, underparts creamy buff. Crown is sooty brown, the cheeks white. A white nape patch can be seen only at close range.
VOICE Squeaking calls.
HABITAT Ponderosa pines.
RANGE Patchily distributed through the Rockies, other mountain systems and foothills.
MOVEMENTS Resident.
BREEDING Ponderosa pines with clearings and dead trees; April-May.
NEST AND EGGS A hole in a dead tree excavated by the birds themselves, though sometimes also an old woodpecker hole; the 5 to 9 eggs are white, speckled reddish brown.

INCUBATION The eggs take 16 days to hatch, incubated by the female.
COMMENT This, the smallest of our nuthatches, has a range that closely parallels that of the ponderosa pine in the western half of North America, except in California where it frequents bishop pines.

BROWN-HEADED NUTHATCH

Sitta pusilla   4½in/11cm

IDENTIFICATION Typical, short-tailed nuthatch, with blue-gray upperparts and creamy-buff below. Distinguished by chocolate-colored cap and black eye-stripe bordering white cheeks.
VOICE Double squeak.
HABITAT Loblolly pines.
RANGE South-eastern US from Texas to Virginia.
MOVEMENTS Resident.
BREEDING Mixed, as well as pure conifer, forests; March-May.
NEST AND EGGS A cavity in a dead tree, or beneath loose or broken bark; the 5 or 6 eggs are white, spotted reddish brown.
INCUBATION Lasts for 14 days and incubated by the female.
COMMENT A regular member of the flocks of chickadees that roam through the woodlands in winter.

BROWN CREEPER

Certhia americana   5—6in/13—15cm

IDENTIFICATION Easily overlooked, brown and buff-streaked bird, that climbs trunks and major limbs of trees. White underparts, long, decurved bill and sharp-pointed tail-feathers are all good marks.
VOICE High-pitched *see-see-see*. Attention is usually attracted by call than by a sighting.
HABITAT All kinds of woodland and forest.
RANGE Breeds right across North America in conifer zone and southward through western states and Appalachians.
MOVEMENTS Winters throughout most of US as far as Gulf coast.
BREEDING Mature forests of a variety of types; April-May.
NEST AND EGGS The cup-shaped nest is usually situated beneath a piece of loose bark or in a broken snag; the 4 to 8 eggs are white, speckled with reddish brown.
INCUBATION The eggs take 15 days to hatch, incubated by the female.
COMMENT Though separated from the Treecreeper of Europe, this may be the same bird that ranges right across Asia.

RED-WHISKERED BULBUL

Pycnonotus jocosus   7in/18cm

IDENTIFICATION Brown above, white below, marked by bold crest, red cheek patch, and red undertail coverts. Asiatic species.
VOICE Noisy chattering.
HABITAT Suburbs.
RANGE Established near Miami, Florida.
MOVEMENTS Resident.

WRENS & DIPPERS

ALTHOUGH placed consecutively in almost every systematic order of birds, these two families are quite distinct. The New World is home to all of the world's 60 species of wrens, only one of which also occurs outside the continent. North America, however, is home to only nine species, though they are among the most familiar and well-loved of all birds. Wrens vary in size from the tiny Winter Wren that moves southward across the U.S.A. to winter in the southern states, to the thrush-sized Cactus Wren of the southwest. They have long, decurved bills ideally suited to probing bark crevices in their search for small insects, spiders, and their eggs. Their tails are mainly short and frequently held cocked over their backs. Mostly these are ground dwelling birds that skulk among dense vegetation, though they will also perch quite openly to sing. The Winter Wren is the only species to have crossed the Bering Straits and colonized the Old World. It is now found right across northern Asia as far as the Atlantic coast of Europe.

Here, it has even colonized small, isolated islands, become resident, and evolved into distinct subspecies. It seems strange that this bird doubtless owes its success in the Old World to its long-distance migratory habits, yet, having colonized some remote rock, it then loses the habit and starts to differentiate from its neighbors. Along the way it has been able to occupy habitats that, in the Americas, are the domain of related species. Thus, in Europe the Winter Wren can be found around houses and gardens that in North America would be home to the House Wren; among rocky hillsides that would seem more suited to the Rock Wren; in damp woodlands that one would feel more likely to hold the Carolina Wren, and so on. The new opportunities offered by a wren-less landmass have been fully exploited, making the Winter Wren undoubtedly the most abundant member of its family.

There are only four species of dipper in the world, though between them they occupy every significant landmass save Africa. Though they differ in plumage pattern, all are structurally very similar and share the remarkable ability to walk underwater. The American Dipper is confined to North and Central America, being replaced to the south by the startling White-capped Dipper.

The salmon rivers of the far north-west often attract Bald Eagles and Glaucous-winged Gulls. An American Dipper watches in the foreground (see over).

M.J.PLEDGER.

CACTUS WREN

Campylorhynchus brunneicapillus   8–8½in/20–22cm

IDENTIFICATION Large wren of arid landscapes. Heavily barred and streaked in white, black, and dark brown above; white on breast and creamy-buff on belly, both heavily streaked black. Bold, white eyebrow; long, decurved bill. Tail often cocked.
VOICE Harsh *cha-cha-cha*.
HABITAT Cactus country, dry hillsides.
RANGE States adjacent to Mexican border.
MOVEMENTS Resident.
BREEDING Semi-desert and dry, thorny scrub; March-April.
NEST AND EGGS The large, domed structure, with a side entrance, is strategically placed among the thorns of a cholla or yucca; the 4 to 7 eggs are pinkish, spotted with brown.
INCUBATION The incubation lasts 16 days, and is by the female.
COMMENT The nest of the Cactus Wren is a large structure that resembles nothing more than a hay-stack among the thorns of a cactus.

ROCK WREN

Salpinctes obsoletus   5½–6in/14–15cm

IDENTIFICATION Crown, back and wings are gray, spotted white; rump and tail brown, and similarly spotted. Underparts whitish becoming creamy on belly; slight streaking. Short, pale eyebrow.

VOICE *Tic-ear* and trilling.
HABITAT Rocky gullies, hillsides.
RANGE Whole of western US from central Texas northward. Also south-western Canada.
MOVEMENTS Northern interior populations are migratory.
BREEDING Rocky cliffs and screes, earth banks and crumbling cliffs; March-April.
NEST AND EGGS A crevice is lined with grasses and the entrance hole is often decorated with small stones; the 4 to 8 eggs are white, lightly spotted reddish.
INCUBATION The eggs are incubated by the female alone.
COMMENT The habit of collecting small stones at the entrance to the nest hole is not unique to the Rock Wren, but it is a useful clue to its presence.

CANYON WREN

Catherpes mexicanus   5½–6in/14–15cm

IDENTIFICATION Easily identified by rufous body contrasting with gray crown and white face, throat and breast. But often difficult to see.
VOICE Loud, rich descending notes that stutter to a conclusion.

HABITAT Dark canyons and gullies.

RANGE Mountain systems and foothills from Canadian border to central Texas.

MOVEMENTS Some high-altitude breeders descend in winter.

BREEDING Cliffs and screes often in canyons; March-April.

NEST AND EGGS A crevice or small cave is used as a nest, lined with leaves and grass; the 4 to 6 eggs are white with brown speckles.

INCUBATION The eggs are incubated by the female.

COMMENT Though a natural cliff nester, this wren has taken well to roughly constructed stone buildings, especially when neglected.

CAROLINA WREN

Thryothorus ludovicianus   5 – 5½in/13 – 14cm

IDENTIFICATION Medium-sized wren with plain, deep buff below. Brown back, barred wings and tail; bold white eyebrow; mottled ear coverts.

VOICE Pleasantly warbled three-note song.

HABITAT Thickets in suburbs, streamsides, damp woods.

RANGE South-eastern states and somewhat northward.

MOVEMENTS Resident.

BREEDING Dense, bushy areas often along wooded streams; April-May.

NEST AND EGGS Cavities and holes in trees, banks or buildings, lined with twigs, roots, and a soft lining; the 4 to 6 eggs are white or creamy, spotted with brown.

INCUBATION Lasts 12 to 14 days and is by the female.

COMMENT Like other small birds that do not migrate, the numbers of Carolina Wrens may be decimated by a harsh winter.

BEWICK'S WREN

Thryomanes bewickii   4½ – 5in/12 – 13cm

IDENTIFICATION Well-marked wren with long, graduated tail, that is wagged from side to side high above the back. Upperparts brown or gray brown with black barring on wings and tail; underparts white. Bold white eyebrow and dark barring on ear coverts. Bill, long and decurved.

VOICE Buzzing warble.

HABITAT Thickets, scrub, woodland clearings.

RANGE Breeds across much of the west, local and declining in Appalachia.

MOVEMENTS Largely resident, but eastern birds move southwards to winter along Gulf Coast.

BREEDING Dense bush in open woods, farmsteads, and suburbs; April-May.

NEST AND EGGS Uses a variety of nest cavities including old woodpecker holes, buildings, nest boxes; the 5 to 7 eggs are white, spotted with brown.

INCUBATION The eggs take 10 to 14 days to hatch and are incubated by the female alone.

COMMENT Like most other birds that utilize natural holes in which to nest, a wide variety of material is used as filler before the nest chamber itself is constructed of soft materials.

HOUSE WREN

Troglodytes aedon   4½ – 5in/11 – 13cm

IDENTIFICATION A widespread and common small wren. Chunky shape and short, "cocked" tail are characteristic. Upperparts only faintly barred and underparts paler than similar wrens. Generally grayer with no prominent facial markings.

VOICE A loud rising trill, plus various scolding notes.

HABITAT Broadleaved woods, thickets, often alongside water.
RANGE Breeds across US extending northward into southern
Canada.
MOVEMENTS Whole population moves southward to winter
along Gulf and Mexican border states.
BREEDING Woods, shelter belts, farmsteads, suburbs; April-
June.
NEST AND EGGS A cavity filled with leaves, grasses and all
manner of other materials lined with hair and feathers; the 6
to 8 eggs are pale pink, spotted reddish brown.
INCUBATION The eggs hatch after 13 or 14 days and are
incubated mainly by the female.
COMMENT The variety of nest sites used by this bird is
remarkable. Virtually any cavity will serve its purpose,
including a hole in a building, car, a pocket in a jacket or even
a shoe.

WINTER WREN

Troglodytes troglodytes   4in/10cm

IDENTIFICATION Tiny, brown bird very similar to House
Wren. Upperparts barred brown, buff, and black; underparts
brown, heavily barred on belly. Very short tail often held
cocked over back. House Wren has longer tail and lacks
barring on belly.
VOICE Rich, explosive trill.
HABITAT Conifer woods with dense scrub.
RANGE Boreal Canada extending northward into Alaska and
southwards along Pacific coast and the Appalachians.
MOVEMENTS Canadian birds migrate southward to winter in
southern and eastern states.
BREEDING Mature conifers with open clearings and
secondary growth; March-June.

NEST AND EGGS A domed structure of grasses tucked among
tree roots or a pile of brush; the 5 to 8 eggs are white,
speckled reddish.
INCUBATION The eggs take 14 to 17 days to hatch and are
incubated by the female alone.
COMMENT This is the only wren to have colonized the Old
World where it ranges right across Asia to Britain and the
Faeroes. In many areas it behaves like a House Wren.

SEDGE WREN

Cistothorus platensis   4½in/11cm

IDENTIFICATION Similar to Marsh Wren, but has white,
streaked crown; faintly white streaked back, and buffy
underparts. Pale eyebrow neither as bold nor as long as Marsh
Wren. Formerly called Short-billed Marsh Wren.
VOICE Chattering trill.

HABITAT Shallow, overgrown marshes.
RANGE Breeds north-eastern US and southern Canada extending into the prairies.
MOVEMENTS Winters along Atlantic and Gulf coasts.
BREEDING Damp, marshy areas with bushes such as willow or alder; May-June.
NEST AND EGGS A neat, ball-shaped nest of vegetation, attached to grass or sedge, with a side entrance; the 4 to 8 eggs are white.
INCUBATION The eggs take 12 to 14 days to hatch and incubation is performed by the female alone.
COMMENT This is a shy species, more often heard than seen.

MARSH WREN

Cistothorus palustris   5in/13cm

IDENTIFICATION Rich, rusty wren found in association with wetlands. Upperparts, rufous, heavily barred black with series of bold white stripes on back. Crown, black brown with lengthy, white eyebrow. Throat and upper breast, white. Formerly known as Long-billed Marsh Wren.
VOICE Scolding rattle.
HABITAT Reed swamps.
RANGE Right across North America except for Rockies and south-east interior states. Also southern and prairie Canada.
MOVEMENTS Mostly a summer visitor; winters in southern and coastal states.
BREEDING Marshy vegetation, especially cattail; April-May.
NEST AND EGGS A large, domed structure, woven to tall,

emergent vegetation, with a side entrance; the 5 or 6 eggs are brownish, spotted dark brown.
INCUBATION Lasts for 13 days and is performed by the female alone.
COMMENT The eggs of this bird, being brown in color, are quite unlike those of any other wren.

AMERICAN DIPPER

Cinclus mexicanus   7−8½in/18−22cm

IDENTIFICATION A chunky, all-gray bird that is seldom, if ever, found far from tumbling, rocky streams. Rotund body, thick neck, short, rounded wings and tiny, often "cocked" tail are best field marks. Bounces on rocks, swims and wades in water.
VOICE Loud song and characteristic *zeet* call.
HABITAT Fast streams with boulders, long stony glides, weirs.
RANGE Resident in western Alaska, Canada and US, in Rocky Mountain chain.
MOVEMENTS Some local movement, especially where streams ice up in winter.
BREEDING Banks of streams, bridges, culverts; April-May.
NEST AND EGGS An untidy, domed structure of grasses in hole or crevice overlooking water; the 4 or 5 eggs are white.
INCUBATION Lasts 12 days and is performed by the female alone.
COMMENT It is rather strange that the Dipper is confined to the west when there are plentiful streams elsewhere in North America.

OLD WORLD WARBLERS, THRUSHES, KINGLETS, GNATCATCHERS & WRENTITS

THIS is a diverse group of closely related birds that is widespread in the northern hemisphere and which has its origins in the Old World. Most numerous in North America are the thrushes. All North American thrushes are, to some extent, migratory, though it is somewhat surprising that the one bird which is resident over much of the U.S.A., has been given the scientific name of *Turdus migratorius*.

The American Robin breeds throughout the area, extending northward well into the Canadian Arctic where only dwarf vegetation covers the ground. It is equally at home in parks, suburbs, and gardens as far south as Florida and Mexico. The fact that these abundant birds leave Canada almost completely in winter and perform long and obvious migrations doubtless accounts for the early ornithologists naming them as they did. The English name of "robin" certainly stems from their red breast, for English colonists had a remarkable propensity to call any bird with such markings after their own familiar European Robin, no matter where it was found or what its relationships. In fact, the North American Robin is a thrush, while the European Robin is a chat.

Most other thrushes are brown above, pale below, and well spotted on the breast. They vary somewhat in size and are mainly only summer visitors. Several species, notably Swainson's and Gray-cheeked Thrushes, together with the Veery, pose interesting identification problems, particularly when faced with a solitary individual on migration.

A closely-related group of birds are the bluebirds, with three distinct species being found within North American boundaries. The familiar Eastern Bluebird is one of the most colorful of North American birds, but it has suffered a quite serious decline in recent years due to competition for nesting holes with the alien House Sparrow and European Starling. Fortunately, these lovely birds have responded well to special nest boxes, and in places where enthusiasts have designed and erected them there is evidence of a comeback. A national campaign may well be required to bring this species back to its former numbers. No doubt a similar story could be told for the Western Bluebird.

The two kinglets are predominantly birds of the

northern forests, though they extend southward through the mountain chains. They prefer conifers, but will frequent a wider variety of woodland and other well-treed areas in winter. Both are migratory, though the Ruby-crowned Kinglet is almost completely so, and its flights rival those of some of the hummingbirds in terms of distance flown. They usually feed high up in trees and are best located by their continuous high-pitched calls.

Were it not for their longer tails, the three gnatcatchers would be equally as small as the kinglets. They too are active little birds that spend every waking hour scouring through vegetation in their search for food. Most abundant is the Blue-gray Gnatcatcher, which is a summer visitor through most of the U.S.A. In winter it joins the Black-tailed Gnatcatcher along the Mexican border. The third has recently been split by ornithologists from the Black-tailed Gnatcatcher. It is the California Gnatcatcher, a species found only in southern California and in adjacent Mexico.

Though several Old World warblers and chats occur as vagrants in North America, only a handful have managed to spread to this continent to breed. Thus, the Arctic Warbler can be found in western and central Alaska among the scrub willows that clothe the sheltered valleys. Western Alaska also holds the colorful Bluethroat. A species that may perhaps make the transition from being an Old World to a New World bird is the Northern Wheatear. This sprightly chat breeds in Alaska and migrates, like the Arctic Warbler and Bluethroat, across the Bering Straits to winter in Asia. But it also nests in Greenland and among the Canadian archipelago, and migrates eastward across the Atlantic via Iceland and Britain to Africa. Perhaps one day Wheatears will start to move southward through North America, as doubtless other species did in the distant past.

ARCTIC WARBLER

Phylloscopus borealis   5in/13cm

IDENTIFICATION Small, active, Old World warbler with fine, pointed bill. Olive-green above, with single narrow wing-bar. White, washed yellow below; pale legs. Long, clear supercilium extends beyond eye and turns upwards; clear dark eye-stripe.

VOICE Hard *tchack* or a buzzy song.

HABITAT Tundra thickets.

RANGE Western Alaska.

MOVEMENTS Summer visitor, returns to Old World.

GOLDEN-CROWNED KINGLET

Regulus satrapa   4in/10cm

IDENTIFICATION Tiny, ever-active bird, greenish above, with black wings marked by double, white wing-bar, and black tail. Male has complex "face" pattern of black eye-stripe, white eyebrow and vivid, orange-red crest. Female is similar, but with yellow crest.

VOICE Thin *see-see-see*.

HABITAT Conifer woods.

RANGE Boreal Canada together with western mountains, Appalachians and northern US.

MOVEMENTS Northern birds migrate to winter throughout US.

BREEDING Conifer woodland, or conifer dominated mixed woods; April-June.

NEST AND EGGS A rounded ball of mosses lined with feathers is suspended between a horizontal fork at the edge of a conifer, usually quite high above the ground; the 5 to 10 eggs are white, spotted brown.

INCUBATION The female incubates the eggs for 14 days.

COMMENT Ever-active little birds that spend most of their time in high canopy.

RUBY-CROWNED KINGLET

Regulus calendula 4½in/11cm

IDENTIFICATION Similar to Golden-crowned Kinglet with greenish upperparts and black wings with double, white wing-bar. Both sexes show plain face, lacking the distinctive stripes of the Golden-crowned Kinglet. Male has red crest, but this is seldom a prominent field mark.

VOICE Thin *see-see-see*.

HABITAT Conifer woods and thickets.

RANGE Boreal Canada extending southward through the US Rockies.

MOVEMENTS Migratory, wintering southern, western and eastern US.

BREEDING Conifer forests and other more open woodland; May-June.

NEST AND EGGS A spherical nest of mosses held together with cobwebs and usually placed high in a conifer; the 5 to 11 eggs are white, spotted brown.

INCUBATION The female alone incubates the eggs for about 13 days.

COMMENT Most kinglets are located by their thin, high-pitched *zi-zi-zi* calls. On migration they may appear in a wide variety of cover including low, deciduous, bushy areas.

BLUE-GRAY GNATCATCHER

Polioptila caerulea   4½in/11cm

IDENTIFICATION Small, long-tailed, active and conspicuous bird. Male is bluish gray above with white eye-ring, black eyebrow, black wings, and long, black, white-edged tail. The underparts are pale gray.
VOICE Nasal *wee*.
HABITAT Woods, scrub.
RANGE Breeds across most of US, though absent from north-central and north-western states.

MOVEMENTS Summer visitor, but resident along Atlantic and Gulf coasts and along Mexican border.
BREEDING Though it frequents a variety of woodlands, mature trees are an essential ingredient; April-June.
NEST AND EGGS The neat nest is placed across a high branch of a tree and consists of vegetation bound together with spiders' webs; the 4 or 5 eggs are pale blue, spotted brown.
INCUBATION The eggs take 13 days to hatch and incubation is shared between the pair.
COMMENT Though a totally New World family, the gnatcatchers are clearly related to the Old World warblers.

CALIFORNIA GNATCATCHER

Polioptila california   4½in/11cm

IDENTIFICATION Very similar to Black-tailed Gnatcatcher, but dusky below and darker above.
VOICE Cat-like mewing calls.
HABITAT Brushlands.
RANGE Coastal southern California.
MOVEMENTS Resident.

BLACK-TAILED GNATCATCHER

Polioptila melanura   4½in/11cm

IDENTIFICATION Gray above with black cap, blackish wings and black tail with white margins. Female lacks black cap, but has much less white in tail than the Blue-gray Gnatcatcher.
VOICE Repeated *gee*.
HABITAT Arid brush country, sagebrush.
RANGE US along Mexican border.
MOVEMENTS Resident.
BREEDING Dry, arid semi-desert with low bushes; April-May.
NEST AND EGGS A neat little cup is placed low in a bush, often mesquite; the 3 or 4 eggs are pale blue, spotted brown.
INCUBATION The eggs take 14 days to hatch, incubated by both sexes.
COMMENT Where the range of the gnatcatchers overlap there may be significant problems in identification.

BLUETHROAT

Luscinia svecica   5½–6in/14–15cm

IDENTIFICATION Breeding male has blue breast with central red spot and white supercilium. Female has clear white breast with dark border. In all plumages base of outer tail feathers is rusty.
VOICE Hard *tic-tic*.
HABITAT Arctic scrub.
RANGE Northern Alaska.
MOVEMENTS Summer visitor, migrates via Asia.

NORTHERN WHEATEAR

Oenanthe oenanthe   5½−6in/14−15cm

IDENTIFICATION Active, ground-dwelling bird that shows bold white rump. Male is gray above, white below with black wings and tail band, and clear-cut black mask. Female and immature males are buffy, but show rump pattern.
VOICE *Chak-chak*.
HABITAT Tundra, rocky slopes.
RANGE Alaska and eastern Canadian archipelago and Greenland.
MOVEMENTS Migrates to Old World with western birds flying west and eastern birds flying east in fall.

EASTERN BLUEBIRD

Sialia sialis   6½−7in/17−18cm

IDENTIFICATION Male is bright blue above; rusty below with white belly and undertail. Female has only a touch of blue on the crown, with bluish wings and tail; underparts a pale rust. Sits openly, dropping to catch insects on the ground or in the air.

VOICE Melodic *chur-lee*, repeated.
HABITAT Woodland edges, clearings, orchards.
RANGE Eastern US and Canada.
MOVEMENTS Birds from northern half of range migrate.
BREEDING Frequents woodland clearings, margins, farming country; March-June.

NEST AND EGGS A tree cavity, including old woodpecker holes, or nest box is lined mainly with grasses; the 3 to 7 eggs are very light blue.
INCUBATION The eggs take 12 days to hatch and are incubated by the female with some help from her mate.
COMMENT The provision of suitable nest holes is the essential of every territory of this bird.

WESTERN BLUEBIRD

Sialia mexicana   6½−7in/17−18cm

IDENTIFICATION Structure and behavior as Eastern Bluebird, but male darker, purple blue above and dark rust below; belly gray rather than white. Female similar to female Eastern, but darker rust on breast.
VOICE A repeated *few*.
HABITAT Woods, farms, orchards.
RANGE Western US as far north as British Columbia.
MOVEMENTS Northern birds migrate, but resident near Pacific coast.
BREEDING Haunts woodland clearings, burnt-over areas, orchards; May-June.
NEST AND EGGS A tree cavity or nest box is lined with grasses; the 4 to 6 eggs are pale blue.
INCUBATION Lasts for 14 days and is performed by the female assisted by the male.
COMMENT Eastern and Western Bluebirds share a very similar lifestyle and have clearly evolved into distinct species by being separated by the treeless prairies.

Mountain Bluebird

Sialia currucoides   6½−7in/17−18cm

IDENTIFICATION Male is blue above, with deep-blue wings and tail; underparts pale blue becoming grayish on belly. Female is gray above and below, with blue in wings and tail. Plain featureless "face" lacks eye-ring of other female bluebirds.

VOICE A warbling *tu-lee*.
HABITAT High-level grasslands.
RANGE Western US as far north as Alaskan panhandle and as far east as the Dakotas.
MOVEMENTS Northern and interior birds migrate southward to Mexican border and beyond.
BREEDING Park-like woodland with scattered trees, but also similar areas of farmland; April-June.
NEST AND EGGS A cavity in a tree, old woodpecker hole, nest box or hole among rocks is lined with grasses; the 5 or 6 eggs are pale blue.
INCUBATION The eggs take 14 days to hatch and incubation is shared by both sexes.
COMMENT The exact roles of the sexes in incubation for the three bluebirds has not been properly defined.

Townsend's Solitaire

Myadestes townsendi   8½−9in/21−23cm

IDENTIFICATION A slender, gray bird marked by short bill and pale eye-ring. Orange in wing, and white outer feathers of long tail are particularly obvious in flight. Perches openly, sometimes catching insects in the air. Juvenile is brown, spotted and barred above and below.

VOICE Pleasant warble.
HABITAT Mountain conifer forests.
RANGE Mountains of the west from Alaska to Mexican border.
MOVEMENTS Alaskan and Canadian birds move southward to winter.
BREEDING Open forests, parkland and burnt-over areas; May-June.
NEST AND EGGS The nest is a cup of grasses and bents placed among tree roots or against the wall of a cutting or bank, the 3 to 5 eggs are white, spotted brown.
INCUBATION The eggs are probably incubated by the female alone.
COMMENT A member of a totally New World genus that has close relatives among the forktails of Asia. The name of flycatcher-thrush has been aptly applied to a closely related genus.

Veery

Catharus fuscescens   6½−7in/17−18cm

IDENTIFICATION Warm rufous-brown above, with warm buff on throat and upper breast, delicately streaked; white below with grayish wash on flanks. Pale lores, and ear coverts speckled. Rufous upperparts separate from all other thrushes except Pacific form of Swainson's Thrush.
VOICE Series of fluty notes on a descending scale.
HABITAT Damp woodlands and riverside thickets.
RANGE Breeds across the continent either side of the

US-Canada border, southward through the Rockies and Appalachians.

MOVEMENTS Summer visitor.

BREEDING Inhabits deciduous and mixed woods with clearings covered with a dense growth of shrubbery; May-June.

NEST AND EGGS A cup of twigs and grass, lined with leaves and hair usually placed on the ground; the 3 to 5 eggs are greenish blue.

INCUBATION The eggs take 12 days to hatch and are incubated by the female alone.

COMMENT One of those birds that is named after its call, this is actually a typical small thrush.

GRAY-CHEEKED THRUSH

Catharus minimus   6½−7in/17−18cm

IDENTIFICATION Small, earth-brown thrush; white underparts clearly spotted brown on the breast, and with a grayish wash along the flanks. Dull-gray lores and ear coverts, together with insignificant eye-ring, give this bird a somewhat featureless "face".

VOICE Nasal, Veery-like song.

HABITAT Conifer forests, also mixed woodland.

RANGE Northern taiga zone from Alaska to Newfoundland.

MOVEMENTS Summer visitor.

BREEDING Conifer woods, often near the tree-line, but also along coasts; dense growth seems essential; June-July.

NEST AND EGGS A cup of grasses placed in a tree, usually quite low and occasionally on the ground; the 3 to 5 eggs are green blue, spotted brown.

INCUBATION Lasts for 12 to 14 days and is performed by the female alone.

COMMENT One of the most northerly of small passerine birds that makes a length of the continent migration to southern Mexico and beyond.

SWAINSON'S THRUSH

Catharus ustulatus   6½−7in/17−18cm

IDENTIFICATION Earth-brown above with buffy eye-ring and lores; underparts are warm buff on breast, heavily spotted with brown; belly whitish, flanks brown gray. Western form is a warmer shade of brown.

VOICE Rising series of whistles.

HABITAT Wet scrub, thickets, damp woods.

RANGE Boreal and western mountain zones.

MOVEMENTS Summer visitor.

BREEDING Dense shrubs among conifer or deciduous woods, but also overgrown clearings; April-June.

NEST AND EGGS A neat structure of twigs and grasses placed at no great height, usually in an evergreen; the 3 or 4 eggs are blue, blotched brown.

INCUBATION The eggs are incubated for 12 days by the female alone.

COMMENT Though widely distributed and quite common, this is a self-effacing bird that must be definitely searched for during the breeding season.

HERMIT THRUSH

Catharus guttatus   6–6½in/16–17cm

IDENTIFICATION Small thrush with brown upperparts and rust-red tail. Underparts white with large splodges of brown and gray, particularly on the breast. Pale, narrow eye-ring. Colors vary somewhat across North America, but the rufous tail is virtually a constant feature. *See* other small thrushes.

VOICE Fluty warble.

HABITAT Woodlands, scrub.

RANGE Breeds through the boreal zone southward through the Rockies.

MOVEMENTS Most birds are migratory, though resident along the Pacific coast throughout the year. Winters along the Atlantic and in southern US.

BREEDING Conifers or mixed woods, with clearings, swamps and other open areas; May-June.

NEST AND EGGS A cup of twigs and roots usually placed on the ground among tree roots or other snags; the 3 or 4 eggs are greenish blue.

INCUBATION Lasts 12 days and is probably entirely by the female.

COMMENT Though it spends most of its time among ground vegetation, this dainty little thrush requires tall trees for song posts.

WOOD THRUSH

Hylocichla mustelina   7½–8in/19–20cm

IDENTIFICATION Largest of the "brown and spotted" thrushes. Upperparts are rich chestnut on crown and upper back, remaining parts brown. Underparts white, boldly spotted black. Bold, white eye-ring is excellent clinching field mark.

VOICE Melodic three- to five-note phrases.

HABITAT Deciduous and damp forests, suburbs.

RANGE Eastern US.

MOVEMENTS Summer visitor.

BREEDING Found among secondary growth of mature, deciduous woodlands; May-June.

NEST AND EGGS The nest is made of grasses reinforced with mud and lined with roots; the 3 to 5 eggs are greenish blue.

INCUBATION The eggs take 13 to 14 days to hatch and are incubated by the female alone.

COMMENT Though officially placed in a genus by itself, many authors consider this bird better placed with the *Catharus* thrushes.

CLAY-COLORED ROBIN

Turdus grayi   8½–9½in/21–24cm

IDENTIFICATION Dull, washed-out brown and orange-buff thrush with white-streaked throat. Highly secretive.

VOICE *Cheery-cheer.*

HABITAT Thickets and undergrowth.

RANGE Southern Texas.

MOVEMENTS Rare breeding visitor.

AMERICAN ROBIN

Turdus migratorius   9½–10in/24–25cm

IDENTIFICATION Well-known, common bird marked by brown upperparts and rich-red underparts. Other field marks include boldly broken, white eye-ring, streaked white bib and white tips to the outer tail feathers. Juvenile shows same basic pattern, but is heavily spotted above and below.
VOICE Melodic, three-note warble, repeated.
HABITAT Suburbs, parks, woodland.
RANGE Breeds throughout North America.
MOVEMENTS Canadian, Alaskan and north-central US birds leave in winter.
BREEDING Coniferous and deciduous trees around farms, suburbs and woodland edges; April-June.
NEST AND EGGS A neat cup of grasses and mud placed in a bush; the 3 to 5 eggs are pale blue.
INCUBATION The eggs take 12 or 13 days to hatch and are incubated by the female alone.
COMMENT The ability to live alongside man and take advantage of the changes he has wrought on the countryside have made this the most successful of American thrushes.

VARIED THRUSH

Ixoreus naevius   9–9½in/23–24cm

IDENTIFICATION A dark thrush with blue-gray of back extending to nape and tail; underparts rich, rust-red with bold, black breast-band. Black wings with bold, rust-red, double wing-bar. Female has earth-brown, not blue-gray, upperparts, but is similarly patterned with rust-red eyebrow being more prominent.
VOICE A slow and variable trill.
HABITAT Conifer and other forests.
RANGE From Alaska along Pacific coast as far as northern California.
MOVEMENTS Northern birds move southward as far as southern California in winter.
BREEDING Inhabits a wide range of woodland types at different altitudes, but always prefers dark and damp places; April-June.
NEST AND EGGS A neat cup of grasses and mud is placed in a tree; the 2 to 5 eggs are blue, spotted with brown.
INCUBATION The eggs are incubated by the female for about 14 days.
COMMENT Though essentially a western bird this species does wander eastwards in winter, sometimes as far as the east coast.

WRENTIT

Chamaea fasciata   6–6½in/16–17cm

IDENTIFICATION A small, brown bird with a long tail.
Upperparts dull brown, underparts richer brown and
streaked; southern birds are a dull buffy below. Bill is short
and pale yellow eye is a good feature.
VOICE A trilled *pit-pit-pit-r-r-r*.
HABITAT Chaparral.
RANGE Pacific coast of US.
MOVEMENTS Resident.
BREEDING Dry, thickly vegetated scrub;
February-May.
NEST AND EGGS A neat cup bound by spiders'
webs is hidden among dense, low
vegetation; the 3 to 5 eggs are bluish.
INCUBATION The eggs take 15 or 16 days to hatch and are
incubated by both members of the pair.
COMMENT Taxonomists still debate the relationships of this
strange little bird. Some consider it an Old World flycatcher,
others that it is a member of the parrotbills of Asia.

MOCKINGBIRDS & THRASHERS

THE thrashers are a New World family of some 30 species, no less than ten of which breed in North America. The family includes the Gray Catbird and Northern Mockingbird, both of which are familiar right across the continent. Of the thrashers proper, no less than eight are found, but only one species, the Brown Thrasher, has managed to extend very far eastward. The rest are dry ground birds of the west that spend most of their time scratching a living from the earth with their heavily decurved bills.

These are generally soberly colored in shades of gray and brown, and with heavy, well-formed bills. Several species are well streaked, and the tail is often long and frequently flicked upward. They are pre-dominantly ground or near-the-ground feeders, and are generally fond of dense vegetation. These are highly vocal birds, producing a wide range of calls, some of which, by sheer law of averages, are bound to coincide with those of other birds. Pure mimicry, from which their family name is derived, is a relatively small part of their vocabulary.

By far the best known species is the Northern Mockingbird, held high in the esteem of many Americans, including song-writers. This fine songster can be heard singing from rooftops and television antennae, continuing until well after dark. It will certainly mimic other birds' calls and songs, as well as whistles and other less natural sounds. Almost as familiar is the Gray Catbird, another member of the family that has learned to live easily alongside man. Though by no means a competitor of the Mockingbird, the Catbird's cat-like miaowing is equally as familiar in suburbs and gardens. It too may become a proficient mimic.

The Sage Thrasher is gray and streaked like a Mockingbird, but behaves like a thrasher. It occupies much of western North America, being replaced to the east by the rufous Brown Thrasher. All of the other thrashers are more or less confined to the southwestern U.S.A. and are dry-ground birds.

GRAY CATBIRD

Dumetella carolinensis   8½in/21–22cm

IDENTIFICATION Uniformly slate-gray bird with black cap and black tail that is often held cocked over back. Rich chestnut undertail coverts.

VOICE Cat-like *me-ow*.

HABITAT Dense cover in woods and suburbs.

RANGE Breeds across southern Canada and much of US, though absent from south-western quarter of the country and the Gulf coast.

MOVEMENTS Migratory, winters Florida and Gulf Coast and along Atlantic coast.

BREEDING Dense thickets in a wide variety of situations; May-July.

NEST AND EGGS A large, bulky nest of twigs is lined with grasses and roots and placed in dense vegetation; the 3 to 5 eggs are greenish blue.

INCUBATION The eggs take some 12 or 13 days to hatch and are incubated by the female alone.

COMMENT Named after its cat-like whining, this bird is also a noted songster that, unlike its closest relatives, does not repeat phrases.

NORTHERN MOCKINGBIRD

Mimus polyglottos   9–10in/23–25cm

IDENTIFICATION Dull-gray crown, back and rump; contrasting black wings and tail, both showing bold areas of white in flight and display. Underparts, pale gray. Bill, slightly decurved. Readily associates with suburban man.

VOICE Accomplished mimic of other birds and natural and unnatural sounds.

HABITAT Suburbs, thickets, open woodland.

RANGE Breeds across entire southern half of US and northward along east coast.

MOVEMENTS Northern interior birds move southward in winter.

BREEDING Scrub and thickets, hedges and suburban shrubbery; March-June.

NEST AND EGGS A large cup of twigs and grasses at variable height in a tree; the 4 or 5 eggs are bluish, spotted with brown.

INCUBATION The eggs take 12 days to hatch and are incubated by the female alone.

COMMENT The amazing ability of this bird to imitate the songs of other species is strangely more developed in the east than in the west.

SAGE THRASHER

Oreoscoptes montanus   8½in/21–22cm

IDENTIFICATION A gray-brown thrasher heavily streaked below. Pale eye; white, double wing-bar, and pale tip to tail are all good field marks.

VOICE Extended warbling with no mimicry.

HABITAT Sage brush country, semi-desert.

RANGE Great Basin and interior western states.

MOVEMENTS Migrates southward to winter in Mexico and bordering US states.

BREEDING Dense thickets and sagebrush in dry, arid areas; April-May.

NEST AND EGGS A semi-domed, loosely woven structure of twigs placed in low vegetation or on the ground; the 4 or 5 eggs are greenish blue, spotted with brown.

INCUBATION The eggs are incubated by both members of the pair for about 15 days.

COMMENT Though commonly found in towns in semi-desert areas, its natural home is sagebrush country.

BROWN THRASHER

Toxostoma rufum   10½–11½in/27–29cm

IDENTIFICATION Rich, rufous brown above with bold cream and black, double wing-bar. Tail long and rounded; bill decurved; eye yellow. Underparts cream, heavily streaked black. Common bird of woods and hedges. The closely related Long-billed Thrasher of south Texas has gray face, longer bill and orange eyes.

VOICE Phrases repeated two or three times.

HABITAT Woodland edges, suburbs, hedgerows.

RANGE Breeds throughout eastern US as far west as the Rockies and northward into adjacent Canada.

MOVEMENTS Winters in southern and Atlantic states.

BREEDING Thickets, hedges and field corners, secondary woodland; April-May.

NEST AND EGGS The loosely woven nest consists of twigs and is lined with roots; the 4 or 5 eggs are white, washed with blue.

INCUBATION Lasts 11 to 14 days and is shared between the sexes.

COMMENT The distinctive habit of repeating each phrase of its song makes it easy to distinguish from the similar song of the Catbird.

LONG-BILLED THRASHER

Toxostoma longirostre   11–12in/28–30cm

IDENTIFICATION Very similar to more widespread Brown Thrasher, but with longer, decurved bill, grayer face and bright orange eye.

VOICE Repeated phrases.

HABITAT Thickets and undergrowth.

RANGE Rio Grande and adjacent Texas.

MOVEMENTS Resident.

BENDIRE'S THRASHER

Toxostoma bendirei   9–10in/23–25cm

IDENTIFICATION Gray above; dirty buff below, spotted dark gray. Similar to Curve-billed Thrasher, but bill significantly shorter, with pale base to lower mandible. To be identified with care.

VOICE Warbled song, repeated notes.

HABITAT Brush country, arid farmland.

RANGE Arizona and surrounding states.

MOVEMENTS Most leave the US in winter.

BREEDING Low vegetation in dry areas often with cactus; March-April.

NEST AND EGGS A structure of twigs lined with grasses and roots placed in a low, dense bush; the 3 to 5 eggs are greenish, spotted with light brown.

INCUBATION Undescribed.

COMMENT More inclined to fly than other thrashers, even though it remains a ground-dwelling bird.

CURVE-BILLED THRASHER

Toxostoma curvirostre   10–11in/26–28cm

IDENTIFICATION Large, gray thrasher with long, uniformly dark, decurved bill. Gray upperparts with double, white wing-bar; underparts heavily mottled, or virtually uniformly gray.

VOICE Pleasant, variable trills and a *wit-wheet*.

HABITAT Hillsides, bushlands.

RANGE South-western US.

MOVEMENTS Resident.

BREEDING Dry country with cholla cactus; March-April.

NEST AND EGGS The nest is a dense mass of twigs and cactus needles woven tightly together and placed in a cholla cactus; the 2 to 4 eggs are light greenish blue, spotted brown.

INCUBATION The eggs take 13 days to hatch and are incubated by both members of the pair.

COMMENT The extraordinary ball-shaped nest of this species is a fortress of cactus spines that seems to defy penetration.

CALIFORNIA THRASHER

Toxostoma redivivum   11½–12in/29–31cm

IDENTIFICATION Large, dark thrasher, with long, heavily decurved black bill. Earth-brown above with pale eyebrow and clear moustachial streak; underparts brown, warmer on belly. Tail long and graduated.

VOICE *Chuck*.

HABITAT Brushland, chaparral.

RANGE California.

MOVEMENTS Resident.

BREEDING Thickets of dense shrubbery among foothills (chaparral), but also in suburban gardens; December-April.

INCUBATION The eggs take 14 days to hatch and are incubated by both members of the pair.
COMMENT Very similar in habits to the California Thrasher and similarly feeds by using its long bill as a pick on hard, desert ground.

NEST AND EGGS The nest is constructed of twigs and is placed in a low bush; the 2 to 4 eggs are blue green, spotted with brown.
INCUBATION The eggs take 14 days to hatch and are incubated by both members of the pair.
COMMENT This is a ground-dwelling species that forages among leaves and is very disinclined to fly.

LE CONTE'S THRASHER

Toxostoma lecontei   10½−11in/27−28cm

CRISSAL THRASHER

Toxostoma dorsale   10½−11½in/27−29cm

IDENTIFICATION Dark gray thrasher with long, decurved bill. Upperparts dark gray, paler on rump and crown. White throat accentuates bold, black, moustachial streak. Underparts pale brown. Undertail coverts are rich chestnut. A secretive bird of dense, low cover.
VOICE Pleasant repeated *chiderip*.
HABITAT Dense, low vegetation in arid areas.
RANGE US states bordering Mexico.
MOVEMENTS Resident.

BREEDING Hot, dry desert with streamside brush and thickets; February-April.
NEST AND EGGS The nest is a mass of twigs hidden among mesquite and other tangles; the 2 to 4 eggs are greenish blue.

IDENTIFICATION Uniform pale-gray thrasher of desert areas that spends most of its time on the ground. Gray body with white chin and fine, black, moustachial streak; tail black; undertail a warm rufous. Bill is long, black and decurved.
VOICE *Tu-eep* call, melodic warbling song.
HABITAT Open semi-desert.
RANGE Southern California and adjacent states.
MOVEMENTS Resident.
BREEDING Dry, arid bush country with cholla cactus; January-April.
NEST AND EGGS A substantial nest of twigs and grasses is constructed in a cactus or thorn bush; the 2 to 4 eggs are greenish blue, spotted brown.
INCUBATION The eggs are incubated by both members of the pair for about 16 days.
COMMENT A decidedly scarce bird that spends most of its time avoiding the heat of the day and is most active at dawn and dusk.

WAGTAILS & PIPITS

THIS is a well-defined family of long-legged, long-tailed, ground-dwelling birds, consisting of 54 species, only nine of which are admitted to the American list. Of these, three are found only in westernmost Alaska, and a further four are no more that rare vagrants. Thus, only two species – the American Pipit and Sprague's Pipit – are at all regular and widespread in North America.

The pipits are generally brown-gray birds heavily streaked both above and below. They have medium to long tails, longish legs with a well-developed hind claw, and fly easily with a slight bouncing action. Their identification is usually problematical, especially during the winter, and is based on features such as outer tail pattern and, particularly, on calls.

Wagtails are similarly slim, but with longer tails that, as their name suggests, are wagged vertically. All have bold, white outertail feathers and most have an association with water. The Yellow Wagtail exhibits a wide range of subspecific forms, and those that breed in Alaska are differentiated as *Motacilla flava tschutschensis*.

YELLOW WAGTAIL

Motacilla flava   6½ – 7in/16–18cm

IDENTIFICATION Slim, elegant, ground-dwelling bird with yellow underparts and olive-green upperparts. Long tail with white outer feathers. Highly variable subspecies, mainly in head pattern. Pumps tail while walking.
VOICE High *tsup*.
HABITAT Marshy edges, tundra, bushy fields.
RANGE Northern and western Alaska.
MOVEMENTS Summer visitor, moves southward into Asia in fall.

RED-THROATED PIPIT

Anthus cervinus   6 – 6½in/15–16cm

IDENTIFICATION In summer face and breast washed rusty: in winter throat shows plain creamy patch. Streaking above and below more contrasting and clear-cut than any other pipit.
VOICE *See-eep*.
HABITAT Tundra, marshes.
RANGE Westernmost Alaska.
MOVEMENTS Summer visitor, scarce along Pacific coast.

AMERICAN PIPIT

Anthus rubescens   6 – 6½in/16–17cm

IDENTIFICATION Previously known as Water Pipit. A slim, long-tailed bird, brown-gray above, lightly streaked; buffy below with fine streaking on the breast; much heavier streaking in winter. White, outer tail-feathers. Spends much time walking; dark legs. Habitual tail-wagger.

VOICE Thin *pee-eet*.
HABITAT Tundra, mountains.
RANGE Northernmost Canada extending southward through highest Rockies.
MOVEMENTS Winters south to most areas of US, except the interior.
BREEDING Rocky areas at high altitude or high latitude; June-July.
NEST AND EGGS A neat cup of grasses placed on the ground and sheltered by a tussock or rock; the 4 to 7 eggs are gray, heavily spotted brownish.
INCUBATION Lasts 14 days and is performed by the female alone.
COMMENT Having been recently separated from the Old World Rock and Water Pipits, the name American Pipit, seems well chosen.

SPRAGUE'S PIPIT

Anthus spragueii   6 – 6½in/16–17cm

IDENTIFICATION Similar to American Pipit, but with pale margins to feathers of upperparts producing a "scalloped" effect. Dark eye with no obvious stripes; streaking on breast clear-cut; belly white. More white on outer tail than American Pipit; pink not dark legs. Tail-wagger.
VOICE Loud *squeet*.
HABITAT Grasslands.
RANGE Canadian and north-central US prairies.
MOVEMENTS Summer visitor; winters Texas and adjacent states and into Mexico.
BREEDING Open grasslands and prairies; May-June.
NEST AND EGGS A cup of grasses well hidden, and often overhung, with grass; the 4 to 7 eggs are gray, spotted with brown.
INCUBATION The eggs are incubated by the female alone.
COMMENT This is a secretive, ground-dwelling bird that is often difficult to locate.

Waxwings & Silky Flycatchers

THIS is a group of two closely related families which together number only seven or eight species worldwide. North America is fortunate in having two of the three waxwings and one of the four or five silky flycatchers in the world.

Though both waxwings breed in the north, the Cedar Waxwing is by far the more familiar and regular visitor southward. In large, often huge flocks it roams throughout most of the U.S.A. in search of berries, finding them along hedgerows and in gardens. The Bohemian Waxwing is a more erratic winter visitor southward, particularly in the east. In fact, its visits are more irruptive in character, with a total absence for several years being followed by mass arrivals. Inevitably, such years are warmly greeted by eastern birders.

These are gregarious berry feeders which may descend on a hedgerow and strip it clean in a matter of hours, before moving on elsewhere in search of further supplies. In fact, glutinous is a word that comes easily to mind when describing these, nevertheless, attractive birds.

The two species are very similar in appearance and both share the colorful, waxy protrusions to the tips of the inner wing feathers from which the species is named. The world's only other waxwing is found in Japan, for while the Cedar Waxwing is a North American bird, the Bohemian Waxwing ranges through most of the boreal Northern Hemisphere.

The Phainopepla is a member of the New World family of silky flycatchers, named for their soft, silk-like plumage. Though they are berry-eaters like the waxwings, they are also expert flycatchers, exhibiting considerable aerial agility. In North America this is a bird of the Mexican border country.

BOHEMIAN WAXWING

Bombycilla garrulus   8–8½in/20–21cm

IDENTIFICATION Chubby, olive-brown bird with bold crest, dark "face" pattern and black wings, with white bar. Tail is shortish and tipped yellow. Waxy marks on wings seldom obvious. *See* Cedar Waxwing. Note rusty undertail coverts.

VOICE Buzzy notes.

HABITAT Conifer woods.

RANGE Alaska and western Canada.

MOVEMENTS Regularly winters north-western US, but irrupts eastward every few years to areas where it is otherwise unknown.

BREEDING Mostly conifer forests, but also mixed woods; May-June.

NEST AND EGGS A cup of twigs is constructed in a conifer, often at some height above the ground; the 4 to 6 eggs are pale blue, spotted black.

INCUBATION The eggs take 13 or 14 days to hatch and are incubated by the female alone.

COMMENT Though a bird of conifer forests, in winter the Bohemian Waxwing will occupy hedges and thickets as long as they bear plentiful berries.

CEDAR WAXWING

Bombycilla cedrorum   6½–7in/17–18cm

IDENTIFICATION Smaller, browner version of Bohemian Waxwing, with similar crest and cross "face" pattern. Gray rump, white undertail and yellow belly are best means of distinction. Large flocks in winter.

VOICE Quiet trilling.

HABITAT Conifer and mixed woods.

RANGE Breeds right across temperate North America in a broad belt on both sides of the US-Canada border.

MOVEMENTS Northern birds regularly migrate over whole of US.

BREEDING Open woods with scattered trees, both deciduous and conifer, marsh-side trees; May-June.

NEST AND EGGS A large cup of twigs and other materials placed in the outer branches of a substantial tree; the 3 to 5 eggs are pale greenish blue, spotted black.

INCUBATION The eggs take 12 to 14 days to hatch and are incubated by the female alone.

COMMENT The large, untidy nest of this bird often contains a wide variety of material, both natural and artificial.

PHAINOPEPLA

Phainopepla nitens   7–8in/18–20cm

IDENTIFICATION Male is all-black "flycatcher" with deep-red eye. A sharp, ragged crest and long, boat-shaped tail are best features, though in the air the primaries show boldly white centers. Female is uniformly gray, with darker wings and tail.

VOICE Whistling *werp*.

HABITAT Arid brush.

RANGE Mexican border states.

MOVEMENTS Some birds winter along the border.

BREEDING Dry country with berry-bearing trees; February-April.

NEST AND EGGS A saucer-shaped nest is placed in a tree, often alongside water; the 2 to 4 eggs are pale green, spotted brown.

INCUBATION The eggs take 14 to 16 days to hatch, incubated by both sexes.

COMMENT This essentially tropical bird prefers trees with a substantial growth of mistletoe, the berries of which act as a supplement to its insect diet.

SHRIKES & STARLINGS

PURISTS will, I trust, forgive dealing with these two quite distinct families of birds jointly. Though there are 70 distinct species of shrikes in the world, only two occur in North America. Similarly, there are no less that 106 species of starlings worldwide, but only two occur in North America, and both of these are the result of human introductions.

The Northern Shrike is among the world's most successful small birds, with a completely circumpolar distribution. Like the Loggerhead, it sits patiently atop a prominent perch awaiting the opportunity to pounce on an unsuspecting insect or small bird. The large bill is hooked, like that of a bird of prey, to enable larger prey to be dismembered. It also shares the unendearing habit of impaling food items on thorns as a sort of larder.

The Loggerhead is the only American endemic shrike and is clearly closely related to the Northern Shrike. Its calls are very similar, and it may well be that the two species share a common ancestor.

The story of the introduction of the European Starling into North America is too well known to be worth more than a mention here. It is a busy, aggressive bird that flourishes alongside man, but may be harmful to the interests of other species with which it competes, particularly in its search for suitable nest holes. The related Crested Myna is an Asiatic species that was introduced in Vancouver at the end of the nineteenth century, but which, fortunately, has not spread farther than the immediate area around the city. It is readily recognized as a "starling."

NORTHERN SHRIKE

Lanius excubitor 9–10in/23–25cm

IDENTIFICATION Medium-sized, gray bird of predatory habits. Crown and back, pale gray with black wings and tail, white rump and black facial mask. Underparts lightly barred; bill large and hooked. Perches openly. In flight, shows bold-white wing flash. *See* Loggerhead Shrike.

VOICE Harsh *chack-chack*.

HABITAT Open scrub north of boreal zone.

RANGE Sub-tundra zone of Canada.

MOVEMENTS Resident south Alaska otherwise moves southward to winter across temperate Canada and northern US.

BREEDING Open, bushy country with scattered trees, often near bogs and marshes; May-July.

NEST AND EGGS A huge structure of twigs, placed in a bush, and lined with soft hair and feathers; the 4 to 7 eggs are off white, spotted brown.

INCUBATION The eggs take 15 days to hatch and are incubated by the female with some help from the male.

COMMENT A ferocious killer of small birds and insects that can often be seen sentinel-like atop a low tree.

LOGGERHEAD SHRIKE

Lanius ludovicianus 8½–9in/21–23cm

IDENTIFICATION Very similar to slightly larger Northern Shrike. Smaller bill; larger, black mask extends above eye and over base of upper mandible; smaller; white wing-patch; and darker shade of gray are the main features to look for.

VOICE Harsh *chack-chack*.

HABITAT Brush covered areas of scrub.

RANGE Breeds throughout US northward into temperate central Canada.

MOVEMENTS Canadian and birds of central northern states move southward to winter.

BREEDING Bushy country, but also hedges and other scant vegetation; March-June.

NEST AND EGGS A substantial nest is constructed of twigs with a lining of soft material; the 4 to 6 eggs are gray white, spotted with brown.

INCUBATION The eggs take 13 to 16 days to hatch and are incubated by both members of the pair.

COMMENT The nest of this shrike is lined with hair, feathers, and soft plant materials as well as polythene, paper, and rags.

EUROPEAN STARLING

Sturnus vulgaris   8½in/21−22cm

IDENTIFICATION Introduced from Europe and now widespread. Iridescent green and purple sheen on back in summer; heavily spotted white and buff in winter. Short tail, pointed wings, and yellow bill characteristic at all times. Gregarious and aggressive.

VOICE Wheezes and mimicry.

HABITAT Cities, villages, farmsteads, woods.

RANGE Temperate and boreal North America.

MOVEMENTS Some movements, but found throughout breeding range in winter.

BREEDING From woodland to city centers; April-June.

NEST AND EGGS Virtually any cavity, from a tree to a woodpecker hole, to holes in buildings, will provide a place for this bird to build its rather untidy nest; the 5 to 7 eggs are pale blue.

INCUBATION Lasts 12 to 15 days and is shared by both sexes.

COMMENT The success of the Starling is partly based on opportunistic feeding, but also on its ability to use a wide variety of nest holes.

CRESTED MYNA

Acridotheres cristatellus   9½−10in/24−25cm

IDENTIFICATION Relative of the European Starling, with similar walking behavior. All-black with bold, white wing patches in flight. Yellow legs and bill, small forehead crest.

VOICE Loud cackles and whistles.

HABITAT Suburbs.

RANGE Vancouver.

MOVEMENTS Resident, introduced from Asia.

VIREOS

THERE are 43 species of vireo in the world, 12 of which breed in North America. Mostly they are clothed in shades of gray, green, and olive, and all have rather short and stout bills. Many are picked out by a double wing-bar, eye ring, or prominent head pattern. In general, those with wing-bars also have eye rings, whereas those without show a prominent head pattern. Though there is a considerable area of overlap, the most widespread species are the Red-eyed in the east, the Solitary in the west, and the Warbling virtually throughout the continent.

Vireos are mainly woodland birds, though they prefer dense secondary growth to the canopy. They scour bushes for food, but are neither as active nor as graceful as the warblers. In fact, they can be quite ungainly as they reach forward or hang beneath a leaf to obtain a hidden insect. These are highly vocal birds and the Red-eyed is noted for the persistency with which it sings throughout the day. Nevertheless, they are hardly the most melodic of songsters, despite the 3000 songs an hour produced. Males will even sing while performing a stint of incubation, for as one would expect in birds where the sexes are similar, both members of the pair take a share in sitting on the eggs and they are probably the most abundant birds of deciduous woodland. Though they feed mostly on insects through the summer months, Red-eyed Vireos turn to berries in the fall. This abundant food supply is probably essential for they need to take on food in the form of fat before setting out on their lengthy migrations to the forests of Columbia and Venezuela.

WHITE-EYED VIREO

Vireo griseus   4½–5in/12–13cm

IDENTIFICATION Olive gray above with double wing-bar, yellow-washed flanks and yellow spectacles. Eye is white, but difficult to see in the field.
VOICE Slurred five- to seven-note warble beginning and ending *chip*.
HABITAT Damp thickets.
RANGE Most of eastern US.
MOVEMENTS Winters Florida and Gulf coast.
BREEDING Dense undergrowth, often associated with swamps; March-June.
NEST AND EGGS A neatly woven structure of grasses lined with lichens and spiders' webs, hung inside a dense thicket; the 3 to 5 eggs are white, spotted with brown.
INCUBATION Lasts from 12 to 16 days and is shared by both sexes.
COMMENT Though this is a common bird over the eastern US, its tendency to keep deep within dense thickets makes it a difficult species to see well.

BELL'S VIREO

Vireo bellii   4½in/12cm

IDENTIFICATION Olive-gray vireo, with pale-white, double wing-bar and eye ring. Variable plumage, some have indistinct eye ring and only one faint wing-bar.
VOICE Rapid warble of harsh notes.
HABITAT Woodland and scrub.

RANGE South-western and central US.
MOVEMENTS Summer visitor.
BREEDING Woodland edges, but particularly in dense thickets along streams and gullies, sometimes also in dry brushland; April-June.
NEST AND EGGS A cup is woven of grasses and suspended from a bush; the 3 to 5 eggs are white, spotted with brown.
INCUBATION The eggs take 14 days to hatch and are incubated by both members of the pair.
COMMENT The parasitism of this species by cowbirds, particularly in the west, has led to a decline in some areas.

BLACK-CAPPED VIREO

Vireo atricapillus   4½in/11cm

IDENTIFICATION Black cap with bold-white eye-ring and white loral stripe of male precludes confusion with any other vireo. Female has slate-gray head and less boldly marked "spectacles". Small size; upperparts green; yellow wash on flanks; bold, double wing-bar. Tends to be secretive.
VOICE Twittered and slurred notes.

HABITAT Scrub.
RANGE Mainly central Texas.
MOVEMENTS Summer visitor.

BREEDING Thickets of deciduous shrubs and trees, especially oak and juniper; April–May.

NEST AND EGGS The nest is well-constructed of grasses and slung between a fork of a dense bush; the 3 to 5 eggs are white.

INCUBATION The eggs are incubated by male and female for about 16 days.

COMMENT More like a chickadee than a vireo in its active feeding behavior. It often hangs upside down to feed.

GRAY VIREO

Vireo vicinior   5–5½in/13–14cm

IDENTIFICATION Gray above with pale, double wing-bar, but only a rudimentary eye-ring. Underparts white, grayish wash on breast. Only the Rocky Mountain form of the Solitary Vireo is all gray, but this bird has a prominent eye-ring. Chunky vireo-type bill.

VOICE Pleasant warbling *chu-eet*.

HABITAT Dry, bush country among rocky cliffs.

RANGE South-western US.

MOVEMENTS Summer visitor; winters southern Arizona.

BREEDING Frequents pinyon- and juniper-covered hillsides and dry chaparral; April–May.

NEST AND EGGS The nest is suspended between the arms of a fork in a bush; the 3 or 4 eggs are white, speckled with brown.

INCUBATION Lasts 13 to 14 days, incubated by both sexes.

COMMENT The washed-out gray coloration and the characteristic habit of flicking its tail from side to side is more reminiscent of a gnatcatcher than a vireo.

SOLITARY VIREO

Vireo solitarius   5–5½in/13–14cm

IDENTIFICATION Widespread, but variable vireo. Eastern birds have gray heads, green upperparts and yellow-streaked flanks. Birds in the Rockies are gray; those on the West coast have olive-green heads. All have bold "spectacles", double wing-bars and streaked (not washed) flanks.

VOICE Melodic *chu-eet, cheereo, chuwee*.

HABITAT Deciduous and mixed woods.

RANGE From the boreal zone southward through most of the west and New England, through the Great Lakes and Appalachians.

MOVEMENTS Winters Florida and Gulf coast.

BREEDING Open deciduous woods and mixed woods; May–June.

NEST AND EGGS The nest is a beautifully woven structure hung from a conifer branch and consisting of grasses and roots; the 3 to 5 eggs are off white, spotted brown.

INCUBATION The eggs take about 13 days to hatch and are incubated by both sexes.

COMMENT The nest is truly a work of art with plant fibres bound together to form a purse that is camouflaged with moss, lichens, and bark fragments.

YELLOW-THROATED VIREO

Vireo flavifrons   5–5½in/13–14cm

IDENTIFICATION Olive above, green on "face" with yellow "spectacles" and lores. Rump gray, breast yellow and belly white.

VOICE Slow three- or four-note song, repeated endlessly.

Habitat Woodland edges, parkland.

Range Eastern US.

Movements Mostly summer visitor; some winter Florida and Gulf coast.

Breeding Mature deciduous woodland and similar large trees in suburban areas; April–June.

Nest and eggs A deep cup bound together with spiders' webs and suspended from the branch of a tree; the 3 to 5 eggs are white or pinkish and heavily spotted brown.

Incubation The eggs take some 14 days to hatch and are incubated by both sexes.

Comment The need for mature deciduous trees limits the population of this attractive eastern vireo.

Hutton's Vireo

Vireo huttoni   5in/13cm

Identification Dark olive-gray above, whitish below with yellow wash over flanks. White eye ring, loral spot and double wing-bar. The eye ring is broken at the top – a good field mark if approached within close enough range.

Voice Repeated *chee-eet*.

Habitat Damp woods.

Range Pacific coast and Mexican border states.

Movements Resident.

Breeding Dry oakwoods with thicket undergrowth, often in ravines; March–June.

Nest and eggs A purse-shaped nest is woven of grasses and lined with feathers, suspended from a branch of a bush; the 3 or 4 eggs are white, spotted brown.

Incubation Lasts for some 14 days and is shared by both members of the pair.

Comment A tiny vireo that could easily be mistaken for a Ruby-crowned Kinglet, though lacking the eye-ring of that species.

Warbling Vireo

Vireo gilvus   5–5½in/13–14cm

Identification Grayish vireo with washed-out, pale foreparts. Back is olive gray, underparts white; light supercilium and clear gray eye-stripe. Like Red-eyed Vireo and Philadelphia Vireo lacks wing-bars.

Voice Pleasant warbling.

Habitat Deciduous woodland.

Range Most of vegetated North America, though absent from much of Texas and south-easternmost states.

Movements Summer visitor.

Breeding Deciduous and mixed groves, suburbs, parkland, and orchards; June–July.

Nest and eggs A neatly-constructed cup hung from a tree fork on the outer edge of a tree; the 3 to 5 eggs are white, lightly spotted brown.

Incubation Lasts 12 to 14 days and is shared between members of the pair.

Comment Elms are a favored nesting tree of this species and the male often utters its gentle song from the nest itself.

RED-EYED VIREO

Vireo olivaceus   5½–6in/14–15cm

IDENTIFICATION Olive-brown upperparts marked by gray crown, black, lateral, coronal stripe, white supercilium and black eye-stripe. Only Black-whiskered Vireo of coastal Florida can be confused. Red eye may be difficult to see in field.

VOICE Variable song produced at great length.

HABITAT Woods.

RANGE Eastern US extending northward through the boreal zone of Canada.

MOVEMENTS Summer visitor.

BREEDING Frequents deciduous woods and thickets, often along streams and around ponds; May-June.

NEST AND EGGS A well-constructed cup is suspended between the arms of a forked branch; the 3 or 4 eggs are white, spotted reddish brown.

INCUBATION The eggs take 12 to 14 days to hatch and are incubated by the female alone.

COMMENT Though the most widely distributed of the vireos, migration is mainly through the central and Atlantic flyways indicating an eastern origin.

BLACK-WHISKERED VIREO

Vireo altiloquus   6–6½in/15–16cm

IDENTIFICATION Virtually identical to Red-eyed Vireo, but with prominent moustachial streak.

VOICE Series of phrases similar to Red-eyed Vireo.

HABITAT Mangroves, coastlines.

RANGE Florida coast.

MOVEMENTS Summer visitor.

WOOD WARBLERS

THE Emberizidae is a huge family represented in North America by no less than 132 species. It can be divided among several well-marked tribes, of which the wood warblers are the largest.

Of the world's 125 species of New World warblers, no less than 52 breed in North America. These are mainly small, brightly colored birds that are active and elegant as they move through vegetation. They are mostly found in woodland and scrub, though some species are virtually confined to marshes. Many species are sexually dimorphic, with the male much more boldly and brightly marked than the female. In spring the males are among the most colorful of birds. Despite such bold markings, there are several groups that should be identified with the greatest of care. Nevertheless, the problems are as nothing compared with those that arise in fall. Fall warblers are the birding beginner's nightmare and have caused even the most experienced considerable loss of sleep. With the bold colors of spring gone, these birds are among the toughest of all to name correctly and good views are essential.

Careful note should be made of leg color; the presence or absence of wing-bars; the position and color of wing patches; bold eye stripes; bold supercilia (eye-brows); prominent eye rings; rump patches; flank streaking, and so on. In fact, identifying an unknown warbler requires the fullest of field descriptions both in spring and fall. Fortunately, these birds are a lot easier to identify on their breeding grounds. At this time factors such as distribution and habitat can swiftly reduce the range of possibilities to more maneagable proportions. With the more confusing species, songs can be the clincher.

Probably the most widespread of all warblers is the aptly named Yellow Warbler, which breeds in damp areas from Alaska to Florida, and from California to Labrador. Coincidentally, it is also one of the easiest of spring birds to identify. The rarest and most restricted species, in contrast, is Kirtland's Warbler, a gray and yellow-streaked bird that breeds only in burnt-over jack pines in Michigan, and winters in the Bahamas. Only 500 of these birds are known to exist and great efforts are made to ensure they survive. Being long-distance migrants, the warblers are particularly prone to vagrancy, and there are reports of birds hundreds of miles off-course every year. Numerous "Eastern" warblers have appeared with regularity during migration time on the west coast.

BLUE-WINGED WARBLER

Vermivora pinus   4½–5in/12–13cm

IDENTIFICATION
Male has yellow
head and underparts
broken by clear black
stripe through the eye. The
back is olive, the wings blue
gray with bold-white, double
wing-bar. The blue-gray tail has
white spots visible from below.
Often hybridizes with
Golden-winged Warbler to create a wide
range of intermediate types some of which are of regular
enough occurrence to have been given names: e.g. Brewster's
and Lawrence's Warblers.
VOICE A buzzing similar to Golden-winged Warbler.
HABITAT Scrub and regenerating woodland.
RANGE North-eastern US, but expanding.
MOVEMENTS Summer visitor.
BREEDING Overgrown bushy areas, clearings in woodland with
undergrowth; May-June.
NEST AND EGGS Usually on the ground sheltered by vegetation
or a tussock; the 4 to 7 eggs are white, lightly spotted brown.
INCUBATION Lasts 10 or 11 days, performed by the female.
COMMENT Persistently sings motionless from a single
prominent perch.

GOLDEN-WINGED WARBLER

Vermivora chrysoptera   4½–5in/12–13cm

IDENTIFICATION Breeding male is gray above marked by yellow
wing coverts and fore-crown. Black ear coverts and large bib
create a unique face pattern. Female is similar, but with less
extensive yellow in wing and on crown and with gray rather
than black face pattern. Undertail shows white spots.
VOICE A buzz of four or five notes.
HABITAT Woodland margins and neglected grassland.
RANGE North-eastern US into southernmost Canada
southward through the Appalachians.
MOVEMENTS Summer visitor.

BREEDING Woodland clearings with
undergrowth, overgrown
areas; May-June.
NEST AND EGGS The nest is
constructed of grasses and
placed on the ground
among a tussock; the 4 to 7
eggs are white,
spotted brown.
INCUBATION Lasts for 10 or
11 days and is performed
by the female alone.
COMMENT Hybridizes freely with Blue-winged Warbler,
producing distinctive types of young.

TENNESSEE WARBLER

Vermivora peregrina   4½–5in/12–13cm

IDENTIFICATION Summer male has olive-green upperparts,
white underparts and gray crown. Female lacks gray crown
and has yellow wash on breast. Non-breeding birds are
greener above and below with clear supercilium, single
wing-bar and white undertail coverts.
VOICE Repeated *seet* on descending scale.
HABITAT Deciduous and mixed woodland, feeds in canopy.
RANGE Boreal zone of Canada and Alaskan panhandle
extending across US border in east.
MOVEMENTS Summer visitor; winters Mexico to northern
South America.
BREEDING A wide variety of woodlands from pure conifers to
pure deciduous as well as thickets and tangles; May-June.
NEST AND EGGS A well-constructed, often
domed nest of grasses and mosses
placed on the ground; the 4 to 7 eggs
are white, spotted with brown.
INCUBATION Lasts about
12 days, performed by
the female.

COMMENT Named by Alexander
Wilson, who discovered this bird in
Tennessee, though it does not breed
much south of the Canada border.

ORANGE-CROWNED WARBLER

Vermivora celata   5 – 5½in/13 – 14cm

IDENTIFICATION Dull, greeny-yellow warbler marked by lightly streaked underparts. The orange patch on the crown is seldom visible. Color varies from bright yellowish western birds, to dull olive eastern ones. Immatures are generally greener, like young Tennessee Warblers, but lack white under tail coverts of that bird.
VOICE A repeated trill.
HABITAT Thickets, open woodland, forest margins.
RANGE From Alaska through the boreal zone to Labrador and southward throughout much of the west.
MOVEMENTS Winters mainly in Florida and along the Gulf Coast, but also along Atlantic and Pacific coasts.
BREEDING Deciduous woods and scrubby thickets and tangles; April-June.
NEST AND EGGS A neat nest of grasses placed on the ground, or sometimes in a low bush; the 4 to 6 eggs are white, spotted brown.
INCUBATION Lasts about 12 days, performed by the female.
COMMENT Surprisingly common in the west and decidedly scarce in the east.

NASHVILLE WARBLER

Vermivora ruficapilla   4½ – 5in/12 – 13cm

IDENTIFICATION Dark upperparts and yellow underparts. Male has gray head and white eye-ring. Female has darker, brownish head and lacks yellow on throat. Fall birds are duller still, with eye ring the only prominent feature.
VOICE *See-weet*, high-pitched and repeated, followed by a trill.
HABITAT Regenerating woods and damp spruce woodland.
RANGE Breeds north and south of the Canada-US border in eastern and western populations separated by a gap through the prairies.
MOVEMENTS Summer visitor; winters southern, coastal California and south-west coast of Texas.

BREEDING Mainly secondary growth with scattered trees and plentiful bushes; May-June.
NEST AND EGGS A nest of mosses and grasses is lined with hair and placed on the ground among dense vegetation; the 4 or 5 eggs are white, spotted reddish-brown.

INCUBATION The eggs are incubated by the female for 12 days.
COMMENT The division between the eastern and western populations has already resulted in the appearance of plumage differences.

VIRGINIA'S WARBLER

Vermivora virginiae   4½ – 5in/12 – 13cm

IDENTIFICATION Male in summer has gray head and upperparts, with paler gray chin, a yellow breast-patch and yellow under and upper tail coverts. The belly is a dingy white. Bold, white eye-ring. Female is brown-gray with less yellow.
VOICE An accelerating series of notes.
HABITAT Scrub and thickets at altitude.
RANGE Southern Rocky Mountain states.
MOVEMENTS Summer visitor
BREEDING Dry brushland and pinyon-juniper woodlands; May-June.
NEST AND EGGS A cup is constructed on the ground among dense cover; the 3 to 5 eggs are white, spotted reddish-brown.
INCUBATION The eggs are incubated by the female.
COMMENT Seeing this undistinguished warbler is made all the more difficult because of its habit of singing within dense scrub.

COLIMA WARBLER

Vermivora crissalis   5½–6in/14–15cm

IDENTIFICATION Gray-headed species, with clear eye-ring and chestnut-orange flanks and rump.
VOICE Trilling.
HABITAT Mountain slopes.
RANGE The Chisos Mountains of Texas.
MOVEMENTS Summer visitor.

LUCY'S WARBLER

Vermivora luciae   4½in/11cm

IDENTIFICATION Gray above, paler below, with rusty rump and chestnut crown patch. Female has paler rusty areas and immature female may lack rust on crown completely.
VOICE A pleasant trill terminating with a series of clear, whistled notes.
HABITAT Mesquite scrub, often along dry river beds.
RANGE South-western US as far as southern California.
MOVEMENTS Summer visitor.
BREEDING Dry scrub and desert, often along watercourses and cottonwood; April-May.
NEST AND EGGS A neat cup of grasses in a tree cavity or hole; the 4 or 5 eggs are white, lightly spotted brown.
INCUBATION The eggs are incubated by the female.
COMMENT Hole-nesting among the warblers is remarkably rare, though this species prefers a cavity beneath loose bark, like a creeper.

NORTHERN PARULA

Parula americana   4½in/11cm

IDENTIFICATION A small warbler with blue-gray upperparts marked by a bold, broken eye-ring and bold, double, white wing-bar. The male has a yellow breast, divided by a black and rust breast band; a white belly with a hint of chestnut along the flanks. The female is duller, with no breast band. Fall birds are identified by a combination of wing-bars, broken eye-ring and yellow underparts.
VOICE A trill terminating with a single *zit*.
HABITAT Conifer and mixed woods, often near swamps.
RANGE Eastern US and Canada.
MOVEMENTS Summer visitor; winters southern Florida.
BREEDING Various woodland types, but always with a strong growth of lichens or Spanish moss; May-June.
NEST AND EGGS A suspended lichen (old man's beard) is hollowed out and lined with grasses; the 4 or 5 eggs are white, spotted brown.
INCUBATION Lasts from 12 to 14 days and is performed by the female alone.
COMMENT Finding the nest of this species among woodland littered with hanging lichens is a time-consuming business.

TROPICAL PARULA

Parula pitiayumi   4 ½in/11cm

IDENTIFICATION Dark blue above with black mask and double, white wing-bar. Underparts yellow, washed orange on breast. Undertail white. Lacks eye-ring.
VOICE Buzzing trill.
HABITAT Woodlands.
RANGE Lower Rio Grande, Texas.
MOVEMENTS Resident.

YELLOW WARBLER

Dendroica petechia   5−5½in/13−14cm

IDENTIFICATION Male is yellow above and below, liberally streaked chestnut on the breast. Female is paler and greener, without streaking. Fall birds are similar to female and best identified by pale spots in the spread tail.

VOICE Six or seven *sweet* notes.

HABITAT Damp thickets of willow as well as gardens.

RANGE Virtually throughout North America south of the tundra, but absent much of Texas and Gulf coast.

MOVEMENTS Summer visitor; winters southern California.

BREEDING Scrubby swamps with willow and alder; May-June.

NEST AND EGGS The nest is placed in a bush and is well constructed of grasses; the 4 or 5 eggs are white, often with a wash of blue, and speckled brown.

INCUBATION The eggs take some 11 days to hatch and are incubated by the female alone.

COMMENT This bird will use whatever material is at hand to construct its nest, including a wide range of artificial materials such as baling twine or cotton wool.

CHESTNUT-SIDED WARBLER

Dendroica pensylvanica   5−5½in/13−14cm

IDENTIFICATION Heavily streaked black and gray above with yellow crown and broad, black eye-stripe and moustachial streak. Underparts, white with rich chestnut along flanks. Female similar, but with less yellow and patchy chestnut. In fall, yellowish-green above, grayish-white below with yellowish, double wing-bar.

VOICE A whistled six-note song with accent on the second to last note.

HABITAT Regenerating deciduous woodland.

RANGE Eastern North America either side of the US-Canada border.

MOVEMENTS Summer visitor.

BREEDING Deciduous bushy areas and thickets; May-June.

NEST AND EGGS A neat cup of grasses lined with softer material and placed in a low shrub; the 3 to 5 eggs are white, spotted brown

INCUBATION The eggs take 12 or 13 days to hatch and incubation is by the female alone.

COMMENT The decline of farming in the north-east, together with the subsequent growth of scrub, has suited this dainty warbler perfectly.

MAGNOLIA WARBLER

Dendroica magnolia   5−5½in/13−14cm

IDENTIFICATION Breeding male is black above with gray crown, white supercilium and black mask. A bold, white, double wing-bar merges to form a broad patch in the closed wing. The underparts are yellow, streaked black, the streaks merging to form a black band across the breast. The rump is yellow and there are white patches at the sides of the tail. The female has no black mask or breast band, but is otherwise similar. Fall birds have a gray crown, grayish breast band, pale supercilium, double wing-bar and yellow rump.
VOICE Musical warble.
HABITAT Conifer woods.
RANGE Boreal North America, southward through Appalachians.
MOVEMENTS Summer visitor.
BREEDING Regenerating conifer woods, open brushy areas in mixed woods; May-June.
NEST AND EGGS A nest of grasses lined with hair is constructed in a low conifer; the 3 to 5 eggs are white, speckled brown.
INCUBATION Lasts 11 to 13 days and is performed by the female.
COMMENT Though it breeds right across Canada, this is an eastern bird on migration, being decidedly scarce along the Pacific coast.

"face". Fall birds are paler versions, though male retains white wing patch. Yellow rump in all plumages.
VOICE High pitched *see-see-see*.
HABITAT Spruce forests.
RANGE Boreal Canada.
MOVEMENTS Summer visitor.
BREEDING Open conifer and mixed woods; May-June.
NEST AND EGGS The nest is constructed of grasses and twigs lined with hair and feathers and is placed high in a conifer; the 4 to 9 eggs are white, speckled brown.
INCUBATION The eggs are incubated by the female.
COMMENT The easterly migration of this coast-to-coast breeding warbler takes it over the east coast to the West Indies.

BLACK-THROATED BLUE WARBLER

Dendroica caerulescens   5−5½in/13−14cm

CAPE MAY WARBLER

Dendroica tigrina   5−5½in/13−14cm

IDENTIFICATION A dark, heavily streaked warbler. Summer male is olive, streaked black, above; yellow, streaked black, below. Best field marks are white wing patch and yellow "face" with chestnut ear coverts. Female is similar, but has narrow, double wing-bar and only an orange wash on the

IDENTIFICATION Male is dark blue above with black "face", throat and flanks, and a white patch at the base of the primaries. The underparts are white. Female is olive above and orange-buff below, with pale supercilium and tiny pale patch at base of primaries.
VOICE Slow wheezy notes.
HABITAT Deciduous forests.
RANGE South-eastern Canada and north-eastern US extending southward through Appalachians.
MOVEMENTS Summer visitor.
BREEDING Clearings and felled areas in deciduous woodland with strong, bushy vegetation; May-June.

NEST AND EGGS A substantial nest is placed in a low bush; the 3 to 5 eggs are white, heavily blotched brown.

INCUBATION Lasts 12 days and is performed by the female alone.

COMMENT A very well-marked bird in the male, that utters a lagubrious 'I am so lazy' song while his mate cares for the nesting duties.

YELLOW-RUMPED WARBLER

Dendroica coronata   5½−6in/14−15cm

IDENTIFICATION Formerly divided into Myrtle and Audubon's Warblers. Basically gray above, streaked black; white below with black breast band and flank streaks. Males have yellow on crown, sides of breast and (in some populations) on throat. Double, white wing-bar, often nearly forming a white wing panel. Female and fall birds are brownish with pale supercilium and streaked breast. Yellow rump in all plumages.

VOICE Pleasant warbling.

HABITAT Woodland.

RANGE Widespread in northern and western North America.

MOVEMENTS Winters over much of southern, eastern and western US.

BREEDING Open woodlands of many types; April-June.

NEST AND EGGS A large nest of twigs and grasses is placed in a conifer at variable heights; the 4 or 5 eggs are white, spotted with brown.

INCUBATION The eggs take some 12 or 13 days to hatch and are incubated by the female.

COMMENT The amalgamation of the Myrtle and Audubon's Warblers into this single species is not without its critics, even though the two interbreed in many areas.

BLACK-THROATED GRAY WARBLER

Dendroica nigrescens   5−5½in/13−14cm

IDENTIFICATION Male is gray above, lightly streaked black; the underparts are white with black streaking on the flanks. Whole of head, throat and breast are black with bold, white supercilium and moustachial streak. Female is slate gray rather than black on head.

VOICE Wheezing song.

HABITAT Dry woods and scrub.

RANGE Much of western US to southern British Columbia.

MOVEMENTS Summer visitor, resident southernmost California.

BREEDING Open conifer and mixed woods with a good understory; April-May.

NEST AND EGGS A nest of grasses is lined with hair and placed at variable heights in a tree; the 3 to 5 eggs are white, spotted brown.

INCUBATION The eggs are incubated by the female.

COMMENT This is essentially a west coast bird that is no more than a vagrant to the Gulf Coast and exceptional on the east coast.

TOWNSEND'S WARBLER

Dendroica townsendi   5−5½in/13−14cm

IDENTIFICATION Olive-gray above with bold, double wing-bar; yellow below, streaked black; but with white belly. Distinctive "face" pattern of dark crown, ear coverts and bib

BREEDING Mature conifer forests of the tallest trees in North America; May-June.

NEST AND EGGS A neat cup, that includes fir needles, is hung over a branch high in a redwood or Douglas fir; the 3 to 5 eggs are off-white, spotted with brown.

INCUBATION Possibly performed by both sexes, lasting about 12 days.

COMMENT Though most nests are placed less than 50ft/15m above the ground, the bird spends the entire summer in the top of massive trees and is remarkably difficult to see.

against a background of yellow. Female has yellow, not black, bib.

VOICE Buzzing with clear notes to end.

HABITAT Conifers.

RANGE From Alaska to Oregon and into the Rockies.

MOVEMENTS Winters coastal California.

BREEDING Mature conifer forests; May-June.

NEST AND EGGS The nest is usually placed high in a conifer; the 3 to 5 eggs are white, spotted with brown.

INCUBATION The female incubates the eggs for about 12 days.

COMMENT Though it will use various types of wooded and bushy country during passage, this is a bird that spends the entire summer high among the tops of conifers.

BLACK-THROATED GREEN WARBLER

Dendroica virens   5 – 5½in/13 – 14cm

HERMIT WARBLER

Dendroica occidentalis   5½ – 6in/14 – 15cm

IDENTIFICATION Slaty-gray upperparts with double, white wing-bar; whitish below. Both sexes have yellow head and black bib. Female duller than male.

VOICE Pleasant warble.

HABITAT Conifers.

RANGE Pacific US.

MOVEMENTS Winters coastal California.

IDENTIFICATION Dark olive above with black wings marked by double, white wing-bar. Underparts white with black breast band and flank streaks. Male has black throat joining breast band: female has yellowish throat.

VOICE Wheezing *zee-zee-zee*.

HABITAT Conifer and mixed woods.

RANGE Boreal Canada, north-eastern US extending southward through Appalachians.

MOVEMENTS Summer visitor.

BREEDING Open conifer woods with a secondary growth of shrubs; May-June.

NEST AND EGGS A nest of grasses is lined with hair and feathers and usually placed in a conifer; the 4 or 5 eggs are white, spotted brown.

INCUBATION Lasts 12 or 13 days and is performed by the female.

COMMENT A relatively common warbler, with a decidedly easterly migration pattern.

GOLDEN-CHEEKED WARBLER

Dendroica chrysoparia   5½in/14cm

IDENTIFICATION Summer male is black above with double, white wing-bar; yellow face with black eye-stripe. Black extends to breast; belly white streaked black. Female less black.
VOICE Buzzing song.
HABITAT Woods of ash juniper.
RANGE The Edwards Plateau of central Texas.
MOVEMENTS Summer visitor.

BLACKBURNIAN WARBLER

Dendroica fusca   5−5½in/13−14cm

IDENTIFICATION A black and yellow warbler, marked in the male by a bright orange throat and bold, white wing patch. Immature male and female are blackish-brown above with double, white wing-bar. Head and breast are yellow, broken by complex pattern of black marks; underparts are pale yellow with streaked flanks. Pale tail margins in males and some females.

VOICE High notes followed by thin trill.
HABITAT Conifer, mixed and deciduous forests.
RANGE Eastern Canada extending across US border and through Appalachians.
MOVEMENTS Summer visitor.
BREEDING Conifer and mixed woods, both mature and secondary; May-June.
NEST AND EGGS A nest of twigs and grasses is placed at variable heights in a conifer; the 4 or 5 eggs are white, spotted with brown.
INCUBATION Lasts 12 or 13 days and is performed by the female alone.
COMMENT The orange breast of the summer male makes this one of the most distinctive of the warblers.

YELLOW-THROATED WARBLER

Dendroica dominica   5½−6in/14−15cm

IDENTIFICATION Upperparts gray with bold, double, white wing-bar; underparts white with bold streaking (spotting) on flanks. Male has yellow throat and upper breast and white supercilium (sometimes yellow on lores), separated by black. This distinctive "face" pattern is shared only with Grace's Warbler of the west, but the present species has a white patch behind the ear coverts.
VOICE Descending whistled notes.
HABITAT Mixed and deciduous woods.
RANGE South-eastern US.
MOVEMENTS Winters Florida and Gulf Coast.
BREEDING A wide variety of wet and dry forest types; April-May.
NEST AND EGGS A nest of grasses is lined with hair and placed in a tree among Spanish moss; the 3 or 4 eggs are greenish, spotted brown.
INCUBATION Performed by the female, and lasting about 12 days.
COMMENT A warbler that spends much of its time creeping along high branches.

GRACE'S WARBLER

Dendroica graciae   5−5½in/13−14cm

IDENTIFICATION Very similar to Yellow-throated Warbler of the east, with gray back and yellow throat, but with yellow supercilium and no white patch behind ear coverts.
VOICE Pleasant chipping on same note.
HABITAT Conifers, especially yellow pines and mixed woods.

RANGE South-western US.
MOVEMENTS Summer visitor.
BREEDING Pines and mixed forests in the mountains;
May-June.
NEST AND EGGS The cup-shaped nest is constructed of roots,
lined with hair and placed high in a conifer; the 3 or 4 eggs
are white, speckled with brown.
INCUBATION Undescribed.
COMMENT A canopy-dwelling bird that is very difficult to
observe.

PINE WARBLER

Dendroica pinus   5½−6in/14−15cm

IDENTIFICATION Male in summer has olive-green upperparts
with double, white wing-bar. Underparts yellow with
streaking on sides of breast. Female is duller, with less yellow.
Fall birds are browner above. A rather undistinguished
warbler with a heavy bill.
VOICE A pleasant trilling.
HABITAT Pine woods.

RANGE Eastern US and adjacent Canada.
MOVEMENTS Winters southern and eastern US.
BREEDING Pine woods of various types; May-June.
NEST AND EGGS A cup of grasses and stems is lined with pine
needles and other soft material and placed at variable heights
in a pine; the 3 to 5 eggs are white, spotted brown.
INCUBATION Lasts 12 days and is perhaps performed by both
sexes.
COMMENT Behaves more like a nuthatch than most other
warblers, often crawling along branches and trunks of pines.

KIRTLAND'S WARBLER

Dendroica kirtlandii   5½−6in/13−15cm

IDENTIFICATION Gray warbler with clear eye-ring and faint
double wing-bar; underparts yellow, streaked black on flanks.
VOICE Loud whistling.
HABITAT Burned-over jack pines.
RANGE North-central Michigan.
MOVEMENTS Summer visitor, winters Bahamas.

PRAIRIE WARBLER

Dendroica discolor   4½−5in/12−13cm

IDENTIFICATION Olive-green above with faint streaking on
back; yellow below with clear black streaking on flanks. Male
has black facial markings enclosing an area of yellow below
the eye. Female has grayish ear coverts and clear yellow
supercilium.

VOICE An ascending buzz.

HABITAT Scrub, open woods.

RANGE Eastern US to southern Canada.

MOVEMENTS Summer visitor; winters Florida.

BREEDING Dry areas with scrub and juniper; April-May.

NEST AND EGGS A neat nest of grasses and roots is placed in low bushes; the 3 to 5 eggs are white, speckled with brown.

INCUBATION The eggs take 12 or 13 days to hatch and are incubated by the female alone.

COMMENT This is a thicket warbler that spends much of its time among low vegetation.

PALM WARBLER

Dendroica palmarum   5½−6in/14−15cm

IDENTIFICATION Dark warbler, with brown upperparts, pale wing coverts and chestnut-brown cap. Eastern birds have yellow underparts washed with chestnut and liberally streaked brown; western birds have yellow only on breast and are streaked gray on white on belly. Spends much time near ground. A habitual tail-wagger.

VOICE Trilling.

HABITAT Damp margins of conifer forests.

RANGE Boreal Canada.

MOVEMENTS Winters Atlantic and Gulf coasts of US.

BREEDING Scattered trees among barren ground with low cover, often among bogs or marshes; June-July.

NEST AND EGGS A nest of grasses and stems, lined with feathers, is hidden on the ground; the 4 or 5 eggs are white, spotted with brown.

INCUBATION The eggs take 12 days to hatch incubated by the female alone.

COMMENT Spends much of its time on the ground wagging its tail as it walks.

BAY-BREASTED WARBLER

Dendroica castanea   5½−6in/14−15cm

IDENTIFICATION Male in summer has black "face" separating rich chestnut crown and throat. The chestnut extends to the breast and flanks and there is a pale, buffy patch at the rear of the ear coverts. The upperparts are blackish with white, double wing-bar; the underparts a warm buff. Female has only a hint of chestnut washed over the breast. Fall male retains chestnut flanks; juveniles are olive greenish with black and white wings.

VOICE Run-together double note.

HABITAT Conifers.

RANGE Boreal Canada.

MOVEMENTS Summer visitor.

BREEDING Conifer woods with clearings and a strong growth of shrubs; June-July.

NEST AND EGGS A nest of twigs and grasses is placed at moderate height in a conifer; the 4 to 7 eggs are white, spotted with brown.

INCUBATION The eggs take 12 or more days to hatch and are incubated by the female alone.

COMMENT This late-arriving warbler is remarkably distinct in spring, but presents real identification problems in the fall.

BLACKPOLL WARBLER

Dendroica striata   5½−6in/14−15cm

IDENTIFICATION Similar to Black-and-white Warbler, but cap completely black, lacking coronal stripe. Male streaked gray and black above with double, white wing-bar, white cheeks and white underparts heavily streaked black. Female

high up in a deciduous tree; the 3 to 5 eggs are white, spotted with brown.

INCUBATION Performed by the female, and lasting about 12 days.

COMMENT Very much a canopy species that is very difficult to observe during the summer. Rare on migration west of the Mississippi.

and fall birds are yellowish on head and breast, heavily streaked.

VOICE High-pitched *see-see-see*.

HABITAT Coniferous woods.

RANGE Boreal Canada and New England states.

MOVEMENTS Summer visitor.

BREEDING A northern conifer-dwelling bird that frequents stunted spruce for preference; June-July.

NEST AND EGGS Constructed of grasses, lichens and mosses and placed low in a spruce; the 4 or 5 eggs are white, spotted with brown.

INCUBATION Performed by the female, lasting 11 days.

COMMENT Though it breeds right across North America, among dwarf conifers, even Alaskan birds migrate eastwards along the central flyway.

CERULEAN WARBLER

Dendroica cerulea   4½in/12cm

IDENTIFICATION Male is darkish blue above with bold, double, white wing-bar. Underparts are white with black streaking on flanks merging to form black breast band. Female is green on crown and back with yellowish supercilium, yellowish throat and breast and gray streaking on flanks. Immature is olive above and washed with yellow below.

VOICE Buzzing song.

HABITAT Damp woodlands and bottomlands with tall trees.

RANGE Eastern US.

MOVEMENTS Summer visitor.

BREEDING Mostly mature deciduous woods, but also in conifers; May-June.

NEST AND EGGS A neat cup of grasses lined with hair placed

BLACK-AND-WHITE WARBLER

Mniotilta varia   5-5½in/13-14cm

IDENTIFICATION Breeding male is boldly black and white, marked by black chin and ear coverts and much streaking on breast and flanks. Female lacks black chin and has gray ear coverts. In all plumages the striped crown is the best field mark. Climbs tree trunks and branches like a nuthatch.

VOICE Thin *wee-see*, repeated.

HABITAT Woodlands.

RANGE Summer visitor to eastern North America extending northward through western Canada.

MOVEMENTS Winters Florida and Gulf coast.

BREEDING Mixed and deciduous woods and thickets; April-June.

NEST AND EGGS The nest is constructed of grasses and leaves and is hidden among the roots of a tree; the 4 to 6 eggs are white, spotted reddish brown.

INCUBATION Lasts 13 days and is performed by the female alone.

COMMENT The peculiar branch-crawling behavior of this dainty warbler is more akin to a creeper than a warbler.

AMERICAN REDSTART

Setophaga ruticilla 5−5½in/13−14cm

IDENTIFICATION Male is black with white belly and distinctive bands of orange-red at bend of wing, across the flight feathers, and at the base of the tail. Often fans tail. Female is olive-green with patches of yellow where the male is red. Young male resembles female with yellow rather than red patches, but is darker and with a hint of orange at the bend of the wing.

VOICE High notes ending in down-slurred flourish.

HABITAT Coverts and damp woods.

RANGE Most of North America except for north and south-western states from Texas to Oregon.

MOVEMENTS Summer visitor; a few winter southern Florida.

BREEDING Open areas of woods, mostly deciduous but also mixed, with growth of shrubs; May-June.

NEST AND EGGS A carefully constructed cup of grasses is placed at some height in the secure fork of a deciduous tree; the 3 to 5 eggs are white, speckled brown.

INCUBATION The eggs take 12 days to hatch and are incubated by the female alone.

COMMENT An ever-active warbler that makes much of displaying the chestnut patches in tail and wing.

PROTHONOTARY WARBLER

Protonotaria citrea 5½−6in/14−15cm

IDENTIFICATION Breeding male has golden-yellow head, breast and belly broken by large, dark eye. Wings and short, rounded tail are gray. Female is less golden, particularly on head and nape.

VOICE Loud *weet-weet*, repeated.

HABITAT Streamside woodlands, nests in cavity.

RANGE Eastern US, but seldom common.

MOVEMENTS Summer visitor.

BREEDING Swampy woodlands and along streams; April-June.

NEST AND EGGS A woodpecker hole or some other cavity in a dead tree, occasionally in a nest box; the 3 to 8 eggs are white, spotted brown.

INCUBATION The eggs take some 12 to 14 days to hatch incubated by the female.

COMMENT The unusual habit, for a warbler, of nesting in tree holes is shared with Lucy's Warbler.

WORM-EATING WARBLER

Helmitheros vermivorus 5−5½in/13−14cm

IDENTIFICATION Olive-brown upperparts contrast with warm, orange-buff head and breast. Black stripes through eye and along sides of crown create a distinctive pattern similar to that of several sparrows.

VOICE Rapidly repeated *chip*.

HABITAT Dense woodland thickets.

RANGE South-eastern US.

MOVEMENTS Summer visitor, occasionally seen on migration westward to California.

BREEDING Wooded hillsides with ground cover and open dry areas; May-June.
NEST AND EGGS A neat structure of leaves and grasses placed on the ground; the 3 to 6 eggs are white, spotted brown.
INCUBATION Lasts 13 days, performed by the female.
COMMENT Spends most of its time frequenting shady undergrowth but, despite its name, is not known to eat earthworms.

SWAINSON'S WARBLER

Limnothlypis swainsonii   5½−6in/14−15cm

IDENTIFICATION A dull brownish warbler marked by long, dagger-like bill. Olive-brown upperparts; buffy-cream underparts. Best field mark is chocolate-brown cap and dark eye-stripe separated by broad, whitish supercilium. Hides in cover.
VOICE Series of slurred whistles rising at the end.
HABITAT Dense thickets near water.

RANGE South-eastern US to northern Florida and eastern Texas.
MOVEMENTS Summer visitor.
BREEDING Dense swampland vegetation and cane belts; April-May.
NEST AND EGGS The nest is a large structure of marshland vegetation placed among canes or low bush; the 3 or 4 eggs are white, washed blue.
INCUBATION Lasts 14 or 15 days and is performed by the female alone.
COMMENT An easily overlooked, secretive marshland warbler that is usually found by its song.

OVENBIRD

Seiurus aurocapillus   6in/15−16cm

IDENTIFICATION A ground-dwelling forest warbler. Olive-brown above, with reddish, coronal stripe, bordered black. White underparts with black streaking. Legs pink.
VOICE Distinctive *teacher-teacher*.
HABITAT Deciduous forests.
RANGE Across boreal Canada and eastern US.
MOVEMENTS Summer visitor; some winter Florida.
BREEDING Dense, mature, deciduous woodland with little undergrowth; May-June.
NEST AND EGGS A domed nest of leaves and grasses placed on the ground; the 3 to 6 eggs are white, speckled brown.
INCUBATION The eggs take 12 to 14 days to hatch and are incubated by the female alone.
COMMENT The nest of this species, on the relatively bare woodland floor among fallen leaves, is responsible for its name.

NORTHERN WATERTHRUSH

Seiurus noveboracensis   6in/15–16cm

IDENTIFICATION A tail-bobbing warbler that walks along the ground near water. Note uniform pale underparts with dark stripes and white eyebrow that tapers behind eye.
VOICE Series of loud notes terminating in a slur.
HABITAT Damp woods, thickets.
RANGE Boreal Canada southward through the Great Lakes and north-eastern US.
MOVEMENTS Summer visitor; a few winter southern Florida.
BREEDING Usually thickets near swamps and ponds with alder and willow favored; June-July.
NEST AND EGGS Constructed of leaves and grasses, decorated with mosses and placed against a bank or among fallen tree roots; the 4 or 5 eggs are white, spotted brown.
INCUBATION The eggs hatch after 12 days, incubation is by the female alone.
COMMENT Though it breeds right across Canada to Alaska, this is only a scarce migrant along the west coast.

LOUISIANA WATERTHRUSH

Seiurus motacilla   6in/15–16cm

IDENTIFICATION Dark olive-brown above, with white supercilium extending and broadening to nape. Underparts white, heavily streaked black with warm, buffy wash along flanks. Pale pink legs; a ground-dwelling tail-bobber. *See* Northern Waterthrush.
VOICE Usually three, clear notes followed by trill.

HABITAT Woodland streams.
RANGE Boreal Canada southward into northern US.
MOVEMENTS Summer visitor; some winter Florida.
BREEDING Dense, wooded areas with streams and ponds; May-June.
NEST AND EGGS A nest of leaves and mosses is placed against a damp bank; the 4 to 6 eggs are white, spotted with browns.
INCUBATION The eggs take 12 to 14 days to hatch and are incubated by the female alone.
COMMENT A direct replacement of the Northern Waterthrush in the eastern US.

KENTUCKY WARBLER

Oporornis formosus   5–5½in/13–14cm

IDENTIFICATION Upperparts olive, underparts yellow. Dark cap and black moustache enclose bright yellow eye-ring. Long pink legs; feeds mainly on ground.
VOICE A repeated *churee*.
HABITAT Damp woodland.
RANGE Eastern US.
MOVEMENTS Summer visitor.

BREEDING Damp woodland and thickets along dark, stream-filled gullies; May-June.

NEST AND EGGS A well-hidden nest of leaves and grass is placed on the ground; the 4 or 5 eggs are white, spotted brown.

INCUBATION The eggs are incubated by the female for 11 days.

COMMENT A highly secretive warbler that is best located by its repeated *churee* call.

CONNECTICUT WARBLER

Oporornis agilis   6in/15–16cm

IDENTIFICATION Similar to MacGillivray's and Mourning Warblers, with olive-green upperparts, gray head and breast, and yellow underparts. Has a clear, complete, white eye-ring in all plumages. Larger than similar species, spending more time on the ground where it walks rather than hops.

VOICE Loud, accelerating, clear notes.

HABITAT Damp conifer and other woods with dense ground cover.

RANGE Boreal Canada and US Great Lakes region.

MOVEMENTS Summer visitor.

BREEDING Frequents a variety of wet or boggy habitats with low or dwarf vegetation; June-July.

NEST AND EGGS The neat nest is constructed of grasses and placed on the ground at the base of a tussock or small shrub; the 3 to 5 eggs are white, spotted brown.

INCUBATION The eggs are incubated by the female.

COMMENT Large, stocky, short-tailed shape and walking habits make this a relatively straight-forward bird to identify.

MOURNING WARBLER

Oporornis philadelphia   5–5½in/13–14cm

IDENTIFICATION Very similar to MacGillivray's and Connecticut Warblers, but distinguished by lack of white eye-ring. Note: this feature needs a close approach to check positively and does not apply to immature birds. Breeding male is olive-green above, yellow below, with gray head and breast, the latter spotted black. Female has dull gray head and also lacks eye-ring. Immature birds have white eye-ring and yellowish throats.

VOICE Slurred, five-note warble.

HABITAT Damp thickets.

RANGE Boreal Canada and Great Lakes area.

MOVEMENTS Summer visitor.

BREEDING Scrub and thicket vegetation in logged and burnt-over woodland, together with other low shrubbery; May-June.

NEST AND EGGS A large nest of leaves and grasses is placed on the ground among dense vegetation; the 3 to 5 eggs are white, spotted brown.

INCUBATION The eggs are incubated by the female alone for 13 days.

COMMENT Though it spends much of its time on the ground, this bird hops rather than walks, a behavioral characteristic that aids identification.

MACGILLIVRAY'S WARBLER

Oporornis tolmiei   5–5½in/13–14cm

IDENTIFICATION Upperparts olive-green without wing-bars. Head, gray with broken, white eye-ring; breast gray, with black speckling in male. Underparts entirely yellow; legs

reddish; bill short. *See* Mourning and Connecticut Warblers.

VOICE Buzzing trill.

HABITAT Scrub and thickets.

RANGE Western US and Canada as far north as Alaskan panhandle.

MOVEMENTS Summer visitor.

BREEDING Woodland margins, thicket-covered, clear-felled zones, brushy areas; May-June.

NEST AND EGGS The nest is constructed of grasses and other stems lined with hair and placed low in a small bush; the 3 to 5 eggs are white, spotted brown.

INCUBATION The eggs are incubated by the female for 13 days.

COMMENT One of three 'dark-fronted' warblers, but the only one found in the western US, where it is a relatively common bird.

COMMON YELLOWTHROAT

Geothlypis trichas 5−5½in/13−14cm

IDENTIFICATION Olive above and yellow below, marked in the male by bold, black facial mask. Female lacks mask. Geographical variation affects mostly the amount of yellow on underparts: western birds being brighter than eastern ones.

VOICE Repeated *witchy*.

HABITAT Overgrown grasslands, thickets.

RANGE Whole of sub-tundra North America.

MOVEMENTS Summer visitor, winters southern and coastal states.

BREEDING Mostly wet ground thickets, but also hedges and woodland margins; May-July.

NEST AND EGGS The large nest of stems and grasses is placed on the ground among dense ground cover; the 3 to 5 eggs are white, spotted brown.

INCUBATION The eggs take 12 days to hatch and are incubated by the female.

COMMENT An abundant and widespread bird that spends much of its time among low cover, but which, when seen, often has its rounded tail cocked vertically.

HOODED WARBLER

Wilsonia citrina 5−5½in/13−14cm

IDENTIFICATION A green and yellow warbler, marked in the male by a black hood surrounding a yellow face. White outer tail feathers conspicuous. Female has residual male pattern with only a faint black breast band. Immatures show a yellow supercilium and white in the tail.

VOICE Pleasant warble with slurred flourish.

HABITAT Thickets among damp woodland.

RANGE Eastern US as far as eastern Texas.

MOVEMENTS Summer visitor.

BREEDING Dense waterside vegetation among mature, deciduous woodland; May-June.

NEST AND EGGS The bulky nest is made of leaves and grasses and placed in a small shrub just above the ground; the 3 to 5 eggs are white, spotted brown.

INCUBATION The eggs take 12 days to hatch and may be incubated by both sexes.

COMMENT A rather secretive bird that is best located by its pleasant musical song, not uncommon.

WILSON'S WARBLER

Wilsonia pusilla   4½in/12cm

IDENTIFICATION Male is greenish above and yellow below with neat black crown patch; this feature is lacking in the female which can easily be confused with other yellow warblers that lack wing-bars.

VOICE Long series of *chip* notes on a descending scale.

HABITAT Ground cover in dense, damp woodland.

RANGE Boreal Canada and southward through much of the west.

MOVEMENTS Summer visitor.

BREEDING Dense thickets around marshes, bogs and other wetland areas; May-July.

NEST AND EGGS A large structure of leaves and grasses lined with hair and is well hidden on the ground; the 4 to 6 eggs are white, speckled brown.

INCUBATION The eggs are incubated by the female for 12 days.

COMMENT Like so many other warblers, this bird was named in honor of a famous ornithologist – in this case Alexander Wilson, born in Scotland in 1766.

CANADA WARBLER

Wilsonia canadensis   5 – 5½in/13 – 14cm

IDENTIFICATION Blue-gray upperparts without wing-bars. Underparts yellow marked by clear black streaking on the breast in the male. Bold eye-ring joined to base of bill. Female has subdued brownish breast streaking and only a hint of a loral line between eye-ring and bill. Immature resembles female.

VOICE Pleasant, variable warbling.

HABITAT Forests with dense secondary growth.

RANGE Boreal Canada extending southward into northeastern US and along Appalachians.

MOVEMENTS Summer visitor; winters South America.

BREEDING Woodland with strong undergrowth, especially along streams and marshes; May-June.

NEST AND EGGS Large nest of leaves and grasses lined with fine roots and placed on the ground against a bank or tree root; the 3 to 5 eggs are white, spotted reddish-brown.

INCUBATION The eggs are probably incubated for 12 days by the female.

COMMENT Though first discovered in Canada, this warbler also breeds south of the border in the eastern US. It is an adept 'flycatcher'.

RED-FACED WARBLER

Cardellina rubrifrons   5½ – 6in/14 – 15cm

IDENTIFICATION Gray upperparts, white belly, with distinctive head pattern of red and black. Immature is less boldly marked with a pink flush on the "face".

VOICE Clear *weet* notes.

HABITAT Mountain forests, usually mixed.

RANGE Arizona and New Mexico.

MOVEMENTS Summer visitor.

BREEDING High altitude conifer forests; May-June.

NEST AND EGGS The cup-shaped nest of grasses is placed on the ground against a tree stump, log or rock; the 3 or 4 eggs are white and spotted.

INCUBATION The eggs are incubated by the female.

COMMENT This bird is found only at altitude and spends much of its time among the higher branches of conifers.

PAINTED REDSTART

Myioborus pictus   6in/15–16cm

IDENTIFICATION A black bird with crimson belly and white patches in wing and outer tail. Often fans tail. Immature is slate-black, with white in wing and tail, but no crimson on belly.

VOICE A pleasant warble.

HABITAT Oak woods at altitude.

RANGE South-western states.

MOVEMENTS Summer visitor.

BREEDING Frequents open pine and oak-wooded slopes as well as ravines; April-May.

NEST AND EGGS The nest is made of grasses lined with hair and placed on the ground; the 3 or 4 eggs are off-white and spotted brown.

INCUBATION The eggs are incubated for 14 days by the female.

COMMENT A summer visitor to Arizona, New Mexico and Big Bend country in Texas, that winters just across the Mexican border.

YELLOW-BREASTED CHAT

Icteria virens   7½–8in/19–20cm

IDENTIFICATION Large, heavy, thick-set warbler. Brown above, yellow below. Short, chunky bill with white loral stripe extending to white eye-ring; short, white moustachial streak. Generally shy.

VOICE Chattering.

HABITAT Thickets and scrub.

RANGE Whole of US except Great Lakes and Florida.

MOVEMENTS Summer visitor.

BREEDING Dense thickets near water; April-June.

NEST AND EGGS Large nest of leaves and grasses placed low in a thicket; the 3 to 5 eggs are white, spotted brownish.

INCUBATION The eggs take 11 days to hatch and are incubated by the female alone.

COMMENT Though relatively common this is a self-effacing bird that spends most of its time hidden among dense vegetation.

OLIVE WARBLER

Peucedramus taeniatus   5–5½in/13–14cm

IDENTIFICATION Male is gray above with bold, double, white wing-bar. Head and breast chestnut brown with black facial mask. Female is yellow rather than chestnut, but has facial mask.

VOICE *Peter-peter-peter.*

HABITAT Mountain conifers.

RANGE South-eastern Arizona and adjacent New Mexico.

MOVEMENTS Summer visitor, some winter Mexican border.

BLACKBIRDS, MEADOWLARKS & ORIOLES

THIS is a well-defined sub-grouping of the great family Emberizidae. Its members enjoy a variety of vernacular names, including grackle and cowbird, as well as those listed above. They are generally medium-sized birds, with well-developed tails and sharply-pointed bills. They fly strongly and direct, vary in color from black to bright yellow and orange, and are mostly highly vocal. Outstanding in this respect are the orioles, with their distinctive flute-like whistles. The Northern Oriole is a widespread summer visitor throughout temperate North America. At one time it was divided into two distinct species – the Baltimore Oriole in the east and Bullock's Oriole in the west. The two differ both in plumage characteristics and in calls and song, but where they meet they interbreed quite freely, producing a not uncommon "mixed" plumage. The orioles show a clear sexual dimorphism, with the males much more brightly colored than their mates.

The three species of North American grackles are uniformly black in male plumage, though each shows a distinct color wash of iridescence. The most common and widespread species is the Common Grackle, which is also the smallest. It is a summer visitor to Canada and the Mid-west, but regularly winters as far north as New York state. In contrast, the Boat-tailed Grackle is confined to the Atlantic and Gulf coasts, while the Great-tailed Grackle is found in the southwest from Texas to southern California. As the names of the less widespread species imply, a major feature of the grackles is their curiously twisted tails.

The blackbirds are (in the males at least) black in plumage with bold splashes of color on head or wing, or in some species a metallic iridescent wash. They are chunky, robust birds, two of which have earned the name "cowbird" because of their habit of feeding on ticks and insects taken from domestic stock. The males take little or no part in the nesting chores, and as a result are promiscuous and polygamous. The cowbirds have developed the habit of brood parasitism, like the European cuckoos.

The Bobolink and the two meadowlarks are all plains birds which feed mostly on the ground. Indeed, the Bobolink has developed the habit of turning stones and earth to become a sort of inland, passerine "turnstone."

RED-WINGED BLACKBIRD

Agelaius phoeniceus   8½–9½in/22–24cm

IDENTIFICATION Male is all black with red, bordered yellow-buff, wing patches. Young male is scaled black with less pronounced wing patches. Female is boldly streaked black above and below with a hint of reddish on the wing. Forms huge flocks.

VOICE *Kouk-la-ree*.

HABITAT Marshes and fields.

RANGE Whole of sub-tundra North America.

MOVEMENTS Canadian and northern US birds are summer visitors.

BREEDING Cattails, sedges and other dense emergent vegetation around marshes; April-June.

NEST AND EGGS Usually a loose structure of vegetation attached to emergent plants, but sometimes among marshside shrubs; the 3 to 5 eggs are blue green, spotted brown.

INCUBATION Lasts 10 to 12 days and is performed by the female alone.

COMMENT Males displaying over their marshy domains are one of the characteristic sights of early spring.

TRICOLORED BLACKBIRD

Agelaius tricolor   8½–9½in/22–24cm

IDENTIFICATION Very similar to Red-winged Blackbird, but male has white border to red wing patch. Female very similar to that more widespread bird, but breast streaking is less clear cut and less contrasting. Forms huge flocks.

VOICE *Ou-kee-kar*, harsher than Red-winged Blackbird.

HABITAT Marshes, damp fields.

RANGE California.

MOVEMENTS Resident.

BREEDING Marshes with strong growth of emergent vegetation and shrubs; March-September.

NEST AND EGGS A cup-shaped nest of aquatic leaves and stems is placed among emergent vegetation; the 3 or 4 eggs are green, spotted with brown.

INCUBATION The eggs take 11 days to hatch, incubated by the female.

COMMENT These birds nest in dense colonies of thousands of pairs, a recent decline has been attributed to marshland drainage.

EASTERN MEADOWLARK

Sturnella magna   9½–10in/24–26cm

IDENTIFICATION Medium-sized bird of open grasslands. In summer, yellow underparts with black "V"-shaped breast band are clear features. At other times streaked upperparts, striped crown, pointed bill and yellow-washed underparts identify. *See* Western Meadowlark.
VOICE Whistling *see-you-see-yer*.
HABITAT Grasslands.

RANGE Eastern US and south-eastern Canada, extends as far west as southern Arizona.
MOVEMENTS Northern birds migrate, others resident.
BREEDING Fields of grass and cereals; April-June.
NEST AND EGGS A grassy cup with a domed roof is placed on the ground and hidden among growing grasses; the 3 to 7 eggs are white, spotted brown.
INCUBATION The eggs take 13 to 15 days to hatch and are incubated by the female.
COMMENT Though the two species of meadowlark are so similar in appearance, the songs are completely different.

WESTERN MEADOWLARK

Sturnella neglecta   9½–10in/24–26cm

IDENTIFICATION Very similar to Eastern Meadowlark and overlaps range. This bird is grayer and less contrasting and has more yellow on "face".
VOICE Bubbling notes.
HABITAT Grasslands, generally drier than Eastern.
RANGE From the Great Lakes westwards.
MOVEMENTS Northern and eastern birds migrate to winter along Gulf coast westward.
BREEDING Grass and cereal fields including open prairies; February-June.

NEST AND EGGS A cup of grasses with a domed top placed on the ground. The 3 to 7 eggs are white, spotted brown.
INCUBATION Lasts for 13 to 15 days and is performed by the female alone.
COMMENT Meadowlarks are not difficult to find and are generally fearless of man, allowing a close approach.

YELLOW-HEADED BLACKBIRD

Xanthocephalus xanthocephalus   9½–10in/24–26cm

IDENTIFICATION Male is black with buffy-yellow head and breast broken by black around eye and lores. Small white patch in wing and thick, pointed bill. Female similar, but with orange-yellow breast and brownish head; generally browner than male.
VOICE Rasping buzz.

HABITAT Marshes and farmland.

RANGE Westward from Great Lakes through prairies to coast and southward to Arizona.

MOVEMENTS Summer visitor; winters Mexican border; resident California.

BREEDING Marshland edges with dense emergent vegetation; May-June.

NEST AND EGGS A hammock slung between the stems of aquatic vegetation and constructed of stems and leaves; the 3 to 5 eggs are white, heavily speckled brown.

INCUBATION The eggs take 10 to 13 days to hatch and are incubated by the female alone.

COMMENT Though they breed in marshes, these birds frequently resort to grain fields in the fall and winter.

RUSTY BLACKBIRD

Euphagus carolinus   9−9½in/23−24cm

IDENTIFICATION Breeding male is all black with long, pointed bill and contrasting yellow eye. Female is slate gray with mottling on breast. Outside breeding season, all birds have rusty tips to feathers of body, wing coverts and tertials that gradually wear away to produce the summer plumage.

VOICE High-pitched *coo-a-lee*.

HABITAT Damp woods and marshes.

RANGE Boreal Alaska and Canada.

MOVEMENTS Summer visitor; winters over whole of eastern US except extreme north.

BREEDING Mostly woodlands with pools and shrubbery; May-June.

NEST AND EGGS A well-constructed nest of twigs and grasses is placed in a low conifer; the 4 or 5 greenish-blue eggs are spotted brown.

INCUBATION Lasts 14 days and is by the female alone.

COMMENT This northern breeding blackbird is among the earliest of long-distance migrants to return in spring.

BREWER'S BLACKBIRD

Euphagus cyanocephalus   9−10in/23−25cm

IDENTIFICATION Male is black with purple gloss on head and green gloss on wings and body. The eye is yellow. Female is dull brown above and below, with dark eye. Some fall males are rusty on the body, but never so obviously so as Rusty Blackbird.

VOICE Harsh, wheezy song.

HABITAT Parks, suburbs, farmsteads, woods.

RANGE Western US and Canada extending eastward to Great Lakes.

MOVEMENTS Northern and eastern birds migrate to southern US in winter.

BREEDING Thickets, hedgerows, streamside tangles; April-June.

NEST AND EGGS A loose structure of twigs and grasses bound together with mud is placed on the ground or in a tree; the 5 or 6 greenish eggs are spotted brown.

INCUBATION Lasts 12 to 14 days and is performed by the female alone.

COMMENT This is a colonial breeder that is now regarded as a regular visitor to the north-eastern US.

GREAT-TAILED GRACKLE

Quiscalus mexicanus   (M) 18–19in/46–48cm
                          (F) 15–15½in/38–40cm

IDENTIFICATION Male has purple gloss over body, with long, "V"-shaped tail; the eye is yellow. Female is brown above, buffy on throat and breast, with shorter, wedge-shaped tail.
VOICE Squeaks and harsh calls.
HABITAT Marshes and open scrubland.
RANGE South-western US from Texas to California.
MOVEMENTS Some northern populations move southward in winter.
BREEDING Park-like farmsteads with scattered trees; April-May.
NEST AND EGGS A large nest of twigs and grasses is bound together with mud and placed in a tree; the 3 or 4 eggs are pale blue, spotted brown.
INCUBATION Lasts 13 or 14 days and is performed by the female.
COMMENT Females of this species found west of central Arizona, are considerably smaller and paler than females found to the east.

BOAT-TAILED GRACKLE

Quiscalus major   (M) 16½–17in/42–44cm
                      (F) 14½–15in/37–39cm

IDENTIFICATION Male is washed iridescent blue with long, "V"-shaped tail. Brown, not yellow, eye separate from Great-tailed Grackle, though some have paler eyes than others. The smaller size and rounded, not flat, crown are reliable features. Female is brown above and warm brown below.
VOICE Variety of squeals.
HABITAT Salt marshes, sometimes freshwater margins.
RANGE Atlantic and Gulf coasts.
MOVEMENTS Resident.
BREEDING Thickets alongside salt and inland marshes; April-May.
NEST AND EGGS A large nest of grasses and other vegetation reinforced with mud; the 3 or 4 eggs are pale blue, spotted with brown.
INCUBATION Lasts 14 days and is performed by the female.
COMMENT Though the two "large-tailed" grackles overlap in range, hybridization does not occur, thus confirming their specific status.

COMMON GRACKLE

Quiscalus quiscula   12½–13½in/32–34cm

IDENTIFICATION Male is black with longish, "V"-shaped tail. At close range a purple gloss on head and wings may be visible, though northern and western birds show a blue gloss on the head and a bronze gloss on breast and back. Female is duller with dark eye, but also has "V"-shaped tail.
VOICE Loud squeaks.
HABITAT Suburbs, farms, fields.
RANGE Whole of North America, east of the Rockies.
MOVEMENTS Northern and western birds are summer visitors.

BREEDING Open woods and parks; March-May.
NEST AND EGGS A large structure of twigs and grasses bound with mud is placed in a tree or bush; the 4 to 6 pale blue eggs are spotted brown.
INCUBATION The eggs take 11 to 14 days to hatch and are incubated by the female alone.
COMMENT These grackles form small colonies during the breeding season which starts when the snow is on the ground in the northern parts of their range.

BRONZED COWBIRD

Molothrus aeneus   8½–9in/22–23cm

IDENTIFICATION Thick, but longish, bill is characteristic in all plumages. Male has dark brown body with blue-glossed wings and tail. A red eye may be distinguished at close range. Female varies from uniform black, to dark brown with slightly paler underparts. All birds have a ruff on hind neck that creates an unusual profile when raised.

VOICE Harsh squeaking.
HABITAT Fields, thickets.
RANGE South-western US.
MOVEMENTS Winters southernmost Texas and Arizona; otherwise only a summer visitor.
BREEDING Farmland, parklands and other lightly vegetated areas; April-June.
NEST AND EGGS This cowbird mainly lays its eggs in the nests of orioles; the eggs are greenish blue.
INCUBATION The eggs hatch after 10 to 12 days.
COMMENT A highly gregarious species that forms huge flocks in some areas.

BROWN-HEADED COWBIRD

Molothrus ater   7½–8in/19–20cm

IDENTIFICATION Distinguished from other blackbirds by stubby bill and small size. Male has chocolate head and black body with greenish gloss. Female is brown above and dirty buff below, with dark streaking. Forms large flocks.
VOICE Harsh squeaking.
HABITAT Parks, suburbs, farms, woods.
RANGE Whole of sub-tundra North America.

MOVEMENTS Northern and western birds largely summer visitors.

BREEDING Wide variety of vegetated areas, often farmlands; March-June.

NEST AND EGGS This bird lays its eggs in the nests of warblers, vireos, flycatchers and other species; the eggs are white, spotted brown.

INCUBATION The eggs hatch after 11 or 12 days.

COMMENT Cowbird eggs may be rejected by their hosts, but most hatch and are reared by their foster parents.

ORCHARD ORIOLE

Icterus spurius   7−7½in/18−19cm

IDENTIFICATION Small oriole. Male has black head, back and breast, chestnut body and black wings and tail. Female is greenish above with double, white wing-bar and greenish yellow below. Female Northern Oriole has warm orange breast.

VOICE Whistling and fluting calls.

HABITAT Orchards, suburbs, woods.

RANGE Eastern US.

MOVEMENTS Summer visitor.

BREEDING Orchards, suburbs and other areas with scattered trees; April-June.

NEST AND EGGS A hammock slung from a tree fork woven of grasses; the 3 to 7 eggs are white, spotted brown.

INCUBATION The eggs take 11 to 14 days to hatch and are incubated by the female alone.

COMMENT This oriole may form loose colonies; in some areas there may be ten or more nests in a single tree.

HOODED ORIOLE

Icterus cucullatus   8−8½in/20−21cm

IDENTIFICATION Male is orange with black face and extended bib, black wings with double wing-bar, and black tail. Female is greenish yellow lacking any warm tones on breast, or white on belly. Bill is distinctly decurved.

VOICE Whistling trills and gentle warbling.

HABITAT Palms and other trees.

RANGE California and Mexican border states.

MOVEMENTS Summer visitor.

BREEDING Parks, suburbs, orchards and waterside vegetation; April-May.

NEST AND EGGS A suspended pouch of grasses is hung in a palm or eucalyptus; the 3 to 5 eggs are white, washed blue gray and spotted brown.

INCUBATION The eggs are incubated by the female for 13 days.

COMMENT A bird that has adapted well to man-made environments and which is generally easy to observe.

SPOT-BREASTED ORIOLE

Icterus pectoralis   9−10in/23−25cm

IDENTIFICATION An orange and black oriole marked by bold white margins to flight feathers forming a distinctive panel and a black bib that terminates in a series of spots.

VOICE Pleasant warbled whistles.

HABITAT Open woodland and suburbs.

RANGE Southern Florida.

MOVEMENTS Resident, introduced from Central America.

ALTAMIRA ORIOLE

Icterus gularis   10in/25cm

IDENTIFICATION Similar to Hooded Oriole; but larger, with thicker-based bill, and orange at bend of wing.
VOICE Varied including harsh calls.
HABITAT Open wooded country.
RANGE Lower Rio Grande, Texas.
MOVEMENTS Resident.

AUDUBON'S ORIOLE

Icterus graduacauda   9−10in/23−25cm

IDENTIFICATION Similar to Scott's Oriole, but back is green not black.
VOICE Quiet warble.
HABITAT Wooded country.
RANGE Southern Texas.
MOVEMENTS Resident.

NORTHERN ORIOLE

Icterus galbula   8½−9in/22−23cm

IDENTIFICATION Formerly divided into Baltimore and Bullock's Orioles. Eastern male has black head, back and breast; black wings with a white bar; and black tail with rufous terminal margins. Body and rump are rich rufous. Western male (Bullock's) has rufous extending over "face" and a bold, white wing patch. Female is brownish above and warm orange below, though western female is much paler, with warm wash only on breast.

VOICE Fluty whistles.
HABITAT Woods and suburbs.
RANGE Most of US and southern Canada.
MOVEMENTS Summer visitor.

BREEDING Deciduous woodland with open glades and other areas of scattered trees; May-June.
NEST AND EGGS A neat pouch constructed of grasses suspended high in a tree; the 3 to 6 eggs are white, spotted brown.
INCUBATION The eggs take some 12 to 15 days to hatch and are incubated by the female alone.
COMMENT The most widespread of North American orioles and frequently seen among suburban trees.

SCOTT'S ORIOLE

Icterus parisorum   9−9½in/23−24cm

IDENTIFICATION Male has black head and breast, yellow body, and black wings and tail, the former with a white wing-bar. Female is streaked green above, with a double, white wing-bar; dull greenish below, with a black mottled bib. Could be confused with the smaller Orchard Oriole in some plumages.
VOICE Pleasant warbling and whistling.
HABITAT Yuccas, pinyons and other arid vegetation.
RANGE South-western US.
MOVEMENTS Summer visitor.
BREEDING Dry scrub, desert and juniper-pinyon woodlands; April-June.

NEST AND EGGS A neatly woven hammock is suspended in a pine or oak where it is well camouflaged; the 3 to 5 eggs are white, washed with blue and spotted brown.
INCUBATION The eggs take 14 days to hatch and are incubated by the female alone.
COMMENT In its favored habitat, this bird may be quite common.

TANAGERS, BUNTINGS, TOWHEES, JUNCOS, SPARROWS & LONGSPURS

THESE are the members of the Emberizidae that remain after the large and homogeneous groups of the wood warblers and the blackbird-orioles have been treated separately. Some might argue that the tanagers would be better treated along with the warblers, and that the longspurs are quite distinct from the chunky-billed sparrows. Nevertheless, the present arrangement does have the advantage of treating these groupings in the order adopted by the American Ornithologists' Union and the American Birding Association.

Most colorful and obvious is the Cardinal, a regular visitor to gardens and feeding stations throughout the eastern U.S.A. and southern Canada. With bright crimson plumage marked by a black mask, a prominent crest, and a pink bill, they are as readily identified as the Robin. Though basically birds of the woodland edge, they are aggressive and have expanded northward and westward during the twentieth century. The closely related Pyrrhuloxia is confined to areas along the Mexican border and has an even larger bill to crack the thick-skinned shells of desert seeds.

The buntings too are colorful birds, often in shades of blue, though the male Painted Bunting is an artist's palette of colors. Purple, red, and green appear in large, bold patches. Essentially a southern bird, the other, more widespread buntings are only slightly less colorful. The Indigo Bunting of the east and Lazuli Bunting of the west both have much blue in the plumage, while the larger Blue Grosbeak, which extends right across the U.S.A., is virtually blue throughout.

A group of long-tailed buntings has gained the unusual name of towhee following the call of the Rufous-sided Towhee, the most widespread member of the group. This is also the most boldly-marked member, but like the others it finds most of its food on the ground. A glance at a distribution map of this species shows a clear divide through the center of North America where birds are found only in winter, or where they are probably only recent colonists. The isolation by the unsuitable open prairies into two distinct populations has resulted in clear plumage differences. Western birds are heavily streaked white in both male and female. These are somewhat secretive birds that keep mostly to densely vegetated areas.

North America is particularly well endowed with sparrows, members of the sub-family

Emberizinae, which in the Old World are called buntings. These are mostly brown-streaked birds that, to the beginner at least, all look very much alike. They may be separated by bold head patterns, but some pose identification problems. The diversity of species found in North America indicates a wide range of habitat preference, and members of the sub-family can be found in almost every part of the continent. The White-crowned Sparrow, for example, is found among the tundra of the extreme north and through the upland plateaux of the high Rocky Mountains, while the White-throated Sparrow is a forest bird that is familiar in gardens. Then there are sparrows, like the declining Baird's Sparrow, which are found among prairies, or the aptly named Swamp Sparrow that lives among densely vegetated marshes. It is the variety of North American habitats that has led to the variety of sparrows in this area.

These are mostly small birds, with the short conical bills of the seedeaters, and strong, perching feet. The wings vary from the short and rounded to long and pointed, the latter particularly apparent on the longer-distance migrants. In fact, most species of sparrow are migrants, breeding in the north, but wintering in the southern U.S.A., where they are either resident or winter visitors. A large number of species are streaked brown and buff above, with brownish streaks on the paler underparts. Though some species have particularly bold head patterns, usually striped, others are more uniformly streaked on upperparts, underparts, and head. The juncos are unusual in being unstreaked and clothed in shades of brown and gray. Though they are inhabitants of coniferous or mixed woodlands during the breeding season, these attractive birds are found in a wide range of habitats in winter. They arrive with the first snows and are often found around buildings. In general, the sparrows are somewhat self-effacing birds, spending much of their time among vegetation, usually near the ground. In spring, however, males proclaim their ownership of a territory by singing loud and long, often from a prominent perch. Most songs are clear, distinctive, and attractive, though some of the marshland species produce an insect-like buzz and behave more like small mammals than birds. Interestingly enough, this behavior has been adopted in the Old World by some of the warblers, rather than by this group of birds.

Several sparrows have, of course, developed quite distinct subspecies. The Seaside Sparrow, for example, formerly called the Dusky Seaside Sparrow, has a remarkably dark form and is now close to extinction. Found only in the area of the St. John's River marshes near Titusville, Florida, the decline of this subspecies has been linked with marsh drainage, housing development and the establishment of the Kennedy Space Center. While it would be reasonable to suppose that security measures might actually protect this bird, the need for mosquito eradication has seriously affected the habitat. Yet another well-marked subspecies is the Ipswich Sparrow, now regarded as a race of the Savannah Sparrow. This bird breeds only on Sable Island off the coast of Nova Scotia. Though numbers remain obscure, this is a very rare bird indeed. The erosion of Sable Island plus coastal development has reduced both breeding and wintering zones.

HEPATIC TANAGER

Piranga flava   8–8½in/20–21cm

IDENTIFICATION Male similar to male Summer Tanager, but with brownish ear coverts and dusky wash over back, wings and belly. A dull, scruffy version of the more widespread bird. Female similar to female Summer Tanager, but with gray ear coverts. Both sexes of Hepatic Tanager have dark bills.
VOICE Harsh whistling.
HABITAT Conifers and oaks at altitude.
RANGE South-western US.

MOVEMENTS Summer visitor.
BREEDING Conifer woodland in mountains; April-May.
NEST AND EGGS The saucer-shaped nest is constructed of grasses and placed on a lower branch of a tree; the 2 to 5 eggs are pale blue, heavily spotted brown.
INCUBATION The eggs are incubated by the female.
COMMENT Though similar in plumage to the Summer Tanager, the habitat difference is usually clear-cut during the breeding season.

SUMMER TANAGER

Piranga rubra   8–8½in/20–21cm

IDENTIFICATION Male is bright red with broad red margins to black wing feathers. Female is greenish-olive above with yellow underparts, variably washed with warm orange. Both sexes have pale bills.
VOICE Rich whistles.
HABITAT Oak-pine woods and cottonwoods.
RANGE Right across southern US.
MOVEMENTS Summer visitor.
BREEDING Open deciduous and coniferous woodland, mostly of mature trees often near water, suburbs; April-May.
NEST AND EGGS A cup of twigs and grasses is constructed in the outer branches of a tree; the 3 to 5 eggs are greenish blue, spotted brown.
INCUBATION The eggs take 12 days to hatch, incubated by the female.
COMMENT Though a colorful bird, this species is never particularly obvious and is best located by call.

SCARLET TANAGER

Piranga olivacea   7–7 ½in/18–19cm

IDENTIFICATION Male is brilliant scarlet with black wings and tail and whitish bill. Female is greenish-olive above, yellowish below with no wing-bars. In winter, male is greenish yellow with black wings and tail.
VOICE Harsh whistling.
HABITAT Deciduous forests.

RANGE Eastern US extending into southern Canada.
MOVEMENTS Summer visitor.
BREEDING Mature deciduous woodland, sometimes pines; May-June.
NEST AND EGGS Loose cup of twigs and grasses placed on the edge of a tree, often at some height; the 3 to 5 eggs are blue green, spotted brown.
INCUBATION Lasts 13 or 14 days and is performed by the female alone.
COMMENT One of the most brilliantly colored of all North American birds.

WESTERN TANAGER

Piranga ludoviciana 7–7½in/18–19cm

IDENTIFICATION Active, forest bird with thickish bill. Male's head is brilliant flame-red; underparts and rump, yellow; back, tail and wings black, the latter with double, yellow wing-bar. Female is brownish above and dull yellow below, marked by double wing-bar.

VOICE Harsh whistling.
HABITAT Forests, particularly conifers, at altitude.
RANGE Most of the western mountain systems.
MOVEMENTS Summer visitor.
BREEDING Conifer and mixed woods with open areas; May–June.
NEST AND EGGS Large structure of twigs and grasses lined with hair and placed in a conifer; the 3 to 5 eggs are pale blue, lightly spotted brown.
INCUBATION Lasts 13 days and is by the female alone.
COMMENT A common bird of high conifer forests in summer.

NORTHERN CARDINAL

Cardinalis cardinalis 8½–9in/22–23cm

IDENTIFICATION Male is red with black "face" and bib, conical pink bill, and sharply pointed red crest. Female is buffy-brown on head, underparts and back with red wings, tail and crest.
VOICE Repeated whistled phrases.
HABITAT Suburbs, woodland margins, marshy thickets.
RANGE Eastern US extending westward along Mexican border.
MOVEMENTS Resident.

BREEDING Bushy areas and thickets in both coniferous and deciduous woodland and around houses, hedgerows and streams; April–June.
NEST AND EGGS A nest of twigs and grasses, lined with hair, is placed at moderate height among bushes; the 3 or 4 eggs are white, spotted with brown.
INCUBATION Lasts 12 or 13 days and is usually performed by the female alone.
COMMENT A highly successful species that has learned to live alongside man and spread northwards during the present century.

PYRRHULOXIA

Cardinalis sinuatus 8½–9in/22–23cm

IDENTIFICATION Similar in shape to related Northern Cardinal. Male is gray with red tail, primary edges, face, breast, and tip of crest. Female similar, but less red. Horn-colored bill is hooked, parrot-like.
VOICE Thin whistles.

HABITAT Arid scrub.

RANGE Mexican border states.

MOVEMENTS Resident.

BREEDING Dry, open country with prickly dwarf vegetation; March-April.

NEST AND EGGS A neat cup of stems placed low in mesquite bush; the 2 to 4 eggs are dirty white, speckled brown.

INCUBATION The eggs are incubated by the female alone for 14 days.

COMMENT This species is easy to locate along the Mexican border states.

ROSE-BREASTED GROSBEAK

Pheucticus ludovicianus   8–8½in/20–21cm

IDENTIFICATION Chunky, thick-set finch with massive white bill. Male is black above, white below with bright red breast. The underparts are white and a white rump shows in flight. Female is brown above; buff streaked brown below.

VOICE Whistled phrases.

HABITAT Regenerating woods, waterside thickets.

RANGE North-eastern US extending into Canada and westward through boreal zone.

MOVEMENTS Summer visitor.

BREEDING Bushy thickets along streams and pools among deciduous and mixed woodland; May-June.

NEST AND EGGS A platform of twigs placed in a tree at some height above the ground; the 3 to 5 green-blue eggs are speckled brown.

INCUBATION Lasts 12 or 13 days and is shared between members of the pair.

COMMENT Though it breeds as far west as British Columbia, this bird is relatively scarce on passage in the west.

BLACK-HEADED GROSBEAK

Pheucticus melanocephalus   8½in/21–22cm

IDENTIFICATION Male has black head, black back and tail, and black wings with double, white wing-bar and primary patch. The rich cinnamon underparts are diagnostic. Heavy, conical bill. Female brown above with buffy, light diffuse streaking on breast.

VOICE Whistled phrases.

HABITAT Woodland margins and clearings.

RANGE Western US into adjacent Canada.

MOVEMENTS Summer visitor.

BREEDING Open woods with bushy growth along streams and pond margins; May-June.

NEST AND EGGS A platform of twigs at variable height among waterside bushes; the 3 to 5 greenish-blue eggs are spotted brown.

INCUBATION Lasts 12 days and is shared by both sexes.

COMMENT The male Black-headed Grosbeak has the unusual habit of singing while it is taking its turn on the nest.

BLUE GROSBEAK

Guiraca caerulea   6–7½in/15–19cm

IDENTIFICATION Chunky, large-billed finch that is dark blue with rusty wing patches in male. Female resembles a large female House Sparrow, but is warm brown rather than gray and has two rusty wing-bars.

VOICE Song is rich warble; calls *klink*.

HABITAT Hedgerows, thickets, damp grasslands and sorghum fields; roadside wires.

RANGE Summer visitor northward across southern half of US, though absent from most of Rockies.

MOVEMENTS Winters southward to Central America.

BREEDING Hedgerows, thickets and scrub; April-June.
NEST AND EGGS A cup of grasses and leaves is hidden among ground vegetation; the 3 or 4 eggs are pale blue.
INCUBATION Lasts 11 days and is by the female alone.
COMMENT The relationships and nomenclature of the various species of grosbeaks changes rapidly and can often prove confusing.

LAZULI BUNTING

Passerina amoena   5–5½in/13–14cm

IDENTIFICATION Male is blue on head, neck and rump; breast and flanks warm rufous; belly white. Bold, white, double wing-bar. Female, warm brown, with pale wing-bars.
VOICE Descending and rising warble with repeated phrases confined to opening notes.
HABITAT Arid gulleys with brush, poor pastures.
RANGE Summer visitor western US, though absent from southernmost states.
MOVEMENTS Winter Mexico.
BREEDING Woodland clearings and burnt-over land with strong, bushy growth; April-June.
NEST AND EGGS A cup of grasses lined with hair is constructed in a bush; the 3 or 4 eggs are white, washed blue.
INCUBATION The eggs take 12 days to hatch, incubated by the female.
COMMENT In the mid-west, where Lazuli and Indigo Buntings both breed, hybrids are far from uncommon indicating a close relationship between the species.

INDIGO BUNTING

Passerina cyanea   5½in/14cm

IDENTIFICATION Male is only all-blue finch. Considerably smaller and more dainty than Blue Grosbeak, with tiny conical bill and paler plumage. Looks black in poor light. Female, rusty-brown with indistinct breast streaks.
VOICE Warbled song with repeated phrases.
HABITAT Scrub, wasteland, bushy pastures, neglected farmland.
RANGE Summer visitor to eastern US.
MOVEMENTS Winters from Mexico to Panama.
BREEDING Clearings and margins of woodland with strong undergrowth, hedges and neglected farmland; May-June.
NEST AND EGGS A cup of twigs and grasses placed in a bush near the ground; the 3 or 4 eggs are white, washed blue.
INCUBATION Lasts for 12 days and is performed mainly by the female.
COMMENT This is another successful species that is extending its range westwards.

VARIED BUNTING

Passerina versicolor   5½in/14cm

IDENTIFICATION Chunky, dark bunting with iridescent colors visible in bright sunlight. Blue face, red nape, chestnut back and blue rump all disappear in poor light. Bill stubby and white.
VOICE Warbled thin notes.
HABITAT Thickets.
RANGE Mexican border states.
MOVEMENTS Summer visitor, though some winter lower Rio Grande.

PAINTED BUNTING

Passerina ciris   5½in/14cm

IDENTIFICATION Male is highly colorful with purple head, yellow-green back, red rump and underparts. Bill conical and silver; eye with red ring. Female greenish above, yellowish-green below; pale eye-ring.
VOICE Variable, mainly clear warbling.
HABITAT Hedgerows, thickets.
RANGE Summer visitor to southern US as far north as Missouri and as far west as New Mexico.
MOVEMENTS Winters Central America, though some stay on in Gulf states.
BREEDING Thickets of a wide variety of types and in varied situations; April-June.
NEST AND EGGS A neat cup of grasses is placed low in a bush; the 3 or 4 eggs are white, spotted brown.
INCUBATION Performed by the female, lasting 12 days.
COMMENT Despite its remarkably gaudy plumage, the male Painted Bunting is a difficult bird to locate among dense thickets.

DICKCISSEL

Spiza americana   6–6½in/16–17cm

IDENTIFICATION Dark crown and ear coverts contrast with bold, pale supercilium. Male has black bib and yellow breast; female has white bib. Upperparts streaked chestnut and black. In all adult plumages there is a chestnut patch at the bend of the wing. Bill black, thick and chunky.

VOICE *Dick-dick-dickcissel.*
HABITAT Fields and grasslands.
RANGE From the prairies eastward to the Appalachians and southwards to the Texas Gulf Coast.
MOVEMENTS Summer visitor.
BREEDING Open fields with tall crops and bushy margins; April-May.
NEST AND EGGS A large cup of grasses and leaves placed on the ground or in a low shrub; the 3 to 5 eggs are pale blue.
INCUBATION The eggs take 12 or 13 days to hatch and are incubated by the female alone.
COMMENT One of those birds that is named for its song. Actually it is related to the cardinals and grosbeaks.

GREEN-TAILED TOWHEE

Pipilo chlorurus   7–7½in/18–19cm

IDENTIFICATION A ground-dwelling finch, with long, rounded tail, typical of the towhees. This is a well-marked species with gray head topped by a rich chestnut half-cap. A bib and moustachial streak are white contrasting with gray underparts. The upperparts are green.

VOICE Whistled song terminating with a trill.
HABITAT Dry chaparral at altitude.
RANGE The interior west.
MOVEMENTS Mainly summer visitor, winters along Mexican border.
BREEDING Dry, open areas of chaparral, sagebrush and other scrub; May-June.
NEST AND EGGS The nest is a large structure of vegetation placed on the ground or in a low bush; the 2 to 5 eggs are white, spotted brown.
INCUBATION Undescribed.
COMMENT A decidedly secretive bird that keeps low to the ground among dense vegetation.

RUFOUS-SIDED TOWHEE

Pipilo erythrophthalmus   8½−9in/22−23cm

IDENTIFICATION Most widespread towhee. Male is black on head, breast and upperparts with white panels in the wing and white tips to the long tail. Western birds are flecked white on wings and scapulars. Underparts are white with rufous-chestnut flanks. Female is brown above, white below with chestnut flanks; the western female has similar white flecking as the male.
VOICE *Tow-whee* (west) or *Drink-your-tea* (east).
HABITAT Scrub and thickets, woodland edges and clearings.
RANGE Breeds over most of US and adjacent Canada, though absent from most of Texas.
MOVEMENTS Central birds are summer visitors; elsewhere resident; winters Texas.
BREEDING Bushy areas of a wide variety of types from mountains to prairie gullies; May-June.

NEST AND EGGS The cup is placed on the ground or in a low bush and is made of loosely woven grasses; the 3 to 6 eggs are white, spotted brown.
INCUBATION Lasts 12 or 13 days and is performed by the female alone.
COMMENT In Mexico this species hybridizes with the Collared Towhee and may well be conspecific.

CANYON TOWHEE

Pipilo fuscus   8½−9in/22−23cm

IDENTIFICATION Brown above and creamy below with large, conical, silver and black bill. Best field marks are a creamy bib enclosed by a necklace of black spots, and rufous, undertail coverts. The closely related California Towhee of the Pacific coast lacks the breast-spot, is darker and calls with a metallic *chink*.
VOICE Trills and hard, sharp *chinks*.
HABITAT Dry brush areas, chaparral, suburbs, usually at some altitude.
RANGE South-west, from Arizona to Texas.
MOVEMENTS Resident.
BREEDING Open woods and chaparral, suburbs; March-May.
NEST AND EGGS A cup of vegetation is placed low in a bush; the 3 or 4 green-blue eggs are speckled dark brown.
INCUBATION Is performed by the female alone for 11 days.
COMMENT Recently the Brown Towhee was "split" into two species, the Canyon Towhee and the California Towhee.

ABERT'S TOWHEE

Pipilo aberti   9½–10in/24–25cm

IDENTIFICATION Brown above, creamy below marked by a black 'face' that extends from forehead to behind the eye.
VOICE A rolling trill.
HABITAT Woodland thickets, orchards.
RANGE South-eastern California and Arizona.
MOVEMENTS Resident.
BREEDING Desert brush, canyon scrub, mesquite and suburbs; February-May.
NEST AND EGGS A cup of stems and other vegetation is placed in a low bush; the 2 to 5 eggs are bluish green, spotted brown.
INCUBATION The eggs are incubated by the female.
COMMENT Though similar to the Canyon Towhee, this is less of a mountain slope bird than that species.

WHITE-COLLARED SEEDEATER

Sporophila torqueola   4½in/11cm

IDENTIFICATION Small finch with brown upperparts, black wings, marked with double, white wing-bar, and rich buffy underparts. Half collar is buff.
VOICE Buzzing song.
HABITAT Brushy grasslands.
RANGE Scarce visitor to Rio Grande, Texas.
MOVEMENTS Migrant from Mexico.

BACHMAN'S SPARROW

Aimophila aestivalis   6in/15–16cm

IDENTIFICATION Large-billed, large-tailed sparrow. Crown and back gray, broadly streaked black; chestnut on wings. Underparts grayish with moustachial streak. Variable with western birds having much more chestnut, warm buff underparts, and largely lacking crown stripes.
VOICE Warbled trill.
HABITAT Pines and other dry woods.
RANGE South-eastern US.

MOVEMENTS Northern interior birds move southward for the winter.
BREEDING Clearings in deciduous and coniferous woodland, overgrown fields; April-May.
NEST AND EGGS A well-constructed nest of grasses, which may have a dome, is placed at the foot of a tussock or bush; the 3 to 5 eggs are white.
INCUBATION Performed by the female and lasting 14 days.
COMMENT Highly localized in south-eastern US where its secretive habits make location difficult.

BOTTERI'S SPARROW

Aimophila botterii   6in/15cm

IDENTIFICATION Similar to Cassin's sparrow. Large, pale sparrow with rows of chestnut streaking over crown and back. Long, rounded tail without white tips, plain buffy breast with hint of a darker band. Secretive.
VOICE Trilling.
HABITAT Scrub-covered grasslands.
RANGE South-eastern Arizona and lower Rio Grande valley of Texas.
MOVEMENTS Summer visitor.

CASSIN'S SPARROW

Aimophila cassinii   6in/15–16cm

IDENTIFICATION Chunky sparrow with heavy bill and long, white-tipped tail. Streaked crown and back; plain buffy underparts lack streaking, with white bib. Secretive. Similar Botteri's Sparrow of south-east Arizona and extreme south Texas, is darker, has a brown tail and a dry tinkling song.
HABITAT Dry grasslands.
RANGE South-western states, north into Nebraska.
MOVEMENTS Resident along Mexican border; more northerly birds move southward to winter.
BREEDING Dry, grassy hillsides with cactus; April-May.
NEST AND EGGS A well-hidden cup of vegetation, hidden on the ground at the foot of a bush; the 3 or 4 eggs are white.
INCUBATION Undescribed.
COMMENT Very much a secretive bird, save only when singing males proclaim their territories.

RUFOUS-WINGED SPARROW

Aimophila carpalis   5½–6in/14–15cm

IDENTIFICATION Grayish, brown-streaked above with characteristic chestnut patch at bend of wing and on folded flight feathers. Double pale wing-bar; long, rounded tail.
VOICE Chipping trill.
HABITAT Dry grasslands.
RANGE Southern Arizona.
MOVEMENTS Resident.

RUFOUS-CROWNED SPARROW

Aimophila ruficeps   6in/15–16cm

IDENTIFICATION A dusky, long-tailed sparrow with chestnut cap. Gray-brown upperparts; pale gray underparts; tail, long and pointed. Chestnut cap extends to nape; thin chestnut eye-stripe; black moustachial stripe make identification straightforward, if well seen. Spends much time on ground.
VOICE Jumble of chipping notes.
HABITAT Rocky slopes.
RANGE South-western states.
MOVEMENTS Mostly resident.

BREEDING From open woods to bushy upland slopes; March-May.
NEST AND EGGS A well-constructed cup of grasses placed on the ground; the 2 to 5 eggs are white.
INCUBATION Performed by the female.
COMMENT Often found among rocky outcrops that form a song post for the male.

AMERICAN TREE SPARROW

Spizella arborea   6–6½in/16–17cm

IDENTIFICATION Attractive, delicately colored sparrow. Upperparts are streaked rich chestnut with prominent white, double wing-bar. Underparts pale gray, extending to sides of head. Most obvious field marks are chestnut cap and dark central spot at breast. Thin line extends from behind eye; chestnut smudge at side of breast.
VOICE Thin warble.
HABITAT Taiga with scattered trees; winters marshes and neglected fields.
RANGE Northern Canada and Alaska.
MOVEMENTS Summer visitor; winters over most of US.
BREEDING Arctic scrub with willows and dwarf conifers, often along streamsides; June-July.

NEST AND EGGS A well-constructed cup of grasses is placed on the ground, sometimes in a low tree; the 4 to 6 eggs are pale blue green, spotted brown.

INCUBATION Lasts 12 or 13 days and is performed by the female alone.

COMMENT One of the most northerly breeding of all sparrows that migrates *en masse* to the US to winter.

CHIPPING SPARROW

Spizella passerina   6in/15cm

IDENTIFICATION A darkish sparrow, marked in breeding season by chestnut crown, broad white supercilium and thin, black, eye-stripe. Gray underparts extend to sides of head and nape. Upperparts dark, with chestnut streaking and white, double wing-bar. In winter, much less obvious with paler chestnut cap and gray nape.

VOICE Rapid, trilling *chip-chip-chip*.

HABITAT Suburbs, farmland.

RANGE Virtually the whole of temperate North America.

MOVEMENTS Largely a summer visitor, but resident in southern states.

BREEDING Woodland clearings, bushy thickets, orchards, suburbs; March-June.

NEST AND EGGS A neat cup of grasses lined with hair is placed at moderate height in a tree; the 3 to 5 eggs are blue, speckled with brown.

INCUBATION Lasts 11 days and is by the female with some assistance from her mate.

COMMENT A common and widespread bird that is a summer visitor over most of North America. Often found in gardens feeding on lawns.

CLAY-COLORED SPARROW

Spizella pallida   5½−6in/14−15cm

IDENTIFICATION Neatly marked sparrow with unstreaked underparts. Head shows light crown stripe; dark lateral streaking; broad, white supercilium; darkish ear coverts; and neat moustachial streak on white bib. Underparts are warm buffy.

VOICE Buzzing.

HABITAT Prairies, thickets.

RANGE Prairie Canada and adjacent US eastward through Great Lakes region.

MOVEMENTS Summer visitor; winters south-west Texas and beyond.

BREEDING Thickets and scrub along rivers and beside ponds, but also dry thickets; May–July.

NEST AND EGGS A cup of grasses lined with hair placed low in a tree; the 3 to 5 eggs are green blue, spotted brown.

INCUBATION Lasts 10 to 12 days and is shared by both members of the pair.

COMMENT A successful species that is slowly expanding its range eastwards and which may be worth looking out for along the Atlantic coast on migration.

BREWER'S SPARROW

Spizella breweri   5½–6in/14–15cm

IDENTIFICATION Similar to Clay-colored Sparrow, but much less contrasted. Streaked crown and upperparts, buffy underparts. Buffy supercilium, dark ear coverts and thin moustachial streak.

VOICE Trilling.

HABITAT Chapparal and sagebrush country.

RANGE Interior west with extension northward into adjacent Canada.

MOVEMENTS Summer visitor; winters Mexican border states.

BREEDING Bushy areas mostly at altitude; April–June.

NEST AND EGGS A cup of stems lined with hair is placed in a low bush, often sagebrush; the 3 or 4 eggs are bluish green, spotted brown.

INCUBATION Lasts 12 or 13 days.

COMMENT A common bird on scrubby areas in mountain meadows and among sagebrush.

FIELD SPARROW

Spizella pusilla   5–6in/14–15cm

IDENTIFICATION A small, pale sparrow marked by a gray head, topped with a rusty-brown cap. The stubby bill and the legs are pinkish; there is a narrow white eye ring. Upperparts are boldly streaked brown-black with gray and chestnut, the rump is unstreaked and there are two bold, white wing bars. The outer tail feathers are gray. Underparts are pale gray with a warm wash on breast and flanks.

VOICE Whistles that roll into a trill.

HABITAT Fields and bushy country.

RANGE Eastern US extending into southern Canada and US prairies.

MOVEMENTS Partial migrant, leaving northern part of range moving southwards into Florida and much of Texas.

BREEDING May–June.

NEST AND EGGS Cup of grasses in low bush; the 2 to 5 eggs are blue gray, spotted brown.

INCUBATION Lasts 11 or 12 days by the female.

COMMENT This close relative resembles the Tree Sparrow, but has a pink bill and lacks the chest spot of that tundra-breeding species. Western birds are generally paler and less colorful.

BLACK-CHINNED SPARROW

Spizella atrogularis   6in/15–16cm

IDENTIFICATION Distinctive gray sparrow with chestnut-streaked back and wings. Male has black around base of bill extending to form prominent bib, lacking in female. Both sexes have pale, ivory bill. Could be mistaken for Dark-eyed Junco, but chestnut back is distinctive.

VOICE Plaintive start to trill.
HABITAT Chaparral and brushy hillsides.
RANGE California and border states.
MOVEMENTS California birds are summer visitors.
BREEDING Chaparral and sagebrush slopes in mountains;
April-May.
NEST AND EGGS A grassy cup placed in a dense low bush; the
2 to 5 eggs are blue, sometimes spotted brown.
INCUBATION Lasts 13 days.
COMMENT Though rather secretive, the song of the male is a
distinctly pleasant trilling that has been likened to that of a
Canary.

VESPER SPARROW

Pooecetes gramineus　　6–6½in/16–17cm

IDENTIFICATION Well-streaked sparrow with short, white-edged tail. Lacks prominent supercilium of many other sparrows, but has dark ear coverts, pale eye-ring and clear moustachial streak. Chestnut shoulder patch usually difficult to see.

VOICE Pleasant trilling.
HABITAT Grasslands, farmsteads.
RANGE Breeds over most of temperate North America, though absent from southern states.
MOVEMENTS Summer visitor; winters southern states.
BREEDING Open, weed-covered areas such as neglected fields and roadsides; May-June.
NEST AND EGGS A cup of grasses, lined with fine grasses, is placed on the ground; the 3 to 6 eggs are white, spotted brown.
INCUBATION The eggs take 11 to 14 days to hatch and are incubated by the female alone.
COMMENT This fine songster was given the name "Vesper" because it was thought to sing better in the evening.

LARK SPARROW

Chondestes grammacus　　6½–7in/17–18cm

IDENTIFICATION Brown above, grayish below with distinctive head pattern and small black patch on breast. Crown and face shows pattern of stripes in chestnut, black and white. In flight, white outer feathers contrast with black tail.
VOICE Extended trills and buzzes.
HABITAT Prairies and other open areas.
RANGE Most of US except eastern coastal states; also south-west Canada.
MOVEMENTS Summer visitor; winters Florida, Gulf coast and Mexican border states.

BREEDING Neglected open areas with bushes; April-June.
NEST AND EGGS A cup of stems lined with fine grasses is placed on the ground or low in a bush; the 3 to 5 eggs are white, spotted black.
INCUBATION Lasts for 10 or 11 days and is by the female alone.
COMMENT A declining species that seems to be withdrawing from the eastern parts of its range.

BLACK-THROATED SPARROW

Amphispiza bilineata   5½in/14cm

IDENTIFICATION Neat brown and white bird, marked by black bib extending to a point on the breast. Brown head shows contrasting white supercilium and moustachial streak. Immature has gray head with bold white supercilium. White in outer tail, small bill.
VOICE Trilling.
HABITAT Dry hillsides and deserts.
RANGE From Oregon and Wyoming southward and east to central Texas.
MOVEMENTS Northern birds move southward in winter.
BREEDING Dry desert with cactus or sagebrush; March-May.
NEST AND EGGS A cup of available stems lined with fine grasses and placed in a bush or cholla cactus; the 3 or 4 eggs are white, washed pale blue.
INCUBATION Undescribed.
COMMENT This bird inhabits some of the hottest and driest desert in North America.

SAGE SPARROW

Amphispiza belli   6–6½in/16–17cm

IDENTIFICATION Large, ground-dwelling sparrow with gray head; brownish upperparts, white underparts with flank streaking and small, black breast spot. White supercilium and moustachial streak are most obvious in much darker Californian form. A great runner.
VOICE Series of thin notes.
HABITAT Dry, arid flats, sagebrush, chapparal.
RANGE Western US.
MOVEMENTS Resident California; inland birds of Great Basin move southward to winter.
BREEDING Chaparral and sagebrush hillsides; April-May.
NEST AND EGGS A cup of vegetation, often sagebrush, lined with softer materials and placed in a sagebrush; the 3 to 5 eggs are white, washed blue and speckled brown.
INCUBATION Lasts 13 days.
COMMENT A very secretive bird that keeps well inside dense cover for most of the year.

FIVE-STRIPED SPARROW

Amphispiza quinquestriata   6in/15cm

IDENTIFICATION Large, dark sparrow with dark brown upperparts marked by narrow, white supercilium and moustachial streak. White bib and gray breast with small black spot. Decidedly rare.
VOICE Trill.
HABITAT Thickets on dry hillsides.
RANGE Southernmost Arizona.
MOVEMENTS Mostly summer visitor.

LARK BUNTING

Calamospiza melanocorys   7−7½in/18−19cm

IDENTIFICATION Male in summer is black, with thick, chunky bill and broad white wing patches. Female is brown above and streaked below, with broad buff wing patch and buffy supercilium extending around ear coverts. Winter male resembles female, but with white supercilium and moustachial streak joining to enclose dark ear coverts. Some black on throat and upper breast.
VOICE Whistling trills, often in flight.
HABITAT Dry grassland.
RANGE Central US and adjacent Canadian prairies.
MOVEMENTS Summer visitor; winters Texas and Mexican border.
BREEDING Prairie grasslands with sagebrush; May-June.
NEST AND EGGS A loose cup of grasses placed on the ground beneath the shelter of a smaller bush; the 4 to 6 eggs are pale blue.
INCUBATION The eggs take 12 days to hatch and incubation is shared between the pair.
COMMENT These are gregarious birds, even in the breeding season when the song flight of the males makes location relatively easy.

SAVANNAH SPARROW

Passerculus sandwichensis   5½−6in/14−15cm

IDENTIFICATION A brown and buff streaked sparrow with shortish, notched tail and some yellow on the 'face'. Highly variable coloration, but all birds have a prominent supercilium (often yellow); a bold, double moustachial streak; and pale

coronal stripe. Otherwise they may be heavily streaked, as in California; plain backed and lightly streaked below, as in Colorado; or totally washed out, as in the formerly specific Ipswich Sparrow of Nova Scotia.
VOICE A repeated *chip* followed by a trill.
HABITAT Open ground.
RANGE From tundra to southern California, but absent from many southern states.
MOVEMENTS Mainly summer visitor; winters southern and coastal states.
BREEDING Wide variety of open habitats from meadows to salt marshes; March-July.
NEST AND EGGS A hollow on the ground lined with grass; the 4 to 6 eggs are white, spotted brown.
INCUBATION Lasts 12 to 14 days and is shared by both sexes.
COMMENT One of the most widespread and variable of North American songbirds ranging from Alaska to Florida.

BAIRD'S SPARROW

Ammodramus bairdii   5½−6in/14−15cm

IDENTIFICATION A well-marked, chunky sparrow with clear-cut pattern of head stripes. "Face" is usually warm buff with coronal stripe, lateral stripe, broad supercilium, double moustachial streak, and white bib bordered below by neat rows of streaks that extend over the breast and continue along the flanks. This is a species that exhibits almost all the facial markings by which sparrows are identified. Upperparts are streaked buff and brown, with rich chestnut on the scapulars.
VOICE Warble and trill.

INCUBATION Lasts 11 or 12 days and is probably by the female alone.

COMMENT It is a peculiar quirk that the scientific name of this species is *A. savannarum*, yet it is not the 'Savannah Sparrow'.

HABITAT Prairies.

RANGE Prairies either side of Canadian border; scarce and declining.

MOVEMENTS Summer visitor; winters Arizona and adjacent Mexico.

BREEDING Long, grass-covered areas with a scattering of bushes; May-June.

NEST AND EGGS A cup of grasses placed on the ground; the 4 to 6 eggs are white, spotted brown.

INCUBATION Lasts 11 days and is performed by the female alone.

COMMENT Highly restricted range both in summer and winter and, as a result, quite definitely declining in numbers.

GRASSHOPPER SPARROW

Ammodramus savannarum   5 – 5½in/13–14cm

IDENTIFICATION A short-tailed, large-headed sparrow of chunky appearance and proportionately large bill. Streaked above; plain buffy below with light flank-streaking only in some sub-species. Most have a clear coronal stripe.

VOICE Double *chip* followed by a buzz.

HABITAT Grassland.

RANGE Breeds over most of US and border Canada, though absent from large areas of the west.

MOVEMENTS Summer visitor; winters Atlantic and Gulf coast states and along Mexican border.

BREEDING Dry prairies and grasslands, preferably a little neglected; April-June.

NEST AND EGGS A cup of grasses, lined with hair, hidden on the ground; the 4 or 5 eggs are white, speckled brown.

HENSLOW'S SPARROW

Ammodramus henslowii   5in/13cm

IDENTIFICATION A thick-set, large-headed sparrow with rich-chestnut upperparts. Olive-gray head with yellow-buff coronal stripe, double moustachial streak, and neat, white bib. Nape is plain olive-gray forming a half collar. Upperparts chestnut; underparts buffy, with neat streaks on breast and flanks.

VOICE *See-lic*.

HABITAT Damp fields.

RANGE North-eastern US.

MOVEMENTS Summer visitor; winters Florida and Gulf coast.

BREEDING Fields of long grass mixed with weeds; May-June.
NEST AND EGGS A cup placed on the ground, sometimes a little above, among weeds; the 3 to 5 eggs are white, spotted brown.
INCUBATION The eggs take 10 or 11 days to hatch and are incubated by the female alone.
COMMENT Although best located by its song, it most frequently sings at dusk and even at night.

LE CONTE'S SPARROW

Ammodramus leconteii   5in/13cm

IDENTIFICATION Easily identified if well seen. Combination of white coronal stripe, black lateral crown stripe and broad, orange supercilium separate from all other sparrows. White underparts with orange breast band is shared only with Sharp-tailed Sparrow which is always darker above. Generally very secretive.

VOICE Buzzing.
HABITAT Damp grassland.
RANGE Canadian prairies and grasslands.
MOVEMENTS Summer visitor; winters Gulf coast and adjacent states.
BREEDING Well-vegetated marshy margins with bushy tangles; May-June.
NEST AND EGGS A cup of grasses placed on the ground or in a tussock; the 4 or 5 eggs have a greenish wash and are spotted brown.
INCUBATION Lasts 13 days and is by the female alone.
COMMENT Though fairly common, the secretive habits of this mouse-like skulker make it difficult to see.

SHARP-TAILED SPARROW

Ammodramus caudacutus   5in/13cm

IDENTIFICATION Dark chestnut above, usually with fine white streaking. Whitish below with warm buff-to-orange wash on breast, sometimes streaked. Best field marks are gray coronal stripe and nape, and broad, orange supercilium. Considerable color variation.
VOICE A trill.

HABITAT Shorelines, lake margins.
RANGE Breeds across Canadian prairies and along Atlantic coast of US.
MOVEMENTS Prairie birds are summer visitors wintering along Florida and Gulf coasts. Atlantic birds are resident.
BREEDING Waterside vegetation, both coastal and inland; June-July.
NEST AND EGGS A cup of grasses is placed on the ground; the 4 to 6 eggs are greenish-blue, spotted with brown.
INCUBATION By the female alone for 12 days.
COMMENT Even during the breeding season this sparrow retains its gregarious habits by breeding in loose colonies.

SEASIDE SPARROW

Ammodramus maritimus   6in/15–16cm

IDENTIFICATION Highly variable. All forms have thinnish, pointed bill; short, pointed tail; and yellow patch between bill and eye. Head, though variable in coloration, is plain rather than heavily marked like many other sparrows; all have a moustachial streak. Gulf coast birds have yellow on head and chestnut back; Atlantic birds are much grayer.

VOICE Buzzing.
HABITAT Tidal marshes.
RANGE Atlantic and
Gulf coasts of US.
MOVEMENTS Resident.
BREEDING Wet areas of saltmarshes; April-July.
NEST AND EGGS A cup of grasses placed in a grassy clump above high tide mark; the 3 to 6 eggs are white, spotted brown.
INCUBATION By the female alone for 11 days.
COMMENT Curiously among the sparrows, this bird does not eat many seeds, but takes mainly small marine creatures and insects as food.

FOX SPARROW

Passerella iliaca   7−7½in/18−19cm

IDENTIFICATION A large sparrow that is variable both in plumage and structure. Most have rusty rump and tail, many have gray crown and back, all have spotting or streaking on underparts.
VOICE Whistling and buzzing.
HABITAT Undergrowth in woodland, hedgerows or willow thickets.
RANGE Boreal Canada and Alaska southward through Rockies.
MOVEMENTS Summer visitor; winters Pacific coast and across southern states.

BREEDING Scrub and thickets of a wide variety of types; May-June.
NEST AND EGGS A cup of twigs and grasses lined with hair is situated on the ground beneath a bush; the 4 or 5 eggs are white, washed blue or green and spotted brown.
INCUBATION Lasts 12 to 14 days and is performed by the female, probably alone.
COMMENT Breeding in a vast area across the Canadian Arctic and the western mountains, a large number of distinct sub-species have been described.

SONG SPARROW

Melospiza melodia   6−6½in/16−17cm

IDENTIFICATION Though highly variable, all Song Sparrows have a broad, gray supercilium; dark, moustachial streak; long, rounded tail, and spotting or streaking on the breast. Most show chestnut in the wings and the breast streaking, though variable, usually forms a solid spot on the breast.
VOICE Varied clear notes followed by a trill.
HABITAT Scrub and waterside thickets.
RANGE Most of North America, except southern US.
MOVEMENTS Canadian birds are mostly summer visitors; winters southern US.
BREEDING Bushy thickets around wetlands, but also in dry locations; April-June.
NEST AND EGGS A cup of grasses lined with finer grasses or hair is placed variably on the ground or in a small bush; the 3 to 5 eggs are blue-green, spotted brown.
INCUBATION Lasts 12 to 15 days and is performed by the female alone.
COMMENT One of the most intensively studied birds.

LINCOLN'S SPARROW

Melospiza lincolnii   6in/15–16cm

IDENTIFICATION Neatly streaked brown and black upperparts, with chestnut in the wing, contrast with whitish belly. Breast is warm buff, finely streaked black. Head pattern has gray coronal stripe, with chestnut and black lateral crown stripes and a broad, gray supercilium; dark ear coverts and thin moustachial streak. Somewhat secretive.

VOICE Pleasant trilling.

HABITAT Marshes and grasslands in summer; dense thickets in winter.

RANGE Boreal Alaska and Canada extending southward into the Great Lakes region and through the interior west.

MOVEMENTS Summer visitor; winters southern US; resident Pacific US.

BREEDING Bogs and marshes with thickets of willow and alder; May-June.

NEST AND EGGS A cup of grasses placed on the ground; the 4 or 5 eggs are white, speckled brown.

INCUBATION Lasts 13 days and is performed by the female.

COMMENT This bird is not named after Abraham Lincoln, but after the little known Robert Lincoln, a companion of Audubon.

SWAMP SPARROW

Melospiza georgiana   6in/15–16cm

IDENTIFICATION A well-marked, rather dark sparrow. In summer has rich chestnut cap that is absent in winter. At all times the gray face, with double moustachial streak, gray supercilium and white bib are characteristic. Shows more chestnut in wings and on rump than other sparrows. Underparts gray with chestnut-streaked flanks.

VOICE Pleasant trill.

HABITAT Well-vegetated marshes.

RANGE Temperate Canada and north-eastern US.

MOVEMENTS Summer visitor; winters southern states; resident north-east US.

BREEDING Cattails and other emergent vegetation around ponds and bogs; May-June.

NEST AND EGGS A loose cup of grasses placed in a marshy tussock; the 4 or 5 eggs are blue green, spotted brown.

INCUBATION Lasts some 12 to 15 days and is performed by the female.

COMMENT A secretive bird that is something of a loner and which needs patience and skill to locate.

WHITE-THROATED SPARROW

Zonotrichia albicollis   6½−7in/17−18cm

IDENTIFICATION Large, ground-dwelling sparrow with typical hunched appearance. Bold pattern of head stripes similar to White-crowned Sparrow, but in some birds coronal stripe is gray and eyebrow a warm buff. In others, these may be white as in White-crowned Sparrow, but with a yellow area at the front of the supercilium. White bib and rich chestnut upperparts are both useful features.
VOICE Thin *dee-dee, diddla-diddla-diddla*.
HABITAT Thickets in woodland and suburbs.
RANGE Breeds over much of temperate and boreal Canada into the north-eastern US.
MOVEMENTS Summer visitor; winters through much of lowland US, especially in the east, but also in coastal California. Resident north-eastern US.
BREEDING Clearings and burnt-over areas in conifer and mixed woods; May-July.
NEST AND EGGS A cup of twigs and grasses, lined with finer materials, placed on the ground in the shelter of a bush; the 3 to 5 eggs are pale, washed gray, or green and spotted brown.
INCUBATION Lasts 11 to 14 days and is performed by the female.
COMMENT Abundant in most areas of North America at one season or another, except the extreme west.

GOLDEN-CROWNED SPARROW

Zonotrichia atricapilla   7−7½in/18−19cm

IDENTIFICATION Large, dark sparrow with yellow and black crown pattern. Upperparts striped black and brown with chestnut in the wings and a clear, white, double wing-bar. Underparts buffy-brown with gray chin extending to sides of head. In winter, the head pattern is subdued.
VOICE Rasped, three- or five-note series.
HABITAT Meadows and waterside thickets at altitude.
RANGE Alaska along Pacific coast of Canada.
MOVEMENTS Winters Pacific coast of US.
BREEDING Shrub-covered areas above the tree-line; June-July.
NEST AND EGGS A cup placed on the ground or in a low bush; the 4 or 5 eggs are greenish buff, spotted brown.
INCUBATION Performed by the female, lasting 13 days.
COMMENT Even in winter, when they descend from the mountains, these birds remain in dense cover and are difficult to see.

WHITE-CROWNED SPARROW

Zonotrichia leucophrys   7−7½in/18−19cm

IDENTIFICATION Streaked buff and brown above; unstreaked grayish below extending to sides of head and nape. Distinctive crown pattern of black and white stripes; only White-throated Sparrow shows similar pattern in some areas. Conical, pink bill.
VOICE Whistles and trills.
HABITAT Open areas, scrub, grassland.
RANGE Breeds across northern Canada and Alaska and southward through most of the west.
MOVEMENTS Southern birds are resident; northern populations winter over much of US.

Breeding Woodland edges, bushy country, thickets; March-July.

Nest and eggs Large structure of twigs and grasses placed on the ground near a bush; the 4 or 5 eggs are pale gray-blue, spotted brown.

Incubation Lasts 9 to 15 days and is performed by the female alone.

Comment Often found with, but outnumbered by, White-throated Sparrow in the eastern parts of its range.

HARRIS'S SPARROW

Zonotrichia querula   7½−8½in/19−21cm

Identification Large, long-tailed, pink-billed sparrow. In summer, has black crown and bib contrasting with gray sides of head, marked with a black comma. In winter, sides of head are buffy. Upperparts neatly striped black and buff with bold, double wing-bar. Underparts white in summer, but with buffy flanks in winter.

Voice Extended whistles.

Habitat Stunted boreal forest; in winter open scrub.

Range Mackenzie and northern Manitoba.

Movements Winters central US.

Breeding Dwarf vegetation between tundra and boreal forest; June-July.

Nest and eggs A neat cup of twigs lined with grasses hidden on the ground at the foot of a shrub; the 3 to 5 eggs are grayish green, spotted brown.

Incubation Lasts at least 13 days.

Comment A far northern breeder that has been little studied in its Arctic headquarters.

DARK-EYED JUNCO

Junco hyemalis   6−6½in/16−17cm

Identification Former division into four distinct species indicates variability of plumage. Male has gray of upperparts extending to breast, with paler or white belly. Head may be black; back may be brown; belly may be washed pinkish. Most have pale, conical bill, and dark eye. Female is brown above and white below. All have broad white margins to tail. Closely related Yellow-eyed Junco of southern Arizona mountains, has yellow eyes, dark lores, and a rufous back

Voice Pleasant trill.

Habitat Woodlands in summer; catholic in winter.

Range From Alaska to Newfoundland southward, through northern US extending south through western mountains and Appalachians.

Movements Northern birds move southward to winter throughout US.

BREEDING Clearings in woodlands, both coniferous and mixed; March-July.

NEST AND EGGS A cup of roots and mosses lined with hair is placed in a crevice or hidden on the ground; the 4 to 6 eggs are white, spotted brown.

INCUBATION Lasts 11 or 12 days and is performed by the female.

COMMENT A widespread bird that is found throughout North America at one season or another.

YELLOW-EYED JUNCO

Junco phaeonotus   6–6½in/15–16cm

IDENTIFICATION Very similar to "Gray-headed" form of Dark-eyed Junco with gray plumage and brown saddle. Underparts buffy, rather than gray. Bright pale eye.
VOICE Whistled trills.
HABITAT Mountain conifers.
RANGE South-eastern Arizona.
MOVEMENTS Resident.

McCOWN'S LONGSPUR

Calcarius mccownii   6in/16cm

IDENTIFICATION Summer male has black cap, moustachial streak and crescent-shaped breast band. Otherwise rather gray. Female is buffy, with broad supercilium and hint of breast band. In winter, both sexes are buffy, the male with a remnant breast band. Thick bill, chestnut patch at bend of wing and black-tipped, white tail are standard in all plumages.
VOICE Warbles in song flight.

HABITAT Shortgrass plains.
RANGE Prairies of Colorado to central Alberta.
MOVEMENTS Summer visitor; winters northern and western Texas and adjacent states.
BREEDING Lightly grassed fields; May-June.
NEST AND EGGS A depression on the ground is lined with a few bents; the 3 to 5 eggs are white, variably marked brown.
INCUBATION Lasts 12 days and is performed by the female alone.
COMMENT In winter, this bird may frequently be found on ploughed fields in company with Horned Larks.

LAPLAND LONGSPUR

Calcarius lapponicus   6–6½in/16–17cm

IDENTIFICATION Summer male has black head and breast broken by white line behind the eye that extends as margin to black throat and breast. Chestnut nape. Female duller, but with chestnut nape. In winter, loses much of summer plumage to become dull brown with pale coronal stripe in some plumages, or with chestnut nape in others. Always shows much chestnut in wings in winter.
VOICE Warbling in flight.
HABITAT High tundra; winters shores and stubbles.
RANGE Arctic Alaska and Canada.
MOVEMENTS Winters across most of US, but not southern states.
BREEDING Damp areas among Arctic tundra often with tussocks; June-July.
NEST AND EGGS A nest of grasses is hidden in a tussock or

under a shrub; the 4 to 6 eggs are greenish with speckling of brown.
INCUBATION Lasts 11 to 13 days and is performed by the female.
COMMENT Performs a delightful song-flight over the open barren areas of the whole of the northern Arctic.

SMITH'S LONGSPUR

Calcarius pictus   6−6½in/16−17cm

IDENTIFICATION Summer male is rich orange below, with orange nape and richly streaked back. Head is black, with broad white supercilium and cheek patch producing unique pattern. Female and winter male have striped crown, buffy supercilium and warm buff underparts, lightly streaked black. White outer tail feathers.
VOICE Warbling ending in a flourish.
HABITAT Tundra.
RANGE Arctic Canada and south-central Alaska.
MOVEMENTS Summer visitor; winters in south-central states.
BREEDING Tussocky tundra well beyond the tree-line; June-July.
NEST AND EGGS A cup of grasses, lined with feathers, is placed in a tussock; the 4 to 6 eggs are greenish blue, spotted brown.
INCUBATION The eggs take 11 or 12 days to hatch.
COMMENT This scarce bird is a distinct loner and never forms flocks, even in winter, though sometimes it associates with Lapland Longspurs.

CHESTNUT-COLLARED LONGSPUR

Calcarius ornatus   6in/15−16cm

IDENTIFICATION Unmistakeable when breeding. Crown, margins to ear coverts and underparts all black; "face" yellow; nape chestnut. In winter, buffy with black scaling on underparts; female buffy. Grayish-white tail, tipped black.
VOICE Melodic warbling.
HABITAT Moist upland prairies.
RANGE Prairies both sides of US-Canada border.
MOVEMENTS Summer visitor; winters north and eastern Texas to southern New Mexico.
BREEDING Prairies and other short-grass plains; May-June.
NEST AND EGGS A cup of grasses placed in a hollow where it is hidden by grass; the 4 to 6 eggs are buffy gray, spotted brown.
INCUBATION The eggs take some 12 or 13 days to hatch and are incubated by the female alone.
COMMENT In spring, the songs of the males are a characteristic sound of the prairies, where they are relatively common.

SNOW BUNTING

Plectrophenax nivalis   6½−7in/17−18cm

IDENTIFICATION In all plumages, shows white inner wing in flight. Summer male is white with black back, wings and central tail. In winter, both sexes have buff washed crowns, with warm buffy tones on sides of head and breast. Similar McKay's Bunting, with less black on wings and tail.
VOICE Pleasant twitters or short buzz.
HABITAT Tundra.
RANGE Northern Alaska and Canada.
MOVEMENTS Summer visitor; winters from southern Alaska and Pacific Canada across whole of US and southern Canada.
BREEDING Breeds on Bering Sea islands and is uncommon in winter on Alaskan mainland or southward.
NEST AND EGGS Rocky crevices and holes under rocks are used to hold the grassy and mossy cup; the 4 to 7 eggs are whitish, spotted brown.
INCUBATION Lasts 12 or 13 days and is performed by the female.
COMMENT A common bird that is gregarious throughout the year, but which breeds farther north than any other perching bird.

MC KAY'S BUNTING

Plectrophenax hyperboreus   6½−7in/16−18cm

IDENTIFICATION Similar to Snow Bunting, but with much less black on upperparts. Male has white back, female white mottled black.
VOICE Warbling.
HABITAT Isolated islands.
RANGE Islands of Bering Sea.
MOVEMENTS Some winter west Alaskan coasts.

BOBOLINK

Dolichonyx oryzivorus   7−8in/18−20cm

IDENTIFICATION Summer male is boldly marked in black with a white bar across the wing, white rump, and a creamy hood on the nape. At other times it resembles the female and immature which are streaked black and buff above, and buffy below. The striped head pattern; stubby, sparrow-like bill; and pointed tail-feathers are the best field marks.
VOICE Loud *bob-o-link*.
HABITAT Grasslands.
RANGE Right across northern US and southern Canada.
MOVEMENTS Summer visitor; migrates south-eastward to South America.
BREEDING Grassy fields and margins, also crops; May-July.
NEST AND EGGS A lightly built cup of grasses is placed on the ground among ground vegetation; the 4 to 7 eggs are gray, spotted brown.
INCUBATION Lasts 10 to 13 days and is performed by the female.
COMMENT Sometimes called 'rice bird' in the southern US, where it consumes large amounts of seeds in winter.

M.J.PLEDGER

FINCHES & WEAVER FINCHES

THIS is a relatively small group of seed-eating birds that, while bearing a strong resemblance to the sparrows, is sufficiently distinct to merit separate treatment. Though closely related, these birds bear a variety of different vernacular names, including grosbeak, sparrow, and finch. By and large they are adaptable and successful birds that have probably benefited from the coming of man. All of the different species have chunky, seed-eating bills, while a small group have become highly specialized feeders and have crossed mandibles to extract the seeds from pine cones. They vary enormously in coloration, with some being among the brightest of all American birds.

The crossbills have crossed mandibles that are perfectly adapted to prising conifer seeds from their hard cones. They are thus highly specialized and are seldom found far from conifers. The Red Crossbill has a far larger and more powerful bill than the White-winged Crossbill, indicating its ability to deal with larger and harder cones than that species.

In sharp contrast, the American Goldfinch boasts a delicate tweezer of a bill that is perfect for picking seeds from the heads of thistles. Watching one of these dainty little finches manipulate a thistle seed with its bill, separating the kernel from its "parachute", before swallowing, is a revealing experience. In summer the male is bright yellow with black cap, wings, and tail and is, not surprisingly, known as the "canary" in many parts of the country. The Pine Siskin is duller, but remarkably similar in size, shape, and bill construction. It too is a picker, but one that specializes in picking seeds from the cones of alders. The Redpoll is similar in structure, though quite distinctly colored. It spends much of its time in buzzing flocks feeding on the catkins of birches, where it frequently hangs upside-down like a chickadee. All in all, this is a successful group of birds which has proved highly adaptable to the changing environment and which brings a great deal of pleasure to anyone who is prepared to provide food at a feeding station.

One of the most successful members of the weaver finches is the House Sparrow which, in a mere hundred years, has spread throughout inhabited North America. Introduced from Europe, and still often called the "English Sparrow," this is, in fact, one of the world's most successful birds. Wherever there is permanent human habitation, the sparrow will be able to find a living feeding on spilled food, waste, and even on food kindly supplied for other species. It nests in homes and other buildings, forming huge flocks in the fall and roaming the fields in search of wasted grain. The other introduced weaver finch is the Eurasian Tree Sparrow which has not spread far from its initial release site of St. Louis.

Garden birds come in all shapes and sizes to a suburban feeding station. A cardinal, Blue Jay, Black-capped Chickadee, and American Robin all feed together at the table. Above, purple martins fly to their tenement, while below, a Ruby-throated Hummingbird feeds at a fuchsia.

ROSY FINCH

Leucosticte arctoa   6–6½in/16–17cm

IDENTIFICATION Formerly divided among three distinct species, now regarded as conspecific. Male has brown back and breast, pink rump and underparts, pink on the wing coverts and a gray nape below a black crest. Though varying from pale to dark forms, there is no difficulty in identifying the males as this species. Female is brown with pale, double wing-bar. Confiding.
VOICE High-pitched chipping notes.
HABITAT Tundra, taiga and mountains above tree line.
RANGE From Alaska southward through the Rockies to northern New Mexico.
MOVEMENTS Resident, but does wander eastward in winter.
BREEDING Rocky areas of tundra and mountains; April-June.
NEST AND EGGS Cavities among rocky areas of many types are lined with vegetation to form a large untidy nest; the 3 to 5 eggs are white.
INCUBATION Lasts 12 to 14 days and is performed by the female.
COMMENT Though they vary in plumage and size, there is no doubting the identity of the various subspecies of Rosy Finch.

PINE GROSBEAK

Pinicola enucleator   9–10in/23–25cm

IDENTIFICATION Largest of the "red" finches, with chunky shape accentuated by smallish head and bill. Male is red above and below, with black tail, and black wings marked by white, double wing-bar. Female lacks red and is warm orange-buff on head and nape, otherwise gray.

VOICE Low warbling with nasal ending.
HABITAT Conifer woods, also deciduous woods in winter.
RANGE Boreal Canada to northern New England and southward through the US Rockies.
MOVEMENTS Northernmost birds move southward on irregular irruptive pattern.
BREEDING Coniferous woods with open glades and clearings; May-July.

NEST AND EGGS A nest of twigs is placed in a conifer at no great height; the 4 or 5 eggs are blue green, spotted brown.
INCUBATION The eggs take 13 or 14 days to hatch and are incubated by the female.
COMMENT Though these are migrants, they tend to keep very much to pines, though hard weather may bring them into gardens and parks.

PURPLE FINCH

Carpodacus purpureus   6in/15–16cm

IDENTIFICATION Male is rosy-pink on head, back and underparts, with pinkish margins to the wing feathers. Female is streaked brown on buff above and below creating a highly contrasting, striped impression. In particular, the pale supercilium is more prominent than in related species.
VOICE Pleasant warble.
HABITAT Conifer and mixed woodland.
RANGE Boreal Canada extending southward through Pacific

states and the Great Lakes area to north-eastern US.
MOVEMENTS Boreal zone birds move southward to winter
throughout eastern US.
BREEDING Conifer and mixed woods with open areas;
May-June.
NEST AND EGGS A nest of twigs and grasses is placed often
quite high, usually in a conifer; the 4 to 6 eggs are blue,
spotted brown.
INCUBATION Lasts for some 13 days by the female, possibly
also by the male.
COMMENT A gregarious finch outside the breeding season
which wanders through suburbs and parks, as well as other
woodland.

MOVEMENTS Resident, but some movement to areas where it
does not breed to south-western states.
BREEDING Conifers at considerable altitude; May-July.
NEST AND EGGS A nest of twigs lined with grass is
constructed in a conifer, often at some height; the 4 or 5 eggs
are blue green, speckled with brown.
INCUBATION Lasts 12 days and is performed by the female
alone.
COMMENT Ecologically separated from the closely related
Purple Finch by its preference for montane forests where it
frequents yellow pines and other conifers.

CASSIN'S FINCH

Carpodacus cassinii   6−6½in/16−17cm

IDENTIFICATION Similar to Purple Finch with wash of pink
over adult male. Differs in having brown nape; contrasting
black and buff streaked back; fine streaking on flanks and
undertail coverts. Female is less contrastingly streaked than
female Purple Finch with less prominent supercilium.
VOICE Pleasant warbling, longer than Purple Finch.
HABITAT Forests at altitude.
RANGE Mountain forests from southern British Columbia to
northern Arizona and New Mexico.

HOUSE FINCH

Carpodacus mexicanus   6in/15−16cm

IDENTIFICATION Male has red band extending from forehead
over eye, and a red breast. Crown and upperparts are brown;
belly buff, streaked brown. Bill is short and stubby. Female is
brownish, streaked dark brown above and below.
VOICE Warbling with some nasal notes.
HABITAT Dry ranchland, suburbs and hillsides to considerable
altitude.
RANGE Western US; introduced in east where spreading
rapidly southwards.
MOVEMENTS Resident, but may winter in new areas prior to
colonization.
BREEDING Wide range of mainly dry habitats in the west but
also suburbs and gardens; March-May.
NEST AND EGGS Cavities in trees, buildings, nest boxes and
disused nests of other species are lined with a variety of

MOVEMENTS Irruptive across much of US on irregular basis.
BREEDING Conifer forests; February–July.
NEST AND EGGS The twiggy nest is lined with moss and placed high on the outer branches of a tall conifer; the 3 to 5 eggs are blue, spotted brown.
INCUBATION Lasts 12 to 15 days and is performed by the female alone.
COMMENT Though often an early nester, starting when there is still heavy snow on the ground, these birds will nest almost throughout the year.

materials; the 4 or 5 eggs are blue, spotted black.
INCUBATION The eggs take 12 to 14 days to hatch and are incubated by the female.
COMMENT The provision of suitable nest sites may encourage these successful birds to breed colonially.

WHITE-WINGED CROSSBILL

Loxia leucoptera   6½–7in/17–18cm

RED CROSSBILL

Loxia curvirostra   6–6½in/16–17cm

IDENTIFICATION Male is red with brownish wings and tail. Large head and crossed mandibles. Female greenish-yellow. Size, as well as size of bill, varies considerably. In flight, short tail and thick neck creates a curiously chunky silhouette.
VOICE Warbling; distinct *jip* in flight.
HABITAT Coniferous forests.
RANGE Boreal Canada southward through western mountains.

IDENTIFICATION Similar to Red Crossbill, but marked in both sexes by bold, white, double wing-bar. Note white tips to tertials and smaller head and bill.
VOICE Warbles; *chet-chet* in flight.
HABITAT Coniferous forests.
RANGE Boreal Alaska and Canada to northern US Rockies.
MOVEMENTS Irregular, irruptive movements southward over much of northern half of US.
BREEDING Conifer forests; February–May.
NEST AND EGGS A nest of twigs lined with lichens in a conifer; the 3 or 4 eggs are pale green, spotted brown.
INCUBATION Performed by the female alone for 12 to 14 days.
COMMENT Like the Red Crossbill, this species is quite capable of breeding at almost any time of the year.

COMMON REDPOLL

Carduelis flammea   5in/13cm

IDENTIFICATION Neat, arboreal finch with pink breast in summer male. Both sexes have red on crown and black bib, throughout the year. Upperparts streaked brown and buff; underparts buffy with brown streaking on flanks. Bill tiny and horn colored.
VOICE Buzzing, nasal calls and trilled song.
HABITAT Conifers, birches, taiga.
RANGE Alaska and northern Canada.
MOVEMENTS Taiga birds move southward to winter.
BREEDING Varies according to latitude, but in whatever shrubs are available; April-June.
NEST AND EGGS Variable from the ground to trees, a neat cup of twigs and grass; the 5 or 6 eggs are blue, spotted brown.
INCUBATION Lasts 10 to 13 days and is performed by the female.
COMMENT Though highly variable in its choice of habitat, conifers and birches are an important element in most circumstances.

HOARY REDPOLL

Carduelis hornemanni   5½−6in/14−15cm

IDENTIFICATION High Arctic equivalent of Common Redpoll, which it closely resembles. In general, a washed-out version with pale, buff upperparts, white rump, whitish underparts, and slightly smaller bill. Pink wash on breast of male, paler and less obvious.
VOICE Buzzing trills.

HABITAT Tundra.
RANGE Northern Alaska and Canada.
MOVEMENTS Resident, but regularly seen southward in Canada.
BREEDING Rocky gullies with scant vegetation in Arctic tundra; June-July.
NEST AND EGGS The cup is constructed of grasses lined with feathers; the 4 to 6 eggs are blue, speckled brown.
INCUBATION By the female alone for 14 days.
COMMENT Variation within the 'redpoll' group makes for considerable debate as to the exact status of the species and subspecies.

PINE SISKIN

Carduelis pinus   5in/13cm

IDENTIFICATION Streaked brown and black above, brown and white below. Black wings show double wing-bar and yellow flash on primaries that is particularly prominent in flight. Thin, pointed bill.
VOICE Wheezy, husky twittering.

HABITAT Conifer and mixed woodland.
RANGE Breeds across boreal Canada and northern US to Alaskan panhandle and southward through western mountains.
MOVEMENTS Winter visitor to most of USA.
BREEDING Conifers, with or without shrubbery or deciduous trees; April-June.
NEST AND EGGS Twigs and grasses decorated with lichens in a tall conifer; the 3 to 6 eggs are blue, spotted brown.
INCUBATION Lasts 13 days by the female alone.
COMMENT Though it nests in conifers, this bird is a frequent inhabitant of shrubs and other woodland with a particular propensity for alders.

LESSER GOLDFINCH

Carduelis psaltria   4 ½in/11cm

IDENTIFICATION Small finch with stubby black bill. Male has black cap extending, in eastern birds, over entire upperparts. In western birds, the back is green, contrasting with black wings and tail. Underparts are yellow. Wings show white wing-bar, tips to tertials and primary patch. Female is green above, yellow-buff to white below with similar white markings on black wing.
VOICE Trilling warble.
HABITAT Fields, farms, hedgerows.
RANGE Western US into central Texas.

MOVEMENTS Birds in mountains move out in winter.
BREEDING Open woods and suburbs with trees and shrubs; April-May.
NEST AND EGGS A nest of twigs is placed in a shrub or small tree; the 4 or 5 eggs are pale blue.
INCUBATION The eggs take 12 days to hatch and are incubated by the female alone.
COMMENT The availability of water, especially in dry habitats and seasons, has an important impact on this Western species' distribution.

LAWRENCE'S GOLDFINCH

Carduelis lawrencei   4 ½in/12cm

IDENTIFICATION Small finch, with stubby pink bill. Male has black facial mask extending to form a bib. Breast and belly are yellow; hind crown and nape gray; wings black with bold, yellow bars and flash; tail black contrasting with yellow rump. In flight, tail shows white centers to feathers. Female lacks black mask, but shows yellow on breast, wings and rump.
VOICE Jingling warble.
HABITAT Dry slopes.
RANGE California.
MOVEMENTS Largely resident, but winters southern Arizona.
BREEDING Bushy and open hillsides with chaparral and stony growth of weeds; April-June.
NEST AND EGGS A neatly woven cup is placed in a bush; the 3 to 6 eggs are bluish.
INCUBATION By the female alone.
COMMENT This species is occasionally semi-colonial.

AMERICAN GOLDFINCH

Carduelis tristis   5in/13cm

IDENTIFICATION Breeding male is bright yellow with black crown, black tail, and black wings marked by white, double wing-bar. Female is green above, pale yellow below with white, double wing-bar. In winter, the male is brown above with yellow confined to the "face" and throat, the female is similar, but grayer.
VOICE Trilling warble.
HABITAT Overgrown fields, regenerating woods.
RANGE Breeds through all but southern US, extending northward across the Canadian border.
MOVEMENTS Northern birds move southward in winter, when the species occurs in southern states.
BREEDING Shrubby areas and woodland clearings; April-July.
NEST AND EGGS A neat cup of grasses lined with plant down is placed in a low tree in a hedge or orchard or garden; the 2 to 7 eggs are blue.
INCUBATION Lasts 12 to 14 days and is performed by the female alone.
COMMENT Though totally different in appearance, the American Goldfinch occupies exactly the same niche as the European Goldfinch across the Atlantic.

EVENING GROSBEAK

Coccothraustes vespertinus   7½−8½in/19−21cm

IDENTIFICATION Thick-set finch with massive, pale, conical bill. Male is a yellow bird, though the tail is black, and the wings boldly marked black and white. Forehead and supercilium, lower back and belly all yellow. Female is grayer.
VOICE A House Sparrow-like chirp.
HABITAT Breeds in conifer forests; visits feeding stations for sunflower seeds in winter.
RANGE Breeds across southern Canada, extreme north-eastern US, and southward through Rockies.
MOVEMENTS Southward throughout northern half of US.
BREEDING Conifer and mixed woods with substantial undergrowth; May-June.
NEST AND EGGS A flimsy platform of twigs placed at some height usually in a conifer; the 3 to 5 eggs are greenish blue, spotted with brown.
INCUBATION The eggs take 11 to 14 days and are incubated by the female alone.
COMMENT Once regarded as purely a western bird, this species has spread rapidly eastwards in Canada during the present century.

HOUSE SPARROW

Passer domesticus   6−6½in/16−17cm

IDENTIFICATION Also called English Sparrow. Male has gray crown, white cheeks and black bib. Upperparts streaked black and chestnut, underparts dirty, gray cream. Female dully colored with distinct creamy supercilium.
VOICE *Chirrup*, repeated.

HABITAT Cities, towns, suburbs, farmsteads.
RANGE Whole of inhabited North America: introduced from Europe.
MOVEMENTS Resident.
BREEDING Buildings from cities to farmsteads, also hedgerows and thickets near buildings; March-June.
NEST AND EGGS A hole in a building, occasionally a bush top, is filled with an untidy ball of grasses and straw; the 3 to 5 eggs are gray, blotched darker.

INCUBATION Lasts 11 to 14 days and is performed mainly by the female.
COMMENT The ability to rear several (usually 3) broods per year is a feature of the success of this bird.

EURASIAN TREE SPARROW

Passer montanus   6in/15cm

IDENTIFICATION Similar to male House Sparrow, but whole crown chocolate. White cheeks have black comma and pale half collar is particularly useful at any distance.
VOICE Emphatic *chup*.
HABITAT Parks, suburbs.
RANGE St Louis area.
MOVEMENTS Resident, introduced from Europe.

COMMON & SCIENTIFIC NAME INDEXES

SCIENTIFIC NAMES

canus 125
delawarensis 125
fuscus 127
glaucescens 128
glaucoides 127
heermanni 124–5
hyperboreus 128
marinus 128–9
minutus 124
occidentalis 127
philadelphia 124
pipixcan 123
ridibundus 124
Laterallus jamaicensis 90
Leptotila verreauxi 148
Leucosticte arctoa 304
Limnodromus
griseus 115–16
scolopaceus 116
Limnothlypis swainsonii 264
Limosa
fedoa 108
haemastica 107
lapponica 108
Lophodytes cucullatus 59
Loxia
curvirostra 306
leucoptera 306
Luscinia svecica 226

M

Melanerpes
aurifrons 177
carolinus 177–8
erythrocephalus 176
formicivorus 176–7
lewis 176
uropygialis 177
Melanitta
fusca 57
nigra 56–7
perspicillata 57
Meleagris gallopavo 84
Melopsittacus undulatus 149
Melospiza
georgiana 296
lincolnii 296
melodia 295
Mergus
merganser 59
serrator 60
Micrathene whitneyi 158
Mimus polyglottos 234
Mniotilta varia 262–3
Molothrus
aeneus 275
ater 275–6
Motacilla flava 239
Myadestes townsendi 228
Mycteria americana 41
Myiarchus
cinerascens 192
crinitus 192
tuberculifer 191
tyrannulus 192
Myioborus pictus 269
Myiodynastes luteiventris 193

N

Nucifraga columbiana 205

Numenius
americanus 107
phaeopus 106–7
Nyctea scandiaca 156–7
Nycticorax
nycticorax 38
violacea 38–9
Nyctidromus albicollis 165

O

Oceanites oceanicus 22
Oceanodroma
castro 23
furcata 22
homochroa 23
leucorhoa 23
melania 23
microsoma 23
Oenanthe oenanthe 227
Oporornis
agilis 266
formosus 265–6
philadelphia 266
tolmiei 266–7
Oreortyx pictus 87
Oreoscoptes montanus 235
Ortalis vetula 79
Otus
asio 155
flammeolus 155
kennicottii 156
trichopsis 156
Oxyura jamaicensis 60

P

Pachyramphus aglaiae 195
Pagophila eburnea 130
Pandion haliaetus 63–4
Parabuteo unicinctus 68
Parula
americana 254
pitiayumi 254
Parus
atricapillus 210
bicolor 213
carolinensis 210
cinctus 211
gambeli 211
hudsonicus 211
inornatus 212–13
rufescens 211–12
sclateri 210
wollweberi 212
Passer
domesticus 309–10
montanus 310
Passerculus sandwichensis 292
Passerella iliaca 295
Passerina
amoena 283
ciris 284
cyanea 283
versicolor 283
Pelecanus
erythrorhynchos 26
occidentalis 27
Perdix perdix 79
Perisoreus canadensis 203
Peucedramus taeniatus 269
Phaethon
aethereus 25

lepturus 25
Phainopepla nitens 242
Phalacrocorax
auritus 28
carbo 27
olivaceus 28
pelagicus 29
penicillatus 29
urile 29
Phalaenoptilus nuttallii 165
Phalaropus
fulicaria 118
lobatus 118
tricolor 117
Phasianus colchicus 80
Pheucticus
ludovicianus 282
melanocephalus 282
Philomachus pugnax 115
Phylloscopus borealis 225
Pica
nuttalli 206
pica 205–6
Picoides
albolarvatus 181
arcticus 182
borealis 181
nuttallii 179
pubescens 180
scalaris 179
stricklandi 180
tridactylus 181
villosus 180
Pinicola enucleator 304
Pipilo
aberti 286
chlorurus 284–5
erythrophthalmus 285
fuscus 285
Piranga
flava 280
ludoviciana 281
olivacea 280
rubra 280
Pitangus sulphuratus 193
Plectrophenax
hyperboreus 301
nivalis 301
Plegadis
chihi 40
falcinellus 39–40
Pluvialis
dominica 98
fulva 99
squatarola 98
Podiceps
auritus 16
grisegena 16–17
nigricollis 17
Podilymbus podiceps 15–16
Polioptila
caerulea 226
california 226
melanura 226
Polyborus plancus 72
Polysticta stelleri 56
Pooecetes gramineus 290
Porphyrula martinica 92
Porzana carolina 92
Progne subis 198
Protonotaria citrea 263
Psaltriparus minimus 213–14
Pterodroma hasitata 19